*Letters My Mother
Never Read . . .*

Letters My Mother Never Read...

An Abandoned Orphan's Journey.....

By: Jerri Diane Sueck

Library of Congress Control Number: 2007900285
ISBN: Hardcover   978-1-4257-5290-3
                   Softcover   978-1-4257-5289-7

To order additional copies of this book, contact:
Xlibris Corporation
1-888-795-4274
www.Xlibris.com
Orders@Xlibris.com
33534

CONTENTS

Dedicated to my mother whose greatest presence has always been her enormous absence.

Preface

This book is also dedicated to all those children who, even as adults, remember the pain of being forgotten and labeled as "second best." If you are, or have ever been, abandoned, know that no matter how you set yourself apart, or how others set you apart, you are important.

Getting lost in an overwhelming system that is based on procedural concerns, rather than on the individual needs of a child, forces some of us into a lifetime search for a place to be rooted in, a place called home, a place called family.

The purpose of this book is multifaceted. It is the story of the wanton, deliberate psychological destruction of a girl-child by some people. It is also the telling of how I managed to cope in the isolation imposed by others so I would not totally disintegrate and disappear. Mostly though, it is telling my mother the triumph of her child, whose purpose is to celebrate the gift of life she gave me. The letters also tell of her role in being part of the process of surviving and living, even though she had always been but a shadow presence in my life.

This book, *Letters My Mother Never Read,* is possible only because of the whispering echoes of a mother I barely knew, a mother who sustained me in my darkest moments and would have approved of this living document so painfully written. Often I think, what would I do if I could exchange the eight years with the mother I had known for a mother who had lived most of my life?

I would never trade a day with my mother, who was able to share only a brief skip in life with me. She was, and is, a blessing to me. It is time to allow her to rest in peace. She shared only the first one hundred months of my physical life, enough for a short introduction to living, but not enough for self-sustaining personhood.

I thank my mother, for touching my face with her existence. Never has a daughter so loved a mother as I have and would have continued to, had fate not stepped in.

Acknowledgments

This book would have never been possible without the many supporting cast members who have nurtured my dream of writing. From the first time my friend Liz told me that I should write a book to the present reality, I have been blessed with companions who journeyed with me at various times on this road of life.

First and foremost, I must thank Claudia Gard and her husband, Paul, for opening their hearts and home to me. Lauren, their daughter, did some grunt work in the beginning with typing. Claudia gave her invaluable support in encouraging me to tell the story as it unfolded, and helped me to resist the temptation to delete parts or sections of the book that I thought were too personal. She constantly reminded me that the essence of the book would be altered, unless I allowed the reader to glimpse the boomerangs that happen when a child grows up surrounded by the absence of the ordinary. For her time and energy and welcoming spirit, I am grateful.

Liz Eshelman, my librarian and Alvernia College friend, always told me that I should write a book. She has been an "umbrella" who provided support and shade when I thought the book was getting too intense. She was instrumental in forming our monthly reading group that involved Linda Fisk, Rosemary and John Deegan, Marilyn Seymour, and Sylvia Kane, who cheered me on, chapter by chapter. My friend Debbie Johnson, who shared a writer's and mother's point of view, thanks. Talk about night-lights in the darkness.

There is Sister Lynn Michele Hartigan, an adult in my youth who became a friend for always. Thanks for the grammar checks. Also, Sister J. Lora Dambroski, OSF, and later Jackie, who acknowledged the shattering of my life experience and chose to mother me and nurture my broken soul. Thanks for the probing questions that always challenged me to grow.

The *Seymour Tribune* has been gracious in granting me the copyright to the newspaper article. Natalie Knable, my vice principal, who opened the school doors early at Franklin Learning Center. She introduced me to the soothing music of David Lanz, especially his *Beloved* tape, which played constantly while I wrote this book.

My thanks to Paula Randazzo for the title page artwork. Also, my gratitude to David Felicano and Jacob Doherty for the artwork on the dedication page. Their energy and creativity have been something for which I am grateful. To all my friends, too many to name, thank you for believing that this was a story worthy of being told.

Finally, my thanks go out to my mother and God, because without their support in the darkest of times, I would never have been able to bring this book into the light of day. They have always buoyed me when the "whisper tears" threatened to drown me in the great sorrows that no child should ever know.

SEYMOUR DAILY TRIBUNE

SEYMOUR, INDIANA, WEDNESDAY, NOVEMBER 11, 1964   522

MOTHER OF FIVE DIES IN TRAILER FIRE

Fatal Mobile Home Blaze Scene-Shown shortly after flames had been extinguished which early today destroyed a large mobile home, suffocating Mrs. Gussie S. Zigga 31, at Hiltop Mobile Homes Park, 115 S. O'Brien St, is the center of kitchen area of the house trailer. This was the most severely damaged section of the home. Front bedroom of trailer in which Mrs. Zigga was found at the right the photographed portion, was less severely damaged part of the mobile home and contents itted by flames which burned with intense heat was estimated at approximately $6.000.

Five Children Not Home When Blaze Strikes

Investigation was being continued today into the cause of a fire which swept through a large mobile home in eastern Seymour early this morning, causing the death of Mrs. Gussie S. Zigga. 31, mother of five children, and destroying the trailer residence.

The five children ranging in age two to ten years were not at home when the fire of undetermined origin broke out in the trailer home, located in the last row of mobile homes on the east side of the Hilltop Mobile homes Park, 115 South O'Brien street.

Death of Mrs. Zigga, who had been in the process of cleaning out the mobile home to show it to a prospective purchaser today, was due to suffocation and third degree burns on her legs and other parts of her body. Victor L. Burkholder, coroner of Jackson County who investigated stated.

Her lifeless form was found by city firemen, lying at the foot of a bed in a bedroom at the front of the trailer, which had no outside doorway. The discovery was made after most of the flames which had consumed much of the trailer home, burning with intense heat, had been extinguished. She was partly wrapped in a blanket, clad in a blouse and underclothing and was wearing tennis shoes, authorities said. They said from the expression on her face, she apparently had been gasping for breath just before her death from suffocation.

After finding the suffocation victim neighbors and authorities became concerned about the safety of her children and a thorough search was made of a blackened ruins of the mobile home's interior. Neighbors said Mrs. Zigga had her oldest son with her about 6 p. m. Tuesday.

State and city police who aided in the investigation learned that Mrs. Zigga and her son had taken a taxicab to the home of her mother southwest of Tampico Tuesday night. The cab driver said she had returned to Seymour in the taxi without her son, so they theorized he was at his grandmother's residence. This was corroborated early this morning when Coroner Burkholder and Trooper Jack Pike, of the Seymour state police post, visited the home of Mrs. Zigga's mother and found her five children including twins, safe at the grandmother's residence where they had spent the night.

Mrs. Zigga had moved some of their belongings out of the mobile home Tuesday, it was learned preparatory to selling or renting the trailer, as she planned to leave shortly for Montana to be with her husband, Zigga, Jr.. stationed with the U. S. Air force there. The children, most of whom had attending Lincoln School here, were planning to make their home with their grandmother and attend elementary school at Tampico.

Efforts were being made today,with aid of the Red Cross, to contact Mrs. Zigga's husband, whom it was learned is in the PADAN Squadron, Cutbank. Montana, and was scheduled to enter a hospital soon.

City firemen estimated loss to the mobile home at $5,600 and approximately $100 to contents, a total loss of about $6000.

State police said they learned William A. Hall, of Austin, on route to work at the H. O. sanfield Company of Indiana, inc, plant at Freeman Field, saw the blazing 55-foot long trailer as he passed on East Tipton street, looking north between the Seymour district state highway garage and the state police post. He drove to the trailer park and beat on the side of the burning mobile home to rouse occupants, he said. Persons living in mobile homes nearby heard him and one of them, Elmer Wagner, summoned the Seymour fire department, who received the call at 3:18 a. m.

The fire was belived to have broken out about 3 a. m. or shortly afterward and the greatest portion of the blaze was in the center section of the trailer, which housed the kitchen and dining are. Rear of the mobile home also was badly damaged, with the front bedroom, in which Mrs. Zigga was found, less seriously burned.

The fire spread to dry grass outside the trailer home and was burning close to a mobile home on the north before it was extinguished by city firemen. Several articles of wash hanging on a line between the rear of the trailer and a state highway garage building were not burned.

Nothing was saved from the burning mobile residence. A smoldering uncovered mattress which had been on the bed near where Mrs. Zigga was lying was pulled out into the yard, along with the other smoldering articles. The mattress top was not burned where the barrel of an unloaded rifle was lying, along with a screwdriver and flashlight, across the bed when firemen entered the bedroom. There was no evidence of foul play and authorities presumed Mrs. Zigga had been gathering those articles together to remove them from the residence when she moved out as she had planned today.

City firemen were at the scene for approximately two hours. In addition to Trooper Pike and Coroner Burkholder, others at the blaze included Trooper Jack Means and Detective First Sgt. Chester Wilson of the Seymour post; Seymour city police and Keith Burkholder, deputy county coroner.

Details concerning survivors and funeral arrangements were not available pending notification of Mrs. Zigga's husband.

The Zigga family was reported to have moved into the trailer park from Texas about six months ago and had resided there since that time. Mrs. Zigga was reported to have visited a trailer park neighbor across the street until after 11 p. m. Tuesday.

Persons nearby said they heard several explosions from fuel tanks during the fire and investigators were attempting today to determine whether an explosion could have caused the blaze or whether a defective heater might have been a reason for the fire.

JACKSON COUNTY HEALTH DEPARTMENT
207 North Pine Street
Seymour, Indiana 47274-2143

CERTIFICATE OF DEATH

THIS IS TO CERTIFY, that our records show:

Name: Gussie S. Zigga

Died on: November 11, 1964   at 2:35 am   at Hill Top Trailer Park, Seymour, Indiana

Age: 31 years   Sex: female .   Marital Status: married

Cause of Death: Smoke Suffocation
Found dead on floor of her fire gutted trailer home

Certified by: Victor L. Burkholder, Coroner
Address: Seymour, Indiana

Place of burial or removal: Vallonia Cemetery
Date of burial: November 14, 1964

Funeral Home: Burkholder Funeral Home
Address: Seymour, Indiana

Filing date: November 13, 1964   Book & Page No.: EK and 185

_____ County Health Officer

SEAL

Issued On: October 2, 1998

"Beginnings"

Beginnings start with a second in time,
Never repeated, always seeking the present.
Where the soul comes to rest,
Only to begin on the road again.

She stands looking askance at the clouds,
Wondering if the wings will follow her.
From heaven to earth she journeys in a flash,
Only now both worlds intertwine in her soul.

Eyes open, mind alert, new steps forward,
Straight and curved no compass in sight.
Guiding hands appear steering towards a direction,
Rootedness takes place in fluid motion.

Feelings, attachment, bonds, so tight,
Only slivers of light show the path.
Where uncertainty of potential become realized,
As a new creation of a child's humanity - begins.

In the Beginning...

In the Beginning

Dear Mother,

Who are you? There have been many conversations and letters written in my heart to you over the years of my life, always longing for that connection, which stopped when you died.

Did you know for years I looked for you in every woman I encountered? I must have been fourteen or fifteen when I realized that the physical person known as Mother had disappeared, and worst, any mothering I was ever to experience ended at the age of eight. I felt so lost. There was a severing of any connection to everyone, even to myself.

I thought perhaps if I started to write down all the experiences of my life, maybe I would find out who you were, and maybe in the process find out who I was.

Life is not always kind to an eight-year-old motherless orphan in search of roots. Your death, your leaving wounded me in ways that would pierce the heart of God. The isolation, the aloneness, the struggle to see if I could put one foot in front of another, and the many stumbles of trying to be a person became almost unbearable.

For as long as I can remember, I wondered about you. What was it like to live in the 1950s and 1960s? What was it like to be married?

What was it like to have children? What was it like to be thirty-one years old and die in a gas explosion from a faulty heater? What were your last thoughts as you tried to wrap yourself up in a blanket, in a desperate attempt to breathe?

What would, or could, you have taught me from the age of eight until now? Why did you marry, first, an abusive, violent man, then, a weak-willed man, who allowed your children to linger in a limbo of existence, denying them a childhood and an adolescence?

Do you know how many times I prayed to God and promised him, that I would be good, if only he would let you come back to me? Did you know that I spent years as a child praying that God would let me die so that I would be with you, so I would not ache so much, so I would not have to face the day?

Love,
Jerri

*   *   *

As far back as I can remember, there had been a chain of events that had shaped my life. Never did I believe that life could turn upside down without me knowing it would happen. Maybe it is that being a child, I felt such control over my universe, and what I didn't know, I knew my mother would always fix up and make right again.

I never really planned to start writing to this woman to whom I have always felt connected, and yet would never know, but life has a way of changing who we are and where we are going.

The splintering moment that redefined the direction of my life started with a simple gas explosion, which threw what I had known to be true and unchangeable into a chaotic life-altering inferno.

Before the fire, or BTF, my life seemed to be humming along rather smoothly, with only an occasional bump.

My biological father wasn't too nice, although I always thought that daddies were supposed to be fun. This father would do bad things and beat my brothers; he even put my brother Tyler in the hospital for a few months by breaking his arms and legs.

I don't know why adults can't get along and be nice all the time. When my mother and my father divorced, I had to stay with these people called foster parents for a few months. This was a scary time because I kept being moved around without my brothers. Eventually, after three months, my life returns to normal.

Living back with my mother was exciting, but I became constantly afraid that something would happen to her, and she would disappear. Even though she kept explaining that the custody battle was over, I couldn't help but be afraid to let her out of my sight. I figure if I keep a close eye on her, she would never leave me again.

Everything starts to fall back into place, moving with the air force, going to school, and being rocked every night. I like this life of mine with my new daddy, who married my mother and adopted us.

My mother would always defend me whenever I went to a new school, because I was born with this birth defect called cleft palate. With a cleft palate and cleft lip, kids always teased me. I was good in school though and liked going to school. Whenever the air force transferred us, I always had to deal with a new set of children laughing at me because I could not speak well.

Your echo to me is, "Sticks and stones may break my bones, but names can never hurt me."

At the last move we were ever to share, the school in Seymour would not accept me and my brothers. All the kids in the school that I am sent to could not read. They keep staring at the wall and could not play games. I soon realize that it was a school for severely handicapped students.

I keep asking my mother if I could go to school with my brothers because they get homework and I didn't. As I sit outside the principal's office and listen to both of them argue, I find it hard to understand why people think I was retarded, just because they could not understand me.

The principal said, "She is going to be made fun of, left back, and mocked." And all my mother said was, "Well, that's her problem, and she will have to learn to deal with it, won't she? I can't always be here to protect her, but she wants to learn, and you cannot help her here."

With that, we march out, hand in hand. Then I went to a school that gave me homework.

I wonder how many hand-in-hand walks I will never know. Just as I had settled into my little-girl routine, my mother tells me about this war in a place called Vietnam. Somehow there are all these people who are fighting each other for freedom. I am told that since my new daddy is a soldier in the air force, he has to go and help in the war.

I love my daddy! He is nice, handsome, and tall. He always sits by my hospital bed at lunchtime whenever I have to go in for cleft palate operations.

I ask my mother if Vietnam is like when Billy, Trevor, Tyler, and I play cowboys and Indians. She tells me that these bad guys from a place called North Vietnam want to take over this country called South Vietnam. As I snuggle with her in the rocking chair, I become afraid. My mother says that daddy has to go into the hospital in Montana for a couple of weeks, before he is sent to Vietnam. She tells me that she will be going to take care of him for a little while.

I ask her if she will be back soon, but I don't tell her that I am afraid to let her go without me. My mother runs her hands through my thick curly hair, telling me that she would never forget to come back. As I look at her face with her dark brown eyes, I know she will keep her promise.

She asks me if I will be a good girl for Grandma, and, of course, I say yes. As she rocks me, she hums a musical tune that she always uses when she paces back and forth as she cooks. This is my favorite time of the night. I just wish I wasn't so scared inside.

I ask my mother why she can't tell the air force to leave Daddy alone so she won't have to go away. She just pulls me closer to her and says that everyone must serve their country, and Daddy is a soldier who must go wherever he is told. She also tells me that I am a soldier's daughter, and I must do my part for my country by being good.

My brothers and I aren't too sure that we like this idea of my mother going to Montana.

Billy is ten years old and one of the smartest people I have ever met. He knows so much stuff about different kinds of salamanders and frogs that we always try to keep as pets. He has dark hair, like me, and blue eyes and is very strong. Billy always beats me at hand wrestling.

On the other hand, there are the twins Trevor and Tyler. They have blond hair and are six years old. They are always running around and making a lot of noise. The best part though is that I can beat them at hand wrestling. For some reason, my mother tells me, "Just wait, someday they will be bigger than you, and they will beat you at hand wrestling." I know that just barely being eight years old, I will always be older than the twins and, therefore, stronger.

Sometimes I wonder what my mother is talking about. She likes to tell me things with a slight smile on her face. She is so beautiful with her lipstick and is very smart; maybe she is right about things down the road.

My sister, Alice, who is two years old, is the most beautiful baby and, like the twins, also has blond hair and blue eyes. My brothers and I love Alice, and we spend a lot of time playing with her. She is such a happy baby and is always trying to follow us around.

Trevor and Tyler are going to be seven years old the day after tomorrow. My mother tells me that she is going to get ready to leave for Montana the day after the birthday party.

I ask her again if I can go with her, and she holds my face in her hands and tells me that I worry too much and that she would never leave me. She says I have to trust her. She tells me that since I am learning to write letters in the third grade, maybe I could write her a letter every day that she is gone so I can tell her everything that is happening while she is in Montana.

My mother kisses me on my forehead and hugs me. I tell her that I am going to write her letters and keep a list of everything that is happening. She laughs and says, "That's my girl."

On November 10, 1964, we have a birthday party for my twin brothers who turn seven years old at Grandma's house, which is in the middle of a cornfield. My mother tells me that we will stay with my grandma, because the trailer has to be cleaned for the people who are going to move in the next day. I ask one last time if I can help her, but she tells me that I'm running a fever, I need to take a medicine and rest.

I keep asking how long she will be away. She tells me that she has to stay overnight just to make sure everything is okay. My mother kisses me on the head, tells me to be a good girl and to take care of my brothers. She turns, walks out of the house and out of my life.

How could I have ever let her leave without me, when I have been so careful to tag along everywhere she went? How is it possible that I could not know that forever without her was about to begin?

I am so sick after my mother leaves. Grandma tells me I have to go to bed early so I will be rested for her return. I wake up to muffled voices in the hallway. As I climb out of bed and look out of the window, I see a police car. It is still dark outside, probably around five or six in the morning.

As I peek around the corner, there is one of the biggest men I have ever seen, telling Grandma that he is very sorry. With that, he turns and leaves.

Grandma is crying. When she sees me, she tells me to go back to bed, it is too early to get up. When I get up later and go into the kitchen for breakfast, I ask Grandma why there was a cop wearing a hat tucked over his head, with a strap that looked like it was choking him around his chin.

She tells me that he is a State Policeman who has to wear a special uniform. My brothers and I want to know why he was here. We are told not to ask questions for now. I ask Grandma if I can go pick flowers for my mother from her garden so that she will have a surprise when she comes to pick us up later.

She says yes.

I wonder why my mother is so late coming back to get us?

It is a Wednesday morning, November 11, 1964, around 3:00 a.m. when a gas explosion happens due a defective heater in Seymour, Indiana. Gussie 'Sandra,' my mother, dies alone, struggling for air.

I hope that my mother did not struggle for too long or feel the intensity of the flames as the trailer burned. She was only thirty-one years old, leaving behind five children: Billy ten, Jerri Diane eight, Trevor and Tyler seven, and Alice two.

Did she know that forever would start before she died? What were her last desperate thoughts?

I keep waiting for my mother to come for us. She said that if Grandma gave her a good report, we would get to go for ice cream.

My brothers and I play hide-and-seek in the cornfields, which is a lot of fun because I can always tell where Trevor and Tyler are hiding.

Grandma gives us a big lunch and says that she will be talking to us later but wants us to stay outside while Alice takes her nap.

For some reason, Grandma's face is all red, as though she was crying. I put my arm around her and ask her if she is okay. She tells me yes but that her heart hurts right now and she needs to be quiet for a little while. I pat her hand and tell her that when my mother comes back, she will fix her up. She smiles at me in a strange way and tells me to go play for now.

This afternoon I ask my grandmother what time my mother will be picking us up. She says she wants to take a walk with me. As she holds my hand, she asks me if I believe that Jesus loves everyone. I say of course, because my mother has taught me that Jesus is everywhere and loves everyone.

Grandma then tells me that Jesus has special plans for my mother and that she has to go away and live with him in heaven. I drop the flowers that I have picked. I tell her no, because she had told me that she would never leave me and would be coming back from that faraway place called Montana. I don't want her to go to heaven to take care of my little brother that died! I want her to be with me!

I tell Grandma that Jesus does not need my mother because he already has a mother. I say I will wait on the front steps until she comes, because she probably will not want to live with Jesus without us.

I sit on the steps waiting. My grandmother tries to tell me that my mother will not come back, that something happened to our trailer; there was a fire. I just know that she will not let a fire keep her from us.

I cannot eat. It is getting dark and chilly. I am told that Daddy is on the telephone and wants to talk to me.

Daddy tells me that my mother had to go away to do some secret special mission for Jesus and will not be coming back. I tell him I do not believe him because they do not know what she had told me, that she would come back, and we would be a family again.

How am I supposed to know that my mother is touching the face of God at the same time I am so desperately longing to touch her face again?

I am so mad at my mother, because Grandma and Daddy tell me she is not coming back. Mother promised me that we would go for ice cream if we were good, and I made sure that my brothers and I were good for Grandma.

Somehow, Grandma keeps crying, and the phone keeps ringing. Grandma keeps rushing to the phone and whispering so we can't hear what she is saying.

There are all these people stopping over, even my mother's middle sister. I like my two aunts; one has dark hair and always lets me play with my cousins.

My mother's youngest sister has blond hair and a new baby. She likes to run her hands through my curly hair, just like my mother, but right now, she lives far away in Colorado with her soldier husband.

I overhear Grandma telling someone that my aunt who lives far away is coming home. Everyone is quiet in Grandma's house, and they are crying about my mother. I don't know why they are upset because my mother will be right back. After all, she promised to come back to me.

Mothers are supposed to keep their promises. I know Jesus wouldn't want my mother because she belongs to me. He has his own mother anyway who always hangs out with him.

Grandma tells me that there will be a lot of people at her house tomorrow. When I ask why, she says she will tell me later.

Today there are all these people at Grandma's house; a man and a woman who say they are Daddy's parents are also there. I call them Grandma and Grandpa Resuba, and they've brought us candy. They take Alice back to the hotel with them for the night.

My mother's youngest sister comes to visit. I like her. She always visits us whenever we move and sometimes helps to take care of us. I just know that if she is here, she will fix everything and make my mother come back. Although her hair is blond, she always reminds me of her.

My aunt and her baby sleep with us at Grandma's house. The boys are sleeping, but I can't because I want my mother so much. It has been two days since I last saw her, and tomorrow, Grandma tells me, we are going to her funeral.

I wonder what a funeral means. At Grandpa's funeral in September, everyone was crying, and then a box was lowered into the ground.

I start crying in bed because it is so dark, and I want my mother. I don't care about what Jesus wants, I need her! My aunt crawls into my bed, rocking and holding me, asking me what is wrong. I keep telling her "I just want my mommy!" over and over again.

My aunt keeps running her hand through my hair, telling me that my mother loved me. I want her to do what she always did and make everything right again.

On Saturday morning, November 14, 1964, I get dressed up and wear good shoes.

When we go into the funeral home, they show me a long box with pretty brown wood and gold handles. It is closed. They tell me that my mother is in there.

I think to myself, That is silly, because my mother will not be able to breathe in a box that is closed. Then Billy suggests that we play cowboys and Indians, which we do for a little while.

After the songs and prayers, we take a ride to the cemetery in Vallonia, Indiana, where the long box is lowered into the ground. As we leave the cemetery, we are told we will be going to the bus station for a long trip to a place called Scranton, Pennsylvania.

I do not want to go because I am afraid my mother will not find me when she returns. I want to stay in Indiana. I am told that her spirit is everywhere. This makes no sense to me, since I know that no one can be everywhere, except God.

As we wait for the bus, I overhear Grandma and Grandpa Resuba, Daddy's parents, discussing that Alice belongs to them but that we are the "bastards."

I never heard that word, "bastard," before. They sound so angry and keep hugging and holding Alice. As we get ready to board the bus, Grandma Resuba says that only Alice can sit near them because she is a baby, and we are too big for them.

I get on the bus, but I am afraid of these two people. I hear my brother Billy telling Grandma or somebody, "Please, don't put us on the bus because something bad will happen!" Grandma just says that nothing bad will happen, that the Resuba grandparents are very nice people.

How do people know how people are? Did my mother know them? Would she have wanted us to go with them?

On the afternoon of her burial, we board the Greyhound bus and head for that faraway place called Scranton, Pennsylvania. I am so small that I have to kneel on the seat to see out of the window. This is also the time I remember a very kind old black woman who shares her sandwich with me. She sits next to me as we are eating; I remember this woman asking me why we are traveling, and Grandma Resuba responds, "Oh, my son's wife died, and we're taking our granddaughter back with us. These are the children from her first marriage."

I just sit there, listening, because my mother said "children should be seen but not heard" when adults are talking. I keep trying to figure out what

Grandma Resuba means by saying only Alice is her granddaughter. I feel at that moment that she might not like us, although I cannot figure out why.

Can my mother hear what is in their hearts? Are they going to love us like she would have loved us if she didn't have to go to live with Jesus? Maybe she could tell Jesus that he is messing up my life and ask him if he could trade her for Daddy's parents?

No matter how often I look around, I can't find my mother. In my mind, I try to desperately remember the last things that she told me about moving to Montana. Maybe I should start writing letters and making lists so that she will know how mean Daddy's parents are to us.

There are all these thoughts and questions inside my head. I just know that I have to write everything down because there is too much for me to remember all the time.

It is so hard to remember that my mother is never coming back. I try not to think about the word *forever* because it makes my head hurt. My teacher in school today looked at me rather strangely when I asked how long forever is.

My teacher said forever is like the numbers that we count in math. If I keep counting, there is no end, and forever has no end. I don't believe her because there has to be some end to numbers, so every night I count numbers and start from where I left off the previous night. I figure if I run out of numbers, then I will find the end of forever, and maybe my mother will be waiting there.

In the meantime, I have to keep track of the people and things in my life so that when I reach forever, I can tell my mother about my life without her.

"Mother's Absence"

Darkness prevails with unsteady steps that start to stop,
Hands of trust slowly withdrawing bringing a chill.
The child has turned her head seeking any direction,
Chaos following as death swirls all around her.

Tap dancing, skipping, her galloping stride hurries,
As she tries to stumble back to what she once knew.
Free-falling through a mist of tears with hands outstretched,
Seeking a catch as the whirlpool of life swallows her.

Light of her path slowly fades, walls closing in,
Brothers as companions huddle together, heads touching.
Looking for the hands that once caressed a gentle safety,
Wondering how she can go back with the retreating warmth.

Unaccustomed noises, names so different now labeling her,
Confusion becomes the norm, splintering happens readily.
When, what, how, where, unceasing questions with no answers,
Hurricane winds of change, force her to seek shelter from the storm.

Around every corner she looks for who sheltered her to appear,
No explanation or excuse for her absence acceptable or understandable.
Her soul tries to return to the place and person she came from,
Only time is not accepting of her choice, stay on earth she must.

Cold winds, biting temperatures, tears freeze on her face as she looks up
Questioning, pleading, begging for her return to no avail,
The hands of protection no longer part of the here and now,
Brothers and she alone, disconnected, no safety net to catch them.

Grandmothers's Cellar: Waiting for my Mother
Ages 8 - 10

Grandma Resuba's Coal Cellar:
Waiting for My Mother

(Ages Eight to Ten)

Dear Mother,

As we arrive in Scranton, I keep thinking that at any time, you will come back and take me home. It is so cold and snowy.

My Grandma Resuba has told me that since I am not her grandchild, I will have to live in one bedroom with my brothers, and I will sleep on the floor. We will not be allowed to use the bathroom in the house; we must use the outhouse on the coal bank. Also, we will eat, do homework, and shower in the coal cellar. A shower would be built.

At no time are we ever to be in the house—no TV and no eating with her family. Alice belongs to them, because she is their flesh and blood. We are not to talk to her or interact with her.

I always thought that if only you had held your breath longer or had fallen asleep in the living room instead of the bedroom, or had you rolled just one more time in the blanket on the floor as you tried to stay below the smoke, then everything would be so different. Mostly though, I spend time fantasizing about being there and rescuing you.

However, all my wishing, all my longing, all the tears not yet cried cannot keep you from being torn away from my heart and from my life. If only I could change back the hands of time and make you come back to me. I don't know if I can live without you.

Who will tell Daddy and the Resuba family that Billy, Trevor, Tyler, and I are the same kids as when you were here? Couldn't you talk to God and tell him that I miss you more than anything in the whole wide world? Please, Mother, couldn't you find a way to come back for me?

During that first night in Scranton, Pennsylvania, it is so dark in the room, and I'm lying on the mattress on the floor. I just know that you will never find me. What is happening to me? In less than one week I have become a different child in the eyes of the Resuba family because you had to go live with Jesus. When will you come back to wake me from this nightmare and tell me that I am only dreaming?

Love,
Jerri

          *   *   *

The first few weeks after my mother died, I keep looking around every corner, just thinking that she might be there. My search grows more frantic because Grandma Resuba starts to treat us meanly openly, constantly screaming, "You bastards, someday we're gonna put you away!" She begins by making us stay outside from the time we get up until nine o'clock in the evening.

I keep hearing Grandma Resuba calling us bastards and wonder what she really means. I never heard my mother use the word "bastard." She likes to call us the "bastard orphans," and I know that "orphan" means "to belong to no one."

In school today, I ask my teacher what the word "bastard" means, and she tells me that it is a nasty word and I should not be using it. I don't say anything, but I wonder why it is wrong for me to use the word "bastard" but not for Grandma Resuba.

When the teacher gives us some reading time, I go over to this big dictionary that is on the back table and decide to look up the word "bastard." I am careful not to let the teacher see me so she won't get mad, but I have to know why I am a bastard so I can change whatever it is and make Grandma Resuba like me.

I read the definition: "a child with no father, born to an unmarried mother," and I wonder what that means. Isn't Daddy my daddy? He said he adopted us. Maybe when mothers go away the family goes away.

I wonder if the reason why Grandma Resuba says we are bastard orphans is because Daddy isn't married to my mother anymore because she left? If this is true, then the only way not to be a bastard anymore is for her to come back and remarry Daddy.

The dictionary also says bastard is "a derogatory name to call someone in a hateful manner." I don't like this part of the definition, because it means that I have to make them stop hating us. It is probably easier for my mother to come back from living with Jesus than to make Daddy's family want and love us.

I wonder if adults use different words than kids because they are in charge, or do they see people differently? When my mother got married to Daddy, did that mean forever, or just until someone dies? How long is forever and ever?

Daddy comes home today after being away at the air force base for two weeks. When he calls us into the coal cellar to shower, I whisper to him that I want to know if he is our daddy, because Grandma Resuba says we are bastards and he is not our father.

Daddy just will not look at me. He tells me I ask too many questions. I tell him that someday I will tell my mother how mean Grandma Resuba is to us, and he just says that she will never come back, and there is no one to tell.

Daddy says that when my mother was here, he adopted us after our father died. I have some memory of a man who was mean to us, but it is mostly this daddy I remember and love.

Daddy says that things are different now since my mother has died and that we will never be how we were. He tells me that I am too young to understand how overwhelmed he and his family are from taking care of my brothers, Alice, and me. In addition, I must understand that Alice is his real daughter and the only one that Grandma Resuba cares about and loves.

Daddy tells me to stop asking questions and trying to change what cannot be changed.

I don't understand how, when my mother was here, she and Daddy were able to travel with the air force and take care of five children all by themselves? She leaves, or dies, and now a whole group of adults can't take care of us.

I guess bastard orphans are even less human than plain old orphans, and daddies and mommies are never the same if life changes.

I wonder if there is a way to get in touch with God and tell him that by keeping my mother, he is messing up everything for my brothers and me? Maybe it is not God who changed, but who else can I go to in order to change the unchangeable?

We spend most of our time outside on the coal bank. It is so cold, and my ears are freezing. Grandma Resuba says that we don't deserve hats, gloves, or scarves. I have such an earache and cannot wait to be called inside so I can ask Grandma Resuba for some medicine. I feel like someone is stabbing me in the middle of my ear with the ice pick that I see Daddy use sometimes.

Grandma Resuba finally calls us in from the outside to the coal cellar, and I am almost frozen because I keep using my bare hands to cover my ears from the piercing winds. Sometimes it feels like the wind is blowing straight through my head.

When I go into the coal cellar, I tell Grandma Resuba that my ear hurts, and she said, "What do you want me to do about it? Quit whining like a sissy, and don't you dare cry." I beg her for some medicine because my ear really hurts. She tells me to leave her alone and take a shower. She says the pain isn't really that bad, and if I don't think about it, it will go away.

The pain is intense, but I try to focus on running through a meadow of flowers on the side of a mountain, anything to stop the stabbing pain. Before I go up the coal cellar steps, I again ask for something. She tells me I'm nothing but a baby who was spoiled by my mother, and if I don't move up the steps fast, she'll give me something to cry about.

I know Grandma Resuba won't take me to the doctor. The last time I went to the doctor was when my mother was here. Ever since she left, I've been trying not to be sick because I don't know what to do to make the pain go away. Grandma Resuba hates me, and I don't know why, except that I am not a flesh-and-blood grandchild. The only problem is that even non-flesh-and-blood kids get sick and need medicine except there is no one to help me.

I wish my mother wouldn't stay away so long because she would know how to make my ear pain go away.

As I lie on the mattress, I press my left ear as hard as I can into my hand, trying to flatten out the pain. It is so incredibly sharp that I force myself to leave this existence and focus on the mountain of flowers.

Maybe when I wake in the morning this will only be a nightmare never lived, and only my mother will be here to wipe away the tears of pain that are leaking out. I have to learn to be tougher.

How do I "protect" myself against things that I have no knowledge of before they hurt me? Why are people so scary and so changeable?

I want to tell my mother how cold it gets in Scranton—a city nestled between mountains. When I first arrived here, it was already cold—colder than Seymour, Indiana.

The first thing we have to do in the morning is to get up, go down two flights of steps through the coal cellar to the outhouse located on a coal bank about fifty yards from the house.

We then eat breakfast on the porch or in the coal cellar, dress, and go to school. It is the same breakfast: one bowl of puffed wheat bought in economy bags. We are all so hungry every day, usually eating the one bologna sandwich in our lunch by the time we get to school.

It is the biting cold wind that freezes my hands stiff that hurts the most, and we don't have gloves, scarves, or hats. When you get really cold, the fingers of your hands won't touch each other, no matter how hard your mind tries to make them touch.

It is so cold that Billy, Trevor, Tyler, and I huddle together, trying to block out the piercing wind and talk about our mother. I often wonder how she could ever leave us with these people who despise us because we are adopted children and orphans. We would stay outside for hours, even after dark. The neighbors would call the police, but nothing happens, nothing changes, and my mother, as champion, no longer has influence in this world. No one listens.

What will happen to us in this swirling chaos of hatred? I wonder if my mother ever knows the intensity of Grandma Resuba's feelings toward her?

I remember the first time I ask why Daddy's family hates us so much. I am in the coal cellar, and Grandma Resuba is screaming at us. She never really talks to us, saying, "You bastards, shut up, don't talk in the house." I will be nine this summer, and I think a lot about the past few months since my mother left. She hates Trevor, Tyler, Billy, and me, especially in comparison to the way she treats Alice.

So that day, I finally ask, "Why do you hate us so much? When Mommy was here, you gave us milk and cookies and let us sit in your kitchen."

Grandma Resuba is so mad and looks at me for the first time since we arrive, telling me, "You are not my responsibility, not my flesh and blood, and I got stuck with you."

Also, Grandma Resuba screams, "My son had no business marrying a woman with four bastards. Your mother was nothing. She should have never married my son. You are taking time away from my granddaughter, who will always be the daughter I never had. I'm sick of people telling me how to treat you. This is my home, and since your mother is dead, you should be lucky for whatever I give you. I will never forgive your mother for marrying my son. I'm glad she is dead. My family is not obligated to take care of someone else's bastard children."

This is the one and only time she has ever talked directly to me. For months, I lie in bed and try to ponder the fact that never, ever, would my mother come back.

Every night I would try to fathom what "flesh and blood" means. One time, I even cut my finger to study my blood. It looks red, but there must be something about it that makes it bastard blood. I check my fingers over and over, but maybe my blood changed by my not having a mother.

They will always hate us. I try to stay out of Grandma Resuba's way. The meaner she gets, the more focused I get on my mother's returning.

Is it possible to restore my blood back to normal blood? Does this mean that bastard blood is noticeable to other people also?

I never knew that the same people could occupy the same space and time yet be worlds apart. That is how my mother's children are treated, with Alice, at two years old, living and breathing the same air, and the four of us—at seven, eight, and ten years old—all occupying the same space. Yet, how differently we are treated.

Every Saturday, Grandma Resuba dresses Alice up in a beautiful dress, puts pink bows in her blond hair, and takes her shopping. We stop and look at her. Grandma Resuba then screams, "What the hell are you bastards staring at? I am taking my granddaughter shopping. Stop looking at her! You're not good enough to look at her!"

We, of course, then turn away. It is just that Alice is our sister. She is such a pretty little girl. We love her, but we are not allowed to speak or play with her, because her blood is different—it is better.

My brothers and I always wear the same clothes: blue jeans and a shirt. For Christmas, Alice has a pile of presents under the tree, and we get a pair of jeans and a shirt unwrapped.

Sometimes I wonder what makes us so different. Is it because she is a girl different from me? This begins a time of great questioning. The more I question things, the more confused I become, feeling eventually out of step with everything that makes sense when my mother was living.

Is it possible for two sets of children, related by blood, to ever know each other if they are kept apart? Was my mother the only connection of family that ever existed with all her children? I feel more and more different, although I used to share the same world with Alice.

Is there a switch in heaven that my mother can flip, and it will open some hidden door for me to come to her? How do I stop Daddy and the Resuba family from making me feel different, when I don't want to feel different?

I keep getting more lonely. So many things are happening; I'm beginning to feel as though I am spinning into a different kind of girl that no one else sees.

Shortly after we begin living in the coal cellar, it becomes routine for us to shower, one by one, with our backs turned. As each one of us finishes, we put on a pair of underwear and nothing else. One by one, we must go up the coal cellar steps through the living room, where Alice is watching TV with her grandfather, and through the kitchen to sit on the steps leading to the upstairs bedroom. I am always the first to undress and shower. Grandma Resuba sits at the picnic table holding a belt, in case we talk. After I finish showering, she always throws my underwear at my face.

Grandma Resuba says she can't trust us to shut up in her house, so she makes us always stay together. She says we have to sit on the steps together in our underwear because she isn't spending one penny for nightclothes for us. She says that we should know that nothing belongs to us.

As the last of us comes up from the shower, we are allowed to go upstairs to sleep with only one sheet—no pajamas, no blanket, no slippers, and no housecoats.

One day, Daddy's younger brother stops over with his wife and baby son. I've always liked him because he is the only one to ever show some kindness to us, sometimes slipping us candy when no one is looking.

He and his wife are the only ones who will buy us a Christmas gift and wrap it. I can tell that Grandma Resuba does not like this son as much as she likes her other two. I know he feels sorry for us.

While we are sitting on the steps waiting for Trevor after taking a shower, he stops over, and, seeing us sitting there together, he says something that will always bother me for years to come. He points to me and says, "She should not be sitting like that with her brothers." Grandma Resuba says, "It doesn't matter, they are all the same. She is no different from the boys, and mind your own business. This is my house. I'll do what I want."

Grandma Resuba is always telling me that I am like the boys and to stop asking what Alice gets when she goes shopping. I know what she is really saying, that somehow without my mother here, I will never be a girl. Only, I wonder what I am supposed to be, because no one pays any attention to me.

My uncle gets quiet; then he and his wife leave, saying they will see us later. As they walk out the door, I want to curl up and hide, because for some reason, he has told me I am different from my brothers, and Grandma Resuba tells me that I am different from my sister.

I feel so lonely and wonder how I am different, and what is wrong? Is there something else that is different about me besides my bastard blood?

While I lie in bed, my eight-year-old mind is going a mile a minute, trying to figure out what has made my uncle so mad and what is wrong with me.

Alice is a daughter and granddaughter, a girl who gets dressed up every Saturday and goes shopping, who is fed at a table with adults and allowed to sit on the couch and watch TV. She lives, what I later find out from kids in school, a normal life.

Sometimes I feel like I don't belong as a girl. I begin wondering all kinds of things. What is it like to be a girl? Why did my uncle say I should not be walking around like that? Why are my brothers boys and my sister a girl? Why am I in neither category? If I am so different, maybe when my mother comes back, she won't want me either.

It is at eight years old, with no one to talk to, that I begin having these conversations with my mother inside my head, trying to make sense of all the confusion. Maybe being a girl is not so important, and if I need a mother, but do not have one, maybe I am different.

I try to remember what my mother looked like, how she smelled, and what she sounded like; but increasingly, she seems to fade from my memory. I ask God to find her, because I am not sure anymore about anything or anyone, even about what I am supposed to think or ask.

I am worried that being a girl, but not a normal girl, will be the reason my mother will choose not to come back to me.

This is about the time that we have a play in school and are supposed to ask our parents to make a costume. I am so afraid of Grandma Resuba. One of the mothers in class volunteers to make me an outfit so I can be in the play. However, I can feel in my mind that I am moving away from people. We are the talk among the adults in school.

How do I stop all the ways that make me different from my brothers and my sister? How do I get back to my mother? Does she even hear me when I talk to God about her?

I wonder when my mother was little, did her grandmother ever threaten her? Grandma Resuba often tells us about these things or places called mine shafts, where people disappear and are never heard from again.

Today Grandma Resuba sees me staring at her again and starts screaming at me not to look at her, before she does something to me. She says that the hole is so deep and dark that not even the police will find us, and if I don't stop watching her, she will find the deepest one and throw me down in it. I tell her, "When my mother comes back, she's going to be mad at you for being mean to me."

I know Grandma Resuba will kill me like that because she already beats the boys with the belt that she likes to hold during shower time. She is always threatening us and hating us.

I wish someone could see what Grandma Resuba is doing, but who am I going to tell? In school, the teachers say that she must have liked us; after all, she took us in. Daddy never says anything when we tell him. I wish for the impossible—that my mother can come back and put an end to this madness before Grandma Resuba really kills us.

I will try not to stare at Grandma Resuba or any other adults. I will avoid looking at them because they might get mad and want to hurt me. I don't want to disappear, just in case my mother comes back to look for me. However, I will make sure that I don't stand too close to the edge of the coal bank, just in case Grandma Resuba tries to come down and sneak up behind me and push me over the edge.

I wish my mother would hurry and come back soon. I just don't feel safe here. Grandma Resuba doesn't want us here, and I'm so afraid of her. I lie awake at night, imagining how deep and dark a mine shaft must be.

Are there really places that I could disappear into forever? Are there mine shafts that are so deep and dark that even God won't find me? How do I stop being afraid of the darkness?

Why do people tease me? In school, the kids sometimes make fun of the way I speak, but I've gotten used to that. I am also teased by my Grandma Resuba about not being wanted by anyone.

One of Grandma Resuba's favorite ways to tease my brothers and me is to stand on the porch holding Alice in her arms and scream at us while we are standing on the coal bank. She always says the same thing. "Hey, you bastard orphans, look at my granddaughter, the daughter I never had. You four are nothing but bastard orphans, and no one will ever want you. You will never be as good as this granddaughter of mine." She then kisses Alice up and down, like my mother must have kissed me when I was a baby, and goes into the house with her, leaving us out in the cold or the heat.

I hate when Grandma Resuba teases us like that, and I wish that I was as good as Alice, or even like Alice, so Grandma Resuba will like me. Maybe she knows about my secret of wanting to be a boy like my brothers so that I can at least blend into their world.

Sometimes I think Grandma Resuba likes looking down on us and making fun of us because my mother is not here to protect us. She says we are nothing but bastard orphans who have no business existing. Only Alice counts. Are there different kinds of orphans?

Is there a special place for mothers who leave their children behind? Does my mother ever think about me?

Why did my mother name me Jerri Diane? Grandma Resuba is mad tonight because she has caught me watching her again. She tells me that I am nothing but a bastard orphan and to quit watching her.

I tell Grandma Resuba that my name is Jerri; then she laughs at me. She says my mother was either stupid for not knowing I was a girl or else she wanted all boys, or she named me a boy's name because she didn't want me.

This isn't true, is it? My mother did want me at one point in my life. What If she didn't? What if Grandma Resuba is right about my mother wanting all boys? I know my mother was not stupid, but how do I prove to Grandma Resuba that she really liked me and wanted me? I am getting confused in my mind about a lot of things.

Grandma Resuba keeps saying, "Get back with the boys, with your boy name. See my granddaughter with her girl name! Look at you, get away from me. I can't stand the sight of you or your brothers!"

As I walk down to the coal bank, I wonder what she, Grandma Resuba, means by names being girls' or boys', and if that means I am not who I think I am. *Alice* is such a beautiful name, and my sister is so pretty and always dressed up.

Look at me, with a name that adults think is funny and a grandmother who hates me because I am a different kind of person from my sister and my brothers.

I keep all my thoughts to myself, lest Grandma Resuba is right about me being a mistake—born a girl when my mother wanted a boy.

Is that why my mother went away? I want her to come back and make Grandma Resuba stop saying these mean things and tell her that I was wanted, even if I was a born a girl.

Could it be that even if I have the most splendid girl's name in the whole universe, it would not make me any more wanted by Daddy's family?

Today in the coal cellar, I overhear Grandpa Resuba saying that his black lung check is late. Then I hear Grandma Resuba say that after breathing that coal dust in the mines all these years, Grandpa Resuba, who is sick with the black lung disease, should have had his check on time.

I look at the coal bin—which is ten feet from the picnic table where Trevor, Tyler, Billy, and I sit—and wonder if we will get the black lung disease. When the coal is delivered, a full dump truck pours it through this thing called a chute.

It does get musty, and it is hard for me to breathe at times in the coal cellar, although I don't dare to complain. Sometimes I wonder if I am getting sick inside.

After the earache episode, I have learned to keep silent about any pain that I feel, mostly because I don't want to hear about how much Grandma Resuba hates my mother. And I don't want her to feel bad in heaven about having a daughter like me, who isn't always feeling well, or who isn't a girl like Alice.

The coal dust permeates the whole coal cellar. Coal is shiny, dusty, and black. Even after it is burned in the coal oven, when Grandpa Resuba shifts the ashes, there is white dust. The coal oven is five feet from the picnic table, and I am always afraid that the burning embers might pop toward us and set us on fire. I am afraid that we will burn to death like Grandma Resuba gleefully tells us that our mother did.

I don't know if Grandma Resuba is telling the truth about my mother and the fire, but if she is, she must have hurt a lot. I hope that heaven can heal my mother quick so she can come back to take care of us soon.

Sometimes I think I am getting the black lung disease because I cough a lot in the coal cellar, and Grandma Resuba gets mad. She says that I'm not allowed to cough in the house. When she is upstairs and I have to cough, I bury my head in my T-shirt so I can muffle the sound. Maybe this is what Grandpa Resuba feels like around the coal, unable to breathe. If we get the black lung disease, I wonder if we will get this thing called a check. We probably won't, because none of us dares to complain.

One time, I ask Grandma Resuba why it is so funny smelling in the coal cellar, and always dusty. She starts screaming at me, saying I am lucky even to be in the coal cellar and that she hopes I choke on the dust.

She is always mad whenever I ask her questions. Grandma Resuba must have a lot of energy because she cleans all the time and screams at us whenever possible.

I look at the coal bin and wonder if the coal comes from the same mine shafts that Grandma Resuba uses in her threats to us. How could something so small and shiny as a piece of coal hurt us with its dust?

In the coal cellar, there is only one little window high above the sink. Sometimes I want Billy to open it because it is hard for me to breathe, but he is too small to reach it. Besides, we all know what Grandma Resuba will do if she catches us. She has a belt that she wraps twice around her hand, and she uses it on the boys for anything, small or big.

I just learn to adjust and breathe through my T-shirt, which I put over my face like the doctors in the hospital.

I also secretly worry that the coal bin will catch fire, because the coal cellar door is next to it. If a fire starts, we won't get out fast enough, so I always keep an eye on the coal bin, just in case I have to get my brothers out quickly.

I just know this: I don't ever want to live in a coal cellar when I get as old as Grandma Resuba.

Do you think that we will disappear in the coal cellar? Why do I have more trouble breathing than my brothers do? Are there dark places in hell like the coal cellar? Will I be sick all the time that I breathe musty air? Does my mother have a spirit line to my heart, in case I disappear like Grandma Resuba threatens?

Sometimes when I listen to Grandma Resuba talk about my mother, I wonder if she hears her in heaven. I hope she doesn't because she might not like what Grandma Resuba is saying about her. I told God to move my mother into a different room so that her feelings don't get hurt, so if she is moved, I hope she knows why.

The adults that live in this house are mean. Daddy is the nicest, but he is never home, and when he is, he rarely talks to us. I think that he is afraid of Grandma Resuba. I know I am afraid of her.

One time I asked Grandpa Resuba if he liked me. He told me to get away from him because I was no grandchild of his. He said that my brothers and I were a big burden and were always bothering his wife. I wonder why Grandpa Resuba doesn't like us either. Maybe when a man is a husband like Grandpa Resuba and he is married to a woman who is a wife like Grandma Resuba, then they must have to think alike and, I guess, to hate alike.

Grandpa Resuba has a lot of silver hair, probably like Solomon from the Bible, but he doesn't appear too smart, too wise, or too good like Solomon. Solomon had to choose for a child; Grandpa Resuba doesn't care and just lets Grandma Resuba be mean to us, although we haven't done anything wrong that I can remember.

Daddy's youngest brother, Uncle Resuba, is tall and mean. He limps from a car accident and says that we are lucky to have two good legs. He laughs when Grandma Resuba threatens us with the mine shafts, saying he'd be happy to toss us over the edge. He tells us that we are bastards, just like his mother said. Aside from kicking us sometimes when we sit on the steps, he likes calling us names and words I have never heard of before. Otherwise, he usually never speaks to us.

I still don't know why God won't send our mother back to us in exchange for Daddy's family.

Why does Daddy's family have to be so mean when I try to like them? When we visited before my mother left, they liked us. Sometimes these adults can be very confusing; they always change their minds and hate my brothers and me because of our bastard blood.

Did my mother know that they hated her before she left us with them?

I am so hungry all the time. My brothers and I wonder what we did wrong to make everyone hate us. Billy says he is tired of having nothing all the time for lunch and dinner, except for a bologna sandwich.

We are still four skinny bastard orphans hovering together on the coal bank, trying to figure out what to do next.

Grandma Resuba must be a good cook because we can smell the food in the coal cellar as we eat our sandwich. I think they have chicken, hamburgers, and steak a lot because it smells like them.

Every once in a while, but not often, Grandma Resuba gives us something hot to eat. She always tells us that we don't even deserve what little she feeds us. She likes to say "You bastards, I wish you would just disappear or die like your mother."

I try not to stare at Grandma Resuba, but I just can't understand what we did to make her hate us every day and feed us different kinds of food. Maybe there is bastard food and family food.

Even on the holidays, which we never get to celebrate with the Resuba family, we eat our sandwiches in the coal cellar in silence, while they have all their relatives over for a big dinner. We can really smell the turkey at Christmas and Thanksgiving.

We can see all these cars in the driveway from the coal cellar door. At times, we can hear this muffled laughter upstairs floating down to us. They probably don't even know we exist down in this coal cellar. I wonder if any of them would feel bad about eating if they knew about us.

Since Grandma Resuba hits the boys with the belt but not me that often, Billy tells me to ask her for hot food. One time when I do, she starts screaming at me that the food is for her family and that they are stuck with us. She told me that we are going to be put away someday, where we will be starved, so we should enjoy the sandwiches while we can. Then she tells me to stop asking questions, because if I don't, she will even stop giving us the sandwiches. I tell her that when my mother returns, I will tell her how mean she is and that she is supposed to treat us nicely because she is our grandmother.

Grandma Resuba is furious and comes toward me, screaming that my mother is dead and never coming back. She screams that I am nothing but an ugly bastard orphan whom she would kill if she could get away with it.

Grandma Resuba says she is tired of the time and space that my brothers and I take up. In addition, she tells me, "You should quit asking questions about things that are none of your business, or threatening to tell your mother about me. She was a wild and loose woman who had no business saddling us with her four bastards.

"Thank God, she is dead, and if the four of you would just die and disappear, then my family would be better off. I will never give you any of the food I feed my family.

"The neighbors can call the cops all they want, but no one tells me what to do in my home. They can't save you, and the police don't give a damn about you.

"I can do anything I want, including starving you to death, and no one can stop me or protect you. Now get outside with your bastard blood, and do not ask me for food again.

"All of you sicken me, especially you with your ugly face and bad speech, always staring at me and questioning me!"

My brothers and I go back to the coal bank where it is freezing. Billy tells me that I did a good job questioning her about the food. Sometimes I wonder if Billy knows how afraid I am of Grandma Resuba and her threats.

Billy says that tomorrow he will try to steal some food from the store for us. He says that stealing isn't good, but neither is starving.

I ask Billy if my mother is dead. He says that she is, in a way, but she is also alive in our hearts.

See, I know my mother isn't dead, no matter what Grandma Resuba says. I just wish she were here, because sometimes it is so hard not to cry. I want her to hold me and tell me everything will be okay.

Is there really bastard food and family food? Does my mother eat in heaven while we starve on earth? What is it about us that makes us so unacceptable?

At Grandma and Grandpa Resuba's house, they always tell us that we can enter and leave the house only through the coal cellar door. It is painted white, while the rest of the house is painted yellow. We have to duck our heads as we enter and leave because it is so low.

I stand on the coal bank, watching the house all the time, because I am always trying to figure out what my mother is going to say to them when she comes for us. I wonder if Grandma Resuba will make my mother go through the coal cellar door, because she talks bad about her all the time. She especially talks about how she had four bastard children that she dumped on Daddy by dying.

Daddy, his brothers, the Orthodox priest, Alice, Grandma, and Grandpa all go through the porch door, not the coal cellar door.

I guess when someone belongs to a family, or is a real flesh-and-blood person, they get to use different doors. If my brothers and I weren't bastard orphans, then maybe we could use the family door entrance to the house. When my mother left us—or died, as Grandma Resuba says she did, that was the time when we had to begin using the coal cellar door.

The neighbors behind Grandma and Grandpa Resuba let their kids come and go through their porch door. They don't use the coal cellar door like we do, but then their parents don't call them bastards or make them stay outside all day into the night.

I wonder if the door to the coal cellar is just one more way of showing that we are different, not real flesh-and-blood kids. Sometimes I look at Grandma Resuba's house and try to imagine how things would be different, if only she would let us belong.

Even at night when we sit on the steps in our underwear, I wonder what it is like to sit at Grandma Resuba's kitchen table and eat family food. But even I know that there is only one way in and out of this house for us, and that is always through the coal cellar door.

Are the doors in heaven different for all the angels? Would my mother be allowed to go through the porch door? God, how many doors will be shut to kids like me?

One thing that Trevor, Tyler, Billy, and I know is how much the neighbors hate Grandma Resuba. They always ask us why she hates us so much. I tell them how much she hates our mother and us for being our mother's children.

The neighborhood knows everything that is going on. They say that what Grandma Resuba is doing isn't right, and they are going to call the police. Mostly, they don't understand how she could hate a dead person and treat her orphaned children the way she treats us.

The neighbor who lives next door to Grandma Resuba's house is nice, and she feels sorry for us. They have a girl close to my age, but Grandma Resuba says I'm not allowed to play with her. She says that I have to stay with the boys, where I belong.

There are the neighbors in the back of the coal bank who are so nice to my brothers. They tell Billy that my mother would be so sad to see what is happening to us. The woman said that she has called the police, just like the neighbors living next door to Daddy's family did. She tells us that we have to be strong because, surely, the police will do something someday.

Billy is a friend to the family who also tries to help us. He said that they are angry that we are left out in the freezing cold all the time and we are all so thin. They worry that we are not getting enough food to eat.

Increasingly, we feel more alone, except for the neighbors' occasional encouraging comments about how they will call the police. We are growing tired of waiting to be rescued.

The neighbors next to Grandma Resuba's house are always fighting with her because of the screaming. On the open porch, Grandma Resuba screams and curses at us, telling us that we are horrible and that no one wants kids like us in their family.

Because Grandma Resuba is so loud, the whole neighborhood can hear her, and that's when this neighbor tells her to stop yelling at us. Then the two of them go at it, screaming at each other, with the neighbor telling her that we are only little kids who stand for hours on the coal bank, day in and day out.

She says that Grandma Resuba or Daddy should make sure that we have gloves, hats, and scarves on and that we should not be down in the coal bank for hours when it is dark. The neighbor doesn't understand why we are hated so much.

Of course, Grandma Resuba is screaming at her to mind her own business, that anything she does for us is more than we deserve. She tells the neighbor that we are the bastard orphans that she got stuck with, and she can do anything she wants to us.

The neighbor tells Grandma Resuba that she will call the police, and this just infuriates her. If the neighbors try to help us, we get into more trouble, with more threats about how evil we are.

I am glad that the neighbors confronted Grandma Resuba even if she treats us worse. I figure that someday she will make us disappear or kill us, and my mother will never find us, anyway, but at least the neighbors will know the truth.

Sometimes I wonder what it would be like to live in a family again, like the neighbors do. I see their kids going out dressed up like Grandma Resuba does when she takes Alice out with her. Like Alice, they can come and go through any door in their house.

The kids in school tell me about their Easter baskets, Christmas gifts, and family celebrations, which are not happening for my brothers and me. I know we are different from Alice because of our bastard blood. Maybe we are different because the neighbors' kids don't live like Trevor, Tyler, Billy, and me. They are not deprived like we are.

Why can't the neighbors take us away from Grandma Resuba and let us live with them? Is it okay to want to belong to another family? Does my mother hear the neighbors' call for help in heaven?

In Grandma Resuba's house, there are three large bedrooms. Trevor, Tyler, Billy, and I sleep in one of them. Daddy's youngest brother sleeps in another. Alice is in a crib in Grandma and Grandpa Resuba's bedroom.

The only time that we are allowed upstairs is after showering in the coal cellar, when we go up in our underwear to sleep. Immediately in the morning, when Grandma Resuba says "Hey, you bastards, get down in the coal cellar," we go downstairs to dress in silence.

In the bedroom at night, it gets really cold sometimes. I think it is because I have only my underwear on and a sheet to cover myself. My brothers say that they are cold too, but we are too afraid to ask for a blanket.

My daddy's youngest brother, Uncle Resuba, has a nice quilt on his bed, but I guess children like us won't get one. Sometimes I see Alice wrapped up in a blanket, being rocked by her Grandpa Resuba as they watch TV.

At nighttime, the thing that always fascinates me is the bathroom. Where we sleep, me on the floor and my brothers sharing one bed, I can see this shiny clean bathroom right near my feet.

I wonder sometimes why we are forbidden to use the bathroom in the house. I know what Grandma Resuba says about us and how we will never use anything in her house. She says that bastards like us aren't good enough to use the bathroom and that the less we are seen, the better.

Yet as I sneak a look at the bathroom, I marvel at how clean and shiny it is. The tub is big, there is a mirror high above the sink, and I can't reach it. There is a rug in it, and it smells clean in there.

Sometimes I want to look in the mirror to see if I am as ugly as Grandma Resuba says.

Mostly, what I hate about the darkness of the night is knowing that if we have to go to the bathroom, we will have to go out into the blackness of the night by ourselves to the outhouse.

I force myself never to need to go to the bathroom. The outhouse is dark even in the daytime and smelly.

We don't dare to use the bathroom in the house, although it is next door to the room we sleep in.

By accident, a few months back, one of the twins wet the bed because he was afraid to go out into the dark to the outhouse. Grandma Resuba made him walk in his underwear halfway down the block in the middle of February. He was crying and freezing.

I hated Grandma Resuba because my brother is only seven years old. Finally she called him back and said to all of us that the next bastard who made a mess in her house would stay outside all night, and she didn't care if we froze to death.

It isn't that we drink a lot. We get only a cup of milk for lunch and dinner. We never get any other liquid, not even water, because we are not allowed to drink from any sink in the house.

Grandma Resuba has separate dishes for us to use, and everything is set out for us before we are called to eat. Billy tells us to drink as much water as we can when we are at school. Only a sandwich and a cup of milk await us when we come home—that is, until we get the bowl of cereal for breakfast the next morning.

I guess for my one brother, it is just too hard to go to the outhouse in the night because it is so dark. Yet Grandma Resuba says she will beat him if he uses the bathroom that is three feet from his bed.

Billy says we cannot let Grandma Resuba see us cry, because then she will think she is right. Trevor and Tyler say they will try, but they are hungry and afraid of the dark when they have to go to the bathroom at night.

Billy says that we can wake him up, and he will walk with us to the outhouse in the dark. He tells them not to wet the bed because he hears them talking about getting rid of us or making us die and disappear.

I know my mother told me I should love everyone, but shouldn't everyone also love us? Why do Grandma and Grandpa Resuba hate us so much? How could there be different kinds of bathrooms, one for bastards like us and one for the real family kids like Alice?

The police are here again; they come quite often. There is a nice family that likes Billy, and they call the police because Billy tells them about how we are being treated. I'm glad there are people who try to help us. The neighbors behind Grandma Resuba's house is always yelling at her about how she treats us, and they call the cops.

Most of the time though, our lives never change because the police don't make Grandma Resuba change. The first time the cop comes out to the house, he calls us from the coal bank to the porch and says that he wants her to tell him what the problem is.

Grandma Resuba says she got stuck with "these four bastards from my son's marriage," and no one should interfere in her life. The cop tells her just to make sure that there are no marks that can be seen.

He doesn't ask how we are or if we need help. He talks to Grandma Resuba as if we are not present.

Grandma Resuba says that the neighbors hate her and want to get rid of her, so they call the cops all the time just to harass her. The cop says he admires her for taking care of all these additional children, who are not her flesh and blood.

Grandma Resuba says that she is in her forties and willingly accepts her real granddaughter. She resents being forced to keep stepchildren, whom her son stupidly adopted, in her home. She says that we should count our blessings.

The cop actually tells Grandma Resuba that he understands how hard it must be being stuck with someone else's children. He tells her to make the best of it because the next cop might not be as nice as he is. He tells us that we need to be good and to quit making trouble so that the neighbors won't call the police. He also says that policemen are very busy and have more important things to handle.

Grandma Resuba is standing behind him, smiling. We just stand there with our heads down. We go back to the coal bank, still wondering why no one will help us.

The police come again and again but never ask us what is happening. We are very good. We never try to come into the house until Grandma Resuba yells for us, and we never talk in the coal cellar unless we whisper. In school, we don't get in trouble.

None of us knows what to do to make the madness stop. Why does the whole Resuba family hate us? That is a question we ask a thousand times; even Billy, who is twelve years old, can't figure it out, and he's really smart.

Billy was always trying to figure out a way, from the time he was ten years old, to make them like us, or to find someone to save us.

Billy remembers more than I do, or Trevor and Tyler. He keeps telling us how our mother always told him to go to the police if he is ever in trouble. He says that Mother told him that policemen are nice, and they protect little kids. He doesn't understand why the neighbors know the truth about the family, and yet, when they call the police, the cops don't do anything.

I look at the police in their uniforms and wonder how they could believe Grandma Resuba and not all the neighbors that call in to report what is happening. Even when it is snowing hard and we are freezing and the cops are called, she says we need fresh air.

Grandma Resuba is always telling them that we are nothing but trouble. She says that kids like us don't know how to behave and that our mother was wild, and that is why we are bad.

I wish God could make the policemen smart enough to see how Grandma Resuba is lying about my mother and us. Couldn't he "zap" Grandma Resuba's family and make them nice to us?

Things are so different without my mother, and I decide to list all the changes in my life since she left me. We have been sent upstairs to bed, and it is so dark in the bedroom as I stare at the stars through the window. The following are ways that I live a life that is different from what I had known with her:

1)   No one tousles my hair, touches me, or hugs me.
2)   No one plays games with me.
3)   No one asks me if I have homework or if I finished it.
4)   No one combs my hair like my mother did.
5)   No one takes me to church anymore or to Bible school.
6)   No one comes to school when other parents do.
7)   No one lets me hang out around the kitchen.
8)   No one asks me if I am practicing my speech.
9)   No one buys me an Easter outfit.
10) No one holds my hand when I cross the big streets.
11) No one lets me eat Thanksgiving or Christmas dinners with them. We have to eat in the coal cellar, while laughter and conversation floats down to us from Daddy's family upstairs.
12) No one tells me stories about God anymore like my mother did.
13) No one celebrates my birthday.
14) No one rocks me on her lap in the rocking chair that my mother had.
15) No one takes me shopping.
16) No one brushes the hair off my face and asks me how school was today.
17) No one tells me I am special or pretty or smart, just that I'm the same stupid bastard.
18) No one defends me anymore.
19) No one tucks me into bed at night, reads me a story, or kisses me good night.

I look at the stars at night and wonder if my mother is shining up there. I wonder if she can hear me pray for her touch? I bargain with God that I will be a good girl, if only he will let her return for just a little while, just so I can touch her.

I wonder if God does bargain with little girls who don't belong anywhere or to anyone? What do I have to offer God in exchange for having my mother back?

Daddy builds a shower with a glass door on it because his mother refuses to let us use the bathroom in the house. Directly across from this shower is the red picnic table with a naked lightbulb overhead that has a string attached to it.

We always leave the house and enter through the basement steps. Grandma Resuba says the less she sees of the bastards, the better she feels. I begin to shut her out of my mind, planning for my mother's return or possibly going back to Indiana.

As time goes on, Grandma Resuba is beginning to feed us less and less. We are so hungry, and I mean really hungry. Billy begins to pick up food and candy in the store because we eat the only sandwich we get for lunch on the way to school.

Billy has been caught stealing candy. When the police bring him home, they tell Grandma Resuba that he tells them his sister and brothers are hungry. The police say that they have been called many times before, and if they have to come out again, they will press charges against her and take all the children.

When the police leave, Grandma Resuba begins screaming that this is proof that we are no good. I can still hear her in my mind, screaming at Daddy to get rid of us before we contaminate Alice. Billy feels bad, but he is only trying to help all of us.

I think this is my first experience of really hating. It is as though we were nonexistent, nonessential, and disposable.

I wonder sometimes, Who are the good people here, us or Daddy and his family?

I begin around nine years old to hate myself and the fact that I am somehow physically different from my brothers and my sister. It is not as though I understand any of the differences.

I just want to be exactly like my brothers because the message to me is very clear: Alice is this girl child; I am just like my brothers. Yet I know from my uncle's comment that there is something wrong with me.

It is as if for two years my brothers and I have been isolated in this secret world, with no interaction with adults, except for school. School is a place where no one yells at us, but none of us, and especially not me, can say anything. Everyone in class has parents. They bring real lunches and do not seem to be afraid of adults.

There is a girl named Lacey who invites me to her house. I go, and I cannot believe how nice her mother is. She hugs Lacey and gives us a snack of cookies and milk. I keep waiting for her to tell me to go away because I know I do not belong, but she doesn't.

When Grandma Resuba finds out, she is very angry, telling me I am stupid if I think anyone will want someone like me hanging around their child. She forbids me from talking to anyone. She says my brothers should be enough for me.

After that visit to Lacey's home, I begin to realize that women make the warmth in a home. I realize that I will never have a home because I would have to be a girl first, and then a woman. I know that at least when my mother was here, she was a woman, and she knew how to have a home.

I begin to drift farther and farther into myself. How do I rise above all the differences?

People keep telling me that my mother died, although I still believe that she has left me only temporarily. It is now May 1965, and the classroom teacher insists that I make a Mother's Day card. I try to tell her that I don't have a mother. She tells me that everyone has a mother; I can just give the card to my grandmother or aunt or some woman.

I tell her that Daddy's mother does not really like me, but the teacher tells me, of course, she likes me! Besides, who would resist a card from a cute eight-year-old? So in third grade, I make my first Mother's Day card and take it home.

When Grandma Resuba yells for us to come into the coal cellar that night and get a shower, I give the card to her. She laughs at me. "What the hell is this? I wouldn't be a mother to a girl like you! Stay over there with the boys, where you belong, and keep away from me! I don't want anything from the likes of you." Then she tears up my card and throws it away.

The teacher asks me the next day if Grandma Resuba liked my card. I say "I don't know" because I am afraid the teacher might agree with Daddy's mother that I am not good enough to give her a Mother's Day card.

I decide that for the next Mother's Day, when I have to make a card, I will just rip it up myself on the way out of class and throw it away.

I begin to believe I will never be good enough to give anyone a Mother's Day card. I'll just start to pretend the day does not exist.

I wonder if my mother would have wanted a card from a freckle-faced, dimpled hard-to-understand, speech-imperfect female child had she been around.

I begin to think that if I could be exactly like my brothers, like a boy, then I will not care about becoming more confused about being a girl and wishing my mother was here to hold me together. I will never celebrate the holiday called Mother's Day.

What is so important about having a mother? How do I stop the incessant longing for my mother to hold me and to tell me everything will be okay? I wonder if she thinks that heaven is really that great with Jesus, without my brothers and me?

Today I overhear Daddy and Grandma Resuba talking about where to put us. His mom is yelling that she has had enough, and she wants us gone. She says there are places where he can get rid of us, and he had better act soon.

I ask Daddy, "Why is Grandmother so mean?" He says that we don't belong in his family, only Alice. I ask him if my mother is ever coming back. I tell him that I have been praying really hard, and I think that God will let her come back. I tell him about the mustard seed from the Bible school, although we have not gone since my mother left.

The Bible says that if I believe with all my heart and all my soul and have the faith of a mustard seed, then my mother will come back. That's what it says in the Bible. My daddy says she is never coming back, and he has to find a place for Trevor, Tyler, Billy, and me. I ask him about Grandma in Indiana.

Daddy tells me that no one wants us. People have their own families, and maybe if I am a good girl, like Alice, then someone might take me. Grandma Resuba comes down the coal cellar steps and yells at me. "No one is ever gonna want you. Look at you, you can't even talk right!"

Daddy never says a word. He just goes upstairs after Grandma Resuba. That night, I ask God to change me. I do not want to be a nine-year-old girl without a mother, because I do not have enough faith. I know that if my mother's family doesn't want me and Daddy doesn't want me, then my mother could never want me. I do have the faith of a mustard seed, but I still cannot move the mountains of hard hearts.

I wish my mother could ask God to send me more mustard seeds so I don't lose hope about her coming back.

I begin hearing the word "orphanage" thrown around and wonder what is going on. I try to focus on my birthday coming soon.

I always think birthdays are supposed to be important. Everyone in third and fourth grade brings a treat. If you have a birthday in the summer, you pick out a school date to substitute for it, and you have to bring a treat to celebrate.

In third grade, I ask Grandma Resuba if she will make me cupcakes so we could celebrate my birthday in school, and she says, "What for? You want me to give you my stuff for school? You don't belong here. Nothing in this house is yours. If your teacher wants to celebrate your birthday, let her bring the treat. I have nothing to do with you. Now get outside with the boys, where you belong, and don't ever ask me about your birthday again!"

I tell the teacher that Grandma Resuba is busy, but I think she knows. After all, by May, during my third grade, I can hear the whispers of the teachers in the grade school, talking about us.

The teacher tells me not to worry about the summer birthday celebration; she will think of something. On the day of the summer birthday party, she calls me in the hall and gives me two bags of candy to give out as my treat.

I never tell Grandma Resuba. She would have hated me more, if that were possible.

I decide I will not celebrate birthdays, either, as I will not expect presents, a party, or even a cake. I begin to realize that if I pretend things don't exist, although they are normal for other people, then I don't hurt too much.

Is it still possible to be like other girls, even without a mother or a family?

Billy ran away during our second year of living in the coal cellar. Daddy and Grandma Resuba are mad because the police bring him back and say that Billy told them they are being cruel to us. I know he is trying to get to this place called Seymour, Indiana.

We always spend hours huddled in a circle on the coal bank, talking about my mother's family. Billy remembers more than I do because he is two years older. All I know is that I had a grandmother and two aunts. I do not know their last names, their telephone numbers, or where they live.

When I am nine, I stop at a pay phone to look in a telephone book, but they don't list people by their first names or by their titles, and besides, I never did learn how to use the telephone.

As my brothers and I try to talk ourselves into believing that we will be rescued, I begin to fantasize about the family who will come swooping down to take us away.

My brothers will go to Grandma and one aunt, and I will go to live with my other aunt. We know that no one can take all four of us at once. What we do is divide ourselves so no one will feel stuck with all of us at once, like Daddy and Grandma Resuba feel.

When Billy leaves to run away, he is going to find these people and tell them how bad we are being treated; then he will come back and save us. The police are mad at Grandma Resuba, telling her they have several complaints about her treatment of us. She had better find a place for us, before they receive another complaint. When they leave, Grandma Resuba is so mad. She screams, "That's it! They're gone!"

I ask my mother, where are our protectors? Who will champion us? Who will nurture us? I wonder if we are truly left on our own. What would she have thought?

Christmas of 1966 is coming, and I still believe that somehow I am not going to be forgotten. The last two Christmas holidays, we ate in the coal cellar. Already, I am becoming so withdrawn that sometimes it is as though I am retreating behind a maze of doors. I begin to visualize, cementing myself inside cinder blocks.

When the first Christmas comes around after my mother's death, I am eight years old and in third grade. I still believe in Santa Claus. I remember, before she died, how she baked cookies, pacing back and forth, humming to herself. She would follow this by rocking me in front of the Christmas tree, telling me that I am a good girl and that she loved me.

However, these images are beginning to fade. Daddy and his family have different ideas about the way Trevor, Tyler, Billy, and I will celebrate and how their family, with Alice, will spend the holiday.

There are so many gifts under the tree, because after the shower, we will walk through the living room and see them.

I am excited. I think that, for sure, Grandma Resuba and Daddy will let us eat with them upstairs and give us presents. I think at least Santa Claus will remember us, maybe even bring my mother back. That is all I wish for Christmas.

On Christmas morning, on the way to the coal cellar, we see Alice opening all these gifts, but there is none for us, except for a pair of jeans and a shirt. We eat by ourselves in the coal cellar and spend the day huddled in the freezing cold on the coal bank.

I learn that there is no Santa Claus and that my mother is not coming back. I decide that Christmas is for other people, and if I shut it out of my mind, I will not need or want to experience the meaning of Christmas.

Maybe we are not only becoming motherless, but also family-less.

I wonder if my mother celebrates Christmas in heaven? Does she feel my loneliness and intense longing for her return?

I can't wait for Easter to come because I remember when my mother would make candy and take us to church. Grandma Resuba took Alice shopping for her Easter outfit and a pretty hat. It is hanging in the living room where we can see it as we walk up the steps from the coal cellar after our shower.

I wonder if they will finally take us to church, and I wonder when I will get my Easter outfit. I know that I will not go shopping, because Grandma Resuba never takes me shopping, but maybe she will buy me an outfit.

Easter comes in 1965. At eight years old, I am so excited because I think, for sure, I will get an Easter basket. I saw one in the living room the night before. Also, I wonder how I will go to church without an Easter dress, shoes, and a bonnet.

When I go downstairs to the coal cellar the next morning, I see the basket is for Alice, and she is all dressed up for church. I ask if we are going to church and if I will get an Easter outfit.

Grandma Resuba tells me, "No, why do you think you are going to get an Easter outfit? You are not part of me, and this is my granddaughter. I have nothing to do with you. Get outside with the boys, and quit staring at my granddaughter!"

It just seems so unfair. All I want is to be like Alice. It's just that I cannot find out what I need to change so Grandma Resuba will like me. I begin to become convinced that nothing I do will be good enough. In school, all that the kids talk about is Easter.

My brothers and I share one coconut cream egg in the basement. I add Easter to my list of things I don't deserve to celebrate.

Who cares anymore? Maybe I can pretend I am a super girl, and I don't need or want anything or anyone, but I don't think my mother wants me to be like that. Do I have a choice?

I am beginning to think that maybe I am a boy. I am so confused about everything. The only people I have to talk to are my brothers. We have no friends, no family, and no other human beings with whom to speak. I feel so overwhelmed by the constant presence of my brothers and the slams I feel coming my way every time I try to enter the female world of my sister and Grandma Resuba.

We are always dressed alike, together constantly, treated as one entity. I don't want to be a boy, but it is getting so hard to hold on to the girl/daughter image I must have had when my mother left.

Sometimes I think so much about this my head spins. My mother probably will not like me like this. I can't seem to hold all of me together anymore. I can't tell anyone, because I have no one to tell.

I am beginning to develop the habit of walking with my arms crossed at my chest and staring at the ground, trying to grow invisible. I wish I could be a better daughter. Also, I wish I could disappear inside myself more quickly. How did I ever turn out this way?

Daddy is hardly ever home. He spends most of the week away at the air force base in New Jersey, sometimes two weeks at a time. I dread it when he goes away—not that he talks to us or defends us, because he doesn't. It's just I keep hoping he will change things and make Grandma Resuba nicer. It's as though he is afraid of her too, which does not help us.

Maybe it's just that I remember a time when he was a daddy in the real sense of the word. My mother must have loved him. I wonder what changes a person? What happened to all of us? How is it possible that just by my mother's leaving, or dying, so many lives could be so disrupted?

Daddy is different now. Now he does not talk to us when his mother is around. He will have a whisper conversation with me if I ask him something, but only when Grandma Resuba is in the house. Grandma and Grandpa Resuba despise our very existence.

I am struggling to understand how people can change. I wanted to remain my mother's loving daughter. I am beginning to forget how to be anything or anyone. I am trying to keep the threats form hurting me. Maybe mothers are the life shields of the family. Since my mother is no longer here, we are left unprotected.

How can I change, even when I don't want to change? Couldn't my mother just ask God to send me another life shield?

In my fifth-grade class, I read about the Spartans and how they toughened themselves so that no matter what happened to them, they would survive. The teacher said that they were stoic. I looked up the word, "stoic" in the dictionary. It said "to be tough of mind without display of emotion." I went back and looked up "emotion" in the dictionary, which listed loving, laughing, crying, etc.

I am beginning to feel that I am at battle with Daddy's family. I am ten years old now. My birthday comes and goes, unnoticed, and I realize that I am not important. I try very hard never to cry about anything, not to show any weaknesses.

Inside I am so desperate for my mother's affection and attention. I want so much to tell someone and have them hold me, but there is no one to go to for this kind of comfort. All these desires are hurting me.

I decide I will be like a Spartan. I will build my fortress very high with many, many rooms. Inside each room, I will have all these boxes, and each time I want to cry or talk, I will put it inside a box and seal it up. As each room is filled, I will cement it up.

I will take all the things that Grandma Resuba has said and place them in different places in my mind. As a Spartan, I will prepare and assume that every person will hurt me and be ready for it.

When I feel like crying because I still cannot stop the feelings of being hurt, I will bite my lower lip and press my hands to the sides of my face. When hurtful thoughts come my way, I will tighten my stomach and keep repeating to myself, "It doesn't matter, it doesn't matter, I don't matter." There are times when even this does not help.

I wonder if there are a lot of Spartans in the world? Is it possible to be stoic and human?

Lately, Grandma Resuba has been on a terror campaign about this dark place that orphan children are sent. She says that children no one wants, like us, will be locked up in closets, beaten, and held in dark places; and this is what we get for having the police come. She seems almost happy to tell us this.

Sometimes I wonder if Grandma Resuba would like this to happen to her. I just figure, sooner or later, we will be sent away, and I will never, ever, learn about my mother, especially whether she could have ever loved a girl like me.

I feel afraid to sleep at night because Grandma Resuba said that there are places where I can be put where no one will ever find me. Every morning I go downstairs, wondering whether this is the last time my brothers and I will live together. Grandma Resuba says we will be separated, and no one will ever know where any of us are.

I try to ask about going to Indiana. Grandma Resuba laughs and says, "If they wanted you so much, they could have you. They don't want to be stuck with you, guys. Besides, who would take you four bastards? Now get outside!"

How can Grandma Resuba love Alice so much and hate us? She laughs when I ask if Alice will come with us. She tells me that Alice is wanted and important, not a nothing like me. How dare I put her granddaughter in the same category as me?

Every day, as it gets closer to Christmas of 1966, she snickers. "Wait till you see the dark dungeon you are going to, where no one will ever find you." What she does not know is that I am already in an unseen dungeon.

Where are the keys that will unlock the doors that have slammed me in places that I never wanted to be? What happens if the dungeon keeps getting darker and lonelier?

It is getting colder outside. Winter is coming. The winds slap my face, and even blowing on my ungloved hands can't warm them. I feel so lost and so alone and know that things are moving beyond my control. Daddy has been whispering to his brother. I can only catch snags of "What can I do, no one wants them," "Maybe Mom will calm down," and "At least Alice will be okay."

I tell my brothers that Daddy is up to something. Billy tells me how he begged Grandma in Indiana and our aunt not to put us on the bus after the funeral. He knew something bad would happen to us in Scranton with these people, and he was right.

We all want to run away. No one, not even Billy, knows where to go. This Christmas, we really don't expect anything different.

We are still sitting on the steps in our underwear after each shower. After two years, I still hate doing this. I don't think I should be sitting like this, but I am not sure why it is wrong.

The day before Christmas, December 24, 1966, Daddy comes home from the air force base and tells us that he has a special surprise for us later. I think maybe he found a place to live, or we might get a wrapped gift this year, or he found my mother's family in Indiana and they changed their minds and have decided to take us.

Around 4:00 p.m., as it is getting colder and darker, Daddy calls us from the coal bank and tells me, Tyler, Trevor, and Billy that he wants to take us for a ride. We get into the car with only the clothes we are wearing and excitedly whisper about the new house that Daddy has bought for us. I get all excited because I still love Daddy, and I know he wouldn't put us away like Grandma Resuba always tells him to do.

Since it is Christmas Eve, this will be a special present. We drive to an imposing fortress of a building called Our Lady of Help Orphanage. We didn't even pack anything, but then there really wasn't anything to pack. He says he can't keep us, and no one wants us.

Does my mother in heaven see what is happening?

"Change Uninvited"

Changes with their relentless waves continue unabated,
Never stopping their batterings present although uninvited.
The girl swirls around in a dizzying rush to try to be,
what has been absent since her aloneness has begun.

Her mind, heart, body, and soul trying desperately to keep up,
With the pulling and tugging that keeps pushing her here and there.
Parents, families, fathers, mothers, sisters, aunts, uncles,
All manners of relating not a reality even though mighty sought.

Guiding with only self as the light she stumbles without direction,
Trying to grasp for ways to be as others surrounding her.
Wondering when rest will come and others will take over
the raising and nurturing that eludes her but she still needs and seek.

All around are images of what once was before the darkness,
The ordinary chokes up her hidden whisper tears in a place.
That is only filled with absences that she tries to shake,
Never realizing that beyond life there are changes that can't be undone.

From mother to death to cellar to orphanage why all the difference,
Where is the order and structure that should be part of her life.
How long will she continue to be sane in the midst of all this insanity,
She tries so desperately to make sense of what is impossible to understand.

Building rooms inside the castle of her soul she asks God,
Where is the life that once was known and no longer exists.
How did changes uninvited become the norm of her existence,
When she only wants to find the mother who once held her world together.

The Orphanage: Entering Adolescence Alone
Ages 10 - 12

The Orphanage:
Entering Adolescence Alone

(Ages Ten to Twelve)

Dear Mother,

It is so dark, and the main entrance of the orphanage is so large that I feel like a tiny ant. The two women, called nuns, have their entire bodies covered, except for their hands and face; they scare me. They look like they are wearing pillboxes on their heads.

I hear Daddy and the nuns talking about us, as though we are not present. He tells them that his mother will raise his daughter, and the older boy, Billy, will go to live at a different orphanage because he is already twelve years old.

He tells them that his mother gave him a Christmas deadline to get us out of the house, and although it is Christmas Eve, this is the best he could do.

The nuns ask if there are any gifts he has brought for us. He says no. The nuns tell Daddy that all the children have gone home to families for the holidays and ask if he wants to take us home and bring us back after Christmas. He says no, it is best for everyone this way.

I don't know whom it is best for, Mother. Somehow the image of being placed in an orphanage on Christmas Eve does not strike me as being in the spirit of the season.

I cannot believe Daddy will just leave us. He tells me that I will understand someday, and if I am a good girl, everything will work out.

Where did everyone go who was supposed to protect me? There is nothing in the English language that best describes despair and being forsaken as the word "orphan"—motherless child, and now family-less child.

How could he do this to your children, especially after I loved him so much? Don't people have to still care, although things are not the same anymore?

Love,
Jerri

*   *   *

Daddy says he has to take Billy to the other orphanage and then go home to be with Alice for Christmas. I ask Daddy if we can say good-bye to Billy, and he says no because it's getting late.

He walks out through the lobby into the darkness and leaves behind whatever relationship, even though it had been threadbare, he has had with me as a Daddy.

I bite my lip and focus on having no feelings. I am not going to let anyone see my hurt. I know from this moment on my mother will not find me, and her return ceases to be a possibility in my mind.

I tell God that all that happened is that my mother died. It seems as long as I am not flesh and blood, I am not worthy of existence.

The nuns take my brothers by the hand. I do not let them touch me. I don't want people to touch me.

They lead us upstairs to where we are to eat supper. They say we can sleep together in the dorm during the Christmas holiday until after New Year's Day when the other children return. Then my brothers will live in the boys' section, and I will live in the girls' section.

I tell them no, I want to stay with my brothers. I do not want to be separated. They say this is impossible "because girls stay on the girls' side, and the twins will stay on the boys' side." All I can do is build more rooms with more compartments. The winds of change are blowing hard.

How can this building called an orphanage ever hope to lessen the pain of my mother's absence? Where is she? Surely Jesus could not be in need of her as desperately as I am, could he? How could all of this be God's will?

The orphanage is the biggest building I have ever seen in my life. In the dining room, there are fifty tables that seat four to eight children each. The nuns tell my brothers and me that all the children eat in this one big room. The nuns have a separate dining room.

We will stand in line, like in a cafeteria, with a plate, and receive our food. There will be almost two hundred children returning after the holidays, and two nuns will walk up and down between the tables to make sure everyone behaves.

As they take us on a tour that night, I see a church on the third floor with beautiful stained-glass windows. I have never met a nun before or heard of Catholics, but at least they do not call us names.

They say we will have to go to church every Sunday, and in the morning we cannot talk because it is prayer time.

The dorm where I will sleep has eight beds, and the dorm is connected to four other dorms that are open at the top and bottom.

The place is so overwhelming, and all I can think about is being separated from Trevor and Tyler. The nuns say we have to take a bath every night. I never remember taking a bath.

They hand me pajamas, and I ask why I have to wear them. They say, "You don't want to show off your body, do you?" After eating, bathing, and touring, we go to bed. They say they will see us in the morning and go downstairs.

My brothers and I lie in bed, wondering what will happen next and how we will ever get back with Billy. We are not bad children; it is just that somehow without our mother, who we are has changed for everyone else.

Could our mother have ever imagined that the children that she loved, more than anything in the world, could have ended up in an orphanage? Is it possible to ever recapture that feeling of belonging?

I spend two years in absolute, total isolation with my two brothers, and now they will live in a different part of the building. I hate that I am a girl because this is one more obstacle in the way of what little family I have left. I am more determined than ever to be like them, like a boy. To be a girl means that they send you away.

I already miss my big brother. I wonder if Billy is as lonely as I am on this night. Who will be my protector now?

This Christmas Eve night, I wonder where my mother is, how a holiday that is supposed to bind families together becomes one more step in the disintegration of the cohesive person I was when she was alive.

I try to fathom how Daddy could leave us, and he did not even die! I am mad at my mother for the first time because I bet that if she asks God to let her come back, he will let her. He does not need her, we do!

I think if I stay mad at her, I won't want or need her so much. Maybe she will not want me. I think it is better that she begins to dislike me; then she will not have to know me and find out about my plans to become a boy.

I know I need her to help me to become a girl, but since it is too hard without her, I will just train myself to have no need of her.

I hate Christmas. I was seven the last time I really celebrated. Without a family, there is no point in celebrating anything. I will never be capable of living in a family.

I feel so old, and I am only ten.

Where is my mother this Christmas Eve night?

The next day, the nuns give us each some candy with a bow on top. They say they did not know we were coming because our adoptive father had not called ahead, so there are no gifts. I say nothing because I did not expect anything anyway. They explain that for the holidays, all the children are sent to different families, unless we have one of our own.

They tell us that most of the children are not real orphans, like us, whose parent died. Most of the children have families who temporarily need to place their children while they are dealing with personal issues. They are called pseudo-orphans, or social orphans. Sometimes, the nuns say, some of the children who are orphaned are sent to family members and adopted, and others are adopted by people who want them.

I keep thinking about the word "adoption." The dictionary tells me it means "to be chosen, to be legally and permanently bonded, to be the same as all other members in the family."

This word is hung, like a carrot on a stick, as a possibility, but only if I have no needs and become the perfect girl. Being twins becomes an identity that further separates me from my brothers. Everyone is attracted to them and constantly refer to them as "the twins."

Do you think it is possible to change yourself just by sheer will? How do I become un-orphaned?

The day I fear most has arrived. All the other children are returning from their visits.

Those who received gifts from their families can keep them. If you get a gift from the host family, it has to be donated to the children in Africa.

One of the nuns tells us that if you are a true orphan, then you would want to share it with someone even less fortunate.

This never made much sense to me. To be no one, to belong nowhere, to not be acknowledged by anyone, these certainly must make that child the most unfortunate.

There are about sixty girls living in the ward where I stay. I have never been around so many female people. I want them to go away.

The head of the orphanage, an old nun, calls me over and introduces herself. She says, "You poor motherless thing, maybe someone will find you a home." She has the kindest blue eyes and looks like she is one hundred years old.

"Motherless girl child" becomes my identifying title, since there are very few orphaned children.

I ask if I can live in the orphanage with my brothers. She says no, because "the boys have different things to do than girls," but she will arrange that I get to talk to them at least once a week.

Although she means well, she only adds to my growing belief that it is better to have been a boy. Without my mother, I do not have a clue what a girl is supposed to do or be.

I feel that I am the only one who knows I exist. On Sundays, I talk to my brothers, but I know that whatever family, although unhealthy, I had with my brothers is coming to an end, with no replacement in sight.

How can all of this happen?

Every morning, the nun in charge calls us to get up, kneel down in the hallway, and say morning prayers. She will then leave for church, and everyone is expected to get dressed.

I am horrified this first morning because all the girls are getting dressed in the dorms; they all look lumpy. I enter the toilet to dress because I don't want anyone to see me.

I really hate this body I cannot identify with or understand. I always wear long sleeves and long pants.

I am determined to rise above this body and treat it like everything else that does not exist. I can make things go away in my mind by pushing whatever I cannot handle into the "It's not important or necessary for me" category. I am not going to be like these girls. I am going to be like my brothers so we can live together.

I begin a campaign inside me to separate whatever the outside world sees or needs to see, so that no one sees the crippled and messed-up way I feel, and I'm still wondering how to be a female.

I decide the first thing I must do is to pretend that my body does not exist. It is only necessary for me to live. I will do the best I can possibly do to draw no attention to it.

I am so afraid that someone will find out that I am not a girl like Alice.

The goal is not to get attached so no one will find out how ignorant I am, and also so that I will not endure further humiliation or rejection.

I wonder how much longer I will have to live like this? Would I have been like this if my mother had lived? Does everyone have a limit to how much they can handle?

Are my expectations of wanting to be like other girls without anyone's help reasonable? If it's not a reasonable expectation, how do I get to the same place everyone else is going to all by myself?

I like the fact that I get to go to church again. Since my mother left, Grandma and Daddy never took us to church or Sunday school.

It is so hard to remember what kind of church we went to when my mother was here, but I think it was something called Baptist.

I have looked around for Baptists, but I haven't met any since we moved to Scranton. I guess they live in certain places.

What I miss most about church are the Bible stories, which always tried to explain things. The one I really remember is the mustard seed story, but Daddy said that it isn't true about getting whatever I pray for, even if I pray with my whole heart and soul.

Here at the orphanage, we go to church every Sunday, but I'm not allowed to walk up and get this thing called the bread of life. I am told that I have to be a Catholic to get what the other children get.

I hope that my mother doesn't mind, but I like going to church with these Catholics, and compared to Daddy's family, these nuns are nice. They never bother me, and they don't make fun of me or mock the way I talk. Plus, they don't make comments about my mother or how I'm not a normal girl like Alice.

I decided that I will become a Catholic. My brothers think it would be a neat thing too. Besides, I want to go to church every week and read the Bible stories like I did when my mother was here. Since the only church people I know are Catholic, I think I will join them.

Maybe there are Catholic people who will adopt me if I am Catholic. Maybe I will belong to a group of people that I have something in common with. I hope my mother doesn't get mad in heaven, but I know I should be going to church every week, and the only church I can find is the Catholic one.

Does every religion worship God in the same way? In heaven, will I be able to come to my mother if I change my religion? Why did she always make sure I went to Bible school?

At the orphanage, there is a school, and the children who come from the outside for day school are called outsiders. The orphanage children are called insiders.

I like school. I have always liked school. It is the only place where I feel it does not matter that I am a girl. Every night we go to our classrooms for study hall from eight to nine o'clock and do our homework in silence.

After the study hour, we line up to take a bath. I loathe those times because I am petrified someone will walk in on me and see there is something wrong with my body, something that it isn't normal.

What I do is race up the steps before everyone else and jam a chair against the door. I take a two-minute bath. I am done within four minutes of leaving the study hall. I then lie in bed so no one will see my pajamas or me.

Even though I am ten, no one bothers talking to me or asking me questions. The nuns think I am one of the quietest children they have ever seen.

Since I rarely talk and don't draw attention to myself and don't bother anyone, I am usually left alone. Plus there are sixty other girls from two to twelve years old.

Are there ways of getting where I want to go without my mother? Can I grow and be normal without being mothered or nurtured?

I am called to the office at the orphanage to meet a man called a social worker. He tells me that it is his job to find my brothers and me a place to live.

My brothers are happy. They think we will be leaving the orphanage soon, but I am wary of strangers, just a slight bit more than I am of people I know. The social worker asks me where I want to go. I tell him about my two aunts and Grandma in Indiana. I tell him I will not be any trouble, I will be really quiet. All he has to do is find them.

Trevor, Tyler, and I tell him we can live with different ones because no one will take four children all at once.

Then he says, "How would you all like to go to a foster home?" He says we will probably be separated though. I ask, "What is a foster home?" He says, "People get paid to watch you, but you would not belong there, because at any time, for any reason, you can be moved, so make sure you do not get attached."

The nuns also tell us not to get attached. I guess it is wrong for someone like me to get attached.

My brothers are excited about the foster home idea because they say they want a family and a mother. The social worker says he will work on calling Indiana and on the foster home idea.

I ask before he leaves if Daddy will ever take us back. He tells me no and that Daddy's family does not want us to ever live there again. As a matter of fact, they never wanted us there in the first place.

He says Daddy said it is too hard on his mother, since she does not think it is a good idea for us to interact with Alice.

I ask about Billy. He tells me we will never be together again. He says I will have to accept that this is the way life is.

I wonder what my mother thinks about what is happening?

When I go to the dorm after the visit from the social worker, some of the kids begin to tell me about foster homes. They say you never really belong. They always choose their own children over you and never buy what you need, never mind what you want.

There are kids who say the best thing to aim for is adoption, if Indiana does not pan out.

Adoption, the children tell me, means that you belong. You have the same last name, and no social worker can ever drive up and just take you away for any reason. Plus, with your parents, there is someone to protect you and not let anyone call you names.

The only problem, I am told, is that people want to adopt little kids or babies and that at ten, I am already getting past the age where anyone will want me.

Most people want a boy or a girl who does not need much time and does not have problems. Hopefully, if I do get adopted, they will treat me like a regular kid and be willing to help me later with any of my problems.

I lie in bed this night and wonder how I will ever belong anywhere, and whether I am normal enough to enter the adoption arena. My brothers are cute, boys and twins. Even though none of us talk about Daddy's mother and her treatment of us, I cannot help wondering if part of me is still back there in the coal cellar.

Maybe if I hide more and try to pretend I am a rock with no feelings, no hurts, no problems, and no past, maybe then the social worker can convince Indiana or an adoptive family that I will be no problem.

I also worry about betraying my mother. I know that I had her for eight years, but that wasn't enough.

Would she be hurt because I want a mother whom I can live with and who isn't ashamed of me?

I love her so much, but I cannot seem to remember her very much anymore. I have no pictures. Since she left, no one ever talks about her. No one tells me what she looked like or what she must have been like.

There is a part of me that wants a mother, a flesh-and-blood person who will love me.

When the other girls go home for a visit, they tell me how their mothers take them shopping, eat dinner with them, and hug them when they are dropped off. It is now going on three years since my mother died, and I have not done the following things the other kids talk about in school or in the orphanage. For now this is my list of what I wish:

—I have not gone shopping at all, or even been to a store.
—I have not eaten with any adult at a table.
—I have not cried, even though I hurt a thousand times over.
—I have not celebrated my ninth, tenth, and eleventh birthdays.
—I have not told anyone how much I don't want to be a girl or a boy.
—I have not told anyone how mad I am because I should have a mother.
—I have not asked anyone for anything.
—I have not talked to an adult about anything except what happens in school.
—I have not told anyone about my desire to be adopted.
—I have not celebrated Christmas, Easter, and, especially, Mother's Day.
—I have not lived in a house.
—I have not taken a birthday treat to school.
—I have not called anyone Mom.
—I have not ever felt safe.
—I have not ever been in a kitchen.
—I have not ever made a phone call.
—I have not had my hair combed by anyone.

Daddy comes to visit once or twice every month. Visiting hours in the orphanage are from two to four o'clock every two weeks.

I stand by a big window on the second floor that overlooks the winding driveway coming up from the valley.

Sometimes I imagine that my mother's family in Indiana will drive up and come to take me to live with them. Other times, I imagine a famous movie actress coming and choosing me to belong to her family.

But I know with a depth of sadness that only an orphan child can know that as the others leave, I will be a very hard sell. I am beginning to build higher walls, because more and more, I am determined to keep to myself so that I don't drown in all my disappointments.

The nuns tell me how lucky I am because Daddy, who isn't even my real father, comes to visit sometimes. One in particular asks me why I look so sad. I tell her how much I miss my mother. She tells me how lucky I am because at least I have a roof over my head, and if God wanted me to have a mother, he would have given me one. Somehow, I don't feel very lucky, and I just know I will not be like the other girls if I don't have a mother.

Does my mother think I will ever belong to anyone?

Nights in the orphanage are the hardest. Invariably, I can hear what I call the whisper tears. Many of the other children will cry softly in their beds at night even though most have families somewhere. The shedding of tears over people who will abandon their children, either physically or emotionally, continues every night.

Some of the little girls who are four and five keep asking me why they can't live with their mothers. All I can do is to reassure them that someday their mothers will come to take them home, although I don't tell them mine never will.

I get so mad inside at the adults who think they can treat the orphanage as a respite care center. They think this has no impact upon their children.

I swear that no one will ever break me by reducing me to tears. I pretend that my having no visitors, no family, and no mother are not issues that I want known outside of me. Besides, it takes all of my energy to steel myself, because I feel intuitively that the slams of life coming my way are still not finished.

I lie in bed at night, surrounded by sixty other bodies, still feeling like the loneliest person on the planet. I ask God to take away the lump in my throat and squeeze my eyes really tight so that no one knows that somewhere inside, locked away, are my orphaned whisper tears.

I keep thinking that someone will come, take me by the hand, and wipe away my unseen tears. I wonder sometimes how deep of a well I must dig to contain all the sorrow I feel.

Maybe someday, when I go to college and make a lot of money, I can buy someone to wipe away my whisper tears.

Is there a limit to how much I can handle without crashing?

I begin to dress in black as much as possible, because somewhere inside, I think it makes me less noticeable, and I think I should do penance for my mother's dying and my living.

I get to pick the clothes I wear from these big garbage bags of clothes that are donated to the orphanage. Usually they are wrinkled and not very clean, but I try to find dark clothes so no one will notice me.

In the orphanage, the nun in charge of the girls calls me the Widow Child. She is in her seventies and likes me in a general way. She tells me I always seem sad.

Another nun tells me I sound like I have the weight of the world on me, because I have a habit of thinking deeply about things, and I periodically let go of a heavy sigh. This habit always gives me time to think about what I might say to someone and to balance my words.

I am seen as a very sad child, although I still do well in school. Even my speech is getting better. I really practice hard in private and sing aloud to myself. I also read poetry aloud. I think that if I can talk better, it might be another "selling point" for adoption.

I find that the best way to overcome a speech impediment, or cleft palate, is to sing aloud to myself and read poetry aloud. These two ways of practicing do more to help me to learn to speak words more clearly than anything else I do.

I still look ugly with the scar on my lip, and my nose is still flat. Somehow I just ignore my looks and think speaking clearly might compensate for my lack of having normal facial features. Maybe if I get adopted, I can have what is wrong with me fixed.

I wonder how my mother sees me? By her dying, this is one more issue for me to cope with by myself. The widow child and the orphan embodied in one.

When I was born, what were her dreams and hopes for me?

Again, Trevor, Tyler, and I are called to the office to have a meeting with our social worker. I am so scared that he will tell me something bad, yet I want with all my heart to be told someone wants us. Trevor and Tyler hang on to him as if he were a good friend, but I know he holds such power over us.

I ask him about going to live in Indiana again, because I know intuitively that that is where I belong. I really want to live with my aunt, but I cannot say it aloud, because if I am told outright she does not want me, it will be hard to keep the whisper tears at bay.

The social worker tells us that he spoke with Daddy, who tells him that no one in Indiana is in a position to take us now. They have their own families, and they come first. Since I am ten years old, I should be able to understand this.

The social worker says he wants to find a foster home for the twins and maybe work on one for me. I ask, "Why can't we stay together?" He tells me that he will try, but a lot of people will not take three children. Since I will be an adolescent in a few years, people do not want the responsibility of a teenage girl. Boys are easier to handle.

I do not know what the word "adolescent" means. I look it up in the dictionary. It says "tremendous physical growth, a difficult time in life, a period of searching for identity."

I don't know. Maybe I was born an adolescent. I have no identity. I wonder if things will get worse for me.

Are there things that I do not know? Is that why God gives children mothers, so they can be with them during adolescence? Will I still become an official adolescent, or will I remain a child frozen in time? Is it possible to go through adolescence alone and still turn out knowing what other kids know who have parents and family?

I try to imagine, or really remember, what it must be like to be part of a family. I spend a lot of time having conversations in my head with my mother and God, because no one talks to me.

It is becoming increasingly difficult to initiate any conversation with an adult, women especially. When I am around them, I feel like stepping into the shadows. It is as though I know I am not good enough or worthy of attention.

Every morning in the orphanage, I wake up with my bed completely unmade, with only the bare mattress on the bed frame. The sheets, blankets, and pillows are on the floor. I don't know how they get there.

I have nightmares no one knows about. I am so afraid I won't wake up from them. My biggest fear is that someone will find out. I try to stay awake as long as possible, many nights sitting in the lighted hallway. I don't like the dark. If anyone finds out, they'll think I'm a baby.

I begin to pray that maybe I can wake up one morning with my bed made. If I don't try to stop these night terrors, someone will find out and tell on me. This may be one more reason for my mother's family in Indiana or for some adoptive family not to take me.

I begin "willing" myself not to move in my sleep. It does not work. I then tie the top sheet to both sides of the bed and wiggle my body between the sheets.

I know I am almost eleven and should not have any problems, but I can't stop the nightmares, fear of the dark, or my fear of people, especially women. Maybe I haven't tried hard enough to be perfect.

What is wrong with me? Will the nightmares continue to be part of my life?

I always make sure I am up before everyone else in the dorm. I hardly sleep anymore. It is usually one or two o'clock in the morning before I fall asleep.

I always get up around five or six o'clock. I fear being seen dressing or being found out that my bed looks like someone attacked it.

I always notice that the other girls' beds are not torn apart like mine.

There are many nights I spend in my sleep chasing my mother. I dream often that she is working for the CIA, and she comes to me around a campfire on dark nights in the mountains, with her back turned to me. I can never really see her face. She tells me that for the good of the country, it is important she does what she must. Just as I reach out to her, she disappears. I begin screaming for her to come back.

I try to stop the nightmares, but I can't. So I figure if I don't think about her, they will go away, but they never do.

There are other major themes to my night terrors. Sometimes I wonder whether I am being punished in my sleep because I haven't done a good job of being a girl, a daughter, or a human being.

I am terrorized in my waking moments and my sleeping moments. There is nothing I can do about the nightmares, so I decide to spend all of my energy controlling my non-sleeping time.

I figure the best I can do, since I cannot sleep except for a few hours, is to always be awake before anyone else and prepare for the day.

Every morning though, I wake up so tired. I begin to fight the desire to curl up in a corner of this room, with my knees tucked underneath me and my arms and hands over my head.

What will happen to me if I never sleep? Does everyone have nightmares?

I am really excited, because today, I got my list of what I will need to go to this place called summer camp. Apparently, for one week, I will live in a cabin, probably something like Davey Crockett.

There are supposed to be all these activities that go on every day, including one of my favorite pastimes—hiking. Every evening, there will be a marshmallow roast by a campfire. We will learn camp songs and be told these scary stories.

The nun hands out a list to all of us who are allowed to go. I think you have to be at least ten. I won't be eleven for another month, but at least the age cutoff is ten years old. The nun says we have to put our stuff in a suitcase if we have one, and for those who don't, she has brown paper bags.

I look at my list of stuff and figure I have almost everything that I need. There are requirements for two sets of pants, underwear, bras, shirts, and socks. I don't know what a bra is, but I will ask later. Also, there are pajamas, soap, shampoo, toothpaste, comb, and sanitary napkins on the list.

I have everything on the list but the bra and the sanitary napkins. These must be extra clean napkins that I will use to clean my hands and face at camp, because I don't think it is a very clean place. Maybe I will ask the nun for some, since I have only regular tissue paper for my nose and the cloth napkin that is at my place in the dining room.

When I approach the nun, I show her that I have everything on the list in my brown paper bag. I tell her that the only two things on the list I don't have are the bra and the sanitary napkins. I ask her where I can get them. She tells me not to worry about those two items; they are for the big girls. I tell her that I don't like germs or getting my hands dirty, and I need these sanitary napkins to keep my hands clean. She tells me that I am too young to be bothered about that stuff and that when I get a mother, she will talk to me. I'm not sure what's she talking about, but if I can't get the sanitary napkins for camp, I'd better take an extra bar of soap to keep the germs away when I'm at camp.

Why do people, even the nuns, always tell me that my mother will explain things to me? Does that mean that she might come back to talk to me? What happens if she doesn't come back and I don't get a mother?

Today we are all called down to the auditorium. Every day at the orphanage, I learn a new thing; only, with every new demand, I feel as if I am getting farther away from the life I once knew with her.

It's been almost two and a half years since I last saw her, and so much has changed; actually everything is so different. It is all the little things that are not the same anymore.

No one here in the auditorium, not the orphans or the nuns, even knows that I am alive inside. Here at the orphanage, all of us are increasingly becoming a group. Who I used to be as a person in a family is fading away. I eat with two hundred kids, go to school with forty students, and sleep in a dorm of fifty girls. No one really knows I exist. I'm only noticed through my nickname, the Widow Child, because I don't smile or talk much. I try to be happy, but I feel like there are these concrete blocks of sadness and despair weighing me down. I try never to cry, although if my mother came back today, I would want to crawl on her lap and beg her never to leave me again.

In the auditorium, the nun tells us that on the third Sunday of every month, three barbers will come to cut our hair. She said that we are to come one after another to sit on the stage to get our haircut. The nun said that there isn't much time, so we are to sit silently in the chair while the barber cuts our hair. She said everyone will get the same haircut so we can't ask for something special.

The barbers are these three men with silver hair, and I notice that they cut everyone's hair the same. When I go up to get my haircut, they talk to each other but not to me. My brother, who is sitting, waiting for his haircut, says

I got a boy's haircut. I tell him to just wait until Mother comes back because then I will have girl's hair again. He tells me he was just teasing, but the curly hair I once had when Mother was here left a long time ago. Now all I have is straight boy's hair. Maybe the male barbers don't know how to cut a girl's hair, or maybe this is one more sign that there is something wrong with me, and I'll never be the kind of girl that is normal.

Do men and women cut hair differently? If I have a boy's haircut, does that mean that other people see me as a boy like Daddy's mother did? Why do I worry about stuff that I can't tell anyone about?

My eleventh birthday is coming. In the orphanage, they celebrate birthdays once a month, on the first Sunday. All the children who have a birthday that month sit together at one table. As a treat, every child in the orphanage gets a can of root beer and a slice of cake.

The birthday children are given a piece of clothing. Any child with a family can go with them on their birthday and celebrate.

My birthday comes and goes without notice. I think maybe Daddy, Grandma, and my aunts in Indiana will send me a card or something, but they don't. I should be used to it by now. I wonder what it is like to belong somewhere.

Many of the children come back from their families, telling us what they did for their birthdays. It only makes me feel very lonely, and very sad.

It has been such a long time since anyone hugged me. I know that I am not like other girls and that I should be able to adjust without a mother, but I miss her so much, and even more, I am beginning to hunger for someone to mother me.

Does my mother mind if I want another mother?

Can you believe it? Already I am in sixth grade. The teacher lets me work in the first group of math.

I hear about college and how if you are smart enough, you can go there and be anything you want.

I hear about how, if you work hard enough, you can make a lot of money, buy anything you want, and live wherever you want. I think this may be my outlet to get what I need. Maybe I can buy a mother.

Maybe if I study hard enough and become successful someday, maybe I will become human. Maybe I can pay someone to love me. Can money buy anything? Can money buy everything? Can money buy those things that could help me feel okay?

In school I am driven to do well, although I know I spend a lot of my energy trying not to space out. Spacing out happens often lately.

I can go through the motions of living, but my mind is a thousand miles away. It is as though I pour a bucket of numbing fluid over my entire body and I no longer feel anything.

Now it is almost as though I have all these boxes open inside me, ready to accept any comment, any experience I do not understand, or cannot handle; and they just slide into a box that automatically closes. I don't feel a thing.

There are changes in me I do not understand. My body hurts and is getting bigger.

Since everyone wears donated clothing, we pick out what we want. No one pays attention to me. I always find something big and dark colored with long sleeves.

I do not want anyone to see me or the lumps, so I become even more withdrawn. When you live in an orphanage, it is so easy to disappear, even in public, although I do not think my mother would have let me disappear.

Where am I going in my haste to disappear? How do I hide things I do not want to be a part of me? Why am I changing when I don't want to?

At the beginning of sixth grade, I am told that there is money from the air force for me to get braces on my teeth. I go to the orthodontist in Scranton once every two weeks, which is a twenty-five-mile ride from the orphanage. The nun drops me off in front of the office building. I always have to walk a few blocks to be picked up in front of this large department store.

It is at this time I begin the habit of leaning against the wall of the department store and watching people, especially mothers and daughters. I always have a two-hour wait to be picked up, so I begin to imagine what kind of life they must have.

At times, I feel as though I am in a zoo, watching a species different from me live life. I try to imagine if my mother and I would have had a close life, had she lived. Would she have touched me, tousled my hair, taken me shopping, acknowledged me in public, or left me for four hours, at eleven years old, to go to the dentist by myself?

Sometimes in the winter, when it gets dark early, I get scared someone will kidnap me. Of course, I am not really worth anything, but I am scared anyway.

I always watch mothers and daughters, wondering how people know how to talk to each other.

Do they hesitate a thousand times, like I do, when they need something? Do the daughters have a thousand boxes no one sees? Am I the only one like me in the entire world who feels I don't belong to anyone?

What if I am losing the skills to be a daughter? Who will want me? So far, there are no takers.

Are there classes I can go to in order to learn what has never been taught to me? How will I learn to love and be in a family if I never know that experience? Why can't I be satisfied with the crumbs of life?

It is getting closer to Thanksgiving. Already, it is the third anniversary of my mother's death, and I am still heartbroken that she is not here. All the children are called into the auditorium where we are given a set of rules. All of us will be sent out for the holidays to either our families or to a host family. All the children who are going to their own families are dismissed, after being told to behave themselves and to be helpful. The rest of the children, about twenty of us, have to stay in the auditorium.

We are told how lucky we are that anyone even wants to take us into their homes for the holiday. Therefore, the following rules are applied:

1. Remember, you are a guest, not part of the family.
2. You must not get attached or think you will be able to live there.
3. Never take anything the refrigerator. That is not your food. Be grateful they even feed you.
4. Never argue with their children. They have first say in everything, and these are their parents, not yours.
5. Never use the phone. That is not your home.
6. Be packed at least a day or two before returning to the orphanage, because you do not want to overstay your welcome.
7. Do not anticipate returning at Christmas or Easter; we never send you to the same family each holiday.
8. Anything you receive will be donated to the poor in Africa, because only what you get from your blood families can you keep. (One of the nuns says that if we weren't orphans we wouldn't get the gifts and that the children in Africa are poorer and worthier than we are.)
9. Do not ask for money, gifts, clothes, or anything else. Nothing belongs to you. Be happy that you can see how real people live like.

If I am so lucky, why don't I feel lucky?

Thanksgiving is coming. It will be the first spent at the orphanage. I am told that I will not be able to spend the holiday with my brothers, because a family interested in the twins wants to take them home for a few days.

The nun in charge of the orphanage tells me she has found a nice older couple who want to share the holiday with me, but they are not interested in anything more. "Do not think that there is the possibility for anything other than a visit," I am told.

She tells me she will be looking for someone else to take me for Christmas. I ask her how come I cannot go with my brothers. She tells me that this couple, the Smiths, is only interested in the twins, because they already have two sons. She says they are not interested in getting involved with a girl. The woman told her she can handle boys, but girls are too much work.

The nun tells me if my brothers have a chance of living with the Smiths, she will try to convince them to keep us together. I am told to remember that older children, especially girls, are very difficult to place, but she will do her best.

The week before Thanksgiving, I see my brothers in the playground. They are excited because the social worker tells them he might have a home for them, together, with a couple who have a biological son and a foster son. They feel bad at this point, because I am not going along with them.

Sometimes my nights are so long because I have so much to think about, most of which I have no control over. I now realize that there is a possibility that I might be separated from my brothers.

How do I stop this final separation from happening? Is this what happens to orphaned children who have no one? How could my mother not ask God to stop people from destroying what little I have left of my family? What will it be like to be lost forever?

For the Thanksgiving holiday, I go with this couple the nuns found for me. They are very nice. They have their grown children and grandchildren over to visit. I am allowed to sit at their table and eat, but I am too scared to talk much, plus I am too busy trying to notice everything, without being noticed.

The woman tells me that she and her husband have retired and just wanted to share their home with someone less fortunate, and that is why I have been invited. She wants her grandchildren to see how lucky they are, because they could be like me—living in an orphanage with no family or friends.

I feel very self-conscious. I feel like the poster child for the motherless or family-less. I remember very carefully all the little rules from the orphanage, because even though I know I stopped celebrating the holiday, I do not want to ruin anything for someone else.

Besides, even though I am here as a warning to their grandchildren, the old couple mean well and are nicer than Grandma Resuba, who made us live in a coal cellar, where the food was less than adequate.

I also get to go sleigh-riding with their children, who are very nice, although they ask me how come I must live in an orphanage, and do I think anyone will ever come for me. I tell them I do not have any parents and that maybe my aunt or someone from Indiana will come for me.

They also ask why I do not have clothes like them. I tell them I have not gone shopping yet, but a relative will take me. I realize more and more that I begin to cover the gaps that set me apart from other children, even to the point of inventing stories.

How can I tell anyone that my mother died, and no one wants me? Mostly, I wonder if there are words to describe the confusion that I feel in every area of my life.

My brothers come back and tell me what a wonderful time they had at the Smiths' and how they called them Mom and Dad. I am flabbergasted that they are so easily able to fall into the family routine. I do not think I can ever call anyone Mom.

They tell me they are invited to the Smiths' next Christmas, which means the Smiths are serious about the twins, since usually you do not go to the same family for the next holiday.

I saw the social worker the following week. Again I asked him to call my mother's sisters and mother in Indiana about taking at least me. I know my brothers are excited about the foster home, and I know I am not included in the "package deal."

Every night becomes longer than the night before. I am worried about drowning in my own thoughts. Without my brothers, there will never be any way to prove that I once belonged to a family. If I lose them, there will be no way that we will ever be as we once were, brothers and sister.

The social worker says he will try again, but I should not expect anything. Even blood relatives sometimes are reluctant to take another child. He tells me that if he continues to get good reports from the nuns, he will try to convince the Smiths to take me, even though they do not want a girl.

That night, I again think of being second best. Maybe there is something wrong with my blood. Daddy said we are not the real thing, and I have not heard from my mother's family. Now if I get a home, it depends upon my being perfect and a social worker begging for me to be taken.

Would anyone ever want the real mixed-up me? I wonder if there are enough adults in the world to go around for every child?

I am eleven years old, and Christmas is coming soon.

The last time I celebrated Christmas with my mother, I was seven years old, and now four years later, I wish I could still crawl up on her lap in the rocking chair, as I did then, with her running her hand through my hair, telling me she loves me.

I feel isolated and different, like in a zoo, being one of a kind. My hair is cut by a male barber—it is very short. I hardly ever smile. I am always ready to move at a moment's notice. I am afraid because I never know if tomorrow I will have something to eat or a place to live.

I try desperately not to think of my mother anymore, because I am afraid that what she would have raised as a daughter would clash with the reality of what is happening now. Mostly, I fear her anger because I am not the same anymore.

I don't know how it happened, but one day, I realized I forgot how to engage in conversations with adults. It is this lack of stability that has made me increasingly afraid of adults, especially women. Maybe I fear what I need most: a role model who can nurture me.

Everything is based on what I present to the outside world, even though it is not true on the inside. I try not to be angry because I fear it makes me less desirable for adoption. I try, especially, never to get angry because it might let the lid off a lot of other things.

Is there a place that I can go, where my mother and God could meet me? I get so mad sometimes at both of them, because while they are enjoying heaven, the hell I feel burning in my soul is a reality I can't shake off.

Doesn't my mother get mad because of what is happening to me, or does heaven offer such happiness that there are no backward glances to those you left behind?

Sometimes at night, while everyone is asleep in the dorm, I start rocking in bed because it seems to calm me. At night the beds look like cages with white prison bars. They are metal with bars at both ends. I rock for a little while, hoping to lose the reality that is crushing me.

I know that Christmas is coming, and I want to fast-forward this whole life experience. This is the beginning of discovering different ways to numb myself so I will not feel the twinges of the emotional rivers that sometimes overflow from my boxes.

One of my favorite things to do is to go flying. The orphanage is on the side of a mountain, with a lot of property behind it and a huge playground in the back. Every evening, for a half hour, I go outside. I am not sure how it started, but one day, I just started running and flapping my arms, imagining that I was a bird in flight. It feels so good, almost as though I can leave all this pain and rejection behind!

Sometimes I imagine entering into flight in a total immersion experience. Then maybe, just maybe, I can brush against my mother's wings.

I often think that if I thought hard enough and wanted something beyond all measure, it would become real by sheer desire.

The hardest part about being eleven and flying is that you have to land, and it is always a crash landing into reality. But for a few brief seconds, I imagine I am released from this life.

Could I will, with every fabric of my being, change in my life that will keep me from crashing and keep me from the engulfing despair?

I am called to the office by the person in charge, who tells me that I will be spending Christmas with some old friends of hers. I ask about my brothers. She tells me that if this visit goes well, along with a few other visits, my brothers may have found themselves a home with two other boys.

She must sense my sadness because I don't say anything; I just keep staring at the same spot on the wall. She tells me that she will see how this visit goes with my brothers, and maybe she will ask if I can go to live with them.

I again remind her of my grandmother and two aunts in Indiana, but she tries to explain to me that my daddy tells her that no one is interested, because he has already spoken with them. She tells me they are all very poor and have no room for me, but I shouldn't worry because God will provide for me, if I believe.

You know, it isn't God I worry about providing for me, it is people, especially when I feel no one knows I exist. This is probably because no one does know I exist.

Sometimes I feel like an afterthought. How will I ever learn to be a person if I continue to be invisible to the people who are supposed to care?

There is one thing I have learned since my mother's death three years ago, and that is unless you have a direct link to a family, you can float around or away forever because no one feels a responsibility for you. It is like if I do homework, fine; if I do not do homework, fine. No one has vested enough time on me to be bothered one way or another about something as basic or mundane as homework.

Does God send parents to provide for their children? What happens when God takes them away? Is it enough to believe that God provides? What is wrong with me? Do I ask too much of my mother or God? Do I worry needlessly about who is going to love me? Shouldn't she and God be enough?

I prepare to spend Christmas with a couple picked out by the person in charge, well aware that they are her friends. I must be extra perfect so that they will take another child for Easter.

Unlike the older couple at Thanksgiving, this older couple is very formal. All I can do is sit on my hands at the table and keep my eyes downcast, lest I bring attention to myself or make a mistake.

They have all these spoons and forks just at my place. I don't eat very much on this visit because I don't want to seem like a fool with no table manners. They give me nice gifts and have their friends over for coffee to show me off as someone less fortunate. By now, it is as though I am in a room separated from myself, watching me surrounded by all these people. They don't have a clue as to my thoughts or my existence.

They are nice people, but I am getting so tired of pretending that I can function like other girls my age, without having the same advantages and knowledge that they do. I know I am different, I just don't know how to get back to being normal.

What if I can't stop being shuffled around?

When I return to the orphanage from my Christmas visit, I see my brothers jumping up and down, telling me what a great time they had at the Smiths' home.

They excitedly tell me how much they love these people who have two sons, older than them. They say that if things work out, maybe I could come with them and eventually we will all be adopted.

I tell them that I have been told by the social worker that the Smiths do not want a girl. My brothers tell me I worry too much, and all I have to do is believe that we will all go together. They say being a girl is not a big deal. "Just be like us—they might want a tomboy."

I begin to tell the social worker every time he comes that we cannot be separated, because if I say it a thousand times, he might finally relent.

Even though I secretly want, more than anything else, to be adopted and have a mother, I put this on the back burner of my life, so I won't be separated from the only family I have left—my two brothers.

I trade a lot of what I need just so I won't lose the only connection that is part of my mother.

I have already lost Grandma and my two aunts and a life in Indiana. I have lost Daddy, Alice, and Daddy's parents, who are really no great loss. I lost Billy and, in some ways, Trevor and Tyler.

I just can't let what is left of my relationship with the twins disappear. We are the only proof that our mother ever existed.

Sometimes I wonder if anyone thinks about her, misses her, yearns for her, needs her as I do, almost all the time, every day. I wonder where she is buried and if she has a pretty grave.

I wish she were here now to see my wounded heart, to wipe away my whisper tears, and to reassure me that I will be okay.

What will happen to me when I someday get tired of pretending that everything will work out?

One of the nuns pulls me aside in the dining room to tell me that she wants to talk to me. I know that I must be in trouble because no adult talks to me about anything. She tells me that she is very disturbed because my brothers tell her I want to go to the foster home with them.

She is very angry with me, demanding, "Who do you think you are, trying to butt in on your brothers' good fortune and ruin it for them?" This nun tells me that I should understand that people don't want girls who will be teenagers soon, because they cause too much trouble.

She tells me I have no business forcing myself into this foster home, especially when the Smiths specifically asked only for the twins. Besides, she tells me, boys need more attention and parenting, and I seem to do well in school and not need parents like my brothers. She says someday, when I get married and have children, I will see that girls are self-sufficient.

I feel sick inside because she will not let me say anything. I know she likes the twins. Everyone likes Trevor and Tyler, who, unlike me, the watchful and silent type, are happy-go-lucky. They are much more open with their emotions, more gregarious and accepting. They already call the Smiths Mom and Dad.

I know that somewhere inside me she is right, to a certain point, but she does not know what it is like to be eleven years old and a thousand years old at the same time.

She does not know what it's like to have no mother, no family, and no one to call your own. All I have left is a sliver of my past life in the form of Trevor and Tyler. It is too much to ask of me not to be with them, even if she is right?

Could my mother teach me how to know what the right thing is, even if she is living in heaven?

The school year is coming to a close, and I did really well in the sixth grade. My teacher, a nun who wears army boots, tells me she thinks I did really well—as well as the best outsiders. Usually the insiders, the children living at the orphanage, never do as well as the kids with families who just attend school here.

I think I am as smart as the other kids in my class. Sometimes though, I often have to refrain from hitting some of them when they make fun of the way I talk. What really hurts is when they make fun of the fact that I have no one and that I live in the orphanage instead of with a family.

Sometimes they say I must have done something bad because I have no parents.

When I have a hard day at school and I feel as though the walls of darkness are closing in on me, I lie in bed at night and try to relive what the kids say. Then I try to block it out.

It is just that somewhere along the way, I crossed over the line into believing that, indeed, I had done something so wrong, so terrible to receive the ultimate punishment in a child's life. Not only was I left without a mother or father, I was also left without any semblance of a family.

I beg God on days when I am teased about being so bad or not having parents to just transport me somewhere where no one will see me. I lie in bed, trying to remember or imagine what it is like to belong somewhere.

Whenever the kids tease me about not belonging, I tell myself that someday I will be chosen for adoption, and then I will be just as good as they are. Sometimes I wonder if they know what it feels like not to have anyone. I like to think that I am immune or hardened to the insults, but they hurt immensely.

When you die, does that mean that you stop being a part of everyone you loved? Who is supposed to take care of us and finish our mother's unfinished business?

It is June, and I hear talk that the social worker and the Smiths will take me as part of the package deal. They say they will consider it, and I think, all right! Now I won't be separated. I think maybe if I don't say anything about the coal cellar, or my doubts about me not being good enough for a family and the mixed gender identity swirling around inside me, everything will work out.

In July, I will be twelve years old, and if everything goes according to plan, in September, I will go live with my brothers. It is a warm day in June, and school is finished. I am playing in the playground. I can't wait to go live with my brothers.

Over the past few months, things have been happening that I cannot tell anyone about. Some kids from outside who attend school at the orphanage tell me that I am bad, that is why I do not have parents. So I cannot tell anyone about the two lumps growing on my chest. I think this is one more sign that I am not a normal girl, or maybe I am changing into a boy, or becoming a freak.

Over the last few weeks, my stomach has been really beginning to hurt me. The pain is so bad I want to double over, but, of course, that would draw attention to me and the fact that there is something wrong with my body.

It is on a Saturday morning in June when I go into the bathroom and see blood on my underwear. I just freak out! I keep saying to myself, "What happened?" Something is terribly wrong with me. I think for sure that I am going to die and quickly have to figure out a way to hide this, because I could mess up my last opportunity to ever live with my brothers.

No one ever told me about the blood, so maybe I should keep quiet. There is something wrong with me, but I have to be careful because I don't want anyone to know that I must be a freak, or a boy, which Grandma was always trying to tell me I might be. No one seems to notice anything different about me, so maybe the blood isn't important.

I know now that I have to make the blood go away before someone finds out. I already have a thousand and one things to handle, but to figure out how to make the blood go away is probably my hardest challenge.

If I put the blood into the farthest box in my mind and just become pure spirit, will this make me acceptable? What am I turning into? How can I stop what I don't know about or understand or want? Are all these changes one more sign that nothing is right with me?

Did my mother know this stuff—the lumps, the stomachaches, and the blood—would happen? Why didn't she warn me? Maybe I am being punished for not being like Alice and for not trying hard enough to be a boy, and, mostly, for wanting my mother or some adoptive family.

Who will want me now with this body that I do not recognize? I don't want to be like this. This body is changing me into something I have no control over. Maybe the blood won't come back, but I still have the severe stomachaches. Sometimes I have to grit my teeth so no one notices how much I hurt.

I cannot let anyone notice the blood. I spend the next few weeks relieved because the blood has gone away. With my twelfth birthday coming, I think I have everything under control.

One week after my twelfth birthday, I go to the bathroom and find the blood again. I really freak out this time, trying to figure out what is going on and how I will stop it. Plus there is still all this pain inside my stomach, like a boxing match is taking place in there.

I use globs of toilet paper, hoping it will go away. I decide never to tell anyone about the "body," as I now refer to myself, because they will think I am an abnormal girl and, worse, a freak. I must hide myself like I have never hidden before in my life.

Is there a way that I can exist without a physical body? Do daughters have mothers because they know the secrets of girls? What have I missed by her absence?

Maybe this is what the nun meant by telling me no one wants girls that turn out like me. I still think I am not trying hard enough to be acceptable to someone who would like to adopt me.

While all of this is going on, I am called to the office by the person in charge. She tells me to sit down because she has good news. The Smiths have agreed to take me on a temporary basis when school starts in September, next month. They say they will "try me out," although they really want only the boys.

The person in charge tells me that I am lucky because I have cleft palate and am already twelve years old. She says that very few people will take a chance on a girl like me.

She tells me not to ask for anything. She also says not to say anything about my past because people are not interested, and I might ruin it for my brothers. The nun tells me that I am different from my brothers. She says, "There is a sadness in you, and although you are very intelligent, I wonder what is really going on in your head because you never talk to anyone, and you always have your nose in a book."

The person in charge again reminds me that this is a foster home and I should not get attached. She warns that I can be moved at any time for any reason. I ask her if they might adopt us. She says, "No, they have no interest in adoption because they get paid as foster parents." Besides, she says, I am too big to want to be adopted.

Without my mother, how can I ever hope to even be somewhat normal? Who will teach me the life skills I need to live?

I go to find my brothers to tell them I am going to live with them. We are all so happy, but I am very careful not to say that I am going on a trial basis. I know for sure that whatever is changing inside me and the body problems cannot be told to anyone because then I will be sent away.

I cannot have any problems, and I have to make sure I am ready for any surprises that might bring unwanted attention to me. This upcoming move means I have to practice harder to speak clearly and hope that my face will look normal. I will make sure I spend two hours a day reading poetry and singing aloud to myself. It is so important that I learn to speak correctly and clearly.

I make it very clear to myself that I will never speak of myself or of the weird things happening to the body, or even acknowledge its existence. This also means that if I ever get sick or am in intense pain, like I am periodically, I will not tell anyone.

Most of all, just in case the blood comes back again, I have to be on special guard, because I can never let anyone know. I cannot bear to be told I am not a normal girl like my sister.

I think maybe, if I ever get adopted, just maybe but probably not, I might venture to ask if I am normal. Since I cannot accept the possibility of being told I am not normal, I know I will always have these secrets held inside me.

I wonder if anyone even knows that I exist. I am beginning to feel more and more overwhelmed. I want so much to disappear.

I almost feel like I am splintering into several different directions, and there is not enough of me to hold myself altogether.

Is there a special glue that people use to heal the cracks in the soul? What will happen to me if I keep splintering apart and not even "willing" myself together works? Will God ever make people care, or do they have to want to care on their own? Who will stop the splintering of my mind and my soul?

Tomorrow we will go to live with the Smiths. I am going into strangers' home with my two brothers, my last semblance of a family.

As I lie in my bed in the orphanage, I am so scared inside. Already I feel such pressure to be perfect. It has been almost four years since Mother died. How will I adjust tomorrow, especially knowing that I have forced my way into this foster home?

I really wish it was an adoptive family, or that I was going to live in Indiana. I am having tremendous doubts about going into this foster home. But who else wants me? I will again ask the social worker to talk to my grandmother and two aunts in Indiana, because if I were given the choice to live with them, I would take it in a heartbeat.

My brothers are so different now. They want to play and have a good time. Me, I just want a mother of my own. I want to be adopted so no one can send me away.

Mostly, what I want, but will never be able to do, is to change the clocks back in time and have my mother come back so that she can hold me and tell me everything will be okay.

How many years do I have to wait to find an adoptive family?

"Girl Set Adrift"

Going backwards and forwards, surrounded by
mirrors,
Of self-reflection of confusion and blankness.
Wondering how to find the beginning of
direction,
Or the end of a time of being lost in isolation.

Where once was a certainty of tomorrow without
changes,
Now is replaced by a non-ending, circular
motion.
Of wanting what once was and can never be
again,
A safe haven from the slaps of life's unexpected
sucker-punches.

Ports of safe harbor in a distant past and far
away future,
Vessels of security off on the horizon as far as
she can see.
Wait for the child's swim against the currents,
Of choppy emotional waters that continually try
to pull her
Below the ocean of whisper tears.

Home once a reality; shuffle madness now the ordinary,
Attachment and taking for granted no longer
assumed.
When all that is real is the opposite of what had
been known,
She realizes that she journeys in the company of
one.

The First Foster Home: The Wrong Decision
Ages 12 - 13

The First Foster Home:
The Wrong Decision

(Ages Twelve to Thirteen)

Dear Mother,

It is early in the morning, and I wonder what it will be like to live in a house. The Smiths are supposed to pick us up later. My brothers tell me they are really nice. They know because they have spent a lot of time with them.

We are called to the office, where I am introduced to them. They say they will try the situation out. They live about forty miles from the orphanage, in a city called Wilkes-Barre. I am told, when we arrive, that I have a room, and my brothers will share another room.

Mrs. Smith introduces me to Chris, her biological son, and Mike, her other foster son. She tells me that I am to call her Mom and her husband Dad, like my brothers do. Before I realize it, the words are out of my mouth. "You are not my mother. I will never call you Mom."

Then, shocked by my statement, she slaps me. Needless to say, I am stunned. I know immediately that I have made a big mistake coming here. She tells me I am a foster child who is lucky to be here, because all she wants are the boys.

She then calms down, telling me never again to talk to her like that, and we will get along. You see, Mother, there are words I cannot get out of my mouth like "Mom" or "the body" or "the coal cellar." I cannot call her Mom, but I am not given permission to call her anything else.

I will never call her by any name the whole time I live here. I know she has been coerced into taking me and resents me. Maybe this is my fault, like the nun told me.

With the resounding echo of her slap, I resolve never to be broken. I also decide I will try to tough it out for the sake of my brothers, placing my needs on the back burner. I am also determined to make the social worker contact Indiana again.

I want to be adopted. I do not want to be a foster child. Will it ever be possible for me to be able to give up my desire to be adopted in exchange for staying with my brothers?

Love,
Jerri

*   *   *

As I lie in bed that first night in a room all alone, I wonder what I've gotten myself into. I realize for the first time that there is a need deeper inside me that is more important than being with the brothers I love and adore. That need is to be adopted, to have a mother, to belong to a family where all my secrets will be safe.

Now I understand what the other kids in the orphanage meant when they said a foster home is never safe and you never will belong. They told me that adoption was the only guarantee. I know now that the Smiths never intend to adopt any of us, and that means to always be on guard, to be ready to be moved, and not to have any friends.

I also know that if I want to have a chance to go to Indiana, I will have to make a plan so that I will be attractive to them. Maybe they remember that I am not pretty, cannot talk right, and am sickly. Perhaps they also think, as I get older, they will have problems with me because I am not a normal girl like Alice.

I draw up a short list that I will work on, so the social worker can ask my aunts, or someone from my mother's family, to adopt me.

This night I promise myself that I will work on the following:

A.   I will study really hard. Maybe they will like me if I am smart.
B.   I will pretend that no body issues exist. This might hide all physical things I do not understand anyway.
C.   I will practice my speech. I know people think I am retarded because they cannot understand me. Sometimes I don't feel so smart myself.
D.   I will never complain or ask questions. They might think I need attention.

Is life always going to be so hard?

Today I have to go to this big school called Myers High School, for grades seven to twelve, and I am in the seventh grade. I have to admit that I am jealous of Chris, the biological son, because he gets to go to Saint Albert, the Catholic grade school. He, Mike, and I are all twelve years old. Trevor and Tyler are eleven.

There are so many kids in this high school, and it is in a big city. The woman in the office keeps asking where I lived last year. There are all these people standing around.

I whisper that I lived in an orphanage. She repeats in a loud voice, "An orphanage? Don't you have a family?" I reply that I live in a foster home.

Then there is a big discussion about my last name when I tell her what it is. She says it is different than the Smiths', how come? Again, I have to explain, with all these people staring at me, that I live in a foster home. I am told I need a document proving that I have a different last name.

By then, I am beet red. I wish the ground would open up and swallow me. Some of the kids standing in the office say, "How come you don't have a family? What happened? What did you do?"

What is the big deal about letting me use a different last name so I can blend in? Sometimes I wonder if my name is supposed to define who I am, even if I am not.

I just put my head down, because they don't know how humiliated I feel. I hate having a different last name. How will I ever make it in such a big school? I have to get good grades.

How do I shake this sense of shame I feel creeping up on me?

When I get home from school, only the boys are home, because the Smiths work every day and are not home until five or five thirty. I am having trouble calling them anything, and I do not feel comfortable around them. I think part of the reason is that this is just a foster home and not permanent.

Also, I have discovered that I feel intimidated by the foster parents. I am especially afraid that Mrs. Smith will want me to be different from my brothers. She said last night that I should be excited about this high school. I will meet cute boys there and go to dances. I am really repulsed by what she says. I do not want to meet anyone. I have more important things on my mind, like trying to get a mother and a permanent home.

Tonight she starts by saying, "Someday, when you get married and have children, you can live in a house like this."

What is she talking about, getting married? I don't know how to get married or where children come from. I don't want to be forced to get married. I have to shut her out because I have other goals.

How can I marry and have children if I am not normal? Don't I have to be in a family first, learn how to belong, and have a mother to teach me everything? I feel pressured because she keeps talking about these dances at school. I feel like I am suffocating from being forced into some kind of social scene.

I wish Mrs. Smith would just leave me alone! I have a lot of things on my mind. I feel like a swirling mass of confusion inside. I wish I could stop the madness. Here I am, motherless and family-less, and yet I am supposed to be like everyone else. I don't know what people want from me.

Why do I feel I can't act like a twelve-year-old in seventh grade? Why do I feel so mixed up and so alienated from everyone?

If I am going to be a saint in the making, as the nuns tell me, I have to try to be the most perfect kid with no problems.

I have read a lot of books on the saints, and they say that if I do no wrong, then I can go straight to heaven. Unfortunately, I mess up sometimes, because I know that I could be nicer to Mrs. Smith. It's just that I know that adoption is the best thing for me, and I don't want to be stuck in this foster home.

Maybe I will try to stop competing with Mrs. Smith's son, Chris. Even though we are both twelve, I feel compelled to be better than him in every way, and I don't know why. It's just that in the end, he will always be Mrs. Smith's real child, no matter how much I beat him at the dishes, cleaning, or studying.

Sometimes, when Mrs. Smith is around, I just want to disappear. She is always talking about boys, dances, and makeup. I got her to leave me alone by saying that my mother was plain and didn't have anything.

The truth is I don't remember much about my mother anymore, but I don't want to be involved in anything that is not permanent. Here in this foster home, my only goal is to be perfect in my speech so I can become adoption material.

I want to become a saint, so that when I die, I can return to my mother. I plan to do everything as perfectly as I can so that I can become heavenbound when God tells me it is okay to die.

When I get to heaven, I hope my mother will like me like she used to when I was little. Although I know that I need to move on to another place to live, or die and go to heaven, I will try to be nicer to Mrs. Smith.

Are there kids in heaven who want to come back to earth? God, could I trade places with a kid whose mother is still alive? Is it only the saints who make it to heaven? Can bastard orphans become saints?

Evenings in this foster home are hard. For the most part, I am left to my own thoughts, since I never speak unless spoken to directly. I am terrified of the adults around me. The house is so small. Mostly I spend time in my room, reading aloud and practicing my speech, so I will be considered good enough to live in Indiana.

There are things I do not understand. One is, why do Mr. and Mrs. Smith share a bedroom? Is this what happens when people get married?

Another is, what is all this talk about my brothers needing so much help and attention? Mrs. Smith spends a lot of time with Trevor and Tyler, although she seems partial to Tyler, who hugs her all the time and calls her Mom. She gets mad because I walk ahead of her and everyone else and stare at the ground. It really bothers her that I never look at anyone when I speak or am spoken to.

There is so much I don't understand. How will I ever be able to sort out all this life stuff alone?

This junior high school is not hard; I like english and math, but what I really hate is gym. There is a big indoor pool that the gym teacher insists we must get into in order to pass her class. When it dawns on me that I will have to undress and put on a swimsuit, I freeze. I notice that a few other girls do not swim because of health reasons.

I tell the teacher I have a bad cut on my leg, hidden by my pants. Every week, I think of something new, so I will not have to go to the locker room. I have to be so careful to not let anyone see the body.

Already, some of the kids in school tease me about being a foster kid and not being a real kid who belongs to a family. Plus they make fun of me because I do not look at or talk to anyone. It is just that I do not think I am as good as they are.

I keep to myself because I have all this stuff churning inside me. Sometimes I think I will explode and go crazy, but I always maintain my control.

I put swimming on the list of activities I will never do. Each day I feel more in denial of anything female. I know I do not want to be a boy, so I think I will be a nothing, just a pure mind.

So who, or what, am I? Maybe if I get to live in Indiana, or with an adoptive mother, I will learn what I am. I think I will start making a list of things I will want to talk to my adoptive mother about.

Why does life always seem so confusing to me?

Things are not going well in school, though I do have good grades. A group of girls likes to tease me about going for speech therapy and the fact that I do not fit in or belong anywhere.

I just try to ignore them, because I do not want to ruin my opportunity to live in Indiana. I know I need to go for speech therapy, and no matter what they say, it will not change my mind. I will go. Besides, deep down inside, they can never imagine how inferior I feel to them. I can never be as good as they are, even if I try.

The foster home is not going well either, because I am not really prepared to go to dances or to be interested in boys.

What people do not understand is that the boy/girl issue has no reality for me, other than to make me more confused.

I know Mrs. Smith thinks I am different, not like other girls. I know she feels stuck with me, and it does not matter to her if I leave. Her only redeeming grace is that she really seems to like my brothers, especially Tyler.

For some reason, she does not seem to take to Trevor too much, even though he calls her Mom and is affectionate with her.

I want only one thing: to convince my social worker to beg my aunt to adopt me into her family, or any family, so that I will never be sent away again.

I know deep down in my heart that it is only a matter of time before I will be told to leave. I am not wanted and cannot make myself fit in. I am afraid I am so messed up by so many things and secrets that I probably will never fit in or belong anywhere.

How come some children have permanent parents?

It is the summer of my thirteenth birthday. I will soon be that thing that I have been warned against—a teenage girl. I have a job on a family farm in Wilkes-Barre. Just think, someone is paying me fifty cents an hour to pick cabbages. I never had a job before. It is hard and dirty work. The farm is next to a river, where mostly older teenagers are working.

Trevor and Tyler say the work is too hard, so I share my pay with them and buy them soda. Just think, I will work from six in the morning to six at night, six days a week, and I do not have to deal with being in the foster home for ten hours a day, six days a week.

They pay me $30 a week. I feel so rich. Maybe if I work hard enough, I can pay someone to find my aunt or someone in my mother's family in Indiana. Mrs. Smith tells me I can work, as long as I am home by six thirty. She says I am so different from my brothers, that I do not need or want anyone. She says she has some thinking to do about me. I know what this means.

At the job, the older kids find out I am in foster care. For the first time, they do not make fun of me. They nickname me Cinderella because even though no one wants me, someday a family may come along and take me into their home. They are very kind to me and teach me how to pick the cabbages without hurting myself.

Whenever I return to the foster home, I feel more and more isolated because I know that sooner or later, they will get rid of me. I just hope I can see it coming so I will be ready when it happens. Then I hear that the social worker is coming soon and that he has told Mrs. Smith to make sure I am home.

I wonder what he wants to tell me?

School has started, and I have to quit the job. Mrs. Smith says there is something wrong with me because I avoid any conversations with anyone, including her. She says that all I do is read books and communicate through my brothers.

There is a public library that I go to all the time. I have a library card that allows me to get three books at a time. What I read are mostly books about adoption and saints and biographies. I figure if I read about different people's lives, I might learn how to improve on myself and become more adoptable for the social worker.

Mrs. Smith got us a dog named Mighty Mac but got rid of it because, she says, I loved the dog more than people. More and more, she watches me and seems angry with me. The social worker comes to see me and tells me he is disappointed to get bad reports about me. He says that I am now thirteen and should be fitting in more and more and calling the Smiths Mom and Dad, like my brothers do.

He tells me Mrs. Smith is disappointed in my boyish behavior and my being so silent all the time. She is not sure that she can keep me. The social worker tells me I had better not ruin it for my brothers and reminds me that no one wants a thirteen-year-old girl.

What can I say to him? He does not know what it is like to be me, never belonging, never telling anyone about the messiness inside me. It isn't that I dislike Mrs. Smith, it is just I cannot give away any time or energy to a person who does not want to adopt me.

I have too many problems that tear my waking and sleeping moments apart. I have to work hard at spending time trying to be something I do not want to be, namely, a foster kid.

I know I am ugly, not too smart, and cannot talk well. I know that as much as I would like to be a normal girl and be accepted and adopted, there is too much wrong with me to ever be normal.

How am I going to learn to be normal?

Today Mrs. Smith calls me into her office and says she does not think things are working out and that it was a mistake for her husband and her to take on so many children at one time.

Mrs. Smith asks me if I want to leave, because Trevor and Tyler require so much more attention and have so many more needs. I say yes. She says that Trevor will probably also be leaving because he has problems that are too much for her and her husband. Mrs. Smith says that with her working full-time and overtime on Saturdays, three children will be more than enough.

The social worker is coming to talk to me tomorrow. I will have to convince him to get a new family who wants to adopt me, or to get in touch with Indiana. This may be my last shot at being taken in by someone who feels I need attention and that I have some problems that only a mother could solve.

I am happy because this is my opportunity to beg the social worker to find me an adoptive mother.

I don't dislike the Smith family. They never intended in the beginning to have me as part of their family, but at least they are committed to my brother. I begin thinking about what I will tell the social worker.

I also begin to formulate a twenty-six-point list of what I would want or need from an adoptive mother, because I just know she might be somewhat disappointed in how backward I am.

I might finally get my own parents and have a family, like other kids at last. When this happens, I will not be different, and maybe this new mother will not think I am a freak, although I feel more and more like one.

I wonder if my mother in heaven could make the social worker get me adopted?

The social worker is here today to tell me I cannot stay with the Smiths anymore because they have their hands full with the boys, and I do not fit in. He tells me that I will have a female social worker from now on, because he feels that at age thirteen, I need to have a woman handling my case.

It is almost Christmas of 1969. He tells me I will be moved in a few days, just as soon as a new home is found. I tell him that if he tries to get in touch with my aunt, surely she might consider taking me. I tell him how helpful I can be, how my grades are good, and how I am practicing my speech.

The social worker says he will pass the word to the next social worker, but not to get my hopes up. He tells me that I do not talk to adults. He says that I do not interact with other kids my age, and I am not considered socially acceptable because of my lack of affection and emotional expression, compared with my brothers.

The social worker also tells me I am too tomboyish and isolated within myself, but he will see what he can do.

I tell the social worker I want to be adopted, if not by someone in a family, then by some woman. She does not even have to be married. I have read recently that single people adopt older children. He laughs at me. He says he would never consider a single woman and that I will probably be in foster care for a long time. I am too old to be thinking about adoption anyway, because that is only for younger children.

I do not say anything more because he is wrong about adoption. Maybe at thirteen I am too old to need a mother, but what am I supposed to do about the eight-year-old, the nine-year-old, and the parts of me that long to be nurtured, stroked, and loved?

Are the eight years I had with my mother supposed to sustain me and prepare me to be like everyone else? If so, then what is the point of having parents, if I am supposed to be able to function like all the other girls who have parents?

As I wait for the social worker to come in the next few days and move me from this foster home, I begin a list that I will present to an adoptive mother. I know in my heart of hearts that someone will take me, before I drown in this sea of confusion.

I like to think this is preparation for possible adoption; then no one can ever make me live with strangers who can always trade me in for a new or better kid. I am convinced that the social worker will have success in getting me back to Indiana. Then I begin to daydream about what it will be like.

I also imagine that there will be this big banner welcoming me. My aunts and Grandmother will tell me how much they love me and miss me. They will hug me and say they should have acted sooner, and now they will never let me go.

I imagine that they will tell me stories of how my mother loved me and wanted me to be a wonderful daughter.

Finally, imagine my one aunt running her hand through my hair, and I won't even tell her I do not like to be touched, like my mother used to do when she was living. I like to think that she will tell me that thirteen is not too old to have a mother and that there is so much she wants to teach me.

Finally, I imagine that they will tell me that I will never have to move and live with different people again. I will be adopted into the family and be legal forever.

I am so excited about the prospect of going to live with my mother's family. I am so happy and can't wait to find out what the social worker has to say.

I wonder if I should get my hopes up really high?

I am making a list of twenty-six things I want from an adoptive mother when I go to live with her. These are things that I would want someone to do:

1) *I would want to talk about my mother.* No one ever talks about her. I don't even have a picture of her. I need to know that she loved me, because more and more, I do not believe she could love a girl like me. I want to hear stories about her and know that her existence counted for something, that she was important to other people besides me. I wonder if Mother did matter to other people?

2) *I want to ask, why did my mother have to die?* I want to know if I am in any way responsible for her death. I tried to be good, and I loved her. I wanted her always in my sight and, mostly, I have always needed her. Maybe someone can explain her dying to me. No one has ever asked if I missed her, if I understand why or how she died.

3) *I want to tell my adoptive mother about the coal cellar.* Since my mother is not here, I want someone to know about the coal cellar and how mean Grandma Resuba was to us. Maybe someone can tell me that I am a normal girl like Alice, that Grandma Resuba is just an evil woman for hating me so much. I wonder if my mother in heaven would think it is okay for me to tell everything?

4) *I want to tell my adoptive mother about my confusion over girl/boy identity.* I've been wondering lately if I would be more acceptable if I don't have any identity problems. I want someone to help me sort out these different pieces that don't make sense. It's not that I want to be a boy, it's just I don't know how to be a girl like the other girls with mothers. I feel so alienated at times; I just hope that my new mother won't be repulsed by my needs and that she won't think I'm a freak. I hope that she will know how to help me. Does every girl go through this crisis?

5) *I want to ask about the blood; I feel like a hunted animal.* Ever since a month before coming to this foster home at the Smiths', I have sought

hard to be extra watchful in making sure no one finds out about the blood. It takes a lot of energy to hide, and it uses up all my waking moments to appear normal. I have to make this work. I am so tired sometimes of carrying all this baggage around. I don't understand the blood and see no point to it. I am practicing on willing it away or spacing out when it comes, so it does not exist for me. It is possible to be a whole person, isn't it?

6)   *I want to tell my new adoptive mother about how much I hate this body.* Sometimes I feel like I don't know what the rules are to being a female. It is as if I just want someone to take me back to where my mother left off when she died. This body of mine is almost a separate part of me. It's something I view from afar but am not connected to. If I could will it away, I would. Will this new person be repulsed by my self-hatred, which is even bordering at times on self-loathing?

7)   *I want to go shopping with this adoptive mother for clothes, because I have not gone since my mother died.* I want my new adoptive mother to take me to a store and show me that it is okay to shop for clothes, and not to be afraid of stores. I don't know if it is, because they are so big, or if I have to know sizes, which scares me. I know I don't like to try clothes on in front of other people, but how am I going to learn to shop and look for bargains and take care of myself if no one teaches me? Shopping seems to be such a ritual; someone is always going with someone else. The girls always brag about how they did this or did that with their mother. There are times when I daydream about what might have been had my mother stuck around. I guess the closest in reality that I can get to my mother is through another mother. I wonder if this new mother will want to go out with me in public?

8)   *I want her to teach me how to cook.* Sometimes I have flashes of my mother in the kitchen, with a wooden spoon in her hand, walking back and forth, humming to herself. Those are my most comforting memories of her, especially because she must have loved Christmas so much, with all the cookies she made. What would she have taught me had she lived? I wonder if my mother in heaven is okay with my trying to find a mother on earth?

9) *I want her to hug me and show me how to do my hair.* What I miss most due to my mother's absence is when she would rock me at night in her rocking chair, cuddling me and running her hand through my hair. All I want from this new mother is for her to hug me and tell me that everything is going to be okay. I wish she would treat me like my mother would have if she didn't have to die. Sometimes I hate the fact that she died and left me here without any directions on how to grow up. I wish my mother could ask God to give me some crumbs of relief. All I want is a family, especially a mother. It isn't too late to learn how to be in a family even if I am already thirteen years old, is it?

10) *I want this adoptive mother to talk to me about what it means to be a girl growing up and to be a woman and a female.* I am very confused about the changes going on inside me, the body changes, and the desperation to belong to someone. Every month, every year, it gets harder to believe that I am okay. Maybe it would be better if I just went away and disappeared. How am I ever going to grow up like other girls if no one cares about me or helps me?

11) *I want her to know how bad things were, and are, and to tell me it is okay to cry.* The nights are hardest when I try to figure out how all this pain and how all these people who don't really care about me could be part of my life. It is as if I am disconnected from the human race. The whisper tears that threaten to drown me are held back. I just don't belong anywhere, and all these different people just keep shuffling me around. Is crying, even the whisper tears, okay?

12) *I want this adoptive mother to celebrate my birthday.* I remember, the last night I ever saw my mother was when she brought a birthday cake to celebrate Trevor and Tyler's seventh birthday. I was so happy having this family party, with Grandma, my mother, my brothers, and my sister. There was joy with her during our last time together. Birthdays should be important, shouldn't they?

13) *I want to be part of a family on the holidays.* I think about how each family celebrates traditions. I wonder what my mother would have taught me about her family traditions. The kids in school are always excited about the holidays. They plan and brag at Christmastime or

Mother's Day about what they are doing for their parents. Does my mother brag about me in heaven?

14) *I want to tell my adoptive mother how hard it is to talk about my feelings.* Lately I have begun to feel more and more like I am on autopilot. I feel like I keep adding layers of protective clothing, almost trying to make myself bulletproof. Sometimes I'm afraid I will become permanently numb and not be capable of being connected. I feel like I am always trying to find the right family electrical socket so that I can plug myself back in and be reconnected. Is there a way to feel alive again?

15) *I want her to ask me lots of questions, because it is so hard to tell anyone about myself.* Sometimes I think I am becoming a mute in some ways, especially when it comes to talking to adults. How do I break away from this prison of silence?

16) *I want her to tell me I'm normal, because inside I feel like a freak.* Sometimes I worry that I'll always be just a whispered shadow, slinking through life, surviving but never living. I wonder what my mother would have, or could have, taught me about life; the body; relationships; men; women; children; home; family; being a girl, a woman; trust; and other things. I wonder if my mother in heaven thinks I am normal?

17) *I want my adoptive mother to tell me I am smart.* There are times when I think I am going crazy inside my mind because I can't handle everything all at once. No one tells me anything, I have now, at thirteen years and five months old, lived with eight complete sets of different adults in three places since my mother died. No one notices me, and I am having trouble believing that I ever mattered to anyone, even, at times, to my mother who died. Will being smart be able to make up for what I lack?

18) *I want the adopted mother to tell me that someday I will look okay.* Whenever I look in the mirror, I see reflected back to me a life-form with freckles, a slightly off-center nose, a scar from the nose to the mouth, and a mop of unruly hair. My eyes reflect how unhappy I must be, and I wonder how anyone as ugly as me will ever be able

to find someone to adopt me. If I keep moving, I will never get or look better. I know, when my mother was alive, I moved all the time, but she always came with me. Now, when I move, she is not there to smooth the way. My mother is only a whispered presence in my heart. How do I get some consistency into my life?

19) *I want her to teach me table manners.* Somehow this seems important, but I'm never sure what is proper about handling forks, knives, and spoons. How to eat my food? How to sit at a table and handle a napkin?

20) *I want my adoptive mother to teach me social skills.* In the orphanage, the nuns used to tell me that the only kids who get chosen and adopted are those who know how to act in public. Kids who don't embarrass their prospective parents. I wish my mother had more time before she died to teach me what it takes to fit in with everyone else. I wonder if my mother has to know all kinds of things in heaven?

21) *I want my adoptive mother to set guidelines and give me some rules to follow.* There are no rules for me, no limits, because no one expects that there is any need for me to be given any rules. I hope that I can continue with my good behavior.

22) *I want to be told that I will be someone of worth someday.* My mother must have taught me that my worth as a human being is important. It is very painful to exist in a vacuum, and I wish she were still here to take the loneliness away. Does she feel pain where she now lives?

23) *I want to be mothered and nurtured.* At thirteen years and five months, I just can't help these feelings of incompleteness that overwhelm me at times. All I want is to be mothered or nurtured. Mostly, I wish my mother could put her arms around me, squeeze me, run her hands through my hair, and whisper to me that everything is going to be okay. But I know that God isn't going to let her come back, even though I think I need her more than he does. Is it possible for my mother to give God and me what we both want?

24) *I want my adoptive mother to let me hang around her and to notice me.* I remember how my mother used to let me hang around her as she was cooking or watching TV. I miss just being able to be

with her in the ordinary moments of life when she always made me feel welcome. Outside myself, I am not in need of anything or anyone, but inside I am still that eight-year-old yearning for her to help me feel that I belong. How do I become the way I used to be with my mother?

25) *I want to be adopted so I will never be sent away.* It isn't that I don't love my mother, but she can't make me feel safe by being dead. Being adopted means I belong forever and ever, and I never have to be moved at a moment's notice. Without a permanent family, I'll never belong anywhere or be safe with anyone. I know that Daddy adopted us when he married my mother, but he didn't really love us, only her, and since she died, he isn't the same anymore. I just don't want to be a floater all my life, never belonging anywhere or to anyone. I am afraid I might disappear someday, and no one will ever know that I ever existed. Does heaven let my mother watch me sometimes?

26) *I want to have the same last name as my new family.* Maybe if I have the same last name, I'll be treated like one of the family, and this new adoptive mother will teach me how to live and how to feel. How do I convince the social worker or the new mother that having the same name means I finally belong?

I am going to be picked up tomorrow by the social worker. She is new. Hopefully, she was able to get in touch with someone in Indiana, and I won't have to be bounced around and moved to another foster home. I despise being a foster kid. I wish my mother would please ask God to make someone want me. I promise to be good, quiet, and invisible.

I just don't want to be family-less anymore, or motherless; it's already been almost five and a half years since my mother left me. Never once in all these years since she died has she ever answered me. Sometimes I wonder if she really hears me in heaven. I would give anything I have if she would just ask God to let her visit for a little while.

Soon, in three weeks, it will be Christmas, then a new year, 1970. Yet again, I will be shuffled around, and no one will know I exist, or that I am in so much pain.

Did my mother ever love me? I can't seem to remember anymore if she did or didn't. I think, mostly, it is that I have no pictures of her and no one to tell me about her. I am surrounded by people who are busy telling me of my unimportance in this life. Maybe my luck will change tomorrow. Maybe there will be someone who will want me. Maybe I will be wanted enough to be adopted, but then maybe I'm just a loser.

All I want is for some woman to adopt me and want to know about me. I ask my mother in heaven to just get her to take me, and I'll work at being the most perfect child; she won't even know I'm around. All I want is a chance to be normal again. I just want to be mothered and nurtured again. Tomorrow a new stage of my life begins. I hope it is what I have prayed for.

I wonder if my mother ever hears me up there in heaven? Does she ever wish she were with me instead of with God? How does she celebrate Christmas in heaven? Does she ever hear my whisper tears that ache to come gushing to the surface?

Doesn't my mother have any pull in heaven for just a little miracle?

I am so scared about what will happen today; the social worker is picking me up around 10:00 a.m. The best of all fantasies would be if she would give me a one-way ticket back to Seymour, Indiana, which was the last place I ever felt safe and happy. In my fantasy, someone would be there, meeting me, welcoming me, reassuring me, as I imagine my mother would have done if she had not died.

The other unthinkable alternative would be if I am shuffled into another foster home. I have already been told repeatedly that it is getting too late in my thirteen years of life to belong to a family or to need a mother. I just know that unless I find a place to belong, I'll never be a real girl, just a shadow person who breathes but doesn't live or feel.

I don't think I can take much more of the stuff that life is handing out to me. Sometimes I feel like there is this invisible life force pushing me toward the edge of a cliff. I am pushing back really hard so I won't be overwhelmed, but lately I've been getting more tired and discouraged.

No matter which direction my life goes today, I promise my mother in heaven to give it my one last best shot, because I feel like this is the end of the line.

I don't have much to take with me. The Smiths left for work and wished me good luck. My brothers said good-bye and went to school. The only one left here is me. Today will determine whether I have to keep on constant alert and be what this new foster home wants, or if I will be embraced back into my mother's family in Indiana, with the relatives that must have loved her when she was alive.

I wonder if I will ever find what I am looking for?

The social worker, a nice lady, picks me up at exactly 10:00 a.m. She tells me that I got her as my social worker because the male social worker says I would not tell him anything, maybe a woman would be better.

I ask whether I am going to the bus stop to go home to Seymour, Indiana, or to another foster home. I try to steel myself for either answer, because I know the next words out of her mouth will seal my fate; they will set me free or further imprison me.

The seconds between my asking and her telling me are an eternity for me.

She tells me I will be going into another foster home, and I blank out for a second.

I really wanted to go and live in Indiana. The social worker tells me that she has spoken to one of my aunts, but she couldn't remember who. She says the person told her that no one in Indiana could take me. They said everyone had their family to consider, and I would be a handful, since my mother had spoiled me.

The aunt told the social worker that I had given my mother a hard time once, when I was six years old, by telling her that I hated her. Apparently, the aunt said, I refused to eat something, and I got mad at my mother.

I don't remember saying I hated my mother, but I must have said it if the adults in her family said I did. I'm really sorry if I said it, I didn't mean to get mad at her.

The aunt said my mother didn't even get upset and that she just told my aunt that all kids go through this phase. My aunt said my mother was too easy on me.

The aunt also told the social worker that my mother's mother, my grandmother, was not in good health. Billy visits her periodically, and that is all my grandmother can handle.

Also, there is concern about my cleft palate condition and the financial hardship it would place on the family.

Believing that if I can talk to them maybe they will see that I will be no trouble at all, I ask if I can have their phone number. I am told that the aunt doesn't want the phone number given to me.

Whoever it was said the decision was final, and they didn't want their mother to be bothered. The aunt told the social worker that I would be better off living with someone else, that maybe she could find me a family that will want me.

The fact that I am a teenager now will make it harder for me to be part of a family, the social worker said. I ask again whom she spoke to; she couldn't remember.

The big question is, now what? Does my mother still remember my hating her when I was six years old because I didn't want to eat something? If what I did once, when I was six, didn't bother her, why does it bother her family?

I feel like I am now completely on my own in life. I will never belong anywhere or to anyone, except to my mother. It is as if the social worker has knocked the wind out of me, and I'm being crushed under the weight of life.

The social worker tells me that since Indiana is not a possibility, I will be going into another foster home and that this is my last shot at family life. She tells me that this woman in the new foster home wants a baby girl, but since none are available, she will settle for me on trial basis.

The sting of rejection and betrayal from Indiana really hurts, and now I have to compete with a baby girl that didn't materialize. It's as if I'm back in the coal cellar, being compared to Alice. With all this mind-blowing splintering going on in this same conversation with the social worker on the way to the new foster home, I now know my wants and desires from the list I have made to give to a new mother are useless.

Well, from here on out, I will not use up any more of my energy on Indiana; the Smiths; Daddy; and his family, the Resubas. Those chapters in my life are closed.

I will give my entire energy, heart, and soul over to making this new foster home work. I sort of feel like this is my waterloo; I just hope that this last stand turns out differently for me than it did for Napoleon. Maybe I didn't win this battle for a different family life, but I'll be ready for the next round.

I wonder how many slaps in life it will take for me to give up on my goals of having a mother and a family?

The social worker tells me how hard it is to find a home that will take a thirteen-year-old girl with a cleft palate. She says that I am very lucky that anyone wants to take a chance on me.

I just slink farther down in the car seat. It is as if I hear her talking to me, but part of me is separated from myself, almost viewing me from afar. Maybe this is the key: when things are painful, I will just go away inside myself until someday, when I get all I need, I can come closer to me.

The social worker tells me that Mr. and Mrs. Wesson have four sons, and I groan inwardly, because unlike the Smiths, who wanted my brothers and not me, Mrs. Wesson will expect a normal thirteen-year-old. I can never share with her the list I made to give to an adoptive mother. I will have to make a new one.

The social worker keeps talking about how this woman is disappointed in having to take me since she really wants a baby girl, but Mrs. Wesson is told that for the time being, I am all that was available.

I have a sinking feeling about this, but I know that this is my last shot at having a mother and being adopted. Maybe I could pretend to be everything she wants in a thirteen-year-old girl, and when she likes me, maybe I could tell her the truth, that I need so much help.

How am I ever going to pull this off, being normal and not letting her see how I'm drowning in uncertainty at the same time? I just want to open the car door, jump out, and go away forever into oblivion.

The social worker tells me that with Christmas approaching, I should be grateful that anyone wants to take me before the holiday. This is my last shot, so I have to make the best of it. I think from now on, I have to move cautiously through this field of life that has many hidden land mines.

What if her expectations of me are so high that even with my pretending I can't reach them?

"Places of Roots"

Home is a place of permanency where often,
Mother is a person of unconditional acceptance.
Love tries to make a family come together so that.
Permanency can be a welcome respite from the endless chaos of
disconnection.

Relationship with others is more complicated as she grows older,
Bonding continues to elude her grasp as she seeks shelter.
Rooted in ways that could define her past and future,
Adoption is the only chance that offers a place called family.

Incomplete for the time being but she is still seeking and,
Yearning for the path that will again invite her inside,
Craving for the embracing that could allow her to stop,
Hungering for the holding that her mother used to bring into her life.

Existing alone but not really wanting to keep on.
Soul rooted to a journey of finding life so confusing,
Human identity the prize sought by the child so that she won't feel,
Incomplete as she moves from place to place, people to people.

Hungering for the shuffle-madness to end as abruptly as it started,
Nurturing desperately the desire of healing the brokenness.
Magnetic pulls in all directions within and outside trying to bring about the,
Full-circle of returning to the place where she once was held in
Love and connectedness.

The Second Foster Home: Adoption Denied
Ages 13 - 14

The Second Foster Home:
Adoption Denied

(Ages Thirteen to Fourteen)

Dear Mother,

As we pull up to the driveway of a beautiful home, the social worker, again, warns me that I have to be perfect, because if this home doesn't work out, I will be sent back to the orphanage. She reminds me, again, about how lucky I am to have the opportunity to be part of any family. All I can think of is, how am I ever going to be good enough?

As we go up the steps, the social worker turns to me and says, "Don't say anything about yourself or your background, unless you are asked. She knows that your mother is dead, but the rest you can tell her someday, in the faraway future, if she asks. People don't like to take kids who have problems, so the less you say, ask, or need, the more likely she will keep you."

She rings the doorbell, and this really pretty woman answers the door. There are all these little kids, all boys, running around. Her home is spotless and well lit, with a Christmas tree, and the TV is on. The home is so beautiful, and I hope she likes me.

We sit at the table, she gives me a glass of milk and asks me my name. I tell her Jerri Diane. She tells me how she loves Christmas, but she did not expect me so soon. She says she will have to ask the monsignor at Our Lady of the Springs Church for money to buy me gifts. I just sit there and listen. I am intimidated by her and feel like I am under a spotlight.

Mrs. Wesson is very beautiful, with short dark hair, and she is thin. Both the social worker and Mrs. Wesson talk to each other as if I were not present. I keep thinking to myself that this foster home is another mistake, but I have no choice, I have to get adopted. I wish you would come back from heaven just to teach me what I should know from the age of eight to thirteen. Mrs. Wesson sounds like a woman who is already disappointed in a foster kid like me.

How do I change into what she will want me to be, without losing me?

Love,
Jerri

*   *   *

The social worker and Mrs. Wesson are talking to me, but I am having a hard time looking at them. Mrs. Wesson tells me that she really wants a baby girl. The social worker tells her that she is working on it.

Mrs. Wesson says I will be attending the Catholic school here in Clark Summit, because her friend, the monsignor, will let me go there for free. Also, she says that she is not interested in hearing anything about the past thirteen years of my life. She says, "It is irrelevant, and you should never bring anything up, because what happened before you came to my house is not important."

I do not say anything, because I can't. Now I have to keep everything again to myself. The social worker tells Mrs. Wesson that I am a reader and that I like school.

When the social worker says she has to leave, I want to go with her. I always know when I am over my head. That is how I feel, like I'm about to play a game in life of being a perfect thirteen-year-old girl, without the slightest idea of the ground rules.

I am beginning to feel the sting from Mrs. Wesson's statement about not wanting to know anything about my past. I guess that stupid list I made before coming here can't be transferred to this second foster home. Tonight in bed, I will make a new list after I listen to more of her expectations.

I wonder if my mother makes lists in heaven?

As the social worker leaves, she makes arrangements to pick me up every two weeks to take me to the orthodontist. Mrs. Wesson says that although she is home and does drive, it is not her responsibility to drive from Clark Summit to Scranton to take me to see the orthodontist. He is this nice orthodontist who has been working on my teeth that are damaged by cleft palate.

The orthodontist has put this bridge in the roof of my mouth. He has to put a key in it every two weeks to turn it a fraction of an inch to stretch the palate. He wants to put braces on my teeth and fix the damage from the birth defect.

I listen as Mrs. Wesson explains that since I am a foster child, the state is responsible for transporting me. She doesn't want to take time away from her sons to take me to the dentist.

As they are discussing who should take me and why, I just want to curl up and disappear. I can tell that the social worker isn't happy about having to take me to the orthodontist.

I know intuitively that Mrs. Wesson already resents me and that any care, even at a minimum, is making her angry. She says that if her sons need the dentist, it would be different, but I don't really belong to her, so the social worker should make the arrangements.

Now two people are mad at me, and I didn't even say a word. Mrs. Wesson is upset because I'm not a baby girl and have to go to the dentist, and the social worker is disappointed because she is stuck with taking me every two weeks. I am being hit really hard by both people, and I don't have any control.

I wonder what the real reason is behind Mrs. Wesson's not wanting to take me to the dentist?

I can tell that Mrs. Wesson is a little hot under the collar after the social worker leaves. She tells me that she is laying down some ground rules for me.

First, since she didn't get what she wanted—as in, a baby girl—then I will have to be the thirteen-year-old daughter she always imagined she would have. Her sons come first because they are her heart and soul.

Since I am the foster kid, and the oldest, then I will have to think of them before myself. Then Mrs. Wesson tells me, again, never to mention my past and not to tell other people that I am a foster kid living with her.

I can tell she is embarrassed by me, probably because of the way I look, not too pretty. She makes fun of the clothes I wear and tells me that Mrs. Smith, the first foster lady, doesn't know how to dress a thirteen-year-old and that I look like I am wearing baby clothes.

Mrs. Wesson says that when her husband is home, that is his time, and he likes to spend it with the boys, because they need so much attention. I will be expected to be quiet, unless I need something, then I can ask for it.

At school, I am supposed to blend in and not cause her any embarrassment, because everyone knows that she is doing me a big favor by taking me. By now I feel really hot, like I am burning up, and I need to leave the room, but I can't move. I just listen to what she is saying, but I am not inside this body anymore. As she continues about how I would look okay if it wasn't for the scar on my face, I'm moving farther and farther from her in my mind.

I need to strengthen or toughen myself tonight while I am in bed. It is imperative that I make a list so that I am able to face tomorrow. I have to make her like me. I have nowhere else to go, and she knows it, because the social worker told her this is my last chance at a normal life.

Is this home really where I belong?

Mrs. Wesson tells me that she has high expectations of her sons, both socially and academically, and she hopes that I will have no trouble fitting in. I ask her if she is ever going to think about adoption. She laughs and says that I am not up for adoption, and didn't I think it is a little too late for me, since I am so old?

She tells me that at thirteen, she shouldn't have to do much for me, and I should know how to act. I am to let her know if I need anything, as long as it doesn't involve anything that happened in my life before I came here. I know inside that I will have to try really hard to know everything that she expects a thirteen-year-old girl to know. I just know that I have to get adopted, or I will be lost forever or die.

I hate myself for getting so desperate, for wanting or needing a mother, but I can't stop these feelings. Most importantly, I need to scrap that list I made for an adoptive mother. I cannot let the eight-, nine-, ten-, eleven-, or twelve-year-old girl get exposed.

I must be whatever she wants so she will like me. It's okay that she doesn't love, or will never love, me. I know that since my mother died, no one has wanted to love me. The way I've turned out, I guess I don't blame them.

Tonight I will make another list, another plan to change myself into someone who is, at last, marginally acceptable. It's just that as Mrs. Wesson continues to talk about her desire for a daughter, whom she can show off someday and send to dances, I become more intimidated by her.

Mrs. Wesson asks me why I don't look at her, but I don't answer because she said not to tell her anything about my life before today. I just shrug my shoulders and slump lower in the kitchen chair. She says I can go to my room, but I must remember that I am here only on a trial basis. She also says that the social worker tells her that if I don't work out, she can get another foster kid. I need to make a plan tonight.

How many more plans am I going to have to make?

I wish someone could please stop the stings I feel. I am so tired, yet I will need to focus and use all my energy not to crack. More and more, I am not handling the crash landings as easily as I used to. I will make a list of Mrs. Wesson's expectations of me and my responses to them:

Dressing

Mrs. Wesson: "I always wanted a daughter to dress up."

My Plans: I don't know how to dress, since I almost always wear black, and my nickname at the orphanage was the Widow Child. Most of the clothes are from the donated pile of the orphanage, or what Mrs. Smith bought for me. I will pretend I have taste in dressing, maybe she will not notice. How am I supposed to know what I never knew?

Shopping

Mrs. Wesson: "I always wanted a daughter to go shopping with."

My Plans: I haven't gone shopping in years. What am I going to do? I'll just avoid going out with her.

Nonexistent Past

Mrs. Wesson: "I don't want to hear about your past at all, your existence begins now."

My Plans: Ignore the list I made before coming here. It was stupid anyhow. I guess if she wants me to come here as a blank person, I could do it. Besides, it isn't as if I am going to spill my guts about all the darkness that surrounds me and share what I most would want to share with my mother who died. If only life had been different. I don't know if I will be able to pull off this act of a "no problem" thirteen-year-old foster girl. I do know that this is my last opportunity at a life of normalcy and a life of being a daughter within a family. I wonder if I can run a race toward being all that is expected of me without ever having learned to walk? Is it possible to shake the label of foster kid before its weight stops me from wanting to live and to belong? How old is too old to be adopted and mothered?

Adoption Possibly

Mrs. Wesson: "If you're what we want, we might adopt you."

My Plans: If I can just figure out what she wants, even if I have to pretend, then maybe she will make me a part of her family. I just have to be careful not to let her know about how backward I feel I am, how confused I feel, and I will never reveal anything about my previous thirteen years of life. I must focus all my energy on making no mistakes, not drawing any attention to myself, and stuffing the whisper tears that threaten to engulf me. I must make sure that her sons like me, because she says they are all that matter to her.

Unfair Competition

Mrs. Wesson: "I wanted a baby girl, but you were all that they had."

My Plans: I know she wants a baby girl, but if I try to be perfect, maybe I'll be acceptable. I must be careful not to tell her anything about my past, or then she'll know that I am a freak. I know that my being here is a disappointment to her, and she resents being stuck with me, but maybe she will learn to tolerate and eventually to like me. I can't compete with a baby, but I will try really hard to be like other girls. Maybe she will overlook my shortcomings and my empty personality, which is devoid of feelings on the outside.

Came Too Soon

Mrs. Wesson: "I have to get money from the priest for Christmas. You came too soon, I wasn't expecting you."

My Plans: I have learned that holidays don't matter. I don't want her to tell me about the money. I already feel rotten about imposing on this family, where the woman does not really want me, but what choices do I have? If I say Christmas means nothing to me, she might think I'm weird, and I don't want to draw attention to myself, lest I close the door to adoption forever.

Asking Questions

Mrs. Wesson: "If you have any questions, just ask, but nothing about the past."

My Plans: I have to make sure I never ask questions, because she'll know that I'm not normal. It has been so long since I've even talked to adults one on one. School is the only place where I talk to adults, because I know stuff about books. More and more, there is this echo that bounces around inside me when adults talk. I can't always understand what they expect from me.

Expectations

Mrs. Wesson: "You have no table manners, what's wrong with you?"

My Plans: I just don't know how to do what she wants. I really think that I'm in way over my head. How am I going to make her like me and maybe, someday, love me? I can sense her deep disappointment in me. I would probably not blame her if she sends me away, but it will crush me, because it will be the final nail in the coffin of my being human. Why do I seek being normal, being human, when it would be so much easier not to care?

Looks

Mrs. Wesson: "You would look okay if it wasn't for your teeth!"

My Plans: I know I'm ugly and the only thing I know how to do right is to read. Reading isn't going to make Mrs. Wesson like me, but how do I change the way I look? Maybe she will forget about wanting a pretty daughter if she could get a really smart one in exchange. She loves her sons, but maybe she will love me someday, if I work hard on disappearing physically and just become a "star student."

The End of the Line

Mrs. Wesson: "Why are you acting like a tomboy sitting in the tree, reading?"

My Plans: I have to be really careful not to let her see me act like a tomboy, because she wants this perfect daughter, and I desperately want her to love me and adopt me. The reason I sit in the tree is that I practice singing out loud to myself every day for an hour, then I spend another hour reading the poetry book I have. I do this as part of my determination to speak as clearly and concisely as everyone else, and to make myself more attractive for adoption.

Will whatever I do ever be enough? Will there ever come a point where I say no more? When will I know when to give up?

I went to the new school today, it is called Our Lady of the Springs. Christmas is just two weeks away. The eighth-grade class that I am placed in is getting ready for the holiday.

The nun I have for a teacher is Sister Margo. She is dressed in all blue and seems nice. The students are busy making preparations for the Christmas show that everyone partakes in. Sister Margo tells me that I will just watch because I am new.

Before she introduces me, I ask her if she will let me use *Wesson* as my last name, so the kids won't know that I am a foster kid. She says it would be up to Mrs. Wesson, who is standing by the door in the hallway.

While Sister Margo goes to check with her, I see all the girls sitting in different groups, all wearing the same uniform I am wearing. I'm glad that I finally get to blend in and wear the same thing so I don't stand out that much.

Sister Margo returns and whispers to me that Mrs. Wesson doesn't want me to use their name because I am only here on a trial basis. She doesn't want to give the impression that this is permanent. The nun asks me if I understand, and I say yes with my head, but no with my heart.

I want so much to blend in so that Mrs. Wesson will want me to stay. If she does want me to stay, then maybe it will be a sign that I could be like the other kids in my class.

I would change my name, instantly, if it meant I wouldn't be shuffled around anymore, but my name isn't changed, so I am still on the shuffleboard of life.

Why can't Mrs. Wesson let me blend in with her family?

When I get home from school today, Mrs. Wesson tells me that the social worker will be picking me up from school every two weeks to go to the dentist. I ask her if the social worker will always be taking me, and Mrs. Wesson says yes.

Mrs. Wesson repeats that I must understand that she is getting paid to keep me, but going into Scranton from Clark Summit is a bit too much to ask of her. She tells me that her sons come first, and then me. When I get married and have children, I will realize that my flesh-and-blood kids are more important.

I would rather die first than ever have any kid treated like I am or feel the way I feel. Why does everyone keep saying when I get married and have children I will understand?

I am very confused about what to say and how to act. I so desperately do not want to make any more mistakes.

In heaven, does my mother have to be perfect?

It is Christmas, 1969, and as Mrs. Wesson hands me some gifts, she tells me that I have to thank the priest from Our Lady of the Springs Church. She says that he gave her money to buy the gifts because I was not expected until after Christmas, but the social worker said I had to leave the other foster home before the holiday came. She said that she asked the priest for the money, and they are close friends. I guess he knows that I'm not really what they ordered.

Christmas is supposed to be a holiday for children. Maybe because I feel like I am a thousand years old, instead of thirteen, I am never going to immerse myself in the holiday experience.

Mrs. Wesson says I am old enough to understand that presents do not mean anything and that she and her husband have to think of their children first.

Christmas doesn't really matter much to me anyway; it only hurts to be this close to a real family but be left at the back door waiting to be invited in.

I just wish that family wasn't so important, or that Christmas wasn't such a holiday, with its constant bombarded messages of goodwill to others and going to Grandmother's house.

Why did Mrs. Wesson have to tell me that the priest gave her money? Couldn't she let me think that she and her husband bought me the gifts?

I keep watching Mrs. Wesson when she isn't looking, because I find women so fascinating and so incredibly intimidating. How do they know how to have a family and how to be a mother? I know that I am not part of this family, yet I crave for what I see the boys getting.

What really always fascinates me is Mrs. Wesson's interaction with her sons, especially her eldest, Robert, and one of the baby twins, John. She is always touching them, hugging them, tousling their hair, patting their heads when she walks by.

It doesn't really matter how hard I try, no one touches me like I see mothers do to their daughters. I wish Mrs. Wesson would brush my hair off my face, hug me, or see the whisper tears that beg for a nurturing embrace so I wouldn't drown anymore than I do.

Somehow she never touches me, maybe that's because I am so different. I wonder if girls aren't supposed to receive the motherly touch? Yet I see women with their daughters in public, and they seem to give them their mother touches.

I hope Mrs. Wesson never dies, because I wouldn't want her sons to ever know what I know.

Is it possible to be normal—a girl, a woman, and a mother—in the absence of being touched? Are the mother touches only available from a mother?

Mrs. Wesson tells me today that she thinks I am putting on too much weight. In her house, there is a scale, which says I weigh 120 pounds. She says no thirteen-year-old girl should weigh that much.

Mrs. Wesson says that overweight people are disgusting and lazy and don't care about their appearance. She says she is going to feed me less so I don't weigh so much.

I want to do whatever she says, because in the back of my mind, I know that this is the last chance for me to have a mother. I don't want to look any stranger than I do already. Even though I don't feel heavy, maybe I need to lose the weight so I can be more attractive on the adoption market.

It will not kill me to make this home work for me, and all I have to do is make the body smaller and more unnoticeable.

At night, when Mr. Wesson is late coming home from work, I hear Mrs. Wesson on the phone with her best friend, Marie. She is complaining about being stuck with me. She says if I don't become more like the daughter she always wanted, she'll have to send me back.

Maybe I need to try to be what I have never learned how to be—that is, a thirteen-year-old normal girl who is good enough to be a true daughter.

Sometimes inside, I feel like I know only how to be eight years old.

Is it possible to fast-forward, to skip over ages eight, nine, ten, eleven, and twelve and suddenly be a thirteen-year-old? Since there has been no one in my life since my mother died, and I have to be instantly what I am not, I wonder if I am heading for a crash over a cliff that I cannot yet see?

Today I got picked up from school by the social worker to go for my dental appointment. The kids in my class are always curious about me. They say they have never met a foster kid before.

At the bus stop, I am constantly teased about my name being different from *Wesson*. I just tell myself in my head to ignore them.

It is only fate or luck that, at any moment, their life situation could be mine. After all, I didn't make my mother die, and I really believe sometimes that she didn't want to die.

When the social worker knocks at the classroom door for me to go with her, I could just disappear. Right away, the kids want to know who she is and why she is here. I tell them that she is my social worker who has to take me to the dentist.

One of the girls says her mother takes her everywhere, and the other kids in the class nod in agreement with her. I tell them that when you are a foster kid, a thousand people take you a thousand places, just so you never get comfortable or belong anywhere.

One of the kids asks me if this means that I never stay anywhere forever, like they do. I say yes. I could come home today and move with no notice and no explanation. I just always make sure my mind is ready to move.

It's funny, but the kids feel a little different toward me. Some say that they feel bad for me and could not imagine having no mother. They tell me it must be weird changing families, houses, and schools, and never knowing where you'll end up.

One girl, who waits at the bus stop with me, tells me that she didn't mean anything by the teasing and that she would stop it. At least, the other kids consciously thought of what homes and families are.

Maybe I didn't change anything in my search for my family, but I feel less alone today.

I hope my mother in heaven thinks I did okay today.

On the way to the dentist, the social worker asks me how the new foster home is going. I tell her, "Okay." At least, inside me, I want it to be going okay.

She tells me that Mrs. Wesson tells her that I sit in the tree a lot, with my nose in a book. Mrs. Wesson also says that I never look at anyone and that I walk around with my head down.

The social worker tells me that I'm too withdrawn, and if I don't make any outward changes to act like the daughter Mrs. Wesson wants, then I'll be removed. She tells me that she doesn't know where she will place me, since I am a difficult placement.

Sometimes I wonder why the social worker doesn't offer to take me. I guess social workers aren't supposed to get involved with their caseload, even if it's an orphan with no hope of ever belonging.

The social worker tells me she hopes that these dental appointments aren't long, because they take a major chunk out of her day. There are times when I hear what she is saying, but from a distance, even though I am sitting two feet away from her in the car.

She says that Mrs. Wesson still wants a baby girl, but until one comes along, I'll have to stay and try to make it work.

In the waiting room, all the kids are sitting with their mothers, even the big kids who must be in high school. I guess as long as kids have mothers who aren't dead, then the kids need mothers in their lives, no matter how old they are.

I wonder if I will ever be like other girls?

There is a conference for parents at the school tonight, and Mrs. Wesson says she will try to see my teacher, but she first must give consideration to her own two sons.

I want her to talk to my teacher, Sister Margo, because even though I know I am not the girl or daughter Mrs. Wesson wants, I am a good student. Maybe she will overlook my boyishness, my ugliness, and all my failings if she thinks I am smart.

My grades are good, and Sister Margo tells me that I will do good someday in college. I always tell her that I'm going to go to college to become a real person. She laughs good-naturedly and says I'm already a real person. She just doesn't know my truth, my world reality, or that no one really believes I'll ever amount to anything.

I like succeeding in school because it is so cut-and-dry, I either know the material or I don't. I can always study harder to surpass what I knew yesterday. The best part about school is that I don't need people to make me smart. As long as I read and block out every avenue of my existence, then I am able to become more book smart.

Sister Margo tells Mrs. Wesson that I'm a good student, but Mrs. Wesson tells me not to think too well of myself because I'm not like other girls. I just block out that last part of her statement. Someday I will be somebody.

Is it possible to be whatever I want to be, even if I am the only one who believes it?

Robert ran away after school today. He is three years younger than me and Mrs. Wesson's oldest son. For a little kid, he is all right. Sometimes I think he feels sorry for me. I am not sure why he ran away.

I do know that his mother, Mrs. Wesson, has been very moody lately. Sometimes it scares me, but I think I am the only one who notices. It is as if I have to walk on eggshells, trying not to crack any so I don't set Mrs. Wesson off, because 90 percent of the time, I become the recipient of her anger.

I know there are muffled discussions about a thing called job transfer. Maybe Robert is getting the other 10 percent of her moodiness, and that is why he ran away. He should be just like me, just pull the blanket of emotional blocks over himself.

Mrs. Wesson is crying hysterically over him and tells me to get into the car so we can start looking for him. It is around nine thirty at night and very dark. Mrs. Wesson tells me that someday, when I have kids of my own, I will understand how much this upsets her, because Robert is her firstborn.

She says unless you have your own real flesh-and-blood children, no one understands.

She tells me that it is nothing personal, but she can never love me like she loves her sons. She says I should be able to understand that her real children come first.

The whole time, tears are streaming down her face, as she says that when she finds him, he can have anything he wants. I slink farther down into the front seat, because just what am I supposed to understand? "Oh, it's not personal, you are not a real child, but someday you should understand that your flesh and blood comes first."

When we get home, Robert is there with his dad. He says he got into a fight at school and didn't want to be yelled at for it.

Why can't Mrs. Wesson think of me as a flesh-and-blood child?

I want, more than anything else in the world, to be adopted by the Wessons. There is a part of me that knows that I am failing miserably, trying to change into the image of a thirteen-year-old daughter that is worthy of their love and attention.

With Mother's Day coming, Robert is really busy planning a surprise for Mrs. Wesson. I ask him what it's like, celebrating Mother's Day.

He tells me that he gets to thank her for being there for him, plus she makes a big fuss over him for any card or present he gives her. He tells me I should give her a card and that he will get one for me.

I think about what kind of gifts I could give. Even though I have tried, I never called her anything, not Mrs. Wesson, not Mom, and not Mother. It annoys her. It's just that I don't feel good enough to call her anything. So in the card, I ask her if I can call her Mom, although the word has never passed my lips.

Mrs. Wesson opens the card and tells me, "If that is what you want, okay, but just remember I'm not really your mother, and you don't have to give me a card." She gave the card back to me, so I just ripped it up.

I know inside that she doesn't want any connection. How can I be so stupid? What kind of woman would want me calling her Mom? Maybe I will bring my adoption campaign out into the open, and then it will be she who will invite me to call her Mom.

I wonder if my mother thinks that I am doing the right thing by wanting to be adopted?

Today a girl in my class invites me to her birthday party. This is my first time ever to go to a party with my classmates. I ask Mrs. Wesson if I can go. She tells me that I can go as long as I can find a ride, because she is busy.

I shouldn't have a problem getting there, because another girl, who lives in the same development as I do, says her mother will take me. I am so excited, because this means the other kids like me, even though Mrs. Wesson tells me I am so different from them.

When I get to the party, it is fabulous. This girl's house is an old stone building, with a large back deck and land for as far as you can see.

Her mother has these things called favors at each place for every child. Her father is walking around, snapping pictures, while someone is cooking hot dogs and hamburgers on this big outdoor grill that is built into the ground.

Ever since the kids in class asked me what it's like being a foster kid, they have been nicer and don't tease me anymore about my last name.

The girl's mother approaches me and tells me that her daughter tells her I am new to the school this year and staying in a foster home. I must be turning beet red, but she says that it is good to meet me. She has heard how nice and how smart I am.

She tells me that when I told her daughter what it is like to be a foster kid, her daughter came home and hugged her, saying she felt so lucky to have a mother. The girl's mother thanked me for helping her daughter to appreciate what she has.

The mother wishes me good luck in my effort to find a permanent home and to continue having a good time at the party. That is one of the nicest things that any adult has ever told me—that somehow, without trying, I've made a difference.

What is home like in heaven, where my mother is now living?

Today I decide to really bring my desperate desire to be adopted out in the open. I think that if I am adopted and belong permanently, Mrs. Wesson will see me in a different light.

I have been extra careful lately not to ask for anything or draw attention to myself. I have chosen to block out anything that is said about the body—how fat I am, how I am not normal—and to focus on the most cherished prize: adoption. Mrs. Wesson will then have to love and mother me. It's a law that adopted children are the same as real children.

Mrs. Wesson is in the kitchen when I approach her and ask if I can talk to her. She tells me to make it quick because she has somewhere to go.

I tell her how much I want to be a part of this family. I tell her that I want to have a permanent mother. I say that I want most of all to be adopted by her and her husband.

I quickly tell her that I have really improved my speech and gotten good grades. I have caused no problems and will do anything she wants. I will be perfect and never make mistakes. I also tell her that I know I'm not the normal girl she wanted for a daughter, but if I get adopted, all those areas that she sees wrong will go away.

She stops me in the middle of my pleading and tells me to go outside. She says she will have to talk to her husband. She says that there are a lot of changes coming, and she doesn't know if I will fit into their plans.

I feel crushed inside but become even more determined to get them to adopt me. I have so few other choices for a family, for becoming a girl, a woman, or a human being.

I walk out, convinced that they have to say yes, because I can't accept that any other answer is possible.

Couldn't my mother ask God to force the Wessons to want me?

Mr. and Mrs. Wesson call me into the kitchen and tell me to sit down. Mrs. Wesson says that she and her husband have discussed my request and that at the present time, they have to say no.

Mr. Wesson, sensing my disappointment, quickly says that he has urged his wife to keep working with me, since he is being transferred to Wichita, Kansas. He says that if I am very helpful with the boys, after the move, they will reevaluate their decision on my adoption request. He tells me that his wife will be under a lot of stress with this job transfer. I need to do whatever I can to make life easier for her, since he will be away for weeks at a time in Kansas, looking for a place to live.

I hear myself saying, I will be very helpful to Mrs. Wesson, just ask me to do anything, and I will do it. I will turn myself inside out if it means I fit in enough to be adopted.

While I hear myself responding to Mr. Wesson, another part of me has been watching Mrs. Wesson, and I know she is not happy. She is angry about the job transfer and the fact that Mr. Wesson will be away so much.

I like it when Mr. Wesson is around, because Mrs. Wesson is not so mean or caustic in her remarks to me.

I guess my bar of reality has been raised to a new height. Maybe if I am really helpful with this job transfer, Mr. Wesson will talk his wife into adopting me. I really believe that this is my moment to prove that I can make myself into a member of a family.

What will I do if I fail in my attempt to belong?

Eighth-grade graduation will be next week. Of course, that means that I have done my best in school. We had the final exams in school, and I passed with flying colors.

I am determined to develop what brainpower I have so that Mrs. Wesson will be impressed. I studied really hard and knew everything. School is really cool sometimes, because when I sit at a desk, it's only me and this exam.

The battle to pass or fail rests completely on my shoulders. It's different from trying to be human or a girl; that depends on a thousand and one nuances, always involving other people.

I have learned that I can grow brainpower, increase my vocabulary, understand mathematical concepts, and explore scientific experiments.

I often wonder about the different kinds of final exams that I will have to take in life. The book exams, like the ones I took in school, means that I am partially alive. Taking the life exams of emotions, acceptance, and having an identity are areas I'll probably always fail in.

In some ways, I figure, given all my experiences in this prolonged short life since my mother died, any success, even if it's only passing the book exams, is really an accomplishment. Isn't it really sad that only I believe I can learn to increase my ability to be book smart? No one else believes I can do anything.

Someday, when my speech has been perfected and I have learned a great deal of knowledge, it might be enough to buy me a pass into life. Maybe then, someone will notice me, nurture me, and embrace me. Then I will know that I could pass all the other different kinds of exams that life offers.

How much more perfect do I have to be in order to be acceptable?

Mrs. Wesson tells me that she is embarrassed to be seen with me at the eighth-grade graduation, because I am so fat. She says she asked the priest for money to buy me a dress. She says that she will not take me shopping, she will pick it out.

She probably doesn't want to be seen with me in public. Maybe when she sees me graduate, she will feel differently about me. She will notice that I accomplished something. Maybe if I can show her how smart I am going to be, she will be pleased enough to overlook all the aspects of me that she finds so despicable.

Sister Margo wishes me good luck. She tells me always to set goals and never let anyone stand in my way. She says that someday things will work out. I should just never give up!

I tell her how much I want to be adopted, even though I know I am too old to need a mother. I tell her how much I despise being a foster kid.

She laughs in her gentle way, telling me that every child, even a thirteen-year-old girl, needs a mother and is entitled to one. She tells me I am not too old. She says I will never be too old to need a mother. I like Sister Margo because she doesn't think I am really strange, just a kid trying to find my way.

Mr. and Mrs. Wesson come to the graduation Mass, but sit toward the back. I still cannot use their last name, but I just know that someday I won't have to use my name.

When I am handed my diploma, I feel so good. I just wish that I could know where I am going!

I wonder if my mother is at least proud of me in heaven because of my good grades?

The day after eighth-grade graduation, I again approach Mrs. Wesson about adoption. I decide that it is in my best interest to present my side of the adoption discussion.

I learned in school about the rules for debating an issue, and how I always have to really present my side of the argument well. What I did was look up the word *adoption* and the term *foster kid* and put their definitions side by side.

I believe that if I can show Mrs. Wesson the pros and cons of adoption and foster care, she will see that it is in her best interest to adopt me. I write the two lists out in my room and study them really hard so I can present a valid argument in my favor. I write down,

Adoption of Me	*Me Being a Foster Kid*
1) I'll be permanent, never moved.	1) I'll always be shuffled around.
2) I'll have the same last name as my adoptive family.	2) I will have to carry the name of a family who despises my very existence.
3) I'll automatically be a real person.	3) I'll never be a person, a girl, a daughter, or a woman.
4) I'll get a job to give them money.	4) People get paid to keep me.
5) They don't have to give me anything.	5) I don't get anything.
6) I'll have what I want most—a mother.	6) I'll never be loved or nurtured, mothered or touched.

When I approach Mrs. Wesson, I decide that I will not focus on the foster kid list. I'm afraid she will like that side of the argument better. I find Mrs. Wesson in the living room, reading the paper.

I tell her that I have been doing some research and believe that if they adopt me, then I will be able to help support this family. Also, I know that whatever kind of daughter she wants, I can be that, because of my ability to will myself to change.

She just looks at me and says that it will be a few months down the road before they think of adoption; also, the social worker will be here tomorrow to give the okay for me to go with them. I just nod my head okay, but my heart sinks because I don't know how to sell myself.

Couldn't my mother in heaven figure a way for me to get this family acceptance thing to work?

The social worker comes today and asks me if I want to go to Wichita, Kansas, with the Wessons. I tell her yes, because I know that if I stay longer, maybe they will adopt me. I tell her about how much my speech has improved and that it's getting very clear. I also tell her that I passed the final exams in school.

There is no way I will let this opportunity of belonging slip through my hands. I want to go with them. I know, I tell the social worker, that it is only a matter of time before they notice that I can almost fit in.

I just want to be a daughter, so I can be a girl.

The social worker tells me that the Wessons have not mentioned adoption, but she will give her permission for me to go as a foster kid with them. I thank her, but I also tell her that I will not always be a foster kid being shuffled around. I am going to belong permanently someday. She says that I have such a stubborn streak, that I refuse to accept reality.

What does she want me to accept? That I am nothing? That I am so repulsive, that no one will adopt me? That my insatiable hunger to be mothered is so terribly wrong?

I tell the social worker that I will be good and helpful. She wishes me luck and says that if things don't work out, I will be returned to the orphanage. It doesn't matter, I tell her, because if it kills me, I am going to be in a family. Some parts of me already feel like they are dying.

What do I have to lose?

Mrs. Wesson says Daddy will come to see me today. He has to give legal permission for me to leave the state. I have not seen him in two years.

It's funny; on one hand, he is not in touch, but on the other hand, he is still legally responsible for me. The last time I saw him was in the orphanage, before my brothers and I left for the first foster home.

Daddy greets me, and there is a wisp of nostalgia for the times we were all together, traveling with the air force. I quickly brush those memories of what was, what will never be again, away from my heart.

Daddy asks me if I want to go to Wichita, Kansas. I tell him yes. I tell him for the first time how much I want to be adopted and to have a mother. I tell him that I think my mother would be okay with what I want.

He says that I will have a different last name. I think to myself, Yeah, like Daddy's name is a name I want, a daily reminder of how despicable I am and how much Daddy's parents hate my mother. I keep this thought to myself. What's the point of getting into an argument with someone who left me in an orphanage so long ago?

Someday, I believe that Daddy will have to answer to my mother and God, not so much for what he did, but for what he failed to do. He didn't protect us, he didn't love us, and, mostly, he allowed others to continue hating my mother through their neglect and abuse of my brothers and me.

The really sad part is that I loved him. There is a severing that no amount of forgiveness or reconciliation can ever put back what once was. I can still remember how my brothers and I tagged after him everywhere he went, when my mother was still part of our lives.

How could he have not honored my mother by not loving us?

As we prepare for the job transfer, Mrs. Wesson is making me more nervous. She has always been somewhat moody, but now her mood swings are escalating. It is like walking on eggshells and trying not to crack them.

I am so afraid that the slightest thing will set her off and make her angry. As much as possible, I try to fade into the woodwork so that I am not the recipient of her remarks, which are sometimes acid laced and stinging.

The way I figure life, the less I am noticed, the less is expected of me. Sometimes, lately, the bar of reality has been raised higher than ever. I can pull myself up to reach it, but it is getting harder.

We will be going to St. Louis for a few weeks, to stay with Mrs. Wesson's mother. During this time, Mrs. Wesson will fly to Kansas to look for a house with Mr. Wesson. I don't like going to a strange city like St. Louis and staying with people I have never met.

While we are packing, Mrs. Wesson tells me that I had better not cause any problems at her mother's house because I am an added inconvenience. I get a sense that it is not Mrs. Wesson's first choice to go to her mother's, but the house has been sold, and they have to buy one in Kansas.

I promise that she won't even know that I am around, and I will take James and John out every day.

Living with someone, who has severe mood swings, is like being in a house filled with a thousand mirrors for rooms. I am always trying to find my way, by figuring out where one mirror begins and the other ends. I never know when one mood begins and when it will end.

Increasingly, I feel the heat of her anger, especially when Mr. Wesson is not home. Most of the time, whatever she is angry about has nothing to do with me.

How do I seal the cracks in my plans to be a family member? Am I heading for a crash landing and don't know it?

Today we are in St. Louis. Mrs. Wesson tells me that I am not to speak unless spoken to and that I should remember that her mother is the boys' grandmother first.

She says that I need to spend most of the day away from the house, because there are too many people in the small home. There is this park, a couple of blocks away, where I am to go after breakfast, and then I can come home around five or six in the afternoon.

St. Louis is a much bigger city than Clark Summit, in Pennsylvania. At the playground, there is a free lunch given, which is a good thing. Mrs. Wesson tells me not to come home until dinnertime, but she doesn't mention anything about lunch.

I have my goal of adoption, held out to me down the road, so I want to do everything to make it happen. If she doesn't want me around all day, that is a small sacrifice.

Mrs. Wesson says that after she gets the twins changed and dressed, I am to take them in their stroller to the park. At 11:30 a.m., I have to bring them home to her.

When I bring them back to the house, she greets me at the door. She tells me that I can go out until dinnertime. She doesn't invite me in for lunch, and I don't ask.

I wonder what is going on, why I can't eat lunch with the boys. Maybe I did something wrong, although I can't imagine what it would have been.

I just sit on the swing, going over my list and trying to be perfect and to work on whatever I can improve on. There is a mobile library that stops at the park, so I get some poetry books out and start practicing my speech again.

How will I ever learn about people and family if I'm always by myself? Why does Mrs. Wesson care more about her sons than me? Will adoption really be the answer?

Mrs. Wesson is really angry. I have to sleep in the same room as James and John. There are twin beds on both sides of the room. I sleep in one, and the twins sleep in the other. They have always slept in a crib, but in St. Louis, they have only the bed.

James cries all night, and when I tell Mrs. Wesson this, she starts yelling. She says that I must have done something to him for him to cry. I swear to her that I didn't, that he is afraid of the big bed and that it is so dark in there.

She tells me to shut up and not try to defend myself. She says that it was a mistake to listen to her husband about taking me with them. She says that if James cries tonight, she will put me on the first plane back to the orphanage. She knows I have nowhere to go.

When night comes, and James starts to cry again, I take him into my bed and rock him until he falls asleep. I know she thinks I must have hit him or something, but she is wrong.

It's hard to defend myself sometimes, because who wants to believe a foster kid? As I put James back into the bed with John, I look at them and think how lucky they are. All I will ever know is uncertainty, rejection, and confusion over all the changes that life has to offer.

I find it somewhat ironic that Mrs. Wesson thinks I must have hurt James, yet she continues to make me sleep in the same room with the twins. I know in my wildest imagination that if I had kids, and I thought someone hurt them, I wouldn't let them sleep in the same room with that person.

All she has to do is rock them to sleep in this strange house, sleeping on strange beds. If I'm scared and I'm thirteen, shouldn't they be scared when they're not even two years old?

Do the scary feelings ever go away? How do I convince Mrs. Wesson that I am not as bad as she thinks I might be? What will happen to me in this spiral of confusion?

I tell Mrs. Wesson that James didn't cry last night. Of course, I don't mention that I rocked him to sleep. She tells me not to speak to her. When I ask what I did wrong, she refuses to answer me.

I eat my breakfast quickly, while trying to figure out what I've did now to upset her. She is very pretty, smart, and very moody, but I try to overlook that part of her.

As she gets James and John ready for me to take them out for the morning, she tells Robert to tell me, even though I'm standing a foot away from her, that I will come back after lunch to take the twins out again in the afternoon until dinnertime.

I groan inwardly but don't say anything. I wonder if she knows how much work I have to do to keep two baby boys entertained, just during the morning hours, and now the afternoon hours too.

Plus it's so hot outside. Robert and Anthony get to hang around the house. It doesn't seem fair, but then when has life ever been fair for me?

Apparently, Mrs. Wesson is flying to Kansas to check out a house to live in. Her mother is older and doesn't want to have total care of the boys.

Maybe I am not being as helpful as I said I would be. I will take the boys for the whole day, except for the two hours that I bring them home to eat lunch and to be changed.

I have to sit on the steps outside because she still will not give me lunch. I get scared sometimes, because what if something happens to one of the twins? Then it will be my fault.

Why do some adults use silence as punishment? How do I stop the unraveling of my dreams to be adopted, loved, and wanted? Am I doomed to always be on the outside looking in?

While Mrs. Wesson is in Kansas, I continue to take care of James and John for most of the day. Her mother tells me the social worker called from Scranton to talk to me and to see how I am doing. When she calls again, I get to speak to her.

After all the rides to the orthodontist every two weeks over the past six months, I've sort of grown to like her. Sometimes I secretly wish that social workers could adopt kids like me, at least they may not think that foster kids are all that strange.

The social worker asks me what I do during the day, so I tell her what is happening. She says she doesn't like the idea of me watching the babies most of the day. She tells me that I am not their mother and that it is too much responsibility for a thirteen-year-old girl.

She says she'll talk to Mrs. Wesson about using me as a full-time babysitter. I beg her not to say anything, because I already know that things aren't going as well as I planned. Mrs. Wesson still hasn't warmed up to me, and she doesn't treat me like Robert and Anthony. The social worker tells me not to worry about anything.

Mrs. Wesson comes back from Kansas and says that she has found a house. In two weeks, we will be moving. She calls the social worker. When she gets off the phone, she is livid with me. She screams, "How dare you complain about watching the boys all day!"

Mrs. Wesson says that from now on, she will watch her own children. She tells me I have to leave the house after breakfast and not come back until dinnertime.

I begin walking the streets of St. Louis, like I'm walking on a faraway planet. The isolation is growing, and I sense that my plans for adoption are beginning to crumble. In the whole universe, is there any place for someone like me?

We fly to Kansas, where Mr. Wesson is waiting for us. Ever since that conversation with the social worker, Mrs. Wesson won't speak to me. If she has something to say to me, she will ask Robert to tell me.

We have to eat at restaurants for the first few days, while the house is made ready to be moved into. Mrs. Wesson starts in on me about how my table manners are atrocious. I don't say anything, because I think if she is saying mean things to me, maybe she will eventually say nice things. Even though I feel hurt by what she says, at least she is talking to me.

The worst thing in the world is the punishing silence, because I can never figure out what I'm being punished for.

At Mass on Sundays, I sit in the back of the church, while they sit toward the front. I know Mrs. Wesson is so humiliated and embarrassed by me. It's because I never became what she wanted, and maybe in the end, I will never even become what I wanted to be.

I'm trying to figure out how I can fix what is wrong with me. Sometimes, lately, I feel like I'm going crazy inside my mind. Everything is so jumbled up all the time. I keep running around inside, trying to keep control of all my different ages that keep coming out of their boxes.

Unfortunately, all the things happening in this foster home seem to be more than even my stoic self can handle. What I need to do is slow down and focus on winning at the adoption game.

Is it possible to focus my mind, when I don't feel so good about myself inside?

The new place in Kansas, where I now live, is called a townhouse. It is really very beautiful. Someday, maybe when I grow up, I'm going to build a beautiful house, but it will be a big log cabin, like Davey Crockett's.

The only thing I hate about this house is that I have to sleep in the basement with the twins on this big pull-out couch.

The basement seems so large, and it is so dark at night. It is not like Grandma Resuba's coal cellar, but I now know, symbolically, my place in the pecking order of the Wesson family. Upstairs, on the third floor, there are three big bedrooms: the master bedroom, that must be where married people sleep; Robert has his own bedroom; and Anthony has the other bedroom.

Sometimes I try to figure out why Mrs. Wesson is making me stay in the basement with James and John. They are good babies, and often I rock James to sleep, but I'm always afraid that they might fall off the couch-bed, and then I will be blamed. I stay up most of the night so that nothing will happen to them. In my mind, I think that if the twins don't make any noise, maybe Mrs. Wesson will think I am useful.

I hear Mrs. Wesson on the phone a lot with her best friend, back in Clark Summit, Pennsylvania, telling her how nothing is going right. She says that Mr. Wesson is never home, and there is so much work for her to do, and the last thing she needs is this foster kid. She tells her friend that she wants to send me back, because I am nothing like the daughter she imagined.

I sit on the steps leading to the basement, listening to this, trying desperately to stem the waves of the whisper tears that are trying to overwhelm me. I'm trying so hard to be what she wants; only, I am not always sure how to be what she wants me to be.

Why can't Mrs. Wesson just give me another chance to be normal?

Since we have moved to this townhouse here in Kansas, whatever relationship I have with this family is rapidly dwindling. Mrs. Wesson absolutely refuses to speak to me. When I muster up the courage to ask her anything, she just stares past me.

My fourteenth birthday is today, and it is as if it never exists. I stay with my regular routine of getting up and putting the same clothes on every day. I have no breakfast because there is no place set for me at the table.

When I come up the steps from the basement, I pass the kitchen, where Mrs. Wesson is having a lively conversation with the boys. As I pass the doorway to the kitchen, she becomes silent.

Once, when I ask if I could eat breakfast, she tells Robert to tell me that I have to leave and come back in the afternoon, and there will be a sandwich and cup of milk at the table.

She says I am too fat at one hundred and twenty pounds at age thirteen and it is disgusting. There is no breakfast and no dinner, only a sandwich and a cup of milk.

Mr. Wesson is never home; sometimes he is gone for a few days. Every now and then, he returns and takes Robert, Anthony, and me with him when he goes on his day trips to sell Xerox machines. I like this, because he always stops twice to eat; I just wish he would take us more often.

What is so hard to take is the silence and the sense that even this last chance in this foster home is not working out.

What does everyone want from me? All I ever wanted was to belong, to have a mother, and to be a girl; is that too much to ask? I wonder if I really matter to even God or my mother?

It is now August 1970, and the silence continues. I have tried everything. I stay away from the townhouse from morning until seven or eight at night. The only time I return is to eat the sandwich and have the cup of milk left for me. I am always so hungry and so thirsty.

It gets hot in Kansas in the summer, and I guess it doesn't help that I wear long pants and a long-sleeved shirt. At least my clothes are getting bigger and baggier. I think I've lost a lot of weight.

My stomach still hurts a lot, but I don't say anything. I stopped complaining about my body a long time ago.

I met this old couple who clean a place called the club. It is a part of the townhouse complex where there is also a pool attached.

Mrs. Wesson goes to the pool every day, where she sunbathes and reads a book. The babies play in the sandbox, and Robert and Anthony swim.

I can always see them from the club window, but I never go near them, because I don't want to embarrass Mrs. Wesson. She is so pretty, and maybe someday she will get the pretty daughter that she has always wanted.

I realize now that it is no use; it is too late for me to ever learn the skills that would make a girl into a woman. I just need to focus on surviving; I have to find a way to get food and something to drink.

This old couple sees me hanging around and asks me who I am. I tell them that I am a foster kid with nothing to do, and I'm really thirsty. They give me a soda from this big machine.

They tell me that I can have as much as I want every day they are here. I begin to wipe the tables for them so they can set up this thing called a happy hour. I ask what that is, and I'm told that it's when adults come and drink alcohol for free.

I ask if alcohol is different from soda, and they tell me yes. They say that people sometimes lose control of themselves if they drink too much alcohol. I think in my mind that I had better not ever start drinking alcohol so I don't lose control.

I like the older couple, because they let me have as many peanuts and sodas as I want.

From time to time, I look down from the club's big bay window, at the families sitting around the pool. They all seem part of a different world from the one I live in. I feel I am a total disaster and have become the opposite of everything that my mother could have dreamed of or hoped for in a daughter.

I wonder if my mother thinks that I am really as backward as Mrs. Wesson thinks I am?

As in St. Louis, I find myself now walking the streets of Kansas. But here there are no parks that give a free lunch or have a mobile library like in St. Louis.

I have nowhere to go. I can't stay in the townhouse. The pool is off-limits, because I'm a freak. I don't belong with the other kids around the pool, and I know that Mrs. Wesson goes there all the time.

I would bring embarrassment to her. She hates me, yet I keep trying to figure out just why.

The old couple works at the club only on Thursdays and Fridays. The rest of the time, I just walk block after block.

As I walk mile after mile every day, I keep reviewing my list—my good parts, my bad parts, anything—to try to understand how I could have failed. There is nothing going right for me, and I don't know what to do.

I know now, more than I've ever known in my whole life, that it is no use anymore. I just don't have the skills or the raw material to be a person.

Finally the heat of summer ends. In three weeks it will be September and time for school to start. Robert and Anthony are talking about school shopping. I don't know what will happen to me. Maybe Mrs. Wesson won't let me go to school. Sometimes I think that I'm not even smart anymore.

I wonder if I will become more stupid if I use all my energy to survive?

I overhear Mrs. Wesson on the phone again, talking to her friend back in Clark Summit. She is telling her how Mr. Wesson is never home and how much she hates it here in Kansas.

She says she will take the boys shopping next week, but not the foster kid. She says that if the social work agency wants me to go to school, let them come out to take care of me.

Mrs. Wesson tells her friend that if it weren't for my teeth, I might look okay, but I would still be a really strange kid. I just slide down the steps to the basement and curl up in a ball on the couch-bed, trying to rock and to numb myself.

I don't know how to stop the waves of emotions that are battering my inside core. I know some of the neighbors asked Robert if I was his sister. He said no, that I'm a foster kid his mother took in. Robert sometimes lets me ride his bike, but I don't do it too often, because I don't want to fall and damage it.

I just try to imagine that I am someone else, maybe a Kennedy kid or a kid in Hollywood, someone important, essential, and just part of a family. I am so tired of having to worry about living and surviving.

I wonder if my mother thinks that it is okay for me to wish that I were another kind of kid?

Something is happening to the body again. There are big oozing sores up and down my legs. They are the size of a quarter. I don't dare say anything, because I can't take any more condemnation about being different.

The sores just appeared. They ooze with blood and some kind of yellow pus. I think I counted twelve on the right leg and ten on the left leg. No one notices because I wear the same long pants every day. It's really hard not to pick at the sores, because they itch so much.

One of the neighbors sees me looking at my sores and tells me to tell my mother about them. I tell her that Mrs. Wesson is my foster mother, and she is very busy.

The neighbor asks me how long I've been a foster kid. I tell her for six years since my mother died but that I'm still hoping to get adopted. The neighbor tells me "Good luck" and says that I really should tell my foster mother about the sores.

Of course, I can't tell Mrs. Wesson anything about my body, especially the sores. I think of what I might have and decide that maybe I have leprosy.

I know the "lepers" are sent to live on islands in the middle of the ocean. If I have leprosy, this is a sign that I have not lived a good life and I'm being punished. I know from Bible stories that only Jesus is willing to touch the leper.

I wonder if Mrs. Wesson knows that I am a leper, and that's why she doesn't give me the mother touches that she gives to her sons?

The sores are beginning to crust over on my legs. They still itch a lot, but I will my mind not to feel the itchiness. There are other things going on in my life besides the sores from leprosy.

I am so hungry all the time. It has been four weeks since we moved into this townhouse, and Mrs. Wesson has stopped feeding me. I do get the one sandwich and cup of milk in the afternoon.

What I have to do is come home around three o'clock in the afternoon and look inside the kitchen window to see if it is on the table. Then I go in and eat the food by myself and then leave the house. I never touch anything in the kitchen because that would be stealing.

I know that I should be satisfied with what I get, but I am still hungry. The stomach hurts so much, it makes these weird noises that sound like rumbling rocks.

I know I've lost a lot of weight. No breakfast and no dinner for the past four weeks, and there are two more weeks until school starts. I can't take this starving anymore.

I go to a local grocery store and pretend I'm looking for something to buy; of course, I have no money. As I walk up and down the aisles, I secretly eat some cake or perishable item. I try to keep an account in my head about how much money the store is losing by my stealing food this way. I vow that someday I'll repay the grocery store.

The only way I can get food is to steal it. I know I am breaking the law and a commandment, but I can't worry about that now. Someday I will be rich, and no one will ever starve me again, but in the meantime, I need to eat.

Doesn't God ever want to fix things so that I wouldn't be hungry?

The struggle for my soul is on. Every day I think of different ways to stop the emotional battering. I'm torn between suicide and a total shutdown of existence, short of physical death.

Lately, I've been walking around, looking for tall buildings. In my mind, I think of how easy it would be just to step off a tenth floor and fly from this existence into the next. Once I step off, there would be no turning back anyway. My only alternative to going over that edge is to remain an isolated alien, in a world that refuses to embrace me.

In my mind, I constantly try to think of the pros and cons of staying or leaving this world. It is hard to believe that the end is beckoning me, almost luring me to give up.

I started in this world as a beloved child, and after fourteen years, I am a pariah, an embarrassment to everyone. The only two people I can talk to are my mother—yet she is dead—and God, who won't use all his power to force people to care.

While my mother is enjoying the celestial heavens, I keep trying to pick myself back up. But with each fall, it is growing more and more difficult.

My mother's presence on earth was so important, and her absence has left me still reeling from all the devastation that a motherless and family-less child could encounter.

I find I'm on the edge of the cliff, just looking for a reason not to step into the vast oblivion of death.

Is it possible to resist the magnetic pull into a life of no pain, no rejection, and no confusion? What does my mother want me to do?

God and I had a talk today. I now know that all the plans in the world cannot make people care about me. Also, I realize that even God can't change the hearts of those who wish to do their own will.

Today I know that no matter how attractive or how seductive I find the pull to step off a tall building, I will not go there again. Maybe I finally, at least with God, have figured out why he doesn't use all that power to make things right.

The way I see it, this is a battle for my soul and for my physical life. By now I understand I cannot destroy the gift of life that my mother gave me and the gift of free will that God gave me.

If I die by my own hand, then it would be because everyone else used their free will to destroy me. I have to learn not to let that happen, not to let them win, because that would be like letting evil win.

I would love to step off the building that I found, because I know I have no worth, but then I would never know my mother. Only the two people who care about me, my mother and God, would be so disappointed in me.

In my mind, I decide that I will also end the hunt for a mother, even though I know this means that I will now live a totally isolated life. If in the emotional food chain I can't bond with a mother and a family, then all the other human experiences will forever be beyond my reach. I wish someone could tell me that this permanent decision of not needing and wanting a mother is wrong for me.

Maybe free will is just that, the will to freely choose to enter into someone's life and to make a difference. God can't take the gift of free will back once he gives it, even if it is not being used to enhance the lives of others. My mother cannot take back the gift of life, and this keeps me from stepping off the edge.

Does God really think that this gift of free will is such a good thing? How do I reconcile the gift of life and the gift of free will in a world that wishes to repudiate my existence?

Today I know that the human touches will no longer be part of my life. I always remember my mother touching me, rocking me, tousling my hair, and hugging me. I often see other women touching their children, even kids my age, and I'm already fourteen.

It's just that I need to put away the ordinary and the extraordinary hunger to be nurtured, in order to live physically.

I know something else that I have discovered about God. He gets blamed for a lot of stuff that people do or fail to do. I wish I could tell my mother how often adults tell me that everything is God's will. Personally, I think they use God to rationalize away their responsibility to be Godlike.

Many times I'm told that it's God's will that my mother died, or that it's God's will that I don't have a mother. I chatted with God about this, and there is no way that God doesn't want me to be mothered. If people, especially women, don't want to mother me, that is their free-will choice.

Sometimes I feel sorry for God, because how are people going to learn to change and care if they keep turning a blind eye and shoving everything back on him?

My mother must laugh in heaven at this kid of hers, who is always trying to understand people and always tying that knot at the end of her rope, just to hang on for another day.

I also know this: my mother would never have wanted me to be unmothered, unloved, and unwanted. Maybe things do happen in life, but doesn't that mean that other people should step in, if for no other reason than because it's the right thing to do?

I know that in heaven my mother must not have any needs, or experience any pain. Sometimes though, I still secretly think that she is saddened by what has happened to her four children and the dramatic changes in their lives. Part of me will always believe that even though she is in heaven, she must be mad as hell at Daddy, his family, her family, and this whole foster care system. I like to think that she also thinks that people are stupid, who tell her kid that if God wanted me to have a mother, he would have given me one.

How do I save God's gentle nudges for the times when I am almost drowning in my whisper tears? Why does heaven have to be so far away, so silent, and so untouchable?

I'm really struggling with my decision to live. Somehow I know that things are going to change soon. School has started, and Mrs. Wesson did not send me or buy me school clothes.

It's lonely in the neighborhood when you are fourteen and the world is at school. I don't know what to do with myself.

I again overhear Mrs. Wesson talking to her best friend back in Clark Summit, Pennsylvania. She tells her that the foster kid is still here and that she is not going to buy me school clothes. She tells her friend that she should not have to be responsible for the foster kid anymore. "Let the social worker come and take her." I try to press my body to the wall so I won't feel anything.

Mrs. Wesson finds me so repulsive that I am now, and probably always was, "the foster kid" in her mind. How did I ever become an inanimate thing or term in other people's eyes? There are times when I know I shouldn't listen to what she says on the phone.

I wonder if Mrs. Wesson, or any of the foster parents in the world, really ever sat down and imagined what it must be like to be "the foster kid."

1) I will never be a real person.
2) I will never know the mother touches.
3) I will never be able to stop second-guessing my right to exist.
4) I will never believe that people could ever love someone as repulsive as me.
5) I will always be a half step behind other kids. In my heart, I'll be "the foster kid" who never stayed long enough to become "our kid."

Why do I put myself through such torture of trying to fit into a world that doesn't want to know I exist? Was there ever really anyone who was willing to transform "the" into "our"?

It is now the second day of my not attending school, and I think that the neighbors are noticing. I sit on the steps outside the townhouse and overhear one of the neighbor women tell her friend that she filed a report on me.

She says she doesn't like the way Mrs. Wesson treats me. She tells her friend that she knows I'm a foster kid and that I have been left by myself day after day.

The woman is angry with Mrs. Wesson, telling her friend that "the kid is neglected and wearing the same clothes every day." She also sees me walking the streets by myself all the time and notices that I am losing weight.

I just sit there, listening, because it is very rare that anyone notices me or defends me. Why can't people like this neighbor become a foster parent? It hurts me because I know she probably would hate me too if she knew me, but maybe she would like another kid.

Mrs. Wesson is mad tonight. For the first time in a long time, she speaks to me, even though it is in anger. She tells me not to move because the next day, the social worker is coming over.

She says some nosy neighbor reported her. She says she is happy because now they can come and take me away because I am a total failure.

I seem to listen, but I keep trying to pull down the steel doors inside my mind so she can't hurt me.

I am so angry and so frightened. Where will I go when I have nowhere to go?

I wish I could think of some way to keep another kid from becoming like me.

I wonder if maybe the whole country should know how foster kids are treated?

All night, I sit up, trying to think of some way to do something honorable with my life, and to make a difference.

It just isn't right that someone like Daddy could encourage my brothers and me to love him and then abandon us physically and emotionally, but not legally. I wonder if other kids in America live in this limbo of foster care and hate it as much as I do.

Recently, I've heard a lot about how people hijack planes so that they can hold a news conference about something that is wrong. I think that maybe if I hijack a plane, then I could tell America the consequences of forgetting about America's most forsaken children, who end up in a revolving cycle of foster care.

I know there is an air force base nearby, but I don't want to hurt anyone. I am just tired of not existing; I am so tired of trying to belong anywhere. However, if I hijack the plane, then maybe people will say, "What a loser, what kind of mother did she have?"

Maybe my idea of hijacking a plane is wrong, but I enjoy imagining myself pleading with the world to stop this "shuffle madness."

In a couple of hours, the social worker will be here, and I know that I will be moved once again. I don't think I can take much more. I feel death coming—death to my existence, and even to a life I had once known with my mother.

Does my mother think that I am silly at times?

The social worker is here. I have to stand in a corner of the living room, near the top of the basement steps. Mrs. Wesson and the lady are sitting on the beautiful chairs in the living room. I've never been in the living room.

The social worker tells Mrs. Wesson that they've gotten several reports about me being out all hours of the day and sitting for hours on the steps by myself at night.

Mrs. Wesson tells her that she doesn't want me and that the social worker can make arrangements to send me back to Scranton, Pennsylvania. She says that I am not at all the kind of girl she wanted for a daughter.

The social worker says she needs a day or two to make the airplane arrangements. Mrs. Wesson says she wants me to leave by tomorrow, while her sons are in school.

She also tells the social worker to keep her in mind if a baby girl becomes available.

I just keep staring at the floor, standing with my arms folded across my chest, trying to become invisible. The social worker gets up and starts to leave, and then tells me not to run away before I'm returned to the orphanage. I do not look at her, but I mumble, "Okay." Where would I run to anyway?

It hurts more than I care to admit to hear an adult say that I am not the right kind of girl. Maybe I'm just not a girl at all, maybe I never was a girl. I keep beating myself up, but no one stops me.

The social worker says she will pick me up tomorrow and would like Mrs. Wesson and me to express ourselves clearly, so that there can be closure. I wonder what she means by "closure." Mrs. Wesson says she will have plenty to say tomorrow.

Why do I feel like this thing called closure isn't going to make me feel any better? What am I going to do? How do I keep from sliding toward the edge again?

Tonight Mr. and Mrs. Wesson are having a heated discussion upstairs. Apparently, she has told him I'm leaving and that she is glad to be rid of me.

The light flips on in the basement. James and John are already asleep. Mr. Wesson comes downstairs and sits on the edge of the couch-bed.

He says that his wife has told him that I am flying back to the orphanage in Pennsylvania. He tells me that he knows things haven't been easy for me, but I have to understand that his wife is under a lot of pressure. He says that someday, when I grow up and get married and have children, I will understand that things like this happen.

Mr. Wesson says that maybe things will work out for me at the next home. He says he told his wife that taking me in the first place was a mistake, because she really had her heart set on a baby girl.

He realizes now that my being here is wrong for his family, but I shouldn't take it personally. He says he is sure that there is another woman out in the world who will want to be my mother. It's just that his wife has certain expectations of a daughter and a girl. Also, she has not been feeling well for the past couple of months.

Mr. Wesson says he is sorry that things didn't work out and wishes me better luck with the next family. He goes back upstairs and shuts the lights off.

Is this what adults mean by closure? If so, how come I don't feel any better? What does he mean I shouldn't take it personally? What is so terribly wrong about me? Where is my mother tonight? How could she ever choose heaven over rocking me?

I don't want tomorrow to come. How do I prepare for the day of ending the dream of a real family? Is it possible to stop this thing called closure?

Mrs. Wesson tells me I have to wear the same shirt and pants that I wore when I came to this foster home. She says she saved the outfit just in case I didn't work out. She tells me that I cannot leave with anything she bought for me, including the clothes on my back.

It is now September 1970, and after nine months, the clothes are baggy because I've lost a lot of weight. I also must have grown taller, because they don't fit right. I have been wearing the same pants and shirt for the past eight weeks, even to bed. There is a washing machine, but I don't know how to do laundry. Sometimes, at night, I try to wash my underwear by hand so that I won't smell bad. Since I can't use the bathroom upstairs, I wash it by the sink in the basement bathroom with a washcloth. So I will leave this foster home, wearing only the clothes that I arrived in, and return to the orphanage with no physical baggage. At least the scars from the oozing sores on my legs that are beginning to heal won't show.

Mrs. Wesson makes me sit outside on the steps until the social worker comes. I'm so hungry. She won't give me breakfast, and I am too afraid of this thing called closure to ask for food. My stomach hurts a lot, but it is no use complaining, because I won't go to the doctors. It's been a long time since I saw a doctor; besides, I can't say anything about the body, because I already know that I am not normal.

The nice neighbor lady sees me on the steps and asks me if I'm going to school. I tell her no. I tell her that a social worker is coming to take me away and send me back to the orphanage in Pennsylvania.

She asks me why I'm wearing clothes that don't fit right. I tell her that Mrs. Wesson says that I can't have anything she bought for me, and all I have is this outfit that I came to this foster home with. The neighbor lady has tears in her eyes. She tells me that she is sorry that things are not working out for me. I tell her, "It's okay, I'm used to being moved. At least at the orphanage there will be food and water."

Mrs. Wesson comes out of the front door and glares at the neighbor lady. The woman says, "Good luck."

Mrs. Wesson tells me I'll need more than luck, because I will never fit in or belong anywhere. She says, "Just wait until the social worker gets here, because I have plenty to say." She slams the door and goes back into the house, leaving me on the steps in my lonely world of one.

Why couldn't I ever make her love me?

The social worker is here. She asks me why I'm sitting on the steps wearing these clothes. I tell her I'm never allowed in the house and that these clothes are from the other foster home.

Mrs. Wesson opens the door and invites her in. The social worker tells me to come into the house. I don't want to go because I don't have a good feeling about this.

Mrs. Wesson and the social worker sit on the pretty chairs, and I stand near the top of the basement steps, trying to steel myself. In my mind, I know all my shortcomings, but I know I'm not prepared to hear an adult tell me what she thinks about me.

How could my mother die and leave me all alone? I know Mrs. Wesson hates me and what I am, and now she gets to say stuff about me to my face.

The social worker says she has my airplane ticket in her hand, but before we go, she thinks it is important to have closure. She wants us to say whatever is on our minds, so there won't be any hard feelings. She tells Mrs. Wesson that she realizes having a foster kid is difficult, but that maybe by expressing herself, she will feel better.

Mrs. Wesson begins by saying that she never wanted me. She tells the social worker that she did me a favor by trying me out. She says, "Look at her, she is not like any girl I know. She rarely even talks, except in school. I wanted a girl, but she's more boy than girl. If I wanted another boy, I would have asked for one.

"She has no table manners, and all she wants to do is read a book. You know, no one is going to want someone like that in their family. I was expecting a thirteen-year-old girl who could be a real daughter. I know her mother is dead. Maybe it is a good thing, because what a freak she is. She has no emotions; it's like she's dead, but breathing."

At this point, the social worker interrupts Mrs. Wesson and tells her that she can't say these things to me. Mrs. Wesson snaps at the social worker and says that she was told that she could say anything she wants.

Even so, the social worker allows Mrs. Wesson to continue. I decide I can't be here anymore in my mind, so I move away from that physical body that is my shell. I'm across the room, hovering in the air, watching me standing there, just trying to fend off the verbal sucker punches. I will the whisper tears to retreat. I just can't crash now. Mrs. Wesson continues by saying, "Who is ever going to want something like her? She will never be able to marry or have kids. No one will want her. I'm so disgusted by the sight of her. People are going to think she is a freak. She doesn't know how to do anything.

"She gets good grades in school, but she's not smart like other girls. She walks around staring at the ground, never calls me anything, and is really an embarrassment. It's good that she is going back to the orphanage, because I don't think you will find anyone to take her."

"I thought I was going to get a girl who would blend in and want to go to dances, shopping, and be like a best friend. Instead, I get a cold, nonfeeling thirteen-year-old who can barely hold a conversation with any adult. She sits in a tree reading, or on the steps reading.

"There is nothing feminine about her. What kind of mother would want her for a daughter? Even if her own mother came back from the dead, she would be repulsed by what this girl has become. I'm glad she's leaving. She'll never belong anywhere anyway. Just take her!

The social worker asks me if I have anything to say. I fly back to the body and just shake my head no.

How could I ever tell her how hard I tried and still failed anyway?

The social worker stands up and tells Mrs. Wesson that we will be leaving so I can catch the flight back to Pennsylvania. She asks if I have any other clothes to wear, because the clothes I have on don't look right. Mrs. Wesson says no, that I have to wear what I came to her home with, and I will have no luggage.

The social worker tells me to go outside and stand by the car. I just want to disappear.

Some of the neighbors are outside, staring at me. They all know I'm being sent away.

I just can't believe that Mrs. Wesson felt like that about me. All I ever wanted was for her to love me. Only now, I know that she never intended to love me.

There is no hope anymore to ever be part of a family, to ever have a mother, and to ever be nurtured. I just want to die. I should have jumped off that building.

I tried hard to be acceptable to the Wessons, but there's something terribly wrong with me. I can never go into another foster home. Even if I'm nothing, I will never be able to listen to something like what Mrs. Wesson said, and live.

What is it about me that is so horrible, so repulsive? Did I ask for too much? Ever since my mother died, all I ever wanted was someone like her in my life.

Couldn't God just pour some numbing fluid on me? What should I do to be able to exist in this world? Who was the closure for?

The social worker is inside with Mrs. Wesson for about ten minutes, and when she comes out, her face is beet red. She tells me to get into the car. I sit in the front seat, with my hand on the handle, just ready to get out as soon as she tells me to.

In the car, on the way to the airport, she says not to take what Mrs. Wesson says personally. I don't say anything, because I have taken everything personally. I never understand why adults tell me stuff that destroys so much of me and then tell me I shouldn't take it personally, especially when I am shredded to pieces.

The social worker pleads with me to tell her what I am thinking. I tell her not to worry about anything, just send me back to the orphanage. I tell her that I always knew I wasn't good enough to belong to a family.

The social worker tells me that she will promise me one thing, that Mrs. Wesson will never get a child, baby or otherwise, from her agency. She says she is sorry that Mrs. Wesson said that stuff to me. She says this is the first time that a foster parent has ever said such mean stuff to a foster kid. I tell her not to worry, I don't care, and it's not important anymore.

In my mind, I think, what's the point? I can't change people, and people can't take back their words. From here on out, I will always be alone. I am already fourteen years old, and I'm supposed to be too old to need anyone.

I realize I have to make plans so I can survive. Maybe I will never learn to live, but at least, maybe, I can learn to survive.

I'm so sorry because I wanted something so much, something so normal, and I couldn't figure out how to get it. Now I will go it alone.

I ask myself, who will I become with no guidance? What are the possibilities for my life?

I wave good-bye to the social worker as I board this big plane. I try to sit, scrunched up against the window, willing myself to become invisible.

Somehow, I feel sorry for the social worker because she probably thought this closure thing was a good idea. It might be okay between adults, but I don't think it's so good between kids and adults. It's just that adults have the power to build someone up, or to destroy what little there may be left of a kid's self-image.

The plane is leaving the ground. Now I have five hours to change my life so I can survive, because I really don't want to face another day.

No matter what happens from here on out, I must resolve to never live in another foster home, because the next time, I won't be able to stop the slide over the edge of my emotional cliff.

I will go back to the orphanage, because I can survive there. The nuns won't nurture me or become attached or even love me like I want and need to be loved, but neither will they heap further abuse on me. Maybe life is filled with trade-offs.

I just hope that God knows it was never about him giving too much for me to carry. It was always about people who just keep piling stuff on me and raising my bar of reality to such an unreachable height.

I hope my mother also knows that in my human experience, it is people, not God, who refused to invite me into their world.

With the choices that I will now have to make, how am I going to live in people world, without letting anyone know about my hunger to be a real person?

As usual, I decide to make a list. This time, a survival list. It is to answer the question, How do I survive physically so I can exist in a world that doesn't want to know someone like me?

So at the age of fourteen, flying somewhere over the United States, during the first week of September 1970, I decide to make a list of choices that will help me to survive.

Hopefully, this list will enable me to figure out a way to live so I won't be tempted to destroy myself. Foster homes are poisonous to me because they don't offer the permanency that I hunger for. I would rather live in an orphanage than be compared to other children and never know where I will live from one day to the next. This is my survival list:

Being Female

1) *I will never be a woman or a female.* From the time of my mother's death until now, I have been struggling with feeling like I am a freak. For years I felt pushed, even shoved into the boys' world, where I didn't want to go.

    There is so much confusion inside me about being female. I don't want to be a boy, but I don't know how to be a girl.

    Life is a progression. To be a woman, you have to be female, a girl, and then a woman. It's like math: to do algebra, you have to know how to add or subtract and how to do fractions and other things. That's how I am. I was a girl at one time, but when my mother died, no one came along to pick up where she left off.

    How could I ever be a woman, when I never finished being a girl? It takes years to become a woman. How do I give myself what takes years for a mother to give a daughter?

Body

2) *I decided I will never deal with the body.* From this point on, I will separate myself into different parts. There will be the spirit part, which is good, because God and I are buddies.

There is the mind part, which is good, because in school, teachers like me. They tell me that I am smart, even though I know I am nothing inside. There is also the emotional part, which I never deal with, and I try to make it go away.

Finally, there is the body part, which I will never allow to be a part of my life. It complicates my view of myself and makes me hunger for a woman to mother me.

From here on out, I will not allow myself to deal with the body. I will not feel pain or admit to it. I will just be a person of spirit, with no need for the body, except to physically live, at a minimum.

I will never allow anyone into my inner chambers, because I know that all these unnurtured children, locked up inside me, would make people think I'm crazy. I can't believe how stupid I was to think that anyone could want me. I know now I just need to shield myself from further emotional battering.

Children

3)   *I will never have children.* For the past couple of years, I have been confused about people saying "When you have children." It is never going to be possible to have children. If I am a nothing and a broken person, how could I be a mother someday? Since I never *became* anything, how could I ever give birth to someone?

I don't know where children come from. There is something about being married. I know that women have children, but then that means that they are a female, a girl, and then a woman.

God, I know you're listening. If no one loved me after my mother died, who would love any child I had if I died? I could never wish on any child the loneliness and alienation I feel in being orphaned.

Marriage

4)   *I will never marry.* Mrs. Wesson is right, isn't she? No one could ever marry a "thing" like me. I don't understand what marriage is about anyway. I'm confused about all this marriage and children stuff. It's like I'm eight years old and living in a fourteen-year-old body. No one could ever love me. No matter how hard I try, I just can't seem to fit into a world that I'm not equipped to live in.

Men marry women and stay in the same bedroom. They somehow have children and then have a home. Since women get married and become mothers, then I can't possibly do any of that, because I'm not like other girls who will grow up under their mother's guidance and become women.

What was marriage like for my mother and Daddy? How do people know how to be married? How do they fall in love? These experiences, along with the absence of the ordinary, will always be beyond my reach.

Does my mother still love Daddy, even though she is in heaven? Would she have taught me how to have children and how to be married?

Tears

5) *I will never cry.* It isn't that I don't feel such a tremendous sorrow, because I do. I can't allow myself to be swallowed up by the ocean of whisper tears. They just keep lapping at my feet, and I keep moving farther inside.

If I give in to the unending pain and the never-ending losses, I'm afraid I will drown in my whisper tears, and no one will be there to throw me a lifeline. Ever since the coal cellar, I have tried to train myself not to give in to the emotional part of me, because I know I would hunger for someone to love me and nurture me even more. I try not to feel sorry for myself, but sometimes I hurt so much. Life is not fair.

Feelings

6) *I will never feel.* From here on out, I will try not to feel anything. What happened this morning at Mrs. Wesson's house, I was not prepared for. Now I resolve to always wear a shield, so that when people say things that are hurtful, they will slide into a box in my mind. This way, I can deal with them in my own time, and not when someone thinks it's okay to try and throw me for a loop.

Deep down I know that I do feel deeply about things, and I can't stop feelings. I will just pretend, especially to the outside world, that nothing bothers me. It's not like there is anyone waiting in line to help me sort through all these feelings of loss, hurt, pain, or guilt.

So I just decided that it is best if I go it alone in this people-oriented world. I will put all human feelings away as not being important for someone like me.

Does my mother have feelings in heaven? Is every day in heaven filled with such peace that there are no sleepless nights?

Attachment

7)   *I will never become attached to anyone!* How can I be attached to people, if I have never learned to be attached, or no one has ever attached themselves to me?

For the past six years since my mother died, I have tried to get people to be attached to me, but no amount of planning, no amount of wishing, and no amount of hungering has convinced anyone to want to be attached to a "thing" like me.

I hear all the time about God's will, about how I had my mother for eight years, and how if God wanted me to have a mother, he would have given me one. But what I don't hear, or never hear, is how necessary having a mother is for me, just as all the other kids have mothers.

I now believe that I probably am not capable of being attached to anyone, and, besides, who would want to be attached to me anyway?

Touching

8)   *I will never want to be touched.* It isn't that I didn't want to be touched or held after my mother died. It's just that all the mother touches ended so abruptly, without notice, and without explanation.

I vaguely remember, with the snippets of memory I have of my mother, how she was so physically nurturing. What had been so natural, when she was here, no longer exists. Now no one—not Daddy, his family, her family, the nuns, or the foster parents—ever touches me.

I often watch kids with their parents, even the big kids in high school. They touch their kids a lot—patting them on the back, grabbing their elbow, brushing their hair off their faces, or hugging them. I watch mothers and daughters and wonder in awe about the world they exist in and how, in my mother's absence, my world is so different.

I know why I don't get the mother touches. It's because something has changed about me that made people afraid to like or love me. I will drive myself crazy trying to get what is impossible to give myself.

Will there always be a part of me that craves for what should have been, or for what can never be? Yes, even I know the answer to this question, and I know that I can't deny all these needs. I just can't fulfill them, and I can't make other people mother me with the touches that my mother made a part of my life. All I can do is to lock away this part of me so that I can survive, so I will not drown in the desperate need for the mother touches.

How do I know if there are still other kinds of touches, if I don't know first the mother touches? Do women touch their husbands, their children, and their friends because they learned how to from the mother touches they received as children?

Being Invisible

9)   *I will be invisible until I die.* I really yearn to disappear, or to fade into the woodwork of life. More and more I feel like a distant observer of people and of the world. I must try to keep all these parts of me away from public view, until I know that it is safe.

It's almost like there is this strong force shield separating me from others. I can hear what people say and see what people do, but I am convinced they can't see or hear me.

Sometimes, I just want to fast-forward life so that whatever expectations people have from of girl who is fourteen will not exist. I don't want to experience any more life or feelings or desires. The past six years have taught me how limited I am. I believe it will be easier for everyone, especially for me, if I remain invisible to the world.

Hurting

10)   *I will never hurt anyone, and I will also not be hurt again by people.* I have been hurt in ways that my words, even to my mother, fail to really describe the pain.

I tell God that this gift of free will really challenges me sometimes. In religion class, I learned all sorts of stuff, from free will to resurrection to redemption to the sins of omission and commission. I decided that I will never deliberately hurt someone, even if they devastate my life. I used to will that Daddy's parents would go to live with God, in exchange for my mother, like a two-for-one deal. But I think it is better that they live, because someday I'm going to show them how evil they are and how wrong they are about us.

I heard that revenge is not good, but I heard that there is a thing called sweet revenge. I'm not sure I completely understand what it really means, but this is what I think it is: if I do really well in my life and not let Daddy's family, my mother's family, the orphanage, or the foster homes know about the boomerangs of their actions inside me, then I will win by being successful, in spite of these people wanting me to disappear.

I also know that I have reached the outer limits of my hurt line. There is a point or a line that I cannot cross without destroying myself. From here on out, I must resolve to be protective of my limitations.

It has never been about God or my mother. It has always been about people who keep pushing and pushing until I am almost over the edge.

All I really want is the life that I once had with my mother. But then she died and left me before I was a whole person. The absence of her life shield has left me vulnerable to people's compassion or people's meanness.

Women

11) *I will never trust a woman or seek a family.* I know that I used to seek out love from a woman whom I thought would want to mother me, as my mother did before she went away. It's just that the women I have encountered are not like my mother, not even the women in her family love her children. Women have made me feel as if I'm not normal.

Maybe the simple things in life, like girls becoming women or boys becoming men, are so complicated that this evolution can only happen with women helping girls and men helping boys. If this is true, where does this leave me?

As I fly back to the orphanage, I know that I must put aside my needs and my desperate desire to be in a family. It was a big mistake on my part to have ever sought out what should have been given to me in my mother's absence. I just didn't know how else to get what I needed, and in the end, I failed so miserably that I'll probably spend the rest of my life, such as it is, patching myself back together.

Over and over, inside my head, I beat myself up, because I cannot squelch this insatiable appetite for the mother who would allow me to be a part of a family.

I practiced my speech and diction for years. It's really good now. I became book smart. I even studied the dictionary so I could have a big vocabulary. I learned about religion, even though I always knew about God. It's just that beyond the spirit and the mind, I couldn't understand the language of family, of belonging, of loving, and of being a normal girl.

I know that the nuns taught me about religion, school taught me about being book smart, and I taught myself about clarity of speech, but no one ever taught me about life, family, and becoming a full-grown woman. Maybe I'm just one of those people that cannot learn about being normal, just as some people are good in math but not in science. Maybe I'm only a mind in a human shell, without any capability of learning what it is to be a woman.

Do I disappoint my mother in my failure to continue searching for a mother, a family, and my identity as a woman?

No Telling

12) *I will never share my life experiences since my mother died.* The primary thing I must learn is to keep all my experiences during these past six years, as well as whatever is to come, to myself. No one is interested in what I thought I needed, what I yearned for, and what I sought out, namely, the mothering experience. I realize now how important it is that I make plans about how to live the rest of my life in a way that is good, without doing harm to others.

Now, as I am just turning fourteen, I don't know or understand about what is going on inside me that would make people not want to have anything to do with me. I think that I will just pretend that all the past never existed. Things are so complicated that I could not begin to share anything, without having someone understand the whole of my life.

I will be starting high school when I return to the orphanage. I think I'll just tell people that my family is dead, that my mother was an only child and no one could take me. In the end, isn't this the truth? No one wants to know about my mother's death or my life experiences anyway.

Someday, even when I am seventeen and graduated from high school, I will never mention, or tell about, any of this. What if I make friends, and I really share where I've been? Will they walk away?

I know the social worker in Pennsylvania is picking me up at the airport, and she will want to know what happened. I'm too ashamed to tell her anything because I know what I am, and I just resolve to keep it to myself. I am that freak that I never wanted to be. That is why I can't tell her how bad it was for me. Besides, what good would telling her do for me?

Love

13) *I will never seek to be loved or seek to love others.* Love confuses me. I don't think that I have anything inside me, or about me, that is lovable. I have probably become a rock, hardened in ways that I don't want to be but cannot help. When my mother was here, she loved me, didn't she?

I remember that my daddy loved me, although it has been a long time since I have seen him. He encouraged me to tag along after him everywhere he went, along with my brothers. He even would sit by my hospital bed, reading to me at lunch every day, during all those times I had surgery on my mouth. He took his love away after he lured me into loving him as my daddy, just because my mother died.

Daddy's parents, the Resubas, at least pretended to love me, but I didn't know it was a pretend love until after my mother died.

My mother's mother allowed me to love her, and then when my mother died, she forgot to continue to love me.

My mother's sisters invited me to love them, and when she left, they withdrew their invitation for loving.

I have spent an eternity, trying to figure out what love means and how I fit that definition of love into my reality. What was it about my mother, in her life, that invited people to love her four older children and then, after her death, to not only abandon us, but to be cruelly indifferent? How do people just walk away and never look back?

I think love is so complicated. I'm trying to make sense of how I will be able to love, when I have not been loved.

If I cannot be loved, then how can I ever learn to love? How can I ever be married, have children, or have deep friendships if all I know is how to leave someone?

Freak

14) *I will never be anything but a freak.* Could what Mrs. Wesson said about me being a freak be true? Grandma Resuba also said I wasn't a girl like Alice. Could both these adults have been right?

Lately, even I have been glad that my mother died, so that she would never find out how I've became a freak inside. It's hard to lift my head anymore. I find it really difficult to even look at anyone, for fear they will know how much of a freak I am.

Are freaks born or made by life experiences? Would it have been possible, given the past six years since my mother died, for me to have turned out any other way?

Vulnerability

15) *I will never make myself vulnerable.* Never again will I put my hand out to ask for someone to love me. It is so difficult to stand before someone and beg to be adopted and to hear my pleas for adoption denied. Does anyone know what it's like to be so hungry for something, and when you finally try to build your courage up to ask, to have the question lightly dismissed?

When I opened myself up, asked point-blank about adoption and was told no, I knew I could never go back to that asking place again in my heart. I could never allow myself to be hurt this way again.

What do I do about my inner core that aches for the kind of nourishment that I can't find, ask for, or even buy? Do I ever allow myself to be vulnerable ever again?

Dependency

16) *I will never depend on anyone.* It was the lack of food and water that mostly symbolized my life during the summer of 1970. When Mrs. Wesson told me I had to wear the one set of clothes that I knew didn't fit right, I felt humiliated.

I won't let myself depend on people for anything, then they can't take anything away from me. I know this means not only physical dependency, but also emotional dependency. Never again will I let myself need other people beyond the minimum to survive. This makes me sad, but I see no other choice, because I came close to destroying myself, craving for what is a child's right to expect from adults, either emotionally or physically.

Was I so wrong to want to be dependent before I would have had to be independent? Jesus depended on Mary, yet all these religious people tell me I should not have expected to depend on them. Why?

Dismissal of All Other Lists

17) *I will ignore all other lists.* Since at fourteen I am no longer a child, I will put away all the lists before this one.

I realize that in order to survive, I can't let what I needed, what I craved for, yearned for, and what should have been given to me dominate my life anymore. I know I can't do away with what I wanted and needed, but I can seal them off in boxes and push them so far away inside me.

Where do I go with this new definition of me? What is ahead at the orphanage?

I think it is time for me to let go of those people who let go of me a long time ago. I decide that I need to make a list of the dead for people whom I will no longer seek, yearn for, or love. The following people betrayed my mother in her death by not embracing the lives of her daughter and sons that she tried so hard to nourish:

- My biological father, responsible for abusing her children. He never became my daddy.

- y daddy, who left us emotionally and physically, because my mother was not here, and he wasn't strong enough to protect us. Now if I see him, he will be Dad, but I no longer feel anything for him. I don't recognize him as the same person who once was so important to me.

  His sin of omission, of refusing to do the right thing to protect my mother's only asset—her children—is unforgivable. Mostly, he allowed us to love him. He also allowed his mother, Grandma Resuba, to try to destroy who we were and who my mother was to us by his silence.

- Daddy's family, in particular, Grandma Resuba, whose blind hatred toward my mother left her cold, callous, and indifferent to Trevor, Tyler, Billy, and me. She never became the blessing that grandparents are supposed to be.

  She deliberately set out to destroy us, if not physically, then emotionally. Her unceasing neglect and emotional battering of us has set into motion ramifications that go beyond those two years in the coal cellar.

  Mostly, her sins of commission were aided by her husband and her youngest son. I leave them now where they need to be, locked out of my life and, more importantly, out of my heart.

  They only pretended to love us while my mother was alive, and when she died, they celebrated.

- The police in Scranton, Pennsylvania, who let Grandma Resuba continue her reign of terror. They never did anything; they always left us with her.

- Foster homes, because they were never, and will never be, a home.

- y mother's family, as I now refer to them. Their sins of omission will be what they need to answer for in the next life. It is not *just* that they knew, by the time I was ten, about the orphanage, it's not *just* that they didn't come for me, it is the absence of the birthday cards, the Christmas cards, the telephone calls, and other important things. It is as though when my mother died, they acted like her children never existed. So now, they won't exist in my heart.

- And finally, my mother. I know, even at the eight-year-old level that I function at sometimes, that she is dead. I had such a hard time accepting that she died, because then I would have to accept all the other realities since her death.

  Admitting that my mother has died means letting go of any possibility of real life for me. I now know that she will never finish what she started, and no one else is willing to walk with me through this valley of growth.

  I tell my mother to rest in peace, because although she is on my Dead list, there is no sin that placed her on this list, only a death that was unexpected.

  I miss my mother. My heart aches for her at times. My soul hungers for her touch, but she must live in her world, and I must somehow find a way to live in my world.

  I will let her go in peace, and I hope she knows that I don't blame her anymore for dying and leaving me. She probably was no more prepared for her death than I am prepared for my life.

Does heaven know about my mother's connection on earth? Do she and God really know the language that I speak?

Before I get off this plane, I must figure out a way to build a protective shield. I need one to survive the next four years in the orphanage, until I am seventeen and go away to college.

Is there enough numbing fluid in the whole world to ease my pain? Can I ever be human without touching all these feelings? For me the answer is the Novocain Wall.

I am very tired and know that when I meet the social worker at the airport, I must be prepared for the questioning.

In my mind, I begin to put the core of me, which includes all the parts of me that never grew up, inside a box and start building a double-layer lead wall around me. There will be a space between the two layers of lead so that when I am feeling crushed, I can take a bucket of liquid Novocain and fill up that empty space surrounding me.

Just imagining the numbness will help me on the days when I don't want to face the world. I have so many of those days. There are times when

I wonder why I keep trying. Sometimes it's all I can do to put one foot in front of another.

I like the fact that I can imagine things, because it takes the edge off my reality that should never exist.

Now I must find a way to protect what is barely left of me as a person, so that others won't destroy everything. I like being numb sometimes, because the alternative of feeling my feelings might drown me in an ocean of whisper tears, which I can't survive by myself.

In my mind, I also take a ceramic statue that is me and shatter it, so that all the pieces are in front of me. I look at me and place the different pieces in places where I can find them someday, when it is safe.

The body piece goes in the farthest and darkest corner. The spirit and mind pieces, I keep up front, close to me, since is these are what the world outside my self will see. The emotional piece, I shove way back next to the body piece. All the other shattered pieces of the unnurtured children and unfulfilled growth go back next to the emotional piece.

Somehow I feel so splintered, so torn apart that I don't think it is ever possible for me to be whole. I will just have to keep wrapping myself up tightly, so that I can live in a world that seems so chaotic to me.

Sometimes I feel like someone dropped me. I don't think there is enough of the splintered pieces of myself to pick up. I don't think I will be able to put back together what once was.

Once the shattering takes place in my mind, only a Godlike glue can seal the seams back into place, as though the brokenness never happened. I know that God doesn't like to do other people's work for them, so his glue must come from people who choose to work through him in gluing me back together.

It is people that shattered me, and it will have to be people that will glue me back together. Maybe someday I will meet people, who will enter my life and care for me, as God has taught me that I should care for others. So far, the people's batting average is zero, but there is the rest of my life. After all, God didn't do such a bad job on my mother, and she loved me, didn't she?

Someday I'm going to try to do good things for other people, but for now, I need to focus on surviving so I can live someday.

I wonder if there is a difference between God's healing glue and the nourishing glue of people?

I think it is time to not only let go of the people who never were there for me but also to let go of my desires. Although they are normal in the ordinary lives of other fourteen-year-old girls, they make me incredibly sad, and I yearn for what I cannot give myself.

On the top of my list of things to be let go has to be the overwhelming desire to be hugged and to be held by a mother. I not only have to let go of my mother, but also I have to let go of a hunger to be mothered.

Sometimes people just don't get it. If a kid's mother dies when the kid is at the age of eight, the kid doesn't die, and neither do all the needs that a mother provides physically and emotionally.

My mother left me when I was eight, but I didn't know she was going to die or leave. While she was alive, I didn't have the chance to stockpile all the mothering that I would need from the age of eight until I grew up. I thought someone else would come along, but no one did. Now I'm in such a mess. Part of my mess is my refusal to accept that I don't need a mother, that I don't deserve a mother. Now, after six years of looking for the ordinary, maybe I shouldn't seek out what others have sought to deny me, namely, a nurturing role model.

I also need to let go of the following so I can survive, and maybe, someday, live:

- My wanting to show someone my good report cards and hear them bragging of how well I did

- My desire to know how to be a girl and a woman someday, who is worthy of my mother's blessing

- My longing for a family that lets me share their last name, delights in my accomplishments, and wants me to be the best I can be

- My need for someone to gently nurture me back into the land of the living

- My hoping that the world I live in is somehow not so alien

- My trying to make people love me

- My wish to share small moments with an adoptive mother, so that she can change me from a freak into a person

- My habit, which is addictive at times, of watching mothers and daughters and realizing theirs is a world which I can never enter

Since I have made so many devastating choices in my life, maybe I need to make a Someday list. I know that it might be possible for there to be light, even though it is dim, in my life down the road.

I think I will list all the things that I might search out someday, when I can get beyond the surviving. Someday, when or how I don't know, I will do the following:

- I will go to college and become smart, I mean really smart, so that I can accomplish my goal of being half human, but I will be the best half human there ever was.

- I will do good deeds for others so that the intense pain I feel will be lessened for others.

- I will find out where my mother is buried and build her a tombstone worthy of not only the power of her presence in my life but of the incredible hunger I feel in her absence.

- I will definitely change my last name from Daddy's name to Kennedy, White, Rockefeller, Black, or anything but his name.

- I will make enough money to buy what I never had—a role model. I know you can't buy love or people, but with money, surely I might be able to find a close substitute.

- I am going to make right all the destructive things that other people said about my mother.

- I will travel someday to see all those places that I read about in books, like the Grand Canyon or the Smoky Mountains. I will do this for me, because I have a bit of wanderlust in my body. I will also do this traveling for my mother, because she never got a chance to live a whole life.

- I will have pets because I love animals and always wanted my own cat or dog.

- I will become a real person, not just someone going through the motions of living.

- I will have friends who will love me and help teach me a different way to live.

I sometimes wonder where this spark of wanting more than my present reality comes from. Are they the nudges from my mother and God that keep me tied to the land of the living?

The pilot is on the intercom, he is announcing that we are landing at the Newark airport and is asking us to fasten our seat belts. I fasten mine and ask God to give me the courage to do what I must do to survive the coming years.

I know the social worker will pick me up and have a thousand questions, which I don't want to answer. How could I ever tell her what Mrs. Wesson said to me, that I'm a freak? I can't take the chance that she will agree with Mrs. Wesson or defend her. It will be better if I just don't say anything. Besides, how could I ever repeat what was said, when in my heart I know Mrs. Wesson was right about me even if I didn't want what she said to be true?

As we descend, I notice how all the lights that look so tiny from the air grow bigger as we get closer. Everyone in the plane is gathering up their luggage. I just wait until most of the people have gotten off. I don't want anyone to see me any more than they have to because of the way I am dressed.

When I walk down the ramp, I see the social worker waiting for me. As we walk to the car in the darkness, she begins to try to talk to me. I just refuse to answer her, not out of rudeness, but because I can't tell her anything. She says that when we get on the highway, we can talk.

It takes a while to get out of the airport. The social worker asks me if I am hungry. I tell her yes, even though I had lunch on the airplane.

We stop at McDonald's and go in to eat. The social worker then tells me I look like I have lost a lot of weight since June. She also wants to know why Mrs. Wesson let me leave in these clothes. I just tell her that I was not allowed to wear anything I got in the second foster home.

I'm glad the social worker stopped to eat, because except for the lunch on the plane, I hadn't eaten since the afternoon of the day before.

As I listen to the social worker, I ask myself, what will I have to do, as I return voluntarily to the orphanage, in order not to be destroyed once again?

As we get onto the highway, heading toward Scranton, Pennsylvania, the social worker begins to pepper me with a thousand questions. She says she would like to know what happened in Kansas. I tell her I cannot talk about it. As with the other social worker, she pleads with me to tell her what Mrs. Wesson said. I again say that I can never tell her anything.

The social worker says she will look for a new foster home, and in the meantime, I will stay at the orphanage. This is when I tell her that I will never live in another foster home again. I want to stay at the orphanage until I graduate from high school.

She tells me that she could find a good home for me, one that doesn't want a baby or another kind of child. I tell her to never place me in another foster home because I will not survive.

What she doesn't know, and what most social workers fail to comprehend, is that there are some of us stuck in this foster care system, who have no family or hope of going to their biological family. We become a revolving door of "shuffle madness." Instead of pursuing adoption, it is easier for them to put us on the shuffle assembly line called foster care and see how often we can bounce from one place to another. I guess that they are hoping that we stick somewhere until we are eighteen.

How can the social worker, who I secretly think is an all right lady, not understand the difference between adoption and foster care?

I don't know if most people know what it is like to move from people to people, always dragging my trunks with me and, with each move, adding more weight to my trunks. Adoption is not possible for me; neither is family, mothering, or the thousands of ways that my mother would have made me whole if she didn't have to live with Jesus. So it is better for me to live at the orphanage, I tell the social worker. There is a place in my heart that has been crushed by so much, and any more rejection would be beyond any limit I could handle without killing myself.

Why do I yearn for the things that are ordinary for a fourteen-year-old girl?

The social worker tells me that she is sorry that things did not work out. She says that she would be happy to find another foster home if I change my mind about the orphanage. I just say that I want to go to school and learn more.

I beg her not to put me in another foster home. She says she will think about it.

As we get closer to Scranton, I think about the choices that I have made, mostly because of the messages that people have told me. Maybe I am a shadow person, never quite walking in the light for fear of being discovered for who or what I am. Since there is so much that must remain in the shadows of my life and my heart, I will accept that I am to be a shadow person.

I know that being invisible, although probably not normal, isn't so bad. I won't have to be something or someone who, in the ordinary course of events, would have been okay as a girl or a person. I can have all these splintered pieces of me and still look normal to the outside world. All I have to do is to saunter along in the shadowy world of my existence.

I tell the social worker that everything will be fine as long as people stay away from me. I just want to go to school, be nice to people, and be left alone to live with the nuns in the orphanage. I promise not to cause her any more trouble.

In my heart, I know that someday I might be different, but for now, being a shadow person is as good as it gets. It's not bad living in the shadow of life. There is a certain numbness to it all, a certain safety away from the uncertainty of people. It is the absences of so much, those losses beyond my mother's death that weigh so heavily on my heart and soul. Until the right time comes, which I cannot yet foresee, I will just have to do the best I can to become a pseudo—human being.

I wonder if my mother thinks I'll ever become a whole person?

"Walls of Invisibility"

In plain sight she remains invisible,
To those who know nothing of her existence.
She travels to places where she didn't want to go,
Leaving her unable to speak of experiences uninvited.

Try as she might, she can't escape the fog,
That surrounds her at every turn on the road.
To a journey that is not clearly marked out,
On the life map that is a bit crumpled and wrinkled.

She sees the light; she once knew the light,
Now darkness tries to engulf her with every change.
Pushing back, she forces that part of herself that others once knew,
To remain hidden in safety until she is in a place of safety.

Motherless, Fatherless, Familyless, so many ways to define,
The child's way of being labeled by what should never have been.
Now in the vacuum of a life defined by its absences of the ordinary,
She swims against the currents of a world that doesn't have an open door.

Never did she imagine that in her mirrored world reflecting back to her,
Would there be a way of seeing but not knowing.
Ways of living being played out before her and without her,
Being orphaned has a way of locking her in and others out.

Forever it seems as though there is no end to the widening madness,
The uninvited nightmare of living encapsulated her heart.
With no mothering experience that once was her birthright,
Now has been withdrawn and stripping her of her life force shield.

Back at the Orphanage: Refuge From Self-Destruction
Ages 14-17

Back at the Orphanage:
Refuge From Self-Destruction

(Ages Fourteen to Seventeen)

Dear Mother,

As we ride up the long and winding driveway to the orphanage, I realize that this physical fortress is now to be my home. In the dark it seems so foreboding, but if I am to survive, this is where I must be.

The social worker pleads again with me to tell her what Mrs. Wesson said to me. I tell her that I can never tell another human being what was said. In my mind, I lock that experience away until the day when I will feel differently about myself. Right now, I know that I am all those things that she said, but I still have to find a way to survive even if I am not normal.

There is a new person in charge who greets us at the door. She offers to shake my hand, but I tell her I don't like to be touched, so she draws her hand away. I think that it is best if I tell people up front not to touch me, because I know that it is wrong for someone like me to be touched, even with a handshake.

She and the social worker talk a little bit. Then the social worker tells me that she will see me soon, and to think about another foster home.

The person in charge says that there are almost two hundred children at the orphanage now, but I am the oldest girl. She says that the same nun is in charge of the girls, but she is sickly, so if I could be helpful, it would be appreciated. I am told that tomorrow I will catch the bus at the bottom of the hill and go to North Pocono High School, located in Moscow, Pennsylvania.

The person in charge says that she expects no trouble from me and that the social worker will be back to visit.

The nun in charge of the girls is called to the office. When she arrives, she greets me with a hug, saying, "The Widow Child is back." I cringe when she touches me, because I am not worthy of being touched, but she is an old woman who means no harm and really knows nothing about me.

Well, God, how do you think I am going to survive in this anonymous place that offers a warped sense of safety?

Love,
Jerri

*   *   *

The nun in charge of the girls is happy to see me. She tells me that I was always liked because I was so helpful and didn't cause any trouble. She says that she has a bad heart and was away for a long time, recovering from a heart attack. In my mind, I decide that since, at fourteen, I am the oldest girl at the orphanage, I will try to help her out.

Sometimes I look at old people, like the nun, and wonder how they ever lived to be in their seventies or eighties. I'm having a hard time surviving at fourteen. Maybe someday I will learn the secrets of surviving and living without all the hidden lives that I carry with me.

The nun in charge of the girls shows me where I will sleep in the dorm and shows me the storage room. Inside, there are all these clothes that people have donated, along with supplies of soap, shampoo, and other items. She says that there are pads for my period, and to just help myself. She tells me that since I am responsible and the oldest, I can get the keys from her at any time to get whatever I need.

I tell the nun in charge of the girls that if she needs help, she can just ask. I have learned a long time ago that if I am helpful, it draws attention away from me as a person, and this is fine with me. She says that she would appreciate if I would wake the girls up every morning. She controls all the lights to the dorms from her bedroom. Since I am a light sleeper, for many reasons, we agree that she will flip the light on twice from her room. I will get all the girls up, then kneel and say the morning prayer with them, and then tell them to get dressed for the day. I will then go to the dining room to get the breakfast set up to be served. In the meantime, the nuns will be up at the chapel on the third floor for Mass.

It's okay to do this new routine. Maybe this will fulfill my goal of being good and helping others. At least I will have free access to the supplies I need, and I don't have to talk to anyone about anything. Maybe the blood is the period. I will stockpile pads and supplies in case I am moved before I go to college in four years. With the keys to the storage room, I can help myself at last.

I hope I can get everything together inside my head.

It is my first night back at the orphanage, surrounded by all these living people, yet I feel like I am the only one. It has been a long day since leaving Mrs. Wesson's house this morning. My life feels like it's been in a whirlwind of activities, list making, and trying to keep my head above the whisper tears.

As I lie here in bed, I think of the thousands of ways a person could fail, and I think I have managed to find most of them. Maybe what I need to do is to try to refocus my goals and to put some numbing salve on my fractured self.

Tomorrow will bring new challenges that may take me to different places that I'm not yet sure of, or they might take me on an exciting adventure. I hope that this place called North Pocono High School will be okay and let me fit in somehow.

Some of my new goals will include making sure that I learn a lot, but not get good grades. I have to keep all my grades at a D level, until I can be sure that I won't be placed in another foster home. I think I will flunk every other test purposely so that, together with the other passed tests, my grades will average to a D.

The only positive thing that people say about me is how intelligent I am. I need to remove even this attribute from my outside world so I won't be "attractive meat" on the "shuffle madness" assembly line of foster care.

Someone might want me because I'm smart, and if they take me and find out that I'm only book smart but not a girl or a human being, then what will I do with their rejection? So I believe that I must make a preemptive strike of looking, even academically, like a failure.

Later, when I know I won't be in a foster home, then I'll pass every test and become, outwardly, the best half human I can be. My goal is to survive so that someday, I too might live as my mother would have wanted.

One of the important things that I must do is to indulge my hungering appetite by devouring every book that I can get my hands on. On the third floor of the orphanage, next to the beautiful chapel, is this big library. Usually, on weekends, it is open for the orphans to use. It is such a cool place to hang out. It must have at least a million books that tell a million stories about a million people.

For the past couple of years, especially since I was ten, I have been studying the dictionary. It helps me to learn vocabulary and to practice my speech, plus I can always carry it with me. I have read every Nancy Drew mystery and all the Bobbsey Twins books, along with every life story of the saints that I can find.

The library at the orphanage will become my special place of refuge. There is this little crawl space that I found, and I can crawl into it, with the door left open just a crack for enough light so I can read.

My goal, since I will be here for 1,460 days, or four years, will be to read almost every single book, starting with the bottom shelf on the right-hand side. When I read, I am transported through time and space to other worlds that offer me a glimpse of other peoples' lives that I have never known. There is a certain element of excitement to leaving the continuous loneliness of my world for an adventure of being somewhere else. I like reading, and history is the best, because I think it helps me to learn how other people, good or bad, make decisions and manage their lives.

I know that reading could never replace the people's nurturing that I need and hunger for, but in the absence of the mother touches and the human embraces, I will settle for this imaginary substitution. Reading, at least momentarily, will ease the sharp edges of my reality and, even for a fleeting amount of time, let me, in my imagination, live the lives of people in faraway worlds.

Did my mother give me the gift of being a passionate reader? I remember how she and Dad always read to me, especially when I was in the hospital for the cleft palate operations. Reading is like a Novocain shot to my soul.

I wonder if Daddy thinks about how he once loved me and sat reading to me during all those lunchtimes? Does my mother still read in heaven? Will books become the closest substitute for the human connection that I crave?

It is three thirty in the morning, and I had a night dream. I dreamt that my mother was at a campground, sitting with her back toward me, and she was talking about saving the country. I kept trying to get her attention, but she kept going toward the fire. Then suddenly, she was engulfed in flames, and I started screaming for her.

I wake up screaming and realize that I am at the orphanage. I don't like going to sleep, because more and more, I am being plagued by night dreams that terrorize me.

I can barely control my waking moments. What will I do to control my sleeping moments? I try not to think of my mother and everything that has happened since her leaving and her dying.

For the past week or so, since I have accepted that Mrs. Wesson was going to get rid of me, my nights have been punctuated with unusual nightmares. I dreamt of my mother burning and me being in an orphans' zoo, where people walk by without choosing me, and of hurling myself off a cliff.

How do I stop these night dreams that come uninvited? What am I going to do if I can't wake myself up from a nightmare? Do some people have these dreams and never leave them when the morning comes?

I lie in bed, surrounded by fifty girls, and tell myself that I'm being such a baby about these silly dreams. Maybe if I stay awake, they won't come back. I'm so tired, yet I'm so afraid to go to sleep.

Sometimes I wonder if this is God's way of reminding me that someday I will have to face my demons, even if they are given to me by other people. The dreams, my life, and this orphanage are so real. There is chaos inside me no matter where I turn.

I wonder if these night dreams are my punishment for not figuring everything out? I do wonder which is more frightful, my night dreams or my waking reality.

The nun in charge of the girls flips the light on twice, and finally it is safe to be away from the darkness and the dreams. I get the girls up, and we pray in the hallway. Since I am already dressed—I have been awake since three thirty this morning—I go directly to the dining room.

I am excited about my first day of going to high school, where I can get a fresh start. I know that I must purposely be a D student for a while, but I can still learn things. I must keep my mind focused on my ultimate goal, which is college.

As I go to the dining room, I am met by this kid named Ronald. I like him, because he seems to be pretty funny. We have to get the food set up to be served cafeteria-style to the children.

He tells me that his mother was murdered and that there is no one in his family that can take him. I think to myself, I understand my being orphaned from a fire, but how could anyone deliberately orphan a child by murdering their mother?

I just think that when someone kills the mother, they also kill part of that child's life. People have no right to deprive a kid of such a nonrenewable resource. Accidents are one thing, but deliberate acts of violence are inexcusable.

I'm surprised at my spike of internal anger. It's just that there is little forgiveness inside me for people who orphan children, physically and emotionally. Tonight I will have to mull this thought over some more.

I hear the nuns coming from Mass, so Ronald and I hurry up to start serving the food so that I can get to the bus stop. There is plenty of food, and it tastes so good.

There is this nun who is a great cook, and she makes sure that there is enough food, even for seconds. The kids stand in line for the food, like in the book *Oliver Twist*, except there is enough, even extra, food.

This is a new day. Will it bring me a new adventure, or new human challenges? Sometimes I wonder how God even keeps this complex life of growth going.

Last night, after the social worker left and the nun in charge of the girls showed me the storage room, I picked out some clothes from the donated pile. I threw the outfit that Mrs. Wesson made me wear in the trash.

I also hoard supplies of soap, shampoo, pads, toothpaste, and other items under my mattress, in case I'm moved suddenly.

As I walk to the bus stop, I feel like a new beginning is about to take place. At fourteen, I know that there is so much for me to learn, and so much I have to keep to myself.

The balancing act of existing in both of my worlds is ongoing, but if I become more book smart, then maybe my inner world will recede, and I can keep it from gnawing at my soul.

There is this boy at the bus stop who asks me what my name is. I tell him Jerri. He wants to know why I am at the orphanage. "Didn't anyone want you?" I just tell him that my parents have died and that soon I will have a home.

He continues to mock me because of the clothes I am wearing, and he keeps saying that I'm at the orphanage because no one wants me.

I just ignore him because he doesn't have a clue as to how lucky he is. At any given moment, without his parents and family, his life could be like mine. Besides, he is like a gnat, buzzing around my head, because my inner devastation and outer battles eclipse, by far, any bullying or mockery that he can dish out.

Is the bus stop a symbol of my ongoing struggle to merge the reality of my life with that of the world that I must move into?

Someday I will be wanted, different, accepted, and alive, but for now, I need to concentrate on the life race before me of survival and existence. I must not let myself become distracted or derailed by someone's ignorant pettiness.

Does my mother think I dream too high?

The school bus is taking me to this mysterious place called North Pocono High School. It is a long L-shaped two-story building. It glistens from the outside with the sun's rays glancing off it. There is this huge parking lot with a lot of cars. There are all these fancy cars driven by the big kids.

As I walk inside, I am in awe at the cleanliness of this building. I am directed to the main office, where I have to give my name and address and get a thing called a roster.

While in the main office, I give a piece of paper with my name and address written on it, so I won't have to say out loud where I live. The secretary is nice, she asks me to sit down until I get my roster for class.

This is the cleanest and shiniest school I have ever seen, and I feel so out of place. I can't wait for the day to end so I can go back to my refuge, the orphanage.

The person in charge gives me my class list and directs me where to go. There must be a million people in this school. The hallways are so crowded. I'm trying not to be physically bumped around.

The school puts me in the college prep program because I told them that I'm going to college someday. Hopefully I won't fail, even though, for now, I must, because of the possibility of going into another foster home.

I think that I will like this school. Maybe I can even make some temporary friends. Even here, I will have to be a shadow person, but that's not so bad, as long as I get a chance to see real kids up close and see how they live.

I wonder if I try to stay in both of my worlds will I become a real person, or will I splinter into insanity? Somehow four years at North Pocono High School seems like such a long time.

Will I be able to remain faithful to my inner world and the expectations of the world around me?

Finally, the school day has ended, and I have managed to appear normal, even though some kids did make fun of my clothes. In homeroom, I sat behind this really good-looking kid named Peter. He is tall, with blond hair and blue eyes. He has a deep voice when he whispers.

He asked me where I came from because school has already been in session for two weeks. I told him that I live at the Our Lady of Help orphanage, and he said that he couldn't imagine living in a place like that.

When he asked why I live there, I just told him that my parents were dead but that someday someone would come for me. He said that he couldn't imagine not having his parents, because they are really nice, and they do everything for him. Peter said that it must be weird being all alone in the world, and he hoped that someday I'd be lucky, like he is.

I did make one friend, and maybe I can make other friends. At least, Peter didn't make fun of my clothes, and he even helped me with some of my algebra work.

On the way home to the orphanage, I think about what an intriguing place school is. It is an exciting adventure of learning and a scary place filled with many people. Maybe I need to give everything a chance and think about how to focus on the people who are nice to me, like Peter and my English teacher. My English teacher is very pretty. She told me how to catch up with the rest of the class. She's a real woman who showed kindness to me, even though I can never be someone like her.

I lie in bed, also thinking about what Ronald told me about his mother being murdered. He didn't have to be an orphan. Some person deliberately altered his life in such a way that he can never go back to where he had been. He said relatives had taken his younger brothers and sisters, but they didn't have room for him.

How can families pick and choose who they will invite into their circle? How do they sleep at night, knowing that they left a child outside their welcoming embrace?

I think that after being at the orphanage for a few weeks, I have finally gotten into an everyday routine. From the time I get up in the morning, I get breakfast ready to be served, go to school, come home, serve dinner, do homework, and go to bed, I am physically busy.

You would think that with such a busy schedule, there would be little time to be overwhelmed by my personal demons. I wish sometimes that I could stay awake twenty-four hours a day so I would not have to face the night, with its waking nightmares of the past losses that confront me and its relentless waves of uncontrollable dreams. I feel powerless in the dark.

I embrace the busyness of everyday living with an almost frenzied fury. I try to stay active. Yet there are times when, out of nowhere, thoughts of who or what I think I am overwhelm me.

Many times I find myself suddenly daydreaming of being adopted or of my mother coming back for me. I don't know why these thoughts overpower me, because I know and accept the reality of where I am, even though, in a heartbeat, I would change it if I could.

There are even times when I'm still overcome by the need of having a mother to hug me, even though I know that this is impossible. Try as I might, I don't always have as complete a control as I think I do over these forbidden thoughts.

I will continue to remain focused on the here and now. There has to be a way to keep the absence of the ordinary from intruding on my waking time and my daily routine.

As I go from my tasks at the orphanage to school, I constantly have to struggle to stay in this reality and to let go or push back things and places in my mind where I can never be.

I wonder if after all my hard work I might fall apart, or I might end up crazy.

It is nighttime again, and it is such a lonely time in the orphanage. I can hear some of the kids crying their whisper tears into their pillows. They cry over people who couldn't pull themselves together enough to be a safety net for their children.

It always becomes clear to me at this time of the night how lonely it is to be in a place whose very title is reflective of public separation.

Even in school, when the kids find out I'm from the orphanage, they look at me differently, almost in a pitying manner. Maybe if I didn't have to go to a regular high school, with normal kids, I would see the stark differences that exist on an everyday basis, in a less shocking light.

Often, during the times of what I call the lassoing of the past, I find myself staring into space for moments, even hours. I know that my spacing out is happening more and more, and for longer periods of time, sometimes even for days or weeks. It is as if when I am not looking, the past lassoes me and tries to squeeze the life out of me. It is like I know what's going on around me, but I am just not a part of this life.

Sometimes it is as if I'm on autopilot, and I am removed from myself, like I was back at Mrs. Wesson's house. More and more, it is harder for me to pull myself back. I have to spend quite a bit of time talking myself into returning to me.

As I listen to the children crying, I think how sad it is that no one hears them, least of all the people who placed them here.

I have my own problems, I shouldn't be worrying about the other orphans and the pain that I neither inflicted nor can heal. I can't even soothe my own fractured self. But it still does not stop me from wishing that someone would come and ease the incredible isolation and loneliness that are always present in a place like this.

How come that at the age of fourteen I still feel like an abandoned child?

More and more, at school, I am making temporary friends that talk to me about class stuff. I like making school friends because that proves to me that I am not a total human failure. There are some people who like parts of me, even though I know that there will always be limits to how much they know about me.

Peter talks to me every day. He likes to tell me about what his family did over the weekend. There are other students who ask me questions about classroom assignments. I am even able to help them get some answers. The teachers are pretty nice, although I try not to draw attention to myself.

The only things I don't like about school are gym and the bus ride. The boy who lives at the bottom of the hill still makes fun of me. One of the nuns tells me that he will be nicer when he grows up. I'm told to remember that he is only a freshman in high school. I don't say anything, but I'm also only a freshman in high school, and I don't make fun of people. Maybe he is better than me, but I will continue to ignore him and focus my energy on not going crazy or curling up and going to sleep forever.

I hate gym because I have to put on this stupid short uniform. Looking on the bright side, there is no swimming pool. The gym teacher is very nice. She can play all kinds of sports. Because of her, I climbed a rope halfway to the gym ceiling. This is a big accomplishment, since I see myself more as a bookworm and not as an athletic type. Maybe there are undiscovered gifts inside me that I don't know about yet.

Sometimes I wonder why humans need friends, or even want friends. For me, to have a temporary friend means that I have to choose carefully about what I share and don't share. It takes a lot of energy for me just to have temporary friends, but even half humans must have friends halfway. I decide to continue to work hard at having some temporary friends, so I won't be completely lost as a human being.

Who were my mother's real friends while she was on earth? Did she have any? Where were they when we needed help after she died?

I have been at the orphanage now for a couple of months. While some things have changed, other things have remained the same. The boy at the bus still mocks me, and I am still living by my survival list, but I have made new friends in school and at the orphanage.

Most of the nuns like me, except for the person in charge. She likes the orphans that talk to her about their lives. I'm not like that. I prefer not to talk about myself, since there is so much inside me that is not right. No one would understand me and the complications that exist within my soul.

The person in charge and the social worker are always trying to get inside my head, especially about foster care. I really like the social worker, but she goes home to her husband and children. What could she ever understand about my needs? I still harbor in the deep recesses of my soul the kernel of desire to have someone like her mother me. But that will never be a reality. I realize I'm not the type of kid that is "neon light" for adoption.

I've made up my mind and my heart a long time ago that unless real adoption is possible, I am not interested in being a foster child. It is too late at fourteen anyway, and in a few months, I will be fifteen. But I feel I'm still going on eight.

The social worker, God bless her, is always bringing up Mrs. Wesson and what happened. Every time she comes, she begs me to tell her what happened and tries to convince me to go into another foster home. I have become good at sidestepping her questions and tap-dancing around her inquiries. I always tell her that I do not wish to discuss the Wesson family and that I cannot not survive in another foster home. One of the things I wish I knew before I tried so desperately to make Mrs. Wesson like me, then love me and adopt me, was that she never intended to keep me. I spent such an inordinate amount of energy trying to make that foster home work, and, unbeknownst to me, I was never going to be a keeper.

Contrary to my toughened outer shell, I am a broken and shattered kid inside who cannot heal. I also cannot add one more ounce of rejection to my overloaded boat of confusion, which floats on an ocean of whisper tears.

Today in school, I overheard two girls making fun of someone. They kept saying that she ought to wear makeup or something. I wonder if how you look is really important, and if a person doesn't look good, can they change, or should they change?

Oftentimes, even though I try to stop the thoughts, questions, and memories, I wonder if I am as repulsive or as ugly as Daddy's mother and Mrs. Wesson said I was. The person in charge is always preaching about how looks don't count, yet I hear so many conflicting messages about what I must look like.

I have never really looked in a mirror, except to see if my hair looks halfway decent. Maybe what I need to do tonight, after everyone goes to bed, is to stand in front of the mirror and try to see if I am as ugly as I feel and have been told that I am.

Maybe then I will understand why Mrs. Wesson said all those things about me not being normal and not marrying someday and how I'm not like other girls.

The light from the hallway is reflecting on the mirror, and as I look at the face reflecting back at me, I guess I can see what makes me look like an alien. The eyebrows are bushy; my nose, even at fourteen years old, is still a bit flat; and there is that ugly scar on my lip that must have repulsed Mrs. Wesson. My cheeks are sunken, and there is something slightly crooked about my mouth. Only my eyes seem to have life in them, as if they too, in their reflection back to me, are wondering where I went so wrong and how someone so ugly is ever going to make it in a people world.

Maybe the person in charge is right. Looks don't mean anything, but I can't help feeling that if I were more of a real girl and looked normal, maybe the social worker could have found me an adoptive mother, like she did for all the other kids I know. I know that the orphanage isn't forever, yet how can I show this face to the world, when other people will be as repulsed as Mrs. Wesson and Daddy's mother?

Billy once said that he remembered how beautiful our mother was, and yet she produced a daughter that looks like me, so different from her.

Mirror, mirror on the wall, who's the fairest of them all? I decide that I will never again look at myself in the mirror, except to see if the hair is combed properly.

If I were really pretty, I wonder if it would have made a difference to Mrs. Wesson? Why are some people nice looking and others not noticeable at all? Is it possible to be ugly in the face but beautiful in the mind?

I am in trouble with my English teacher and the person in charge at the orphanage. We got our grades today, which will be appearing on our report cards for the first quarter.

In almost all my classes, I got a D or a C. My plan is working well so far.

However, when I get to my English class, I have a problem. My English teacher has given me an F in English. I see her after class and tell her that my average was a 69.5, but she says my average is a 69.4, and she will not give me the tenth of a point.

When I ask her why, she says that she knows through class participation and my written assignments that I know all the lessons.

What disturbed her the most, and what she couldn't figure out, she says, is how I pass every other test and fail others. I kind of shuffle my feet and stare at the floor, then I stammer that I will pass all the tests from now on.

I explain in a mumbling fashion that I didn't want to appear too smart, because I don't want to be moved from where I live. She tells me that she knows I live at the orphanage and wonders what the connection is to my failing and passing every other test. I just tell her that the social worker is trying to put me into another foster home, and I figure that if I don't do well in school, she will leave me alone.

The English teacher asks me if I plan to go to college. I tell her, "Yes, it is what I dream about." She then tells me that they will look at my four years in high school, and they won't want to see any more Fs.

She also says that I'll be in trouble with the person in charge when I go home, because she called her. Apparently, in that standardized reading test given to all the freshmen last month, I placed first or second in the comprehension part. Lucky me. All the teachers are talking about my bad grades and my high reading score, which registered at the college level.

My English teacher says she is angry because she knows I understand what is being taught in class, and the standardized reading test proves her right. She says to expect a lecture when I go home. I think to myself, Great, how am I going to get out of this mess?

My English teacher says she will not change the F, because she wants me to learn a lesson. I guess she is right. I might as well start passing all the tests since I know the material anyway.

I didn't know anyone looked at those scores, because in the past, I have always scored high on the standardized reading tests, but nothing was ever said about it. She says I read well, and my comprehension is on the second-year-of-college level. Then she tells me not to squander this gift.

Now I have to face the person in charge. When I get home, she calls me to her office immediately. She sits behind this big mahogany desk with Monsignor, who is sitting there to the side.

She tells me that she received a phone call from my English teacher informing her of my F in English and my extremely high score in the standardized reading comprehension test.

I tell her that I will never fail a course again and warn her about the other low grades that will be on the first-quarter report card. I promise to have nothing lower than a B from here on out.

The person in charge tells me she never wants to receive a phone call from the school again. She says to remember that everything I do reflects back on the nuns and the orphanage. I promise that there will be no more phone calls, and I will do much better. Then she says that she will be comparing my next report card with this one, and she had better see a vast improvement.

Monsignor reminds me that people in school know that I'm from the orphanage, and I must leave a good impression, because I represent the kids that make this their temporary home. They finally dismiss me and remind me that the social worker will also lecture me on the report card.

As I leave the office, I think to myself that my plan of getting straight Ds is really not worth all this hassle, so I might as well pass everything.

Would my mother have lectured me about poor grades? But then, if she had lived, would I have even needed to try to fail so miserably in school?

It is hard to believe that my freshman year of high school will soon end. I have managed to pull my grades up. It was either get good grades or listen to the lectures from the person in charge, Monsignor, the teachers, and my social worker. My well-laid plans are not worth the aggravation.

With the end of the school year rapidly approaching, the kids and I become nosy. It is a tradition that most of the nuns will be transferred in June, and a new set of nuns will come in during the summer months. In late August, another set of nuns will come in for the nine months of the next school year.

There is one thing every orphan kid learns quickly, even though the person in charge tells us not to, and that is becoming attached in some ways to some of the nuns. Sometimes I wonder if that is why they get moved in and out so often. It is harder on the little kids who wonder where these nuns, these consistent temporary people, have gone. Everyone else leaves them, so why shouldn't the nuns?

We begin to like some of the nuns who come into our insulated world. From the nun who cooks wonderful food to the eighth-grade nun who lets me order paperback books from her class to the nun in charge of the dining room, all these women are nice. They don't become attached or love us in ways that we desperately need, but what really nice people they are.

With the rotation of the nuns comes a time of change, excitement, and the quiet separations. For some reason, we all get comfortable with the consistency of these undemanding, anonymous people who move in and out of our lives.

A couple of the nuns aren't so nice, but most are easygoing. A few offer random acts of kindness that make us feel less lonely. The person in charge is always telling them not to become attached to the children.

In lieu of foster care, at least here there is no hidden or open hatred, and abuse is nonexistent. Many of the nuns feel bad for the kids, and they are the ones I like the most, because they see a glimpse of the great losses.

In many ways, I really like the nuns here. They don't play favorites and are here all the time. It does bother me that they are changed three times a year, but that is to keep them and us from becoming attached, which is a big no-no here and in the foster homes.

Did my mother ever know a nun or a Catholic? In heaven, does she go to different places as she waits for her family to come for her?

Someday when I'm not fourteen anymore, maybe I will try to understand more about these adults called nuns and women, but as with most other things, it is only one more part of a confusing piece of life for me to figure out. I still wonder where someone like me will ever fit in. The nuns were girls first, then they became women, then they eventually became nuns. Women were girls first, then they became women, and then, eventually, they became mothers. The orphans here were children first, orphans next, and, finally, we all became invisible.

The social workers and the person in charge always tell us that the only people we are allowed to become attached to are our families, the flesh-and-blood kind. That certainty does leave some of us out of the bonding experience.

I don't see the nuns as other women who can mother children, or even adopt children. We are always told that they are married to Jesus and can love all children but not any one particular child. I guess, in some ways, it is better not to waste my time allowing any of them into my heart, because I am just one in the sea of many.

Maybe that is why it is okay to hero-worship the nuns, but it is necessary to be careful not to expect anything that could make up for what my mother would have given me, or what might have been if a woman had adopted me. The nuns are not like the regular women, whom I watch with their daughters, walking down the street together.

Here at the orphanage, it is always so hectic with so many children that even if anyone wanted special attention, they wouldn't get any. Everything that is told to us is always told with us in groups.

Sometimes I chuckle to myself at what we are told. The person in charge likes to tell us every Sunday how the nuns give up their whole lives for Jesus. She says that the reasons the nuns don't have children is so they can go, at a moment's notice, to anywhere in the world to care for the lost children. This is why God gave children mothers and families.

Of course, as she says that, she proceeds as usual to tell us, who sit in this room without mothers and families, about how lucky we are that there are nuns who love us, because Jesus loves us. I guess if the nuns didn't love Jesus, then they couldn't love us.

Although she says that some of us without mothers must be lucky, I'm not quite sure about the reasons behind this thinking. Maybe this is why I see nuns as workers for Jesus and women as people who teach girls how to become women. Where that leaves me and other kids here on the bonding road, I'm not really sure.

In heaven, does my mother know all kinds of people?

Freshmen year in high school is finally over, the summer is beginning. I think that each summer I will work on my reading list. So far, in the orphanage library, I have finished three shelves of books. This summer, I will work on six more shelves, since I have a lot of time on my hands. Maybe this summer I will think about a lot of stuff and try to separate more clearly what will add to my life and what will subtract from it.

The person in charge tells me that there is this CETA program that will pay me minimum wage for cleaning for a certain number of hours. She says that she will save the money for me so that when I leave someday, I will have a little bank account.

I clean a lot anyway, so I might as well get paid for it. I am responsible for the dining room, two guest rooms, the priests' dining room, and the hallway, which is ten feet wide and runs the length of the orphanage. And while I clean, I think a lot about myself and what it takes to survive and make a future for myself.

Sometimes I think about a lot of things and how it is possible to live in two different worlds that rarely intersect. Since I learned this year about how important school is, I am more determined than ever to go to college and to make something of myself.

I have slowly come to the conclusion that whatever happens in my life will be determined by my desire to be whoever I want to be. There are no limits set for me, no expectations by others, and no safety nets should I slip or falter.

Soon I will be fifteen years old. I must always be on guard against anything that can hold me back, especially my own private world of chaotic confusion, which swirls at a depth that could drown me if I give in to my darkness.

My goal will always be to live in such a way that I don't allow my inner world to overwhelm the outer world that I must live in. Always, always, I tell myself, I have to focus on what I have and not on what has been denied me.

In the end, there are only two people whom I must somehow honor with my life of positive self-expectations, and is they are God and my mother. Maybe even I, with my great sorrows and shattered heart, owe them a payback for what blessings I do have. Never will I deny both of them any honor by not living an honorable life.

Even I know that there are times when in the darkness of the night, I travel back and forth at high speed between my two worlds of losses and possibilities.

I just have to keep fighting the desire to curl up with my losses, so I don't deny myself the wonderful possibilities of what might be.

Does my mother experience any loses in heaven or just wonderful possibilities?

Summertime in the orphanage is very busy. The person in charge always tells us that "an idle child is a devil's workshop." There aren't too many devils at the orphanage; we are kept very busy.

Every morning after breakfast, all of us must meet outside around the flagpole. We, of course, pledge allegiance to the flag, then sing one or two songs, then everyone goes in different directions.

Usually, I will spend several hours cleaning, then, in the afternoon, I spend time reading in my little hideaway. I still try to read poetry out loud to myself at the playground so that I can keep my speech perfect. Sometimes I'm afraid that if I stop the daily practice, I will lose my understandable speech, and I can never let that happen.

Often I worry that I am not doing enough to outshine the galloping darkness that comes to my soul at night, when the quiet allows everything inside me to surface.

Last week I turned fifteen years told. There was no celebration, no cake, no card, no gifts; and no one noticed me, but I have trained myself to accept this as part of my reality. Of course, on the first Sunday of each month, all birthdays are celebrated together, but it's not like the kids in school who can't wait for their birthday and the family celebration.

I can't believe that it has been almost seven years since I last saw my mother. I often think about the "what ifs," the "what might have beens," and the "what should have beens." Of course, I don't dwell on this too much. It's just that sometimes I wonder what she looked like, how she sounded when she spoke, or if my hungering for her is the same as that of other orphaned or foster children for their mothers.

In seven years, I have done a lot—probably more than I have wanted to do. I have lived in five different places, with eleven sets of adults, including one foster home that wasn't right for me and another foster home that tried to destroy me, but I'm still alive, and I am going to be someone someday.

I wonder if I will always have the energy to try to outshine the darkness?

It's September 1971; I am now fifteen years old, and a sophomore in high school.

I can't believe what is happening in school today. It seems like an ordinary Monday, until we are told by our principal on the intercom to stand for a moment of silence. I want to ask my friend Peter why, but he must be absent today.

Then the principal says that we must have this moment of silence for Peter. He drowned over the summer. I feel like I have been sucker-punched once again by the unexpectedness of life. Peter, wherever you are, I thought you were really nice.

As I sit in school all day, I just can't seem to fathom how I could be talking to Peter about ordinary things like homework in June and praying for his soul in September.

I wonder if Peter suffered while drowning? His parents must be in such incredible pain, probably the kind of pain I am in over my mother's death. I hope that they are able to honor him in a better way than I have honored her.

At least, I'm sure, unlike my doubts about my mother's love and acceptance, his parents must have known how much he loved them, because he was always talking about how much they loved him. At least they should have no regrets or doubts about things left unsaid, because all Peter ever talked about was the fun he had every weekend with his family.

The highest compliment he always gave them was when he would tell me that someday, he hoped I get lucky and am able to find parents like his.

Tonight, as the darkness encloses around me, I ache for the loss of this temporary friend who showed me some kindness in my chaotic world.

Maybe my mother could console Peter and nurture him in my place, until his parents come to be with him.

I don't know if there is loneliness in heaven, but maybe since my mother has no children, and he has to wait for his parents to come, then maybe both of them could hang out together.

I wish that it had been me who drowned, because he is missed by so many people. At least my absence would hardly be noticed.

I wonder if heaven is a place where people continue to nurture one another as they wait for their loved ones? Do Peter's parents ache in the hidden places of the heart that only sorrow knows about?

It is four fifteen in the morning, and again my night dreams remind me of places and people that I wish would disappear from my life. I'm not sure if it is because of Peter's recent death that I am more afraid of the dark than ever before.

Whenever I go to bed, I always try to think about flowers, mountains, and other pleasant stuff. It's nothing personal, but I try never to think about my mother, so I won't dream. This never works, because I always dream of things that I have so little control over.

I really hate it when I dream of almost catching up with my mother, only to have her disappear. Worse are the dreams that involve Grandma Resuba's coal cellar and Mrs. Wesson's humiliation and scorn of me as a girl and a daughter.

I fall asleep at eleven thirty, and I would think that after almost five hours of sleep, I would be well rested. I'm more tired than ever, and in two hours, I will have to be officially up, facing another nonstop, hectic day. The truth is I'm exhausted, and I am more and more tired every morning. The dreams seem to drain almost every ounce of energy from me.

Once I am awakened by a terrible night dream, I stay up and do homework or read a book. The nuns think I am a bit weird because I always have a book with me. I love savoring every free second to catch another sentence in another paragraph of whatever I'm reading, because everything outside myself, especially in a book, is a wonderful adventure of learning something new.

I just wish I could figure out how to either not dream or how to get some rest. Try as I might, one of the things I am learning is that not everything, not even those ages inside me can be controlled by my sheer willpower.

There is no control over the body and my dreams, so I guess I will just funnel all my other energy into those areas that I have complete control over.

It is going to be a long life if I have to be awake during the whole day and half of the night, especially if the other half of the night is spent with dreams that remind me of what is really inside me.

Why are some dreams so real and draining? Why are my daydreams of a different life not the same as my night dreams of my real life?

I have decided that this will be a better school year than last year. With each new year, especially in the beginning, my mind becomes clearer, almost as if I am clearing away the cobwebs that hide or distort my vision of where I am going.

I have two really neat teachers who are opening new worlds for me to explore. In American history, there is Mr. Niceman. He is almost like a storyteller, pacing back and forth, recounting history almost as if it were a family tree that is always connected.

Maybe that is why I love history, because it really is a soap opera of the good guys and the bad guys and everyone in between. Every person's action has a reaction, and no one, good or bad, in history comes to power without a whole history of events in that person's past life.

The other class that I really like is my English class with Mr. Wiseman. This teacher always talks about Flannery O'Connor, a Southern writer who wrote these really neat stories about how each of us must be ready to grasp our moment of grace.

Sometimes at night, I ponder my role in this world, which still seems so alien to me yet fascinates me in ways that continually surprise me. The

English teacher is always talking about how if we listen to the literature of the ages, we can hear the echo of all humanity. I am going to try to read most of O'Connor's works, as well as most of the other masterpieces in literature.

There is never a time when I don't yearn to learn more and more about people and how they feel. Sometimes I get scared that these human feelings that are part of me are locked so far away inside me that they have become like the petrified forest I read about—solid like a rock with no life.

Is there a need where my mother now lives for continuous learning about the complexity of human beings?

It is three in the morning, and the doorbell in the orphanage is ringing so loudly. I hate it when I hear it ring in the wee hours of the morning, because it only means one thing—that some orphaned child is being dropped off.

Maybe it's me, but I think that even in a cavernous, anonymous place like this orphanage, there is a difference between coming here in the middle of the day and coming in in the middle of the night.

I go to the top of the steps and hear two children crying and asking for their mother. There is a police officer with them, explaining to the person in charge that some neighbor brought them into the station, saying that their mother had left them with her a week ago and never returned.

The little girl looks so scared and is holding her brother's hand tightly. There are a thousand separations that begin when kids become wards of the state, and soon the first will be when the person in charge sends the boy in one direction and the girl in another.

I tell God that sometimes I really hate people. There is no reason for this to ever happen, no explanation that will ever be acceptable to me for abandoning children.

These two kids, like me before them, will have their lives altered radically, and their trust in people will be shattered.

The person in charge sees me at the top of the steps and tells me to take the little girl to the girls' department and to wake up the nun in charge of the girls. I hold her hand, and she begins to tell me that she is five years old.

She says that her mommy went out with her boyfriend but didn't come back yet. I put her in bed, after borrowing pajamas from the back locker.

She asks me if her mommy is coming back soon. I tell her yes, as soon as she is finished taking care of her business. She starts to cry, and I tell her that everything will work out, that her mother loves her, which I know is a lie.

How could any woman call herself a mother and walk away? How dare she not listen to the whisper tears that her child weeps for her?

I don't wake the nun in charge of the girls, because I know she is old and tired. I just slip a note under her door. I find a stuffed animal and give it to the little girl and sit by her bed until she falls asleep.

I hate the doorbell, because even though every kid has a different story for being here, we still all end up in the same place. I go back to bed but cannot sleep, because I know that this little girl, like most of us, just wants to go home.

There are some of us who will remain in this foster/orphanage quicksand, and there are a lucky few of us who will find permanency with a new adoptive family.

Whatever the outcome of each of our stories, the perilous beginnings of being lost without a family always start at the same place, the absence of the ordinary.

How do people like this kid's mother or my Daddy's family or my mother's family sleep at night?

How is it possible for there to be so many different kinds of orphans in a world filled with so many families?

I just can't understand why people are like they are. For instance, one of the girls at the orphanage tells me that her mother is an alcoholic.

I ask her what it is like to live with her mother. She tells me that sometimes her mother is really cool. She brushes her hair, takes her shopping, and talks to her, but most of the time, she is drinking and she then becomes someone else.

She says that sometimes, when her mom drinks, it is as if the bottle is more present than her mother. Mostly, the girl says, it's like living on a roller coaster, the drinking binges last for days or weeks; they suddenly stop for a couple of days and then just start right back.

The girl is crying now, telling me that she doesn't understand why she is not important enough for her mother to stop drinking. Her father left a long time ago, saying that he was tired of the "sloppy" house.

I tell the kid, who is only ten or eleven, that maybe, someday, her mother will pull herself together, and in the meantime, she should just remember that it is her mother's problem.

What do you tell a kid whose mother is alive in a physical sense but dead in ways that destroy whatever goodness she is responsible for?

There are times when I get so angry inside my head at the stupidity of people's choices. I just can't imagine not being with my mother if she was alive.

It must be horrible to have a mother that will not, or cannot, nurture her child because something or someone else is more important. I resolve never to drink, because although I have never tasted alcohol, there must be something inside that bottle that changes the inside of a person.

I often wonder, even more, about how some people change, and they don't even have a drinking problem.

Sometimes I think about all the people my mother knew, who cared for us when she lived. Yet in her death, they all walked away, and I have searched for their reasons, like drugs or alcohol.

Maybe meanness and abandonment are not only found in the bottle or the pill, maybe it lurks in the hearts of some people. I hope I never become mean or callous in how I treat people.

I wonder what happens when mean people go to heaven? Do they have to become nice?

Every second and fourth Sundays of the month, from two o'clock to four o'clock, are visiting days at the orphanage. There has been a lot of soul-searching going on as I watch the kids get ready for the visiting time with whatever family they have.

I stand at the window, waiting, knowing that it is unlikely that I will have a visitor. Dad comes maybe once every couple of months. I never expect him anymore. He says that he is very busy working on the house, taking care of Alice, and helping his parents. I have taught myself to have no expectations of people so that I'm not disappointed.

One thing that I think I have figured out, as I watch the children wait in anticipation for whoever might come, is that it is the absence of the mother, for whatever reason, that places most of us as wards of state.

I really believe that if Daddy had died instead of my mother, we would still be together as a family. Most of the kids here have had their fathers leave a long time ago, yet it is only when the mother has left—because of drugs, alcohol, sickness, imprisonment, or death—that we end up in this "shuffle madness." Even in school, I know quite a few kids from single-parent families that are usually headed by their mothers.

I wonder if there are different expectations for men and women? Some of the nuns tell me how lucky I am because my dad still visits me periodically, even though he is not my flesh and blood.

I often hear that fathers are different than mothers. I think this is true, because I have been mostly searching not for the adoptive father but for the adoptive mother who could have nurtured me as my mother would have. I just think that mothers, for the most part, are the final safety net in their children's lives. If there are holes in the net, the child is, at the least, in trouble or, at the worst, is going to drown.

Although some absences of the mother are more permanent than others, any absence can shake whatever unconditional trust that had once existed. At night in the orphanage, it is not for the father that the children shed their whisper tears, but rather, it is the inconsolable loss, whether permanent or temporary, of the mother, who is at the core of every child's heart. A mother is the person that a child hungers for the most.

I wonder if my hidden whisper tears will ever go away?

I really hate to be compared to regular kids! There are times when the person in charge likes to tell me that I won't ever amount to much if I don't do well in school or talk to her. She says that I am too withdrawn, except in my reading world. I'm not sure what she is trying to tell me, but how would it ever be possible for something like me to ever become a someone like others?

I know that in school I dress more poorly than the other students, and some make comments about it. I try really hard not to buy into the family child image. Although I don't want to be seen as different, I know it is impossible for that not to be the case.

From the moment I leave for the bus stop, up until I come home, I feel like I am stepping into a spaceship traveling light years into another galaxy. For the most part, school and the orphanage are okay, but what a total contradiction they are. It is like experiencing total and sudden change every day, and neither world touches the other.

No one at the orphanage has a clue as to who any of my teachers are, what I study, what my desires and ambitions are, or what a tremendous effort it is just to enter the school world. The school does not have a clue as to where I go every day, the constant reminders of how much I lack, or the alien world of heartbreak and loneliness.

Even I sometimes find myself making a comparison between where I am and where I think I should be at this point in my life. There are times when I beat myself up inside for not being like the kids I go to school with, who plan activities, are involved in clubs, and are balancing family, friends, and school.

I don't know why I expect to be like other kids my age, when I have lived in such a lonely, motherless, family-less vacuum. I never try to stay on the comparison track for too long, because then my uncertainty about my own worth grows even more. I just have to keep putting one foot in front of another and keep trying to do the best I can with what I know.

How are the kids of the shadows supposed to find their way into the light of acceptance? Will I ever know self-acceptance and other-acceptance?

Another school year is almost halfway over. Soon it will be Christmastime again. I still love my teachers at school, because they know so little about who I am, and yet, in their not knowing, they treat me the same as other kids and think of me as a real student. The only individual attention I ever get is from the teachers who let me ask questions, and I always do have a lot of questions.

I'm probably a major "nudge" in class, but I hunger to learn so much. There is a drive, a need inside me to do whatever is necessary to fulfill my desire to be the best half human there is.

Sometimes I wonder how anyone finds out where they are going in life and where they find the niche that allows them to be happy. For now, I know how imperative it is that I pass high school, because unlike the kids in my class, if I fail, there will be nowhere to lay my head down.

There are no safety nets that will catch me if I begin to free-fall into the chaos of my internal and external life. It is like a marathon that has no finish line and where the runners never slow down. Maybe everything in my life so far has been a time of training, and at fifteen, I must continue in the race for my emotional life.

Where I belong and where I am going have answers that I cannot yet fathom. I just know how important it is to never look back over my shoulder, so that I can keep focused on the goals, which, every day, is to make it to tomorrow.

To look back at the swirling whirlpool of inner chaos threatens everything on my survival list. I often revisit the list as a reminder of how I must be ever vigilant about things, events, and people who could still destroy the very core of me if I am not careful.

There is often a trick that I use on my bad days of spacing out. I just stare at my feet, focusing on putting one foot in front of another and making it through the day. Surviving is the name of the game. Finding temporary safety niches offer some rest, and living in the distant future is always the goal.

When my mother went to heaven, did she have to have any goals or expectations? Why do all my self-expectations leave me tired at times?

The students from Marywood College and the University of Scranton are here today. The person in charge says that they will act as big sisters and brothers to the kids at the orphanage. When I ask her if I can go to the playground with them, she tells me I'm too old at fifteen and that it is the younger kids, especially the boys, who need the extra attention. I don't say anything, I figure I will just go to the library and read.

I go to the dining room and look out the window, watching the kids running around, having a good time. The students are setting up a picnic for the kids on the playground. I remember when I was ten or eleven I used to play like the kids outside with these students. They are a welcome break from the world that we all live in.

When I was eleven, I became a Catholic. My godparents were students from the University of Scranton and Marywood College. I'm not sure what the purpose of godparents is, but at least someone stood by me at one time.

As I watch the children play, I think what big brothers and big sisters are supposed to be and how being role models is supposed to be so important. Maybe even these temporary people have something to add to our lives, although tonight, I know a few of the kids will wish that today's fun never ended.

Billy is my real big brother. He is two years older than me, although it has been years since I have seen him. He was such a wonderful big brother. My mother would have been proud of him, the way he tried to protect us even though he was only ten years old. Even when he ran away or stole food, it was always to help us, and in the end, all his desires to end our nightmare didn't succeed. In my heart, I will always love him because he tried to be a man in a boy's body, but the events and the people were too much for him. He was, and will always be, my best big brother. I will probably never see him again, but he is a witness to the absence of the ordinary.

Are role models necessary for children to become adult human beings? Do I crave for a role model of maternal nurturing because what my mother gave me was never completed? Are there a lot of Billys in the world, big brothers and big sisters trying to look out for others?

It is going to be wintertime again, and the winds are blowing hard outside. I hear one of the little girls crying in bed. I go to her, and I ask her what is wrong.

She tells me that the family she has been visiting for the weekends these past couple of months wants to adopt her. I tell her that's great, because every time a child is adopted, it is like sweet revenge against all those people in my past who walked away.

If I can't be adopted, I love knowing that other kids have been chosen. It's like a win for us orphans. Most people, including social workers, don't realize how destructive foster care is to us. The revolving door just adds more confusion to our fragile world.

I ask her why she is crying, because this is great news, that she is wanted. They like her, even though she is already seven years old. Most people want to adopt a baby.

She tells me that the social worker said that they are white and she is black. I ask, "What does that mean?" The little girl tells me that the social worker will not let a white family adopt her and that she will be looking for a black foster home.

The little girl asks me what the color of her skin has to do with being adopted by these people she calls Mommy and Daddy. At seven years old, even she knows what the deal is about foster care, because our favorite topic of discussion at the orphanage centers on the differences between foster homes, adoptions, orphanages, mothers, and fathers. We don't talk about shopping, friends, vacations, or school. There are so many other things that weigh more heavily on our minds and hearts.

Even the younger children understand that this life we live is not really normal. I tell her that she is right about wanting to be adopted and to keep talking to her caseworker.

Who cares about the color of skin or the sex of the child or the age of the child? When foster kids are on this side of the "shuffle madness," it is the matters of the heart that beckon each of us to that place of permanency. It is belonging in a way that should have always been.

For us here at the orphanage, we don't get hung up on the obvious. It is the unseen needs and hunger that are at the heart of every child's desire to belong in a way that roots us again to the ordinary.

I tell her that even I don't understand adults, but I will pray that she will be granted her wish. The choices for her, which will be made by people who don't love her, will shape the rest of her life.

I try to calm Joyce down and tell her to see how tomorrow goes, but I know how social workers are; it is easier just to get a foster home.

I ask my mother if there are different shades of color in heaven. How could such a simple thing like color keep people from caring or adopting? And I ask God, how could anyone in their right mind ever think that a foster home is better than an adoptive home, even if its people are not the right color?

I keep thinking about Joyce and how she will be denied an adoptive home because of something as basic as her color. I think about how I have been denied because of age, and how all the other kids here are just different enough not to be acceptable for adoption. I try to tell the social worker how even the best foster homes aren't good if the kid knows that there is no permanency.

Sometimes I wish that people would stop using words together that don't make any sense. The term "foster home" is a contradiction: to foster means to temporarily take care of someone or something for a short time; the word "home" means so much more than I can express, because it goes beyond the physical care of a child.

Home is a place where a kid should feel safe and not wonder every day whether this is the last day, or when he or she will be moved again. Home is where a kid works on life plans and makes dreams, which slowly become real, with parents along for the ride.

"Foster parents" is a contradiction in words. Parents provide stability, permanency, and roots, which are not at all compatible with the term "foster." Maybe social workers should call these types of temporary placements "foster places" with "foster people." This is a more realistic term, and it might motivate people to become more determined to find a home for that child in the "shuffle madness" of life.

Even the best foster home is just that, a temporary place until something else comes along. No kid should ever be a ward of the state for as long as I and the other kids here have been. There are some of us who will never be part of a blood family.

I just think that for us who are the most forsaken, an intensive search should have been done for people whose hearts and minds are larger and more loving than those of our flesh-and-blood family. Not all of us will return to our blood families, yet the longer we stay under the care of foster homes or the orphanage, the harder it will be to reconnect with the ordinary that we all deserve.

Whatever makes us not right for adoption shouldn't keep people from trying to find matches for children and parents who share the same heart.

Why do people try to make kids like me believe in words that don't match? How will all the kids here get what they most want, a place called home?

Sometimes I find myself slipping into my eight-year-old world, and I can't stop the slide. There are times when I am talking or just daydreaming, and I find myself suddenly transported through time and space right back to the coal cellar and the coal bank.

I'm physically present here, but light years away in a past that sneaks up to suck me back to where I don't want to be.

It is like I'm on autopilot and can't really figure out how to snap myself back to the present moment. There are also moments when I am bombarded with what Mrs. Wesson had said, along with other events that I just wish never happened.

I work really hard to stay in the here and now, because I'm afraid that this spacing out will be noticed and will invite unsolicited questions for which I have no answers.

In school, sometimes my temporary friends will snap their fingers in my face or say, "Earth to Jerri," and this will bring me back. I just have to find better ways to handle this "lassoing" by the past, because it is happening more and more.

I am going to try thinking about people and things like a card game. On each card in my mind, I will write down either one problem, one event, or one person. Then I will indulge myself for ten minutes to leave my present reality and come back with whatever is on the card.

At the orphanage, I have an alarm clock, which I set for ten minutes. When I feel magnetically pulled and compelled to go back to a place where I can't leave or don't want to be, the alarm clock goes off, and I snap back to the present. Tonight, I will not allow myself to be lassoed by the past again.

Maybe it's just that I figure if I try to control these battles which are thrust upon me, I can manage the return visits to a past that I wish I never knew. It feels at times like I have never left the war of life, and now I am just trying to control what I can, so that I am not overwhelmed or defeated. Being fifteen going on eight is not always easy or desirable, and it is a nightmare I want to put behind me, forever.

Does my mother ever think about the past in heaven?

It is the holidays again, and most of the kids have gone home or are visiting host families. The person in charge said she would not force me to go to a host family. Besides, they usually request for the younger children, and it is difficult for her to find someone to take me for the holidays. There are always two nuns who stay in the building during this time, just in case some children are dropped off.

It is probably not normal to be the only kid here, but at least I don't spend my energy being something or someone that I'm not.

This time provides me with some opportunities to do some reading and watch TV because the nun in charge of the girls has gone away. Her only fault, at least to me, is that we are allowed to watch TV only on Sunday evenings. She says we have too much to do, and because she tires easily, I never give her a hard time. We watch *Bonanza* and *The FBI*, because she says one is a family show and the other a law-and-order, right-and-wrong show.

I've discovered a show called *The Waltons*. It is about this family of kids whose parents are their safety net, and everyone gets along.

Mostly, during a quiet time at the orphanage, I like to take stock of where I am and what I need to do in order to go where I need to be.

New Year's Eve, for some reason, always sets the tone for those sincere reflections. It has been over seven years since my mother has died, and even the world, as she must have known it, has changed so much.

That war in Vietnam is still going strong. There are all these people marching against it, and in school I hear about drugs that make you feel no pain. Even in my inner world, which is still a chaotic mess, I am trying to manage myself more firmly. At least for now, my living conditions have stabilized, and I just work on doing what I can to maintain balance.

I wonder if everyone takes stock of their life periodically? Will I always have to find the balance between my inner and outer worlds?

Rather than running away from my fears of being alone, I think I will work on embracing the quiet times. I figure that if I choose to spend time inside my head and to be alone with the quiet, unspoken pain, then I am controlling this loneliness. It is better than the unexpected twinges of being overwhelmed by the aloneness that life's experiences have forced upon me.

I read about how Franklin Roosevelt said that "the only thing we have to fear is fear itself." Sometimes I am afraid of more than just fear, but I work hard at keeping my head above water, so that I don't drown in all that has been denied me.

Even in my quiet moments, whether I'm talking to my mother or to God, I have never quite reconciled the loneliness of this people world with the world that I still yearn to live in, namely, a family.

When all is said and done though, it is my conversations with both my mother and God that allow me to keep the curtain of despair from closing in around me. Even in my loneliest of lonely moments—and I have had quite a few of these—there is always that sense of purpose to my existence and a rightness for me to be here.

I have always believed that no matter what has happened, what is happening, or what will happen, I must survive and live, if for no other reason than because my mother and God never abandoned me.

Maybe if I face the loneliness and learn to be comfortable with my silence, then I won't be so afraid of living, even though I'm not sure I have done anything good for others.

I'll always hunger for the nurturing that has eluded me, but maybe someday, there will be a different life for me. I will just continue to look down when I walk and stare at the steps I take and not look too far into the future so I don't get overwhelmed by the mountains of expectations ahead.

Are there always going to be mountains that I will have to climb? In heaven, is my mother always on her way to somewhere else, like I am? How could there be so many different directions in life?

There are things that I am discovering that I enjoy. I have a little transistor radio, and I listen to country music. I got the radio as a Christmas gift at one of the parties that people give to the orphans, and I hid it away from the nuns. I figure the kids in school have a radio, and it is small, so no one will notice I have it. I can get a friend in school to buy me batteries when I need them. I get a dollar or two every once in a while. I hope that my mother and God don't think I'm a bad person.

The music, even the sad songs, sort of reminds me of the life that I must have had with my mother. It's hard for me to remember her, what she looked like, or where she is from, but I think she lived in a place called Hayden, Kentucky. I wish I could remember every minute of my first eight years with her.

Sometimes I listen more intently when Loretta Lynn sings, because she is from that place in Kentucky that I think my mother was from. I'm always trying to know about who she was, but there is no one to ask, and since she died, so long ago, no one has spoken about her at all. There are times when I think I wasn't even born or had a mother. Those are my craziest moments.

I am soothed by the country songs, as they tell the stories of heartache, loss, pain, and, at times, joy. Someday I am going to go to Nashville and listen to the music that now brings me such comfort in my world of alienation. I might even try to find that place called Hayden, Kentucky, just so I can breathe the same air that my mother must have breathed.

The other thing I really enjoy is listening to the Philadelphia Phillies baseball games. I like baseball because I can relate to it.

Baseball reminds me about how I approach life. There can be two outs in the ninth inning and two strikes, yet it's always possible for there to be a hit and a comeback win.

That's how I see life, no matter how down I get, I will myself to still always believe that tomorrow will be a different and better day. I just know that even with all the outs and the strikes against me, I can still get a homerun or a hit in the game of life. Even in my lowest moments, I try to remember the game of baseball and to remember that if I stick around long enough, I will always get another chance to bat.

I wonder if my mother liked country music and baseball? What does she do in her spare time in heaven? I wonder if I will always have the energy to get up when it is my turn at "bat" in the game of life?

It is really quiet in the orphanage tonight. Earlier today, one of the kids ran away, and, of course, everyone was questioned. I can understand why she ran away, although usually, when the kids are caught by the police, they are brought back here. Most of the time, it is not because of the nuns, since they are usually okay. It is because the kids just want to go back to their homes or to what they have always known.

For me, maybe it is just that I have nowhere to go, or no place to call home, and that's why I have never run away. This orphanage is as close to a resting place as I have had since my mother died.

The girl who ran away is about twelve years old, and her mother is dying at a hospital in Scranton. She had been crying and begging to go see her mother in the hospital, but the social worker cannot make any arrangements for her to go yet. When I talked to her, she was almost hysterical with grief, saying she couldn't live without her mother and had to see her before she died.

Who can blame her for desperately trying to seek out the one person who is the center of her heart? I too know that nothing, and I mean nothing, could ever keep me from going to my mother if she were alive and dying.

I pray for this kid, whose extended family has made her, during the worst time of her life, spend it like a trapped animal in an anonymous place like an orphanage. She is only looking for a way to return to her ultimate safety net.

I will never understand how family, whatever family really means, could let a little kid—and at twelve she is little—be all alone in her grief. I hope that when they find her, it will not be until after she has found the mother she so desperately is looking for. It would be a shame to waste all that energy and not let her at least be with her mother for a while, who has so little time left.

I'm only fifteen, but I know the hungering that is about to begin for this kid. Why don't they, whoever they are, let this child be nourished for as long as possible, before she learns what real hunger is?

I don't even know how to stop the core of me from being hungry for the food of nurturing that I can never have. I can only imagine the hunger pains that are about to begin for this twelve-year-old.

Does running away solve anything, or does it only complicate matters of the heart? Where is home for those of us who have nowhere to run?

Already, two years of high school is coming to an end, and in two months, I will be sixteen years old. It seems like time is marching on, and yet, it is as if I am also still standing frozen at eight years old. I must, at times, will myself to move forward to each tomorrow so that I won't slide back to the edge that I once knew but didn't like.

I overheard one of the nuns calling us the throwaways. You know, the kind of children that no one ever comes back for.

I think about how, just as used shoes can never be restored to look as if they were never worn, the broken hearts of the kids that live here can never be restored without the scars. When people mess with the heart of a throwaway, nothing can ever restore their lost innocence of loving and trusting, which all children are entitled to know.

As I know all too well, this shaken trust is so hard to restore, especially as I struggle in my aloneness to make a safer world for myself. Experiencing life is a very complicated matter, with every action depending on another human being.

I try to repair the damage to my heart, although there seems to be little that I can do about the wounds, with their recurring scars that never quite heal. Maybe I will leave the matters of the human heart to that time when I will know how to live, how to really trust people, and how to experience the love that I once had known.

For now, I must continue to bind the wounds of my broken heart, which comes with the territory of being a throwaway. Maybe someday I will learn the secrets of the shoemaker who can repair a set of discarded shoes and make them look as if they were new. Only with me, it will be on a human level that all my splintered pieces are brought back together to make me feel as if I were whole.

I wonder if every throwaway can rebound from all these losses? Why do I still seek ways of wholeness in the midst of my splintering?

Now that I am almost sixteen, I know that within two years I will be leaving Scranton, Pennsylvania. I have decided that when I leave for college, I will never return, because there is nothing and no one to hold me.

Although I am sure that there must be some good and nurturing people in this town, I have never met them. It is probably going to be in my best interest to put everything behind me. I will act as though this nightmare that I have lived since my mother's leaving and dying has never happened.

In school, I always make it a point to have temporary friends, because I know that I will never see these classmates of mine again. Besides, attachment and close friendships are gifts that elude me. Maybe these are the missing ingredients that would make me a whole human being. However, even the temporary friends do offer some respite of camaraderie in the desert of my inner soul, where my heart tries to believe in reasons for my being.

One of my greatest trade-offs in life will always be not having that human closeness, whether through a nurturing mother or through connections with real friends. This is the sacrifice I will have to make in return for surviving.

People, at least to me, seem very complicated and so changeable, sometimes even having a language and a vocabulary that is difficult for me to understand. I will never cease from trying to make my world intersect with the people world I live in. It's just that it takes so much energy to keep putting one foot in front of another.

There are good people like Sister Jessica, who brings over her students from the local high school. Even some of my teachers and the nuns here are really great people. It's just that there is such a distance between both of my worlds. Maybe friends, even temporary ones, do offer some good things, and maybe they are a stepping-stone until I meet the people who will be part of my world.

Why do human beings, even someone like me, crave for that connection with another person? Were friends important to my mother? Are they to God? Do people always learn about their first friendships in a family?

Today is my sixteenth birthday. Of course, no one notices, but it's okay. In school the girls are always talking about their sweet-sixteen birthday parties that their parents have for them. It must be a special kind of party that girls celebrate. If my mother was living, I wonder if the party would have been in the trailer that burned.

Most of the kids I go to school with make turning sixteen sound like an important milestone. They talk about getting their driving license, having a phone, their own television, and just going out to celebrate with their families.

It's funny though, I don't feel any different being sixteen; it is almost like another day. Someday I will learn how to celebrate birthdays and holidays, but for now, I will just keep my focus on my goal of surviving.

I sometimes have to remind myself not to long for the ordinary, so I won't notice all the losses that keep adding up. It has been such a long time, almost eight years, since my mother was part of my reality, and yet I still hunger for her presence.

At times I still, with a wisp of nostalgia, daydream about finding someone to love and nourish me, as my mother would have. I'm not a bad person. Sometimes I am not even a person of any kind. It's just that there is a separateness within me that I can't bring back together. I observe the importance of family, birthdays, and holidays, and yet, I must always remind myself that this need of being connected is not for someone like me.

How are birthdays celebrated in heaven? Would my mother have had a sweet-sixteen birthday party for me? How old will I be before there is no need to yearn for the celebration in an ordinary life?

The person in charge calls some of us down to the conference room so that she can lecture us about how good we have it compared to other people. She likes doing this conference that she calls group dynamics. It is every Sunday, starting at nine o'clock, and it lasts until twelve o'clock. I really think she does this to torture us, because I know I don't feel any better about who I am by the time she is done.

She says that married people struggle hard to feed themselves and their children, and we get everything handed to us. I think to myself, If only she truly understands the terrible price that each of us pays just by entering the "shuffle madness" that comes with being a ward of the state.

I look around this room and see the brokenness that is hidden within us orphans. There is Ronald whose mother was murdered, and there is me who has, in almost every way, been abandoned, not only through death, but also through the crushing abandonment of me by the living. There is Sally, who is slightly retarded, and Joyce who is the wrong color for adoption. There is Billy, who rocks a lot in public and sucks his thumb, waiting for his mother to get out of prison. Maggie, who is ten, cries every night for her mother to come back from some faraway town.

We all have a story that any one of us would trade, in a heartbeat, for the life of the kid we all once knew. I try not to let what the person in charge says infiltrate my reality, but she really does annoy me when she preaches about the fact that we have plenty of food and water compared to the kids out there with no one to take care of them. She just doesn't know about the life on the other side and doesn't have a clue as to the different kinds of hunger pains that can starve a child.

I always beg the other nuns to ring the lunch bell as early as possible so we can be set free from her indoctrination of untruth. As I scan the room of brokenhearted kids, I know that she will never convince me that we have a better life than the other kids who live in families. They are not only fed physical food, but their hearts and souls are nourished as well.

How can I be luckier by being a throwaway than a family child? Aren't there all kinds of different foods for the body, mind, heart, and soul?

Today while the person in charge was preaching to us about group dynamics, about how hard life is in the outside world, I decide to start an adoption among the orphans.

I read in school about how I must have witnesses for what I want to be made legal. So last night, I wrote these adoption agreements with the assistance of the children who live here. I figure it is as close as I'll ever get to adoption.

While the person in charge is going strong about how we don't need or want for anything and shouldn't be feeling sorry for ourselves since we have it so good, I pass around the paper for the other kids to sign. It says,

> From this day forth, I_____do adopt _____
> as my brother or sister, bound by circumstances beyond the ordinary. Dated August 10, 1972. Witnessed by _____
> and _____and God.

We all know that this is not a binding or a permanent agreement, and most of us, if not all of us, will not ever see each other again when we leave this orphanage, but for now, it is a nice diversion from our real life.

Every Sunday, in this conference room, as I listen to someone tell us how we are not as good as other kids or as real as the other kids, I just resolve to someday make things better for some other children who might be drowning in a loneliness that threatens to keep them from living.

No one, not even me, should ever feel such uncertainty about who or what they are, about their place in family, in life, or in relationship with everyone else. For now, I will continue to fight off every effort to make me feel even worse about myself than I already do.

How do those who are not orphaned learn to appreciate what they have? Can people truly love children not born to them? I wonder if parents worry about dying and leaving their children? Since my mother is in heaven without her children, does that make her an orphaned mother? Are mothers without children the same in the heart as children without mothers? Where are the matchmakers?

Now I am a junior in high school. School seems different this year, more lively and fast paced. I like my teachers and most of the kids. One pleasant surprise is that the boy in my class, the same boy at the bus stop, is not teasing me anymore. He is actually nicer to me now. Maybe he grew up and left his obnoxious days behind him.

Most of the kids in my class are all caught up in their driving lessons, phone calls, and activities in school. I know most people would think it is funny, but I have never used the phone, spent a night at a friend's house, gone shopping for clothes, or joined a club in school that requires extra time. I did join the library club, since it's activities are during school hours; and this teacher is trying to get me to join the debate team, since I like to do research in the library.

I ask the person in charge If I can join the debate club, which participates in activities that take place at other schools and sometimes on a Saturday. She says it is okay as long as I can find my own ride. Then I ask her about learning to drive, and she says as long as I don't use the cars at the orphanage or ask the other nuns to teach me, I can learn. The debate teacher says she will take me to the debate mock trials. As for driving lessons, I don't know anyone who can teach me, and I never leave the orphanage except for school, so I guess I will have to wait until I am in college. Maybe if I make some friends, one of them will teach me to drive a car. Sometimes I wonder how the person in charge thinks I'm going to learn anything if I can't ask the nuns for anything or use things that belong to the orphanage. In school, every kid I know is taught by their parents a multitude of things, including driving. They use the phone or the car in their household, and they don't have to have a teacher pick them up to go to a mock-trial meet.

I just have to remind myself that I am not like the kids I go to school with and that I must work with what I have. It's funny, it is only when I go to school that I realize how different my life is.

Would life have been so different if my mother had stuck around a little bit longer? How do parents know how to parent their children? How do I stop this sense of being overwhelmingly tired of being told no, that it is not for me, when I ask for the ordinary?

I don't know if my mother has ever heard of these drugs that kids sell, but that is what happens sometimes in my school. Some of the students are talking at lunch today about how there are kids they know who are doing drugs. I've never heard of this before.

Apparently, there are pills that I can take that will make me feel like I am floating and feeling no pain. They cost money, and I have to keep taking them once I start. Since I have no money and never go anywhere, I guess I won't get the medicine that could make whatever has happened since my mother's death not exist, even at least momentarily.

Probably the real truth is that I don't need any drugs to numb me, because I can do this already inside my mind. If I have to, I can just go away from both my inner and outer realities. It would be nice, though, to find a pill that can make my night dreams go away, or lessen their terrorizing realness.

I wonder why some kids with families have to take drugs to feel differently? Maybe they have hidden lives that they can't tell anyone about.

It doesn't matter. Just as alcohol can orphan children, so can drugs, so I will never take them. Besides, at sixteen, I think I have enough problems without adding something artificial to the body. Plus I wouldn't want to disappoint my mother or God any more than I probably already have.

I listen to a lot of stuff that the kids talk about. Usually I don't understand most of it, like romance or drugs or weekend parties, but that is okay because that is their life and this is my life. Maybe in the faraway future, this part of the splintering of issues that I don't understand will be brought together with everything else inside me that is confusing.

I wonder what it was like for my mother to be an adolescent during the 1940s and the 1950s. Does every teenager want to feel numb about life? Is temporary numbness such a bad thing?

There are some times when I really hate school. Today in biology class, one of the girls mocks me.

I try really hard to blend in with everyone, although my clothes are not as nice as those of the other girls and I get free lunch. This does not bother me, because I figure if I had a mother or if my mother had not died, life would have been different, my lunches and clothes would have been different. I accept this difference as part of my reality, but there are times when what sets me apart has much more to do with other things than just with clothes and lunch.

The teacher is explaining something about a frog, and when I ask how it knows when to give birth, the teacher says that they are like humans. I ask what he means, and one of the girls snickers loud enough for everyone else to hear, saying, "Didn't your mother teach you about sex or anything?" The rest of the class laughs at her comment at my expense.

I didn't hear the teacher or the rest of the class after that. It was as if I was stung by the unexpectedness that I always try to anticipate. I will just close off that class from my mind for the rest of the year. The teacher is nice, but he can't control the comments of the other students.

The student is right though. How could my mother go and die and live in heaven, while I flounder in so many ways that are not visible?

My mother isn't here to teach me anything, and with all the power that God has, he didn't send me an adoptive mother. It doesn't matter, I will just go on as if nothing happened. I resolve never to ask questions in class again, unless it is in the history or math class.

I just have to continue to redefine what is ordinary for me and to put everything that doesn't directly impact me aside. I especially have to not acknowledge the other half of me that could have made me a whole human being, if life's circumstances had been different. Someday I might get all of myself together and not be stung by the unexpectedness of life. For now, I must continue to live by my survival list until that someday comes.

How do I stop from being angry at my mother for dying? What was the definition of "ordinary" when she was here on earth?

The two foster homes that Trevor was in didn't work out. My brother has been with me at the orphanage this past year.

Lately the social worker is pressuring Dad to take us to this house that he built with our mother's money. Apparently the military pays for dependents, and he took the money to build a house twenty feet away from his parents' property.

Dad says that since Trevor is too old to stay at the orphanage where I am, he will take him temporarily.

I will be a senior, and I definitely don't want to go, because I know the family still despises our very existence. Going there would be no different than going to a foster home. I can't be around people who openly hate me.

Besides, why would the social worker think about putting Trevor and me with people who abused and neglected us? They have never been held accountable for their actions.

It took so long for me to realize that my bastard blood will never allow me admission into that family. I still have nightmares about those two years in the coal cellar, and nothing I do can make them go away.

Another thing is that I still secretly feel so much humiliation and shame from the way I had to sit on the steps in just my underwear during those two years. Even worse is the hidden embarrassment over my questioning of my being a girl or a boy.

For some reason, I still know that Grandma Resuba despises us. She is smug in her belief that she could punish my mother, even in death, for marrying her son—by destroying her four children. Plus I have long ago accepted the fact that Trevor, Billy, Tyler, and I have no defenders.

Trevor doesn't want to go either, but the person in charge says he has to leave this afternoon. I beg her to let him stay, and she says no, he is sixteen, it is time for him to go away.

I wonder if at least my mother and God understand why being a ward of the state is so dangerous? No matter what the kid wants or needs, he or she can be moved at a moment's notice.

Trevor sees me and tells me not to worry. If Dad won't keep him, or if Grandma Resuba starts her nonsense, he will go on welfare and finish high school, then enter the navy. He tells me that he doesn't understand people, but he will try to keep in touch.

Trevor knows Dad doesn't want him, and he can't understand, after all the years of abuse and neglect by the family, why he is being sent back. He hugs me and wishes me good luck on my senior year.

Trevor also says that I should do what he, Tyler, and Billy plan to do, and that is to leave Scranton, and probably Pennsylvania, after high school. We should never look back, because there is only heartache here. There are no memories worth preserving.

As I watch Trevor drive away with the social worker, I can't help but think about how unfair life continues to be at times. Trevor is the one brother I have seen the most, and I know that we will never be together again. I just hope he can hold on until high school graduation, because then he will follow his dream and leave for a better life.

I don't understand how, after nine years, any social worker could return a kid to a place of open hatred and continuing abuse and neglect. Dad didn't want to take Trevor, but he was forced into it, and Trevor knows this.

Maybe it is the two years in the coal cellar, but I feel a bond with Trevor, Tyler, and Billy that I don't shared with anyone else. When I think about the cold, the name calling, and the death threats, I realize that we are lucky to be alive.

Does my mother in heaven still love Daddy?

Dad comes to visit today. It has been months since I last saw him. He says that Trevor will stay with him for a while, because the other two foster homes have not worked out.

I think to myself, what kind of father are you who treats taking my brother as if you are doing him a favor? Maybe if he had been a terrible father to us while my mother was alive, I could accept the indifference and abandonment, but he was a wonderful daddy.

When Dad talks to me, I am eight years old in my mind, sometimes still wanting everything that has happened since my mother's death to have never existed. But people change, and not always for the better. I love my brothers. The destruction of our family will always be what binds them to my heart in ways that I can't explain or understand.

Dad tells me that he is sorry that things didn't work out at the second foster home but that I seem to be doing well at the orphanage. I tell him I feel fine staying here and that in a couple of months I will be seventeen and starting my senior year in high school. He wishes me good luck and says that if I want to visit Trevor for about two hours on the next visiting day, he will come and pick me up.

The house he is building is almost complete, and it is right behind Grandma Resuba's house. Alice stays alternately at her dad's and her grandmother's houses.

It has been a long time since I have seen Trevor, so I agree to a visit, although I don't really want to see Grandma Resuba. She, at least in my mind, is the person I hold most responsible for destroying whatever my brothers and I could have become as a family. I really don't want to return in the daylight to a place where I spend many evenings in my terrorizing night dreams.

I love my brother Trevor, and it is only for two hours, so how bad can it be? Again, more of life's trade-offs that are not exactly equal.

What is it about life that keeps changing people? How does Daddy's family sleep? Why do they hate us so much? Is it possible for me to ever understand them?

Dad picks me up today to visit with Trevor and Alice. I have to will myself to look at Daddy's family.

Grandma Resuba stands on the porch, asking me how I'm doing, as though I were away on a vacation. I want to scream, "How could you hate us so much, hate my mother so much, that you broke her four children in ways that will never be seen?" I just stare at her with dead eyes and say, "Okay."

Grandma Resuba begins to tell me about how well Alice is doing, and I think to myself, Of course, she should be doing well. I can't think about Alice's well-being, because it comes at the expense of the crushing annihilation of her brothers and sister, by the people she calls family. She is not to blame for anything, but I am long past the ability to listen to continued comparison between her and us, about how good she is compared to us.

Grandma Resuba says Trevor has a wild streak in him. She tells me that he must have taken after my mother. I just glare at her but do not speak. I tell her that I have to go to the house to see Trevor and will talk to her later; of course, I have no intention of doing that. I can't believe that she talks to me as if nothing happened.

I know Grandma Resuba thinks we are not as good as her family, especially Alice. There is nothing I can do or say to change her way of thinking.

Trevor and I meet a boy who is my age near the coal bank. He is really nice and the only neighborhood kid that hung around us all the time when we were younger. He wants to show us some back trails up near the mineshafts. Trevor says he has to do something, so I agree to go with our friend.

When we get to the back trails behind the houses, he asks me if I want to fool around. I must look startled, I ask, what he means, like running down the mountain fast, or what? He tells me, "No, let me kiss you and fool around like married people a little." I tell him, "No, let's just go back to the house." He says he didn't mean to upset me, it's just that he thought since we knew each other a long time ago, and he likes me, that I might be interested in fooling around just a little bit. He says he is sorry if he has offended me.

I tell him not to worry about it, that I have a lot of stuff on my mind and that I will never be like married people.

I don't tell him how confused I am about what he is saying or asking, since I don't know what married people do beyond kissing and sharing a bedroom. Besides, I don't want him or anyone to think or know that I am a freak.

When I return to the house, the friend stays for ten minutes and then goes home, wishing me good luck when I return to the orphanage. I see Grandma Resuba on the porch watching us; she just goes back into her house. Dad says I have to get back to the orphanage by five o'clock. I hug Trevor. I really miss what we never had, an intact family.

Dad drops me off, saying that he will see me sometime soon, which translates into a couple of months. I decide that I will not return to the Resuba house anymore, for a lot of reasons. There is no place for me there. The truth is that there has never been a place for me there since my mother died.

I don't want to be involved in whatever fooling around is. I also don't want to be in the presence of Daddy's family, who, underneath their civility today, wished we never existed. Mostly, I want nothing to distract me from becoming the best half human I can be.

Is there a lot about life and people that I don't know about? I feel so alienated by so much.

I am in trouble again with the person in charge. She calls me down to her office and says that she has been told that I want to start a union.

I tell her that I have been studying about unions in my history class and how if people band together, they can make changes and better their lives.

I also tell her that since unions, like the UAW, are helpful to the working person, I have been thinking about forming a children's union. It's just that we have no rights as foster kids or wards of the state. Some of us orphans are more unfortunate than others, especially those of us who have no connection to anyone in the world.

It's not that my mother and God aren't enough, but neither one of them can embrace and nurture me in ways that I secretly hunger for. I don't blame either one of them, because I believe that my mother and God can work through other people to give me what I desperately need. I don't tell the person in charge about my conversations with my mother and God. I do tell her that if I formed a children's union, more adults would listen to us. Maybe they would try to make a difference for the kids who have no cheerleaders in their lives.

I tell her that God uses people to do good for others. However, if others don't know that kids like us exist, then they won't be able to do God's work by adopting some of us.

Well, I can tell by looking at the face of person in charge that I must sound like a fool, because she looks at me like I'm crazy. She says, "Where do you get all these foolish ideas? I'm in charge, and I make the decisions around here. You're not going to go far in life with the way you are going. Stop worrying about the other kids here. If God wanted them to have a different life, he would have given them one."

I ask her if she really believes that it is God's will that kids like me and some of the others at the orphanage should exist with no families. I tell her that this is not about God, because even he made sure that Jesus had a mother.

I say that as long as she and other people blame God, then no one will have to be responsible for nurturing kids like us on an individual basis. The person in charge is now beet red in the face, telling me that I am disrespectful. She says how dare I question her authority. She and the other adults know what is best. She also says that I have a lot of nerve telling her how God thinks and asks me where I learned about this stuff. I just tell her that I read the Bible too and that nowhere does it say that God wants us to be orphaned forever. In fact, even Jesus is always talking about the two great faces of loneliness in the world—the life of the widow and that of the orphan. I don't know anything about being widowed, but I certainly know a lot about being orphaned.

The person in charge tells me to stop talking to the other kids about this stupid children's union, or she'll make me leave and go into another foster home. She says that I am not praying to God in the right way. She tells me that I should accept everything that has happened as the way it should be.

I just tell her that I will stop talking about children's union, even though secretly, I still think it is a good idea. I also tell her that we must read different bibles and pray to different Gods. For now, I will go back to my cleaning and try to mind my own business.

She tells me that she is glad that I agree with her and will stop my nonsense. She tells me to concentrate on trying to be someone who accepts this as the way life should be.

I leave the office, but nothing inside me has changed. Somehow though, I feel the sting of her threat to put me into another foster home. I am ashamed of how much I have to stifle in order not to be sent away to a place where I can't survive.

I still think that God puts people here to parent other people's children when they are orphaned, for whatever reason. I still like my idea of a children's union.

Does my mother hear my crazy ideas in heaven? Do she and God ever talk about me?

It is the summer of my seventeenth birthday. In another couple of weeks, I will return for my last year of high school. I know now that I probably will need to work on how I will accomplish my goal of going to college.

When I tell the person in charge that I'm going to be a lawyer or a missionary, she says she doesn't know if I'm smart enough. I just ignore her. After all, she is just one more person in a long line of people who try to hold me back, but they don't matter to my inner core.

Even if I never succeed at first, I will still keep on trying. There is a kernel of stubbornness in my soul that refuses to let life beat me down into total submission.

Yet the night dreams continue to remind me of my inner messiness. I still believe that I have some purpose in life. Every morning, when I wake up, and I am devastated by whatever dream visited me, I still get out of bed, determined that, on this day, I will not be defeated by life.

Day dreams or night dreams, the lassoing by the past, even the spacing out, none of these will ever be greater than my determination to survive and to someday live a full life. So happy seventeenth birthday, kid. When that birthday comes, I tell myself to remember that I am still surviving! Life should be an interesting journey without a road map or a compass. As I wonder what direction my life will take, I wonder what my night dreams are really all about. How long will they continue?

Every now and then in the orphanage, there is a nun or two who reaches out to the children in ways all of us hunger for. Attachment to another person is something that all of us are warned against, especially by the person in charge.

Sometimes some of the kids will meet a nun who touches their hearts and offers them some nurturing in the arid environment that we live in.

Sister Jill is like a ray of laughter and sunshine. She is in charge of the little boys, but has managed to make her mothering presence felt beyond that group. She reminds me of another older nun, Sister Mary, who is always giving lollipops to the kids when they go to the orphanage clinic where she works as the nurse.

Sister Jill and her parents sometimes bring a treat for all the children at the orphanage. I notice how she goes out of her way to talk to the older kids, and she is always a good listener.

She is actually one of the few nuns who want to be here at the orphanage. Most nuns are assigned to come here, and they aren't too thrilled about it. I think it has more to do with the person in charge than it does with the kids.

Sister Jill has gathered the children in the gym tonight for a treat, and she tells us that she will be leaving tomorrow. The little kids start crying, because she has always allowed them to crawl all over her, and she hugs them a lot. I think that what they will miss the most is her always doing the little extras that somehow make this vacant life we live in a little brighter.

Personally, I think that she is leaving the convent, because usually, if someone leaves, it is sudden, and she disappears as though she never existed. I hope she has a good life, and I know that whatever children she deals with in the future, they will be very lucky. She once told me that it has always been her dream to run a place that involves children. I know we are better for having known her.

Sometimes I try to imagine that a person like Sister Jill would want to adopt someone like me. I keep my thoughts of adoption to myself, because I don't want anyone to think I'm a freak still looking for nurturing that I don't deserve or need but desperately want. I know that not being adopted will always be the greatest disappointment in my life.

What makes some people's hearts full of welcoming embraces? How do people like Sister Jill have the capacity to see beyond the limitations that are imposed by such traumatic childhoods? How could the departure of one nun make all the kids cry their whisper tears over her leaving?

I'm getting nervous, because now it is my senior year in high school, and at seventeen, I feel so old and yet so young. It's scary not knowing what will await me when I must leave this isolated cocoon and go out to that people-oriented world that has never made me feel welcome. In my mind, I tell myself that I cannot let myself be defeated by the unknowns or curl up and die, at least not without a fight.

School is so hectic, I feel as if I am being bombarded by the loud noises of growth that I cannot keep up with. Many of my friends are working part-time jobs, dating, involved in school activities, and talking about their future plans, which always involve their families.

No one at the orphanage, not even the person in charge, has asked me what my dreams are. I sometimes hunger for that closeness of family that is so subtle, so unbreakable, so close, and so safe. When I leave for college in August of 1974, I can never return to this place that I have called, for better or worse, home.

There are rumors swirling around in the orphanage about it going to be closed down in a year or two, and all the children will be placed in foster homes. Somehow there is talk about this being a new direction in social work, and how wonderful it will be for the children to live in foster homes.

Obviously, no one has consulted the real experts, we the orphans, who must suffer the consequences of being second best and never quite up to snuff. Closing the orphanage won't affect me, because it won't be for another year or two.

There are so many things at school during my senior year that will require some parental involvement, such as filling out college applications and making plans for the future, yet I find myself having to face these things alone. I must just keep my eye on what my goals are and try to figure out how to accomplish them. There is so much to do and no one to turn to for help. There are so many occasions in school that cost money.

If only my mother could see me now. I'm still here, and I'm still alive! I will make something of my life. Even with my limitations, I will not be defeated by the scary chaos that looms ahead. In heaven, does my mother have any scary moments? Why do I feel so alone and so scared in the midst of the people world? Will anyone ever embrace me and show me how life works?

I have been thinking that maybe I should start stockpiling the safety nets that will protect me from wanting to hide from life. Even if I live by my survival list, there is still so much I could accomplish in my life, if only I keep choosing every day to live in such a way that honors what my mother started, and what God has loved.

In some ways, I have been stockpiling the safety nets all my life, such as composing my survival list, my card game of life, and my refusal to fade away, no matter how seductive the call to just give up on being, at best, half human. I will need this year to make more lists so I can feel safe, until I no longer need whatever lists I make.

My biggest mistake, when I was eight years old, was that I never knew my mother could die and leave me. Back then I didn't have time to prepare or stockpile "nets of safety" that could keep out the absence of the ordinary.

That's why today, I am no more farther along as a girl, a female, or a human being than I was the day my mother left to continue her life in a different way.

Yet I have changed for the good in some ways. If only my mother could hear me speak with such clarity and a pronunciation, that is crisp and clear. Most people don't even notice that I once had a cleft palate. My nose is no longer flat, and, except for a scar on my lip, there is little to notice about what should have been a dominant issue in my childhood. Her death relegated my cleft palate to the bottom of my list of important and relevant things.

I wonder if safety nets really provide security or do they limit how much of life can be lived? I also wonder, if I stockpiled enough safety nets, could they keep me safe until I die? Was my mother the original safety net, just as all mothers are supposed to be for children who are too young and too powerless to help themselves?

Sometimes at night in the orphanage, I sit at the windowsill and watch the stars, which flicker in their dark tapestry. I think about how my mother must be somewhere up there, shining in all her glory. On a night like this, when I talk to her and God, I feel comforted by the twinkling stars, which offer me a sense of balance and a feeling of being grounded.

Even though I feel cheated over my mother's absence, and angry that whatever mothering every girl-child needs to be a woman didn't happen, I still love her and like to think that she Is somewhere up there watching over me.

As I sit at this window and listen to the gentle sounds of sleep that only children can make, I think that maybe we orphans are the miracles. There is no way that labels like "orphans," "throwaways," "bastards," "foster kids," or "wards of the state" could ever do justice to our untapped potential.

How often I think about how much God must have in common with us castaways. He too must have had to search his heart at times to understand the choices and ramifications of how people use their free will in such a destructive manner.

I also think that God must love kids like us in ways that others do not, if for no other reason that, when all is said and done and everyone has walked away, he is still here, and so are we. Maybe we both feel a little less lonely in our expectations of people to return what they have been given.

Just as my mother shines in her world, reflecting back on all that she has left, I hope that I too can make my life a reflection back to her. I wonder if there are other worlds out in the universe where they too struggle with their humanness? Will my mother, God, and the stars always be there to shine a light in my darkness?

Today I have to drive into town with a nun to help her carry stuff.

In town, as it is getting darker, we ride past a building that has a red light on it, and I remark on how pretty it looks. I say, "Maybe when I build my log cabin someday, I'll have one."

The nun who is driving gives me a weird look, especially when I ask why there is a red light on the house. She says, "Didn't your mother ever teach you anything? That's for if you want to be a lady in the evening." I get really red fast and wish the world would open up and swallow me, because I'm not sure what she means, and I don't dare ask her anything else. This must have something to do with those subjects like the body or sex, which is off-limits in my inner world.

Still, I like the red light. Too bad something so pretty is not good. If someone ever calls me a lady of the evening, I will know it is not a compliment. I just have to stop asking questions that I should already know the answers to. I'm not sure what a lady of the evening does and why she lives in a red-light district, but I know when I build my log cabin someday, I will make sure that there is no red light.

As we drive back to the orphanage, I am really quiet. I don't like to draw attention to myself, except in school. The nun asks me if I am okay, and I say, "Sure." What else should I say, that I am a stupid kid, and no, my mother never taught me anything, and I'm not interested in learning anything about life stuff, unless I get an adoptive mother like I deserve? I feel like an eleven-year-old kid, even though I am seventeen. Of course, this is only said in my mind, because who could ever understand the heartache of floundering in a world that requires so much explaining about what others consider ordinary.

Life is filled with so much to learn beyond the book knowledge in school. Does my mother know I still need her to teach me and to protect me?

Ever since I was in the ninth grade, I would use every few dollars I got my hands on to order paperback books from the nun in charge with the eighth grade at the orphanage. It is vital that I read, and so far I have amassed a collection of 350 books.

Since I value reading above everything else, except, of course, talking to my mother and God in my mind, I have to give my books a place of honor. Beginning in the ninth grade, I have been in charge of cleaning the dining room. It has a huge walk-in closet, with dishes enough for two hundred kids.

I don't have any place in the dorm for my books, only a locker that is twelve inches wide and five feet high to hold the few clothes I have. The way I figure it, since I have to clean the dining room, I am entitled to fix the closet anyway I want.

My books, which I believe are more important and honorable than the dishes in the closet, deserve the best space. Starting in ninth grade, I began putting the dishes on the floor, one shelf at a time, and placing my books in the best place in the closet. Some of my books include *Death, Be Not Proud*, *Heidi*, the Nancy Drew mysteries, and books on adoption.

There is a light in the closet, and when I don't want to be bothered by the craziness of the orphanage reality, I just go into the closet, turn the light on, and read, surrounded by my growing collection of life adventures.

Now in my senior year, almost every shelf in the dining room closet is filled with my books, and all the dishes are on the floor. I either really like someone or something, or I don't.

Well, Sister Linda opened the closet door and almost had a heart attack when she saw my collection, which, I tell her, does include many literary classics. She insists that dishes don't belong on the floor, but I try to point out to her how ideas and stories will last longer than old dishes.

We reach an agreement. The dishes are going back on the shelves, and she found some old bookcases that fit under the last shelf of the closet. I still personally like my design better, but sometimes I must compromise and give in to the desires of others, especially if they are in charge.

How come not everyone sees my way of life as normal? Were books and learning important to my mother?

I wonder if my mother has ever heard of this test called the SATs or the Scholastic Aptitude Test. It is a measure of how well I am supposed to do in college. All the kids in school are talking about taking it together at the University of Scranton on a Saturday, in a couple of weeks.

I have the paperwork sent in. Sometimes it is so hard for me to figure out all the directions, especially the information on college. I apply to Villanova University and Alvernia College.

I have had to keep asking the person in charge for this thing called a check; apparently it is different from money. There must be a lot of different things I don't know, even the many ways there are to pay for stuff.

I ask the person in charge how I will get into Scranton on Saturday to take the SAT test. She says I must find my own ride because the cars at the orphanage have to be available for important things. Sometimes I get tired of always trying to find my own way, but what choice do I have?

There is this kid, Jake, in my trigonometry class, who I overheard making plans to take the SATs. I ask him if he will give me a ride, and he says, "Sure, no problem." When I start to tell him where I live, he says he already knows. I think that my mother would have liked him. He is handsome, with gold-rimmed eyeglasses, long blond hair, ruddy cheeks, and a very likable personality.

After the SAT, which is a headache maker, Jake and I meet the other students from our class at the university. They all decide to go for lunch before going home. I don't have any money, because I never do, and I didn't know that people eat out after doing something big.

I tell Jake that I will wait by the car. He must know how embarrassed I am. He says, "Come on, I'll treat you. My father gave me money for both of us when I told him I was giving you a ride."

We all have a good time at lunch. It is the first time I have ever been out with a group of students, and it feels okay. I realize that life can be filled with welcoming kindness when I least expect them.

Did my friend learn his kindness from his father's example? How did his father anticipate my being hungry by giving his son enough money for lunch for the two of us?

If only you could see these college applications and financial aid forms. They seem to me like they are in another language. Everything is so confusing. It is already after midnight, and I am getting cold sitting on the floor with all these papers surrounding me.

At the assembly in school today, the counselors pass out these applications and tell us to have our parents help us fill them out. This, in translation, means that I have to try to understand them by myself and make some sense of still another application world that I know nothing about.

When I'd asked the person in charge for help with the applications, she'd told me that I am on my own, and I shouldn't be disappointed if I don't get into college. I told her that I needed two checks for the application fees. She said that she would give them to me but would deduct them from the money I get for cleaning. It doesn't matter about the money, because I have to accomplish my goal, and that is to leave Scranton and go to college and try to become a person.

No matter what the person in charge says, I'm smart enough to go to college. Besides, if I get rejected, I'll just keep applying somewhere until I'm accepted.

Why are there so many questions on the application forms about family background and family expenses?

It is so late, and I'm getting cold sitting here, but this financial aid package form has to be filled out by tomorrow. It is hard to understand, especially all the questions for the parents to fill out. The person in charge said she wouldn't fill out anything or sign anything, so I must answer the questions as best I can.

When I look at all the blank spaces, I know that this financial aid application makes me look like I was never born or belonged anywhere. I decide to write a letter with my application, explaining that I am a ward of the state and live in an orphanage. I can't leave the parents' side blank and unsigned, but I can't fill it out or sign it either. Hopefully this will be okay.

This is another one of those moments that remind me of how much I have lost by my mother's not being here. It also reminds me of all the ways that are hard sometimes for me. It also forces me to face all the losses that are always present.

How many more "applications" in life are there that I don't know about?

For the most part, I like North Pocono High School. So far I am still holding my own. There are times though when I see how important it is to have parents, people who will stick up for you.

At school there are two adults that make negative comments to me about where I live. One teacher always says that I am lucky to have a place like the orphanage since no one wants me. I usually try to ignore her, which isn't always easy, since I have her for class every day.

At least, with my last name, I'm always in the last seat of the last row in her classroom. There is something to be said about being out of sight and out of mind. Besides, I always tell myself that the librarian thinks, I'm okay, and so do most of my other teachers. I try to remember that there are more people who are nice to me than those who are not.

However, for the past three years, my biggest problem in school is the continuing harassment by this guidance counselor, Mrs. Crusher. She gets a thrill out of calling me to her office and making me feel lower than I already feel.

Mrs. Crusher is always asking me, "What did you do wrong that you have to live at the orphanage?" When I tell her nothing and that my mother died in a gas explosion and my adoptive father didn't want me, she always laughs in a snickering way. She says, "There must be something wrong if no one on your father's or mother's side of the family ever took you."

What really makes me bristle is when Mrs. Crusher tells me how lucky I am. She says that I should be grateful for the clothes that I have and the food that I eat. She says that no one really has to take care of me.

What really sends me off the deep end is when I ask for college forms, and Mrs. Crusher tells me that kids like me can't make it in college. She says, "Look at you, did you ever notice that you aren't like your classmates? You dress differently and don't have their kind of stable family background. The person in charge at the orphanage and I talk about you and believe that you aren't college material. Kids like you should not take loans and scholarship money away from the children with families."

I stop Mrs. Crusher right in the middle of her one-way conversation and ask her, "What do you mean by kids like me? You have no right to talk about kids in the orphanage, whom I consider my brothers and sisters. Don't tell me we aren't good enough. Let me tell you something, those kids know more about heartache and loneliness than you or most people will ever know in a lifetime. You can call me names, tell me I'm a freak and too stupid to go to college, or tell me about me not being normal, but don't you ever talk about the kids at the orphanage. You think you know everything. You and the person in charge are always harassing me about my limitations, and that's fine, just leave the other orphans out of this conversation."

The guidance counselor gets all flustered and starts telling me that I am nothing but a defiant brat who doesn't appreciate what I have. Mrs. Crusher says that she will call the person in charge and have this act of disrespect put into my permanent record. I realize she would never put me down like this if my mother were here to defend and protect me. I'm right about her defending me, aren't I?

I hate those words—"permanent record." At the orphanage, we always hear about how anything bad that we do will go into our permanent record and follow us for the rest of our lives. We are told that we will never get a good job because we are bad kids.

I wonder why nothing good is ever put into the permanent record. I just don't think that it's fair that for twenty-four hours a day, anything I do could be written down in my permanent record and affect my future.

At school, the guidance counselor tells me that I might be emotionally disturbed, and Mrs. Crusher has talked to the person in charge about having me take this stupid personality test in her office. I tell her that I don't want to take it, but she tells me that the person in charge says I have to. She says to remember that I can be moved at a moment's notice and be sent to a different institution or to a foster home.

Why do people use their power to inflict more damage? I just know that if I had parents, she wouldn't be able to talk to me like this. Sometimes I feel like an animal trapped by forces I have no control over.

I finally tell her, "Fine, I'll take the stupid personality test. Both you and the person in charge are hypocrites because you both already think I'm a failure. You think that I am some poor nobody who is asking for a chance that I don't deserve."

Mrs. Crusher snickers and says that I don't know anything about life, and no one at the high school thinks I'll amount to anything either. I tell her that some of my teachers like me and think I am okay, and I did well on the reading comprehension test as a freshman.

Mrs. Crusher laughs and tells me that none of the teachers really like me, they only pity me. I just tell her to give me the personality test so I can get back to class.

Mrs. Crusher is mad because I'm supposed to take it in silence, but I keep muttering under my breath, "Hypocrites, hypocrites." The test will probably prove her right, that I am emotionally disturbed, and maybe even crazy.

I just don't understand why a guidance counselor who has a place of authority would want to drag down a kid like me who is already down and out. I never did anything bad or wrong to be in the orphanage. My mother was the one who died.

After I take the test, the guidance counselor tells me that the kids in the orphanage aren't my flesh-and-blood brothers and sisters. I tell her that there is more to being related than just flesh and blood. She tells me to give her the completed test and to stop having the last word. She says she will discuss our meeting with the person in charge. That it will go into my permanent record.

Mrs. Crusher says that just by quickly looking at the test, it shows that she is right about me being a little disturbed in my mind. I think to myself that I'm not the only one with a disturbed mind.

In high school, it is the guidance counselor that has the information on colleges. Whenever Mrs. Crusher is in the mood, she will call me to her office and hand me the applications, saying, "Have your parents fill this out—oh, I forgot, you don't have parents, do you? Well, I guess you'll just have to do the best you can on your own. Now you know why parents are so important."

I take the material from Mrs. Crusher and just stuff it into my folder. What most people don't realize is that I may not know what it is like to have parents or to have a mother; however, I do know what it is like not to have parents or a mother.

Even though I won't give in and let them see me break, it eats at me to hear some adults get a thrill out of heaping further humiliation upon me.

Neither this guidance counselor, the person in charge, nor any adult hears what I have to listen to every night, and that is the whisper tears of kids like me who are orphaned by drugs, alcohol, abandonment, prison, sickness, or death.

Why do parents have permanent records of the heart, but orphanage kids have only permanent records made of paper?

Being a ward of the state is such a pressure cooker for me, because I always feel a sense of collective responsibility to do well, not only for myself, but for the other kids caught in this "shuffle madness" as well. I have always tried to hold a high moral standard for myself, because I know that what I do reflects back on my mother and God. There is also a part of me that is very protective of the kids I live with, because I know the unseen pain that they live with every day by being outside the family loop.

Sometimes I'm afraid that if I don't try to be good or perfect, then I might make it worse for another kid who might be taken in by a family. I cringe when I hear "Kids like you" or "Those foster kids, you can't trust them because they are bad, not even their family wants them" or "You know those kids will never amount to anything, they're not like our kids."

The funny thing is that we all started out for the most part as innocent, healthy babies like everyone else. Then the family we were born into became insecure. For reasons only the adults understood, we were given over to the "shuffle madness" and told "Good luck" or "See you at eighteen." In the end, we were left to deal with the consequences of a life lived without all the ingredients that are necessary to turn a child into a man or a woman.

I want so much for the other kids to get their shot at being in a family and a life filled with the ordinary and not its absence. In so many ways, I realize now, at seventeen, that I never had the right preparation for an adoptive family, but there are many kids here who have more going for them. I try really hard to be good, not to talk back, get good grades, and not draw attention to myself, just so there will be less negative comments about "kids like me." Maybe then more people will say, "Yes, I will help one kid."

Why do I feel this need to do well not only for myself but also for others?

Today in the school library, I read about how we are getting out of that war in Vietnam. It said that the president has ordered the orphans flown out of South Vietnam so that they can come to America and be adopted.

Maybe I am being selfish because, at first, I felt resentful and jealous. Only as I sit back tonight, reflecting on my day, do I realize that nationality doesn't matter; an orphan is an orphan. The losses are the same.

The way I figure it, even the kids like me who are available for adoption will never be taken because of our age, sex, color, or a thousand other reasons.

The people adopting these babies from Vietnam won't give us a second look anyway. However, if they are caring enough to embrace any orphan from any place into their hearts and families, then that is, at least, one less lonely child.

So I think I will follow this Operation Babylift story and cheer for every kid that gets out of Vietnam. From what I read, not belonging to anyone in that country makes those kids just as forsaken as it does me.

Somehow inside of me there is a spirit of camaraderie with these children who have been displaced and separated from their parents either physically or emotionally. I'm glad that these orphans from Vietnam are coming. There will be great joy and rejoicing in some families and less loneliness in the world.

I also read about kids called the dust of the earth. There is a special hatred for them by the Vietnamese. Apparently, if a kid is half-American and half-Vietnamese, they are the most hated and unacceptable. I can really relate to them because if people get it in their minds that they can love only their own flesh and blood, just as Daddy's family did, then nothing will make them change.

Nothing these mixed-heritage orphans do will ever change who they are and the way their country sees them. I have learned that sometimes in life, no matter what I do or how hard I work, it is not enough to overcome certain expectations or obstacles set up by people.

I could no more make myself into a lovable, pretty girl child than a dust-of-the-earth orphan from Vietnam who is half-Vietnamese and half-American. There is a certain permanency that exists that cannot be changed.

One thing for sure is that orphaned children, no matter how strong their willpower, cannot un-orphan themselves. The best some of us can hope for is that we are young enough, cute enough, and lovable enough so that someone or some people will embrace us into their family circle.

I think that the club of orphans is not something that any one of us wants to keep expanding. It is a win for us when someone is adopted and our circle grows smaller.

I wonder how there could so many children existing without family matches? This senior year is really going fast, almost as if it is a blur. The activities in the orphanage and the busyness of school life leave me with little time to sort out everything in my life. Lately I have begun reviewing some lists that I made four years ago. So far my survival list is still imperative for my physical and emotional life. The list of the dead will never change, but maybe I need to make some additions to the Someday list.

I think I shall add the following to my Someday list: Someday I will

- Tell my story even if it helps only one other kid
- Go to Nashville, listen to country music, and meet Loretta Lynn
- Ride a motorcycle with the wind against my face
- Know that I am loved in spite of my limitations
- Believe to the depths of my being that my mother loved me

- Retrace my mother's steps and savor the stories about who she was
- Set aright the injustice to kids in the "shuffle madness" of life
- Be nurtured as I hunger to be whole
- Know that all the splintered parts will be brought together
- Know that all the different worlds I live in will intersect and know one another
- Not be afraid to be a female, a woman, and a human being
- Not be afraid to let other people into my life and into my heart
- Make my mark and give something back to the world
- Embrace the whole of me, which is nonexistent now
- Hope to change or do away with my survival list

I like having a Someday list. It gives me hope because there are things on it yet to be accomplished. I still look at the children here at the orphanage who inspire me to want better, or to want more than has been expected of me. It is hard to have goals when I am a kid, especially if no one has any expectations of me.

In six months, I will be a full-fledged adult, which is scary for someone who is still a child in so many ways. I know I need to focus on what I can salvage from my life that, in some ways, is still splintered, but yet in other ways has made me stronger and tougher than most others.

What were some things that my mother dreamt about accomplishing? Did any of them come true for her?

I am so excited because today, I received two acceptance letters from Alvernia College and Villanova University in the mail. I was so happy that I danced in the dining room and ran down the hallway to tell everyone I saw.

Just think, I'm going to college. I can't believe it! Me, a ward of the state and a nobody's child, is good enough and smart enough and alive enough to enter the land of the living. This daughter of my dead mother is really going to be somebody someday.

I tell the person in charge, and she says that she hopes I can make it. I understand she has no idea who I really am. She doesn't have to worry about me making it, because inside me there's a hunger and a thirst to better myself. I will never allow anyone to hold me back in the outside world ever again.

The cleft palate kid, the bastard orphan, the foster kid, the unadoptable child is going to go to college. I feel like I am the luckiest kid in the world. This proves that there is nothing I can't do if I keep my nose to the grindstone and stay focused.

I'll probably choose Alvernia College, because there are nuns who run it, and it is smaller than Villanova University. In four years, I will have a college degree, together with dreams, which will continue to live and grow.

If only my mother was here to share this happy moment with me, because she gave me the gifts of love of reading, stubbornness, and dreams. I promise that I will never let her down. If only she could see me now.

Will a college education help me become more whole? Will I always be as excited about things that are as important to me? Are my dreams part of the dreams that my mother had for me?

The buzz around school lately is that there will be a special dance called the senior prom. Apparently, the kid that goes to it spends a lot of money, gets a date, has family over at the house taking a lot of pictures. The girls go dressed in an evening gown, and the guys wear a tuxedo to this fancy ballroom. Even though this experience is not for me, I think it must be exciting for all my friends.

I have never attended any of the dances at school or other activities, but this senior prom must be an extra special affair. Almost everyone I know is going, but I realize how different I am and how I live in three worlds that do not intersect: my inner world, my orphanage world, and my school world.

Still, I do wonder about how people know how to date, how to dress, or even how to shop. I find listening to the kids in the school cafeteria fascinating. It is almost like there is this fourth world that I don't know anything about. How do girls learn about how to be at a dance, at a prom, in a date, or in a life? Are all the activities at school normal for all kids, or just for most kids?

Sometimes I wonder what it would be like to be Cinderella for a night. I try to imagine having all these people taking pictures and making a fuss over me.

The kids in school are talking about how their mothers are excited. Some of them are having their whole family over, including aunts, uncles, and grandparents. It must not only be a school thing but a family thing as well. Then there is the endless conversation about the prom king and queen. I guess they get crowns.

I do like to hear about other kids having a good time because there is enough heartache in life. I believe life should be filled with more celebrations with family and friends. Someday, even though I don't have a family, and can't have a family, when I make some real friends, then maybe I can join in their celebrations, such as birthday or Christmas parties. But for now, I'm glad that there are football games, dates, trips, and even the senior prom, if not for me, then for the other kids.

Would I have been at a prom if my mother were here?

Today a letter arrived in the mail from the state of Pennsylvania, saying that I have been awarded a full-tuition grant, along with room and board to Alvernia College. It says that if I maintain a C average, the grant is good for four years. Now it is official; there is no roadblock to stop me from pursuing my dreams.

I lie in bed tonight, listening to the children sleep, and wonder about the unknowns of life down the road. We who are children of great sadness are also children of great hope.

I realize that it is not my imaginary world of what might have been, or should have been that propels me to do well, but rather, it is this real world of pain and losses that challenge me to do well in my life. I look at these kids and want so much to become a success, not only for me or my mother or God, but for all the kids who are wards of the state and have been cheated out of something that no one can ever give back or make up for.

Maybe all I can do is to live for the kids who aren't as strong or as tough or as stubborn as I am. No one really understands the price that I pay in order to appear "together" so that I can function every day.

I worry about the kids that cry for their mothers who aren't going to come back. If they don't learn to be tougher, they will die inside themselves by inches, and, sadly, no one will notice.

I try to tell some of the kids not to cry in public and not to let anybody see that they are broken. I know that no matter how much pain I am in, I will never give in to the whisper tears. I will not let the past beat me, even though I am crushed nightly in my dreams. I just want to do well for all these kids who may or may not have a chance. Why do I feel this responsibility for all the children in the orphanage? How can I show them how to turn sadness into hope?

I heard this song on the radio today called "I Never Promised You a Rose Garden." It really tells the story about how life is a double-edged sword. It also tells how nothing is promised.

Life is at times bittersweet, with its thorns and flowers, even in the relationships I have with my mother, God, and others. She is part of my soul even though I know little or nothing about who she was as a person. Yet she must have, at one time, loved me in such a way that secured her in my heart and allowed me to be in a relationship with her.

I talk a lot to my mother in my mind. Yet even though I feel comforted by my conversations with her, I wonder if she hears me and knows the impact of both her presence and absence in my life. I would rather that she knows me through these conversations and letters, than let the journey of my life be unknown to her.

I know that although God doesn't interfere with the choices that people have made, or are still making, regarding my mother's orphaned children, I delight in the gift of roses, such as the mind and heart that he has blessed me with. The thorns notwithstanding, I will always try to be the rose that blooms in spite of the pain.

Some people I have met held out only the "thorns" that cause pain, not always seen but leaving scars that are never quite healed. Yet there are other people who go beyond the thorns and hold out a rose to me. People like my English teacher, Sister Margo, and Sister Linda keep me wanting to learn more and to be more than I am. How could a simple saying tell so much about my life and how I feel about my future?

I really miss my mother even more at times. Usually it is during award ceremonies in school where parents are invited that I feel the loss the most. Even though I always try to tell myself how different I am from other kids, it doesn't always cushion the blows of the unexpected hunger to belong to a family.

In high school they have this thing called a ring ceremony, where seniors are presented with the class ring that they purchased. Almost everyone orders a ring, but they are very expensive, so I know that I won't get one. It doesn't bother me, because this is the trade-off for being a ward of the state. Besides, it's only a ring ceremony anyway. What really sucker-punches me is how many parents come to the auditorium to watch. Those of us who don't get a ring sit in the auditorium and watch the ceremony.

I sometimes wonder what it must be like to have parents who are part of their kids' ordinary life. I think about how for the past ten years since my mother's death, no one has ever gone to my school or to a ceremony and said "That's my kid" or "That's my daughter," or felt publicly proud to be associated with me.

I hear my classmates complain about their parents. Yet they rely 100 percent on them for everything. They also talk about the good times when their parents go to bat for them and show up for many school events. Why are parents still so important, even for seniors in high school? What does a class ring ceremony really symbolize anyway? Is it really for the students? Or is it really for the parents? Or a little of both? At any rate, how will I ever know?

Today in school I am called to the office. I wonder what they want, because in school, I keep a low profile. When I get to the office, I am told to sit down.

The teacher who is in charge of the yearbook asks me how I am. I say fine. Then I am told that there is a mistake in the yearbook and that it is too late and too expensive to change it. I keep thinking, What are they talking about?

Finally, I am told that my picture in the yearbook has the name of the last boy in the class under it and that my name is printed under his picture. I am told that it is an honest mistake and they hope I won't be bothered by it.

I tell them not to worry, I didn't buy one anyway, and I have no family who will see it. With that, I am sent back to class.

When I return to class, I tell one of my friends about the meeting in the office. She tells me she overheard them talking, and they were saying, "Thank God, it is Jerri. She is from the orphanage, and we won't have to deal with an irate mother, since she is dead." My friend says that they were lucky it wasn't her, because her mother would be up in a flash.

Sometimes I realize how little people know of me. It doesn't matter about the mistake in the yearbook, because I figure that when things happen, maybe they will learn how not to let them happen again.

I doubt that Harley's family will be so understanding, but then I didn't buy a yearbook, and no one is going to say anything on my behalf.

The only thing I don't like about this yearbook mistake is that it will draw attention to me, and I don't need the questions or the snickers. On a deeper level, I try not to let this incident be further proof of the discombobulation swirling around inside me.

I tell myself that I have more than enough things to worry about than this stupid yearbook stuff. In a couple months, I will embark on a new journey and never see the high school again. I will put the mixed-up me away and move on to things that are more relevant and important. I hope no one knows about my desire to be a blank person.

Would my mother have stopped the publication of the yearbook if she were here?

Today at lunch, some of my friends show me pictures of their families, taken on prom night, as well as their school graduation pictures. They are really neat to look at, especially the ones with their parents hugging them.

The school pictures are expensive, so I don't get any. Then I learn that people hang their kids' pictures all around their homes. Most of the kids are talking about this thing called a package, where pictures come in all sizes. Their grandparents, aunts, uncles, and parents get the big ones, and assorted friends get the smaller ones.

Tonight I tell my mother in heaven that in all the world and in all the homes there is no graduation party being planned for me nor are there pictures of me on anyone's mantle or desk. I wish secretly that I have pictures of her, or that someone would brag about me with my picture in their home. I guess, since I don't belong to anyone, there is no need for a permanent memory or reminder. I have never been introduced as someone's daughter, and there is no picture taken to show that I even exist.

But then I have no pictures of my mother, no letters for that matter, no stories, few memories; and no one who ever knew her has ever told me about her. I wonder if I will become as invisible to this world as she has?

Do pictures remind people of their connectedness to each other? Could I disappear if no one ever sees me? Did my mother have pictures taken of us? What happened to them? And will someone ever again want to have my picture taken?

I wonder if my mother knows how much I like to write about things that are happening in my life?

I carry a notebook so that I can jot down things that people are doing. Sometimes when I am at the playground, or up late at night, I write some poetry in between.

I never show anyone my thoughts because, the theme in the poems is always the same: a child desperately seeking a mother. I know as a teenager, even as a senior in high school, that these hungering needs for nurturing and bonding are abnormal for someone like me. Nevertheless, inside me, hidden from public view, are thoughts and needs that I've never outgrown.

Sometimes when I write my thoughts or poems, I feel a little less lonely. It is like writing becomes a different kind of friend who lets me know that I am not a hard rock, or the tough kid that the world assumes I am. Besides, I think it is easier on everyone if they think I am tough, because then people don't feel like they have to be stuck trying to help me.

These are silly thoughts of a lonely kid, but in my writings and poetry, it's hard to really deny who I am when I am alone with my thoughts and raw feelings. I am careful about letting anyone see what I write, because even though I feel like a freak sometimes, I can't give someone else the opportunity to verify this by reading my innermost thoughts in this notebook.

Sometimes the nuns are curious about what I am writing. I just tell them that I'm making lists of things that are happening. These are my thoughts about what is happening to me.

There are times when I wonder if anyone else keeps notes about their home life, or write poems of wanting to belong to a family or to have a mother.

In some of my notes and poems, I write about my mother. I wonder what she would be like and whether I would allow her to know the messiness that is inside me. I wonder, if she came back right now, if I would ever show her my notebook of observations, desires, and childlike needs in this grown-up seventeen-year-old body?

The whisper tears are so close to the surface when I read the poems. They remind me of the vulnerability and sensitivity that exists deep down inside me and of how, after all these years, I have not been able to toughen myself and make them go away. I want a place called home and a presence called mother.

Is writing about my thoughts and feelings as close as I will ever get to being a human being? Can written words ever adequately express the heaviness that I feel weighing me down, day in and day out? Is my writing another way to keep myself from going crazy, even though I write like the child I still am, wanting a mother?

In eight weeks, I will graduate from high school, and the dreams of this world, both in school and at the orphanage, will be left behind me. As I lie in bed, I am overwhelmed by the unknowns and how I will handle being thrust into a world that I am not prepared to live in. I know that once I leave here, I can never come back.

In five months, I will be in college. Even when I accomplish my goal of going on in life, I shall miss the structure and the acceptance of this isolated world that I know.

Time is going so fast. There are two nuns here who have been looking out for me this past year.

One nun has been helping me go over my essays and my research paper for English. I decided to write paper on Flannery O'Connor, because in some poignant way, the orphanage is reflective of many themes in her writings.

Both of the nuns have gone to "bat" for me with the person in charge over money, and now they want to have a small graduation party for me. I don't know all the details, but I like knowing that this accomplishment of getting a high school diploma will be recognized publicly.

I won't let fear of failure paralyze me from moving forward. Deep down, I must allow the resiliency that exists within to show. I will not be afraid of the shutting of the doors. I will try to embrace whatever experiences that are yet to unfold for me.

There is no room for failure and nowhere to lay my head if I don't make my life work for me.

I ask God to please don't let me slip. I have to make a life for myself that is good, honorable, and necessary.

In my heart, even though no one expects anything of me, or has any goals for me, I know I need to succeed. There are all these children at the orphanage who have been shoved aside that I must do well for.

Do all doors that open offer opportunities for growth? And what happens after the doors have shut behind me? Will I be able to live up to what the world expects of me after I leave the only worlds I ever knew, namely, the high school and the orphanage?

The person in charge wants to see me in her office. She always makes me nervous, because I never feel good enough to be in her presence. I know that even though she must be a good person, I always end up feeling less confident after speaking to her.

I wonder what I did this time, or what she wants, since she usually stays in her office. In three weeks, I will graduate and then I will leave for college in August.

In her office, the person in charge tells me that I need to make some arrangements to find a place to live during the summer. I am stunned. I ask her what she means.

She tells me that since I am graduating in three weeks, I must find a place to live until I go to college. She says that the day after graduation, I must leave the orphanage because that is when the contract for my care is up.

I tell her that I don't have anyone who wants me or anywhere to go. I plead with her to let me stay until I leave for college. She says no, that graduation ends my time as a ward of the state.

I ask her where I will go, and she says I'm an adult now, I have to make my own plans. She does tell me that she has called Daddy's family, but they weren't interested. Also, she says that I have a passbook savings account of $1,200 for the cleaning that I have done. I never question the money, because I figure it must be from cleaning ten hours a week while living at the orphanage.

I ask her again to please let me stay from June to August, but she tells me no. She says that it is best for me to learn how to be independent and to find my own way in the world. I leave her office, shaken. Where will I go? When I go upstairs, two nuns ask me what the person in charge wanted. I tell them that I must leave the day after graduation. They are furious and tell me not to worry about anything, they will take care of it.

Both of them head down the stairs to the main office. I lean over the railing to listen to the one nun who is doing most of the talking. There is a lot of arguing going on about how I should not have to leave the day after graduation and how I need to stay here until I leave for college.

The nun tells her, "You can't put that child out like this. She has no one, and if we are not legally responsible, then we are morally responsible for giving her a place to live. She has done more than most of these poor children will ever do. No one will ever fight for her, and she deserves a chance to be left here until she goes to college. She has no place to go, not even to that idiot family who threw her and her brothers aside like they were trash. It is jerks like that family who have forced this child to fend for herself. They will all have to answer to God for their inhuman treatment and attitude. We shouldn't add to the impossible burden that she already carries. Fortunately, Jerri is one of the most intelligent people we have ever met, and she will go far in life. It is not fair that you add more pain to her isolated world by making her live somewhere for three months from graduation until college."

The person in charge says to the nun, "How dare you speak to me in such a manner. I am done discussing this issue. Jerri is seventeen, and it is time for her to live on her own."

Under the vow of obedience, she orders them not to discuss the matter anymore.

This only seems to infuriate Sister Linda even more, because she says, "I cannot let that kid leave with nowhere to go. Sister Kate and I will find her a place to live. Just mark my words. That kid is going places and will accomplish more than you can ever imagine. Sometimes you ought to talk to her and know how much she has suffered, more than most of us in this building put together, and how different she feels. Maybe then you would appreciate the struggle and the miracle that she is. This is a kid who tells me that she must do well, not only for herself, but for all the kids here. She is still able to think of others, even as life continues to slap her around. She will leave the day after graduation, but we will make sure that she has a place to live."

The charge person says, "Fine," but that I should be able to do things on my own without any help, because there will be no one to help me when I leave the orphanage.

I meet them in the dining room. Both nuns are beet red and furious. Sister Kate says not to worry, she has a grandmother who has an extra bedroom, and I can rent it for the summer.

Both of them tell me just to focus on final exams and graduation. They will make all the arrangements.

My nun friends say that I have to keep focused on my goals and to believe that I am as good as other kids. I like knowing that some people believe in me.

I wonder if anyone knows how scared I am? Do parents make their kids leave home the day after graduation? How could a celebration become a time of dreadful unknowns?

What is going to happen to me when I leave the orphanage? I thought I would have a couple of months to ease the transition into college, but I have only three weeks left in this cocoon. As I look around this large building that has offered me a measure of anonymous safety, I worry about living in a world that I have never lived in. How will I know all that I need to know in order not to fail miserably?

I realize that I need to be careful so that I don't spin out of control inside with all the confusion that is swirling around. At least my nun friends Sister Linda and Sister Kate will help me to find a place to stay for the next three months.

I think sometimes that I am very lucky and blessed to have these people who act as my guardian angels. They often step in and help me on the road of life. There are times when I am not always capable of anticipating the twists and turns.

I wonder what the person in charge means saying that I'm "an adult now?" Does this mean that the day after graduation I will suddenly know everything? I wonder if all my classmates will become instant adults at seventeen and no longer need their parents or live with them? I wonder if anyone knows how young I feel sometimes? Nothing like the adult that I should be. From what I know of adulthood, it looks like a scary world that seems even more alien to me than even my school or orphanage worlds.

I really like being able to retreat to the orphanage every day, because no one notices me, especially all the ways that are not right about me. There are no labels, no expectations, no goals, and no dreams, only what I make up in my mind.

Even I get tired at times of always trying to be my own cheerleader in life. I know that my choices are either to keep moving forward or to curl up and die. Yet I wonder if even my mother or God realize the energy and the struggle that it takes for me to keep choosing a forward motion in life.

I get really tired sometimes, because I'm still afraid that there is nothing salvageable about me as a human being. Maybe I just need to keep putting one foot in front of the other and to try to keep the darkness at bay.

There is so much riding on my future, and I just can't let the past forces win. Who I am and who I will be is bigger than all the people who threw me away from their minds and hearts.

Where will I go if I fail to be the best person I can be? Is safety always a growth experience?

Today I am in great physical pain. Of course, I try to hide it and make it go away. My stomach is killing me, and my mouth hurts so much. Even though I think I have conquered my cleft palate, whenever I get a cold, I realize that it is still a part of me.

The first day of the cold, it feels like someone is punching the roof of my mouth with a thousand needles; then the next day it is all numb. The worst part about having a cold when you have cleft palate is that aside from the pain, there is the bleeding that occurs somewhere in your nose.

It takes me weeks to recover from a cold. I don't know if this is normal; of course, there is no one to ask. I don't even know anyone with cleft palate, but sometimes I wonder if my incredible pain is a common experience among other cleft palate sufferers.

One of the reasons that I don't complain about the body is that I have tried not to give in to any signs of weakness. I think the stomach pain is from all the stress of trying to appear normal and not to bother anyone for anything.

At least with my cleft palate, I have made wonderful strides. It took me until I was fifteen years old to learn how to keep food from going up to my sinus area and coming down through the hole that was never closed from my nose to my mouth.

During those two years after my mother died, while living with Daddy's family, I never went to the doctor, so I was never treated. I remember how when my mother was here, I went every two weeks to the mouth doctor. I must have lost valuable time, and the operation to close the hole wasn't done, and now it is too late.

When people ask me how much the treatment for my cleft palate costs, I just remind them that the air force is paying for it. I overheard Daddy one time saying to Grandma that they made a mistake in my birth, and the air force agreed to pay for treatments of my mouth until I am twenty-one.

I have had to learn to manage the food. My speech is now really good. All I had to do was practice, practice, practice! No matter what happened to me, I always wanted to make this birth defect invisible.

It is bad enough that inside I am a freak, but I didn't want the outside me to reflect anything that would give away who or what I really am. Except for my scar, I am doing well with the cleft palate. Only the colds remind me of its painful existence in my body.

Did my mother really love me even though I wasn't born normal? Is wholeness ever possible for a person like me?

At this country club, there is a senior family dinner dance that is open to all the high school seniors. One of my friends tells me that I should go and that she and her parents will drive me there and back.

Apparently, the students, with their parents, will have a nice banquet. Everyone is expected to wear a gown or a suit.

I tell one of the nuns about it, and she says I should go and tells me to ask the person in charge. When I ask the person in charge if I can go, she asks me if I will feel left out of everything, because I will be by myself. I tell her that I already feel left out of everything in school, but that I would like to go so that I can see how real people are.

She tells me I can go, and to pick out a dress from the donation pile in the storage room. I am so excited because I will be going to my first and last school event.

The only problem is that when people donate clothes, they just roll them up in a ball and throw them in a garbage bag. I find this green dress that looks like some material that the curtains in the orphanage are made from.

My nun friend says it looks hideous and to ask the person in charge for money to buy a gown. I hate asking for things, because when you ask, you must always know that there is a possibility that the answer might be no.

The person in charge tells me that I need to learn to make do with what I have and to be happy that there are donated clothes to pick from. "Besides," she says, "you don't want to look too fancy."

Sister Linda and Sister Kate say they will get the money to get me a proper dress. They go shopping and pick out this really pretty pink dress. They tell me not to let the person in charge know and to enjoy myself.

The person in charge always stays in her office. She really has no idea about the rest of the people in the orphanage.

Some of the nuns always watch out for us, trying to improve our lives, at least with the little things. Often, I overhear them talking about how they feel sorry for us and how happy they are that they have a good family life. Some of them even get angry over how the kids are dumped here, especially either in the middle of the night or during the holiday season.

I am just so excited, because I have never been to a place called a country club. Of course, I must brace myself for being in the presence of so many parents with their children.

I just remind myself of how different I am and that I am not as good as the other students. I will not begrudge them their happiness or good fortune to have what is truly normal—a sense of belonging. I am sure that if my mother were here, she might not have minded being seen in public with me, although with the way I have turned out, I can't be sure.

When I arrive at the country club, I see that it is so beautiful. It is more beautiful than I could have ever imagined. The tables are decorated with bright flowers and pretty white tablecloths.

Almost everyone in my class is here with their parents. It strikes me as odd that there are so many parents all gathered in one place. Maybe to be orphaned is different and unique and doesn't often happen to a child. I guess it is I who is really the odd one out in the normalcy of life.

It just seems weird that there are so many connected people in one room, yet I am disconnected from everyone who is alive in the world. The best I have is my mother—and she is dead—and God—who is busy with a multitude of things.

I just sit back and savor the moment of watching what could have been, and what should have been, even in my mother's absence. I didn't get adopted, but I have lived long enough to know that what I sought would have been okay. I am having such a good time tonight, and I believe that someday I will be in a room of connected people who will have shared their life with me.

Did my mother ever feel connected to anyone? How could parents be so right and so normal for my classmates, but not for me?

I lie in bed, reflecting on the dinner dance and try desperately to keep the whisper tears from overwhelming me. Tonight it has been brought home to me how my life is limited, and how the ordinary is all around me.

Seeing how real parents interacted in a loving manner with their children at the dinner dance almost broke me in half. There were so many women in that room tonight, acting like mothers. There is a good side to the real world out there, because no matter what happens for most of my classmates, they will always have a place called home.

As I sat with my friend, I felt like an intruder, spying on a way of life that surely is acceptable, ordinary, and real. Again, it never ceases to amaze me how people know how to act and what to do. I was especially surprised at how the parents were so nurturing toward their seventeen- and eighteen-year-old kids, even though they would be adults soon.

In spite of all the evil people my brothers and I have encountered, this world does contain parents, these remarkable human beings who, every day, do good for themselves and their children. I just know that if they knew the truth about who or what I am, I would not have been invited to the dinner party. As I lie here in the darkness, willing the whisper tears not to drown me, I wonder how I can be like everyone else in the total absence of everything that most of my classmates have had. Maybe my mother could ask God how I can keep living in this world. How can I be accepted, with all my splintered parts?

In less than a week, I will graduate from high school. I want to tell my mother that I feel terrorized by the unknown. Never have I felt so scared in my life because I don't feel equipped or ready to face a world where I have never felt welcome.

I am going to rent a room in Sister Kate's grandmother's house for twelve weeks. She is charging me twenty-five dollars a week.

I have a job lined up with the CETA program. This is a special government training section that helps people to gain a foothold in the job market.

Listening to the kids in school, I know that they are not going to be put out of their homes the day after graduation. As a matter of fact, some of my classmates won't even go away to college.

They say everything is expensive. At the prom, some students spent close to a thousand dollars. That must be a whole lot of money. The most money I have ever had was six dollars. I can't even imagine having that much money. I vow that I would be rich so I could buy anything I want.

There is one thing that I hope happens when I turn into an adult the day after graduation. I hope that all my night dreams, which continue to haunt me unceasingly, will disappear. My adult life should have nothing to do with the past seventeen years. I hate dreaming.

I hate being reminded of things I wish never happened. I wish that doubts about who or what I am didn't exist.

For me, the world beyond myself has always been a mixture of fascination, confusion, and alienation. I am afraid that there is nowhere for me to go after I leave my school world. Even though college looms ahead, I know that someday I will have to step away from the shadows where I exist.

Only I know that right now I just want to hide and not move forward because, sometimes the fear can be paralyzing.

I wonder if my mother was ever scared about the twists and turns in life? What will I do if I falter or slip? I wish I knew how to make more safety nets. Is determination enough to succeed in life?

Tonight Sister Linda and some of the other nuns give me a surprise graduation party. The person in charge didn't want me to have one, but she is away for the weekend.

The kids in the orphanage are really excited because Sister Renee has gone out of her way to bake a cake. I get a dictionary as a gift from everyone, and there is cake and sodas for all. I'm going to keep this forever as a reminder that I got something very important from nice people.

I love this dictionary because it represents the contribution of all the children at the orphanage, along with that of some of the nuns. No one really has any money.

When the person in charge found out about the party, she was angry and said she wasn't attending my graduation. She changed her mind after several nuns, including Sister Linda, said it was their idea about the party and told her not to punish me.

It doesn't matter who attends my graduation, because the party tonight is great. Amid it's simplicity of just cake and root beer soda, their giving me a gift, with all the kids around me to see, is public acknowledgment of a job well done.

Also, I know that if I could make it out of this system as a throwaway, then maybe the other kids will realize that there are also wonderful opportunities for them.

None of us, including me, is so stoic that we do not want to do well in our lives. I have been blessed in some ways, because no matter what has happened, and no matter the losses, I have stuck it out long enough to see a different life for myself.

I will hold my head up high tomorrow when I get my diploma. Although graduation is an ending, I must also accept that it is an opportunity of growth and new adventures.

Are all public recognitions a double-edged sword? Will my mother and God be somewhere cheering me on? How could a gift like a dictionary speak volumes for kids who gave so much from what little they ever had?

Even though I have so much to deal with, leaving the orphanage and entering a world that I am ill-prepared to live in, I know that I have been lucky. As I look back over these last four years of high school, I realize that I had a wonderful opportunity to make something of myself after the shattering experience I had in the second foster home, which nearly destroyed me.

In a strange way, the orphanage and North Pocono High School have allowed me to gain a direction in my life.

The orphanage, although a poor substitute for the nurturing love of an adoptive mother, saved my physical life from all the other realities of my past, except, of course, for the years of living with my mother.

School, on the other hand, has also provided a safety net. I know I am a very serious person, and I think deeply inside about a thousand and one things.

Yet here at North Pocono High School, the teachers treat me nicely, except for one. The administration is very nice, except for the guidance counselor.

So for the most part, a kid like me is able to blend in and to be part of the school system, even if only on a limited basis.

The library club helped me to become organized and resourceful through books. It also made me aware of how large the world is. People would actually ask me for help on a project or want to know where a certain book was, and I would know the answer. I got to check out the kids' books and get an idea what they are like based on what they read. Here, I am important and part of a team. Plus I like the two librarians, who don't mind if I hang around.

The debate club, with the help of the teacher, helped me to do research and to answer some of my questions. I know sometimes I asked a thousand questions about many things. It is just that I am so hungry to learn, and except for school, I never get to talk to adults on a one-on-one level.

School has allowed me to succeed and to see concrete proof that I am not stupid, at least not academically. Here at North Pocono High School, from day one, I have been building on my dreams to go to college. I have proved that I am not a total failure or loser, only partially.

To the English teacher who, in my freshmen year, refused to let me settle for less than I was capable of, to the gym teacher who taught me how to climb a rope halfway to the ceiling, to my tenth- and eleventh-grade English teachers who taught me about the literature of the ages, and to my American history teacher who made me believe that I am smart by recommending me for the history contests, I am grateful.

Then there is the teacher who provided a way for me to be in the debate club and almost all my other teachers who allowed me to learn and to grow academically. In a secret way, I felt that they approved of me, as a human being, by not making comments that would continue to wound my broken spirit.

I hope Alvernia College will be a haven of growth and acceptance like North Pocono High School has been. School has been a wonderful haven in light of the battering that comes from being a ward of the state.

Are teachers the real heroes for the success of most human beings? I wonder if my teachers know how grateful I am to them?

Today everyone received a final report card. Tomorrow is my graduation from high school.

I have come a long way since my freshmen year, when I nearly failed everything on purpose. I got five As, two Bs, and one C+ in math. Not bad for a nobody. With everything else that is on my mind, it is probably amazing that I did even this well.

See, I knew that even though some people tell me I'm stupid and that a kid like me can't make it to college, I know inside me that that is not true.

Someday I am going to be very well educated, and I will become this, not to prove anything to anyone else, but to continue doing the best I can before I die.

I can't fathom the gifts that surely I must have. Many times, even though I feel so limited, I still believe that if I continue to live an honorable life, I will discover what my purpose is.

I tell some of the nuns about my report card, and they are happy for me. Sister Linda tells me I am smarter than I realize, probably one of the smartest people she has ever met.

The person in charge says that she hopes that this report card is not a fluke. No matter, I worked hard to keep my inner life at bay so I could concentrate on trying to get straight As, and I accomplished most of my goals.

I show the other orphans my report card and tell them that the best way to get back at everyone who has ever done them wrong is to do well in school in spite of them.

Some of these kids break my heart because they don't have the ability to shut out people that try to hold them back, even if only temporarily.

In two days, these children will be gone from my life forever, struggling against such great odds. I wonder if they are strong enough, tough enough, or stubborn enough not to be crushed by everything that has been denied them?

Someday, I hope that if I become a real person, I can do something that will make a difference for kids like these, who have been left behind while everyone else moved on.

Meanwhile, here I sit, still talking to the dead and the spiritual, sharing an accomplishment with orphaned children and some nuns, none of whom will still be part of my life in two days.

I don't even tell anyone about my one-way conversations with my mother and God. On the other hand, I can't think of any other way to keep her alive and God present.

It's been some ride over these past ten years, hasn't it? From a great cocoon of unconditional love and nurturing, to a darkness of total splintering, I have slowly come toward that point of beginning to see light again.

I know in my heart that I will always remember the darkness that has been my unsolicited home for such a long time. It is in the remembering of where

I have been, and where the other orphans have been, that I can someday live a different reality.

I can still bear witness to all that has happened and still is happening to children who are "cast off in the sea of life" with no life jacket to float them for a while. I have been strong enough to swim out of the darkness. Maybe others will follow me if I continue to do well in my life.

Does hard work always pay off? What is it about me that makes me refuse to give up and just disappear from a life that I do not yet know how to live?

Today the social worker and I meet. She says she is closing my case, since I am graduating. One more time, she asks me, "What happened at the Wesson house?"

I just can't tell her, because as time has passed, I feel even more shame and embarrassment over that whole experience of foster care.

I do tell her that I am excited about going to college. I thank her for leaving me at the orphanage, rather than forcing me into another foster home.

In some ways, I will miss her, because, for the past five years, she has been the most consistent adult I have ever interacted with, even if it was only periodically.

There were even times when I would fantasize about her taking me into her home and adopting me. I know that my imagination runs wild, because knowing what she knows about my background, she would never have taken in a kid like me.

Besides, social workers don't get involved or love or become attached to the kids on their caseload. I think it's against the rules. Unfortunately, if they stick around long enough, and kids like me have no one on a long-term basis, we tend to get somewhat attached in ways that I would never admit.

I like this social worker. She did the best she could, given the kind of kid I am. Maybe if I were cuter, softer, younger, more female, more open, more lovable, and more human, I might have been adopted by some family on her adoptive parents list.

I was always hoping that she might be able to know how essential and important adoption was to me.

Maybe it's just for the best, because I wouldn't want her to know how messed up I am inside, even now at seventeen, when she thinks I've turned out all right.

I hope that someday I will be all that is not a part of my life now. As I say good-bye to the social worker, I realize that my time in the orphanage is coming to a close soon, and even she will be gone forever. As I watch her leave the orphanage, I wish her a happy life, because as a social worker, she was okay.

Maybe this is why, even in a general sense, we foster kids and orphans are told never to become attached, because the departures always hurt, even when they are just general good-byes.

Are separations always a time of pain? I wonder if the social worker ever thought about doing things differently with me if she could?

Today I sit at the end of the row of graduating students. It is not easy having your last name begin with the last letter of the alphabet, because you are always last. The person charge came, along with Sister Linda, Dad, and a friend named Jennifer, who used to be a nun.

The person in charge said I had to invite Dad since he is my legal guardian, or something like that. It's been about nine months since I have seen him or spoken to him. I wonder if Grandma Resuba knows he is coming to my graduation. Since being left in the orphanage these past four years, I have seen him only six times.

As I listen to the ceremony, it is hard for me to concentrate, because I know that this is it. In twenty-four hours, I will have to leave everything and everyone I have ever known.

Although I never told anyone about my conversations inside my head with my mother and God, I'm glad I started talking to both of them so long ago. I only wish that both of them were here in the flesh so that my mother could smother me in an embrace and keep out the world that I now have to live in.

They are calling our names one by one, and we go to the front of the gym and receive our diplomas. Finally there will be the proof of my existence on a piece of paper. It reflects that I was able to stick with something and accomplish a goal.

I have a sinking feeling that everything I have ever known will change tomorrow morning. In two months, I will leave for college, never to return to a city that has offered only painful reminders of how there has been no protection, no nourishment, and no nurturing for me. I know that it is not about the people who live here; rather, it is that I just didn't quite measure up to being normal and good enough.

The ceremony is almost ending. Most of my classmates are going to big family celebrations where, they said, they will get a lot of money and presents. Several students are getting cars as their graduation gift. Many are going to this thing called Senior Week. I must just get through tonight and steel myself for the leaving of all that I have ever known.

The ceremony is over. Outside the high school, Dad wishes me good luck and goes to his car. He waves good-bye and goes home.

I go back to the orphanage and prepare for the good-byes, spoken and unspoken. I show the kids my diploma. The little ones are impressed and tell me that they are going to get one someday. I hope all these kids get what they need and want someday.

Does a piece of paper define who I am, or only what I have done? I wonder if my mother would have had a family celebration if she had lived? How come Dad didn't get me a graduation gift or card? How do I stop the racing darkness from consuming me?

Everyone is in bed. I can't sleep, because I know that the end is only hours away.

I pack what little clothes I have in two cardboard boxes. Earlier, I went through the pile of donated clothes and tried to pick out pants and shirts that might fit me.

The person in charge gave me my passbook savings account that has $1,200 in it. That sounds like a lot of money. I'll probably be able to live on it for the next four years of college.

She wished me good luck. I asked if I could come back to visit, and she said no. She told me it was best that I just go away, make a life for myself, and forget about the past seventeen years. The person in charge said that people are not interested in what has happened to me, and they might find me a bit strange.

She says that if I tell anyone about my past, they will wonder if I am like other kids. Besides, she says, I will be an adult tomorrow when I leave, and adults don't dwell on their past. I never did understand why the person in charge didn't like me, or why she thought it was important to be so domineering over kids like me who have no one who cares.

I just have to pretend that whatever happened didn't affect me, and I will not hang around, because there is no place for me here.

Tomorrow Sister Linda and Sister Kate will drive me to the house where I will be renting a room.

I will not be permitted to come back to the orphanage or to call. I'll just have to pretend that all these years, all these people, and all my experiences never existed.

It is so dark, and I am so scared that I won't be able to make it in the real world. I try not to be the eight-year-old kid that I really am inside. It is hard to be seventeen, eight, and every age in between.

Somehow I don't feel as together inside as I thought I would after I graduated from high school. This diploma only makes me look book smart, but I still fail in the real world, where there is nowhere to go and no one to turn to. I just want to curl up and not have to face another day.

Will the unknown overwhelm me with expectations I can't reach? Why doesn't being a grown-up feel like an exciting, liberating experience? Are all life changes this scary?

It is the day after graduation, yet strangely, I do not feel any different than yesterday; I am no more grown-up than I was. I am still seventeen, unwanted and scared. All the stuff I own are in two cardboard boxes. Most of what I have are books that I just have to take with me. The person in charge had already given me my bankbook and wished me good luck in my life.

Sister Kate and Sister Linda take me to the house where I will be renting a room. They too wish me good luck and say they will be in touch.

I talk to the old woman for a little while and then go to my room.

So this is what it means to be an adult. I sit alone in an unwelcoming city, knowing no one, surrounded by my boxes, and wondering, What am I going to do with the rest of my life?

This morning at the orphanage as I was leaving, the kids surrounded me, saying good-bye. Some of the little ones were crying. We all knew that when a kid leaves, we would never see him or her again. I know that I will never see anyone that I have ever known again.

No one will ever know the world that I came from, or believe anything that has happened to me during these past ten years. Now I will become an automatic adult with no training, and I will be expected to act like other people.

I lie in bed, so confused about how I am ever going to function as an alien in this people world. The thing that haunts me the most is that there is no turning back and no hope of ever being nurtured or being in a family.

This is it! The end of all childhood needs and the beginning of adulthood based on a foundation of the absence of the ordinary.

Now comes the really big challenge of trying to be okay when all I want to do is go away into a dark cave and disappear. Nothing has prepared me for anything I am now about to encounter.

Maybe I need to make everything that is missing from my life unimportant, like I used to do as a kid. I will just pretend that whatever happened never did, and if it did, then I wasn't affected. I will be a person with no past, only a future.

Are other kids my age completely shut off or abandoned by their past? If I keep separating everything in my life, will I ever have a whole life to live?

Even though it has been less than a day since I left the orphanage, it already seems like a lifetime, almost as if that whole experience is something separate from my outside life. I will always be secretly grateful that the orphanage existed long enough for me to graduate from high school.

One plan that I have been thinking about in order not to draw attention to myself is to be an observer in life instead of a player. The most obvious reason is that I realize it is not possible for me to function in a world that I know little about. Another reason is that if I observe people long enough, I will know how to interact and to feel like they do.

I believe that there are things about me that are not right; otherwise, I would have been adopted a long time ago. Maybe I can try to overcome these things if I watch and study people.

Someday in the future, I won't always feel so splintered, or so isolated, but for now, I just have to look at everything from here on out as a learning experience. While I really miss the fortress of the orphanage, with its embracing anonymous cloak, I know I can't yearn for what is now over.

Now, at seventeen, is a new beginning, but it will not be based on the past. I will look at the world as if it were my first glance at it. I know this is a tall order, but, hopefully, nothing that has happened during the last seventeen years will have anything to do with my life from here on out.

For the next couple of years, I will continue to become more book smart, and maybe, if I observe enough, I could become people smart.

How do human beings evolve into people who are noticed and accepted by others? In particular, how do kids like me learn to get along in life with no preparation for it so that people just see us as normal?

These first few weeks are going fast. Working, coming back to my room, and trying to get ready for my college adventure keeps me busy. I always read in my room, so that the thoughts of the past don't bombard me. Every day I realize how many different worlds there are outside of my self.

I work at this place that is an army depot. It is like a factory where I do the same job over and over again. I will use the money to pay my rent and to eat out, since I don't know how to cook or where to keep food. After all, I'm only renting a room.

Dad works there also, but he hasn't told anyone that I am his daughter, at least in a legal sense.

In some ways, the dying of my heart toward him is becoming more and more complete. I talked to Trevor a while back, and he told me that Dad isn't good enough to be a father to us. He said that both he and Tyler want nothing to do with him. He also said that it is in my best interest to forget about having ever loved him, because he really never loved us.

Maybe my brothers are right. Why am I the last to let go of something that died the morning my mother did? All I know is that I could never love and nurture a child as my own, invite that child to love me as a mother, and then walk away because he or she is not my flesh and blood.

After all these years I still can't understand or accept that flesh and blood is so much more important than relationship or heart bonding.

Maybe some part of me will always be that kid wondering why my bastard blood can't overcome all the good I try to do.

When I think of the terrible suffering and losses experienced by Billy, Trevor, Tyler, and me in the name of the flesh-and-blood family, I am still, after all these years, unable to comprehend any of their rationalizations.

It is strange how the worlds of family, friends, school, church, and work never intersect with my own survival list and inner world. I think my problem is that I love from such a passionate place in my heart that it is so hard for me to accept that people change and life changes. Maybe that is why my brothers were able to see Daddy's family for what they were a long time before I did. I was trying to still be a daughter, even when he walked away.

If I become more educated, will I understand people more? Did Joseph worry about Jesus not being his flesh and blood? Did Jesus love Joseph as a daddy? Did Joseph love Jesus as a son?

In two days I will be ready for the next leg of my journey in life. Time has passed quickly. It seems like only yesterday that my mother was kissing me good-bye. Now, ten years later, I am leaving everything and everyone I have ever known for a chance at a life that will be different and, hopefully, more inviting.

I sit in my room, looking at what I will be taking with me to Reading, Pennsylvania. There are two cardboard boxes for me to pack. Basically, I have a couple pair of pants and shirts, along with about a hundred books that have taught me about life.

My favorite, a book called *Death, Be Not Proud*, is about the relationship of this teenage boy dying of a brain tumor with his family. I think I have read it about eight times, and with each reading, I have learned something new.

This kid fights to live, and his parents do everything possible to find help and to nurture him. He ends up dying at the end of the book, but what an extraordinary life he lives because of his ability to touch people and make a difference.

I also want to make a difference in life, maybe not by dying of a brain tumor, but by living in such a way that the world is better because of my existence. I know that at this time, as I sit in the lonely city of Scranton, surrounded by my boxes, it won't appear that I have done anything worthwhile, but just wait when I grow and get stronger.

Sometimes I think that God just waits to see what I will do in response to the curves that life throws at me. I am not going to be defeated by anyone or any event, because nothing could begin to compare to the waking nightmare of these past ten years.

What happened should never have happened, and in the end, it didn't need to happen. But people make choices about children, and sometimes the ramifications linger long after the adults have moved on. I just know that I will be okay if I take what I have learned and experienced, and use it to make life work for me, instead of against me.

I wonder, do all moves in life require such heartrending reflections? And then I ask, how will I pack together all the splintered pieces of my self as I move on in life?

Tomorrow is the day that begins the rest of my life. I just know that I will flourish when I get to college, because as long as I can remember, I have wanted to go to a place that would appreciate my mind.

I do have such dreams for myself that I believe can only be accomplished by moving forward. All the packing is done, now I lie in bed thinking about the dreams that I have.

I have made a list of dreams that can only come true by my going to college:

1) My mind will grow, and my hunger to learn will be satisfied.
2) I will make real friends in my school world and my personal life.
3) Maybe I can travel to see places like Washington DC or New York.
4) I hope someday that all the worlds I live in will intersect.
5) Maybe I will find a way of living life that reflects the good things about me.
6) I will live independently and not fall apart.
7) All my uncertainties about identity will disappear.
8) I can finally move closer to changing my name.
9) Maybe I could make this shame I feel go far away.
10) I want to celebrate birthdays and holidays.
11) Maybe I can make a family of friends for myself.
12) Hopefully, I will be respected for my knowledge and hard work.

13) I hope I can know what God wants from my life.

14) I will have proved to myself that I am not a loser or a bastard.

15) I could become that most elusive thing—a whole woman.

I get tired sometimes, and that is why I make lists. When I get overwhelmed and begin to think about myself like other people do, I take out my lists of accomplishments and dreams and re-center myself on what is really real for me.

Why do I feel such power from simple lists of things I want in life? Do the dreams in lists keep my soul from drying up? Are my dreams the dreams all parents have for their children? Or are they the dreams that children have for themselves?

Today is the day that I finally leave Scranton for Reading, to attend Alvernia College. I know I shouldn't blame the people of this city, but all I have ever known here were people who caused me great pain and sadness.

My brothers are also leaving, but they are going to join the military. Trevor says that he wants nothing to do with the state of Pennsylvania and just wants to start a new life somewhere else. He probably has the best idea—just leave, and don't look back, because truly, there is no one, and there really has never been anyone that has ever been here for us.

Trevor has one more year of high school and now lives with Dad. He will be going into the navy when he graduates. He says this is his ticket to a new and better life, and he doesn't plan to ever return.

So today marks an ending to a life that has been splintered beyond recognition since my mother died. It also marks a beginning of new growth with, hopefully, a life filled with dreams of hope.

I pinch myself sometimes because all my hard work toward this goal of college is finally paying off. Although I will not leave Pennsylvania as my brothers will, I will not be returning to the Scranton area, unless Trevor needs me before he graduates from high school.

Maybe a new start is what Trevor, Billy, Tyler, and I need. It has been years since I have seen Billy and Tyler. Trevor and I see each other every once in a while. Since that Christmas Eve separation so long ago, we have been going in different directions.

I think the really sad part is that each of us has suffered such pain and hurt that we need to spend all our energy healing ourselves. There is so little energy left over to try to put together what little threads of connections have been left after all the abrupt separations of the past.

Our blood was so different that we became pariahs to all the people who should have been responsible. We could not change our "bastard" blood, so in the end, we all chose different ways to change ourselves.

Probably the only thing we have in common, besides those two years in the coal cellar, is our desire to outrace a past that we didn't deserve. Scranton has been the symbol of our waking and sleeping nightmare, which will always be part of our life experience. I wonder if the good people in Scranton know about the evil that exists in their town.

How could a place become so frightful that four orphans wait for the day to leave it forever? How could some people living there make a tragedy even more tragic?

I think I need to decide what I will say or not say about my past, because I know how inquisitive people are. Even after four years, the social worker was still asking about the second foster place. Maybe that is how people are, they just want to know things about the past that are sometimes easy to share and at other times rather difficult.

In high school, I have learned that my being at the orphanage invited many questions that I never wanted to answer. It is very difficult to explain to anyone how an entire family, flesh and blood or adoptive, couldn't find room for me or my brothers.

I know with regard to me, at least in the beginning, it was because of my speech defect, my ugliness, and my changing from a girl to a boy, and then, finally, to a nothing. Then as time evolved, with no adoptive mother for me or rescue by a family, it became clear that there were things wrong with me, that no one could love or nurture me.

I can't tell anyone the real reasons why I was never chosen for adoption, because even I don't want to know how horribly I failed as a person. When I go to college tomorrow, I will just pretend that I never existed before now. I think I will do the following:

1) I will tell people that my parents are dead, and my family lives far away.
2) I will never mention my years as a ward of the state, since that will invite questions of why Daddy, his family, and my mother's family never came to take care of us. I get nervous when any conversation turns personal.
3) I will pretend that nothing ever happened since my mother's death, that I am normal like other eighteen-year-olds, although I know this is not true.

4)   I will try never to draw attention to myself.

5)   I will make sure people don't make me feel bad.

6)   I will make sure I don't look at people. It feels as though someone is shining a bright light in my face when I look at people. I think that I am afraid that if I look at them, they will know the truth about me, that I am a freak.

7)   I will also make sure that any friends I make won't end up hating me.

8)   I will just tell people that family is not important.

9)   I will try, to the best of my ability, to blend in with everyone else.

Do people really need to know my past in order to know me now? How come there are so many pieces of me that I feel compelled to keep hidden?

I am waiting for the bus to come. In my hand is my Greyhound one-way ticket out of Scranton, allowing me to go off to follow my dream of freedom.

The buses look so big, and I feel so small. Everyone is carrying these things called suitcases. Actually, they look nicer and better than the two cardboard boxes I am lugging haphazardly.

The taxi ride to the bus station is expensive, almost $7. I have to be careful with my money, since $1,200 has to last for four years. I don't have any money saved from working at the army depot, because I was earning only a minimum wage. I had to pay for rent and food. I also gave Trevor some money and bought the bus ticket for college.

The bus is pulling into the station, and as I begin to get in line, I get nervous. How could I feel so afraid to get on the bus that will take me away from this place called Scranton to that life-giving city of Reading? Maybe I am just scared because there is nowhere to turn.

Now is my time to search for a more hospitable place that will embrace me as I am. I sit in my window seat, and I feel like I'm sitting on top of the world.

Inside me, the body is feeling nervous as the bus pulls away from the station. It is hard for me to breathe sometimes when my stomach is all tensed up. I use my mind to relax the stomach by breathing in and out and just focusing on a mountainside filled with flowers.

The countryside is so beautiful. It makes me want to do a lot of traveling someday. All the houses I pass make me wonder about all the families that live in them. It is a big world, and there is so much land with so many roads. I hope that as we pull into Reading I will have pulled myself together and not appear nervous.

As the bus pulls into the station in Reading, I think that now is my time to be a person. I call for a cab and hope that I am doing the right thing. Hopefully, I will be able to accomplish all my dreams.

Do things like buses also carry other people with dreams like mine? Will I always know with certainty that I am on the right track? How will I know that I have succeeded?

I wait for a cab to come to the station to pick me up and drive me to Alvernia College. I wonder what I am doing here as I stand in this strange city, ready to meet people I have never seen before.

In the real world, people walk fast and just pass by one another on the street, never acknowledging one another. I still can't get over how fast the cars move as I cross the street to the other side, with my two cardboard boxes holding everything I own.

I remember how a long time ago I had asked my daddy if my mother was ever coming back, because I believed with all my heart the parable of the mustard seed.

Truly, no child or adult had my faith and belief that only the mustard seed could provide. When I was told that no matter how much I believed, my mother was never going to be part of my life, I was crushed beyond all measure, and beyond all words. Yet I found a way to make her alive, even if it was only in my heart. Maybe I just found a way to turn my mustard seed of fantasy into a mustard seed of reality.

I know that some fractures of the heart cannot be as they were before the brokenness. My mother's living in heaven almost broke not only my heart but my spirit as well. I had to find a way to make sense of it all before I became so devastated that I wouldn't be able to live without her.

All these years, I made her into my angel, someone that I told every night what happened to me during the day. From fantasy to reality, I have learned that in my mind, I can make most things work in my favor. At least I try to learn some lessons when things don't work out, and I move on with my life.

As I stand here, still waiting for the taxi to pick me up, I know I've spent years pursuing this dream of college, which began as the fantasy of an orphaned child. Now it has turned into a reality of a girl/woman who just keeps believing that all things are possible.

Who would have thought that from the isolation of the coal cellar a "bastard orphan" would stand on the brink of entering a world of acceptance through hard work, perseverance, and determination? Education is a wonderful gateway to life.

Does my mother see me now? Do all people have to climb mountains of doubts before they can reach the mountaintop of acceptance? Does my belief in the mustard seed of reality mean that I have remained faithful to seeking what is needed in my life?

"A New World"

Beginnings start slowly with great caution,
Ways of knowing never fully understood or welcome.
Arrival at the places of the heart takes unexpected turns,
Often leading to experiences that open new adventures of living.

Confusion is sometimes the order of the day,
Roadmaps make the journey more understandable.
As the woman / child tries to find her way in this New World,
That never was known before and therefore not prepared to enter.

People seem so different from one another,
Expectations are as many as the prisms of light.
Which offer both brightness and darkness,
With many colors of gray in between obscuring her view.

She only wants what can be earned with sheer determination,
A way of life that could define what she never knew.
But had in the shadow of her life experience yearned,
To know so that her walk could be in this life not parallel to it.

The past had been the outside looking in,
Years spent in a mirror-like existence always searching.
For the entrance that could open a life experience,
That would invite her to be part of a peopled life and not apart.

Separation, intended and sought by others in her childhood,
is not the dream or reality that she seeks.
Only the merging of what she knew before the childhood plundering,
Could make her feel alive and part of the ordinary.

The College Years: Survival in the Outside World
Ages 17 - 24

The College Years:
Survival in the Outside World

(Ages Seventeen to Twenty-Four)

Dear Mother,

The taxi is finally here. I put my boxes into the trunk, because the cab driver says he can't life heavy things. Since I cleaned all those years in the orphanage, I am accustomed to lifting heavy objects.

As we enter the grounds of Alvernia College, I marvel at its beauty and thank God that I was able to stick with my goals. Finally, I will become a different person, a better person. No one here will ever know about my failure to be normal enough to be part of a family. Here, all that will count is how I am as a student.

I do hope that I can make friends. The world is mine to conquer. At least in college, I will be on equal footing with everyone else for the most part.

There are a thousand and one questions that kids always want to know when they meet someone new. I have already decided that the following will be answers to the standard questions like, Who are you? Where did you come from? Who are your parents? What do they do for a living? and other similar inquires.

1) *I have lived in upstate Pennsylvania but traveled a lot because my parents were in the military.*

2) *My parents are dead, and I have no living relatives, except for my brothers, whom I haven't seen for years. As the person in charge said, no one is interested in my past; I should just pretend nothing happened and start with a "clean slate."*

3) *I will be extremely protective of my inner turmoil and confusion about life. I especially need to pretend that my life has been like that of other college students, so no one will ask curious questions. I need to make sure*

247

that I keep all the different ages in their boxes, so no one will think that I am immature or not really a whole human being. Even though I can only be half human, I cannot let other people know this part of myself.

4) *I must make sure that my conversations with you and God stay in my head, so I don't appear crazy. I will probably die by the time I reach thirty-one years old, because I shouldn't outlive you. It is important that I take the time that is left on my hands and use it wisely, without drawing attention to myself.*

5) *I have to become as educated as I can, so that I can make up for all the ways that set me apart. In some ways, I am so unsure of who or what I am. Maybe if I get educated, I can compensate for what I lack. I must study harder than the other kids so that I don't flunk out.*

6) *I still need to practice my speech because I'm not sure if it is clear or crisp enough. No one wants to listen to someone who can't speak properly. Even after all these years of practice, I still work on beating the cleft palate. There is still the severe pain in the roof of my mouth, and there is still blood when I blow my nose when I have a cold. I also have a slight lisp when I speak. However, I have come a long way from when you were alive.*

7) *I also must never tell these real friends about the years in foster care, the coal cellar, or the orphanage. I'm afraid no one would accept me as a friend if they knew how rejected and unwanted I was. I will live by my survival list, because I don't know how else someone like me could survive and live. I want people to like me and not feel repelled by where I have been. I have had enough rejection to last a lifetime.*

Does everyone protect parts of themselves that are scary and confusing as much as I do? Mother, if you were alive and knew the whole truth about me, would you continue to be proud of me?

Love,
Jerri

*   *   *

As I get out of the taxi and pay my bill, a female student named Becky greets me. She says that she is on the welcoming committee at Alvernia College. She asks me where my suitcases are, and I tell her I have two boxes in the trunk with my stuff in them. I lift them out and begin to follow her into the dorm. In the dorm, I am being introduced to the nun who is in charge of the student life, and a woman with a lot of red hair. Both people seem rather nice.

Becky says she will show me to my room, which I will be sharing with one other student. Afterward, we will take a tour of the campus, and then I can go to the picnic planned for the incoming freshmen. I leave my boxes in my room. There is a lot of space for one person. I don't own enough stuff to fill the closet or the drawers.

As I start on the campus tour, the other students arrive with their parents. They all have much more stuff than I do. Mostly, what I notice are all the pretty suitcases that the students have. None of them have arrived by taxi or carrying cardboard boxes like I did. Maybe this is another way in which it is apparent that I have lived such a different life. I decide that the next time I move somewhere I will make sure that I have suitcases. I can't do much about the parent part, but at least I can do away with the cardboard boxes.

In the orphanage, no one had luggage, especially nothing as pretty as some of the suitcases that the freshmen are moving in with. Usually the kids came and went so often that they carried everything they owned in a brown paper bag. Someday, I'm going to own a really pretty set of luggage, so I won't stand out that much. In the people world, the kids live so differently.

So far, I have been greeted with kindness—from Becky's welcome, to my welcome by the staff at the dorm and at the freshmen's picnic. I hope that I will find my niche and be able to blend in in this school.

I wonder if my mother ever went to college? Did she own suitcases? Does the kind of luggage I own represent where I have been and where I am going? Do cardboard boxes hold all the things a person can own?

The picnic is really nice. It is hard to believe that I am here at college. There are so many faces and names to learn, not to mention the personality behind each person.

People are introducing themselves by shaking hands. Apparently, shaking hands is a standard form of introduction among human beings. Even though I don't like to be touched, I force myself to greet people with a handshake.

There is plenty of food and talk about what everyone is going to study. Here, for the first time in my school life, I feel like it is okay to talk about how excited I am about being at Alvernia College.

I tell these people that I'm going to study history so that I can be a lawyer someday, or a missionary. I am asked repeatedly, a thousand times over, about my background and where I come from.

I begin by saying that my parents were in the air force and that they were killed in an accident. I tell them that I'm not really from anywhere and have no living relatives except for a brother out West. Also, I say that I don't like to talk about my past, I just want to focus on the future.

I realize that this version of my life is not exactly on target. However, I have no living relatives to speak of. My mother did die in an accident, and I really don't belong anywhere and never have. So maybe I just told a slightly altered version of the truth.

It would be impossible for me to tell the truth—that I am nobody's child and was a ward of the state, a foster kid, an unadoptable orphan whose entire family walked away. Even now I still feel such shame and embarrassment that I never became good enough to be chosen.

Explaining one's life, or lack of life, can be very complicated at times. College is a new world. Since I have never fit in anywhere before, I don't want to blow the opportunity of belonging by having these people think that I am a freak and that no one wanted me. I will continue to keep my inner world hidden.

How could I ever tell these potential friends about the things that happened to me without them turning their backs on me too? Does the truth always set us free? Does everyone's past reflect on the possibilities of their future? Will the fear of discovery ever go away?

I have a roommate, but only temporarily. Tomorrow I will be given a single room, which I will pay some extra money to have.

I tell the nun in charge of the dorm that I snore very loudly, and I need to have my own room. I don't want to cause any problems, and I know that there are things wrong with me.

My roommate is really nice, except that she has this *Playgirl* calendar, with a picture of a naked man, thumbtacked on her wall. I never knew that there was such a physical difference between naked men and women. I didn't say anything because maybe, at eighteen, I should know everything.

The only problem is that the longer I stay in this people world, the more I realize that I know very little about people on all levels, from physical to emotional.

I can also now make sense of that one memory I have of my biological father and the car ride in the desert. I have asked for a single room because I just want to be left alone in my isolated inner world that no one can understand. I won't really say why I want to be by myself, because everyone walking into our room thinks the pinup calendar is really cool.

What is wrong with me? It isn't just the *Playgirl* calendar that makes me want to have my own room. It is also that I don't want anyone to find out about my night dreams and the fact that it sometimes takes me hours to fall asleep.

At the orphanage, I would sit in the hallway by the night-light, reading or thinking for hours. I would then crawl into bed after all the other kids had stopped crying their whisper tears and had fallen asleep.

Here at college, people tend to watch each other and pop into each other's rooms unannounced. With my own room, I will be able to balance my school life and my private world so that I won't draw attention to myself. I tell my roommate that I get up early to study every morning, so I'm getting my own room so I won't bother her. I don't mention the *Playgirl* calendar because I don't want her to think I'm weird.

I also have to remember that some taxpayers or private individuals have put hard-earned money into a scholarship for me. I want to use this opportunity that has been given to me to study and not squander this gift.

I can't deal with the inside of me, or the stuff about the *Playgirl* calendar. I need to focus on what is relevant for my survival and for the next couple of years.

How do I keep focused on my goals with all the distractions that life has to offer? Can nourishing only the mind and soul make me almost totally human? Are there a lot more things about men and women that I don't know about? Is life knowledge important for someone like me?

Here at college, I feel like I have come from a faraway planet and was dropped in the middle of an alien world. From the suitcases to the *Playgirl* calendar to TV watching, I feel at times overwhelmed by everything.

There is very little in this college life that resembles my experience as an orphan. Sometimes I feel like I am running a marathon without a chance to rest. Part of me wants to be this eighteen-year-old adult woman, but the reality is that I haven't a clue about what I am doing and how I am supposed to be. It is like I am eight years old, fast-forwarded ten years by the total absence of the ordinary, and now I'm eighteen and still going on eight. Hopefully, I will find a way to be a person without the benefits of the ordinary. Maybe I could be like the roadrunner, always getting up and trying to outsmart the darkness.

On weekends at this college, most of the kids go home for the two days. The dorm on a Friday night has an eerie quiet about it. Only about ten students out of ninety are left, most of them are from out of state.

One of the neatest things about dorm life is that I have access to a TV any time of the day or night. There are no rules here, except for the ones I make for myself. In the orphanage, we never watched TV that much, except on Sunday evenings. One thing that I have discovered is that I like getting up on a Saturday morning and watching cartoons. I have never watched cartoons before, as far as I can remember. I think about how creative people must be in order to make a cartoon that is bright, colorful, fast, and funny.

Sometimes I wonder if there is something wrong with me because I want to get up and watch cartoons. I know that I am eighteen years old now, but inside I feel so young. I just want to experience what I have missed. I am hoping that somehow I can come close to almost catching up with the other kids that are my age. Maybe cartoons are just a symbol of the missing child pieces that got lost in the "shuffle madness" of my past.

Do adults always need to grow up first? Can large chunks of ordinary growth be stepped on and still allow a kid to turn out normal? Will I always still be going on eight years old inside?

I think I am finally starting to make some friends among the college students. There is this boy named Matthew who likes to sing a lot. He says that he is going to be a psychologist someday—someone who fixes a person's mind. He says he also loves to act and sing.

Even though he is a commuter, he spends a lot of time on campus even after classes are over. There is a piano in the administration building down by the auditorium, where we gather to listen to him play and sing.

Sometimes there are four or five of us there, just listening and enjoying being in each other's company. One of my favorite songs that Matthew sings is *The Wedding Song*. It is about how adults learn to love one another with the blessing of God and other people. I like the song because I think that it must be really neat to love other people, even for men and women who end up getting married.

I know that marriage is not possible for something or someone like me, but I like listening to the songs anyway, because they tell me about people's experiences that I will never know.

Matthew is so alive and really enjoys what he does. He has so much talent, and there is an excitement about life when I am around him. He tells me that he has a wonderful family, right down to his little sister, Faith, and a cat named Chuck.

He says he is sorry that I don't have parents because his mom and dad are the best. In his family, he is surrounded by sisters, but they are okay. Mostly he says that he is happy to be in college, where he can learn as much as he can and do some singing and acting.

When I ask him why he wants to become a psychologist, he says he thinks it is the best way to help people with their problems. Matthew figures that he has had a good life and now wants to give back some of that goodness someday to other people.

I know that I will have a friend in Matthew and, hopefully, in other students I am meeting. I did make the right choice to come to Alvernia College, and will make the best of every opportunity that comes my way.

Do people who become friends become a support system to each other? Are friends necessary for learning how to live? Will people like Matthew help me become a more adjusted person for having known him?

One thing that I am learning is that there are all kinds of people in the world. In the Bible, I have always read about how the most forsaken in the world are the orphans and the widows.

I have met many orphans, but today, I met my first widow. Her name is Celeste, and Matthew tells me that her husband died a while back. She has two children close to our ages, and she is returning to college to get her education.

When Matthew introduces us, she reaches out to touch me, but I tell her, rather abruptly, "Please, don't touch me." She apologizes, but then I tell her that I just don't like to be touched, it's not her fault. She has very kind eyes and a ready smile.

Celeste will be a history major like me, and she might become the oldest friend that I will make here at Alvernia. We spend some time exchanging pleasantries, and I find out that we have a lot of classes together.

She says that her two children are still in middle school and high school and that she has to work her schedule around them. She also says that her husband died a few years ago, and she wants to move on with her life, so she is going to college.

When Matthew and Celeste leave, I sit on the grass, trying to sort things out. When Celeste talks about her husband, I sense such great pain and sadness in her. It is probably her son and daughter who keep her going, yet I wonder if they are enough to ease her out of her darkness.

I also sense that she must have a lot of spirit, because she loved, on a level that I will never know, a man who was her partner and the father of her children. To have loved someone as intensely as she did her husband and then to have lost that someone when they died in the midst of their life together, that must have rocked her world.

I guess when someone loves someone deeply, the unexpected losses of life can also shake the life that a person like Celeste must have known.

Marriage must be an intense relationship. I guess if married people love their children passionately together, then for someone who is widowed like Celeste, she must now have to do double work alone in order to keep living in this world. She probably has to love her children as both she and her husband planned, but by herself.

Maybe that is why Jesus always talked with such tenderness about the widows and the orphans. In some ways, Celeste and I must know the shared experiences of being intensely loved, wanted, and needed, and we both were left behind.

How does the widow ever learn to live again? Do widows have the same ways of living with their losses as the orphan child? Is Celeste better for having loved and lost or would it have been better never loving at all and not losing?

Sometimes, here at college, I feel like a little kid in a candy store, only, it is really a "people store." There must be a thousand different kinds of people that I encounter every day. I've met a widow who actually kept her children after her husband died. I am also meeting the people in my classes, all of whom are different from one another.

As much as I love history and learning, it has always been people who have held such fascination for me. Even at eighteen years old, I still desire to learn how to be a normal human being. I often get scared that I might not accomplish the goals and dreams that I've set for myself. Sometimes I am afraid that all the messiness since my mother's death and the confusion about so many things will come spilling out, and everyone will know that I am only half human, and maybe not even that.

I figure if I am around people, maybe I could absorb their good qualities and learn how to push myself toward fulfilling my dreams of being acceptable and okay. Sometimes I think that there are parts of me that are childlike—like being afraid of people and the dark, or wanting so desperately to fit in somewhere. I think that if I keep meeting all kinds of people, then maybe I will find a way to become a real person who isn't afraid of her own shadow.

There are times when I wonder whom I should trust and how to make people like me. It's hard to concentrate on making friends and going to classes. I always have to weigh everything against my "Do not let anyone know" list. I also wouldn't want anyone to know that I carry all these versions of me at different ages that never grew up inside me, because even though I am now eighteen, in some ways I'm still eight years old.

People make me nervous and yet intrigue me in ways that I don't understand. Part of the reason is that I try to make up for what I have lost since my mother's death. I worry that people will resent it that I want to be around them, or they might think I want attention from them. All I really want is a chance to catch up and not feel a half step behind all the time.

How come people still fascinate me even with my history of abandonment by people? Will I ever be able to absorb enough people knowledge that will make up for all that has been denied me?

One of the girls makes a comment about the clothes I am wearing. She asks me why I wear men's clothes so much. I get red in the face and tell her that I'm going to go shopping soon.

There must be a difference between men's shirts and pants and woman's shirts and pants, but I don't see the difference.

In the orphanage, I always tried to pick out clothes from the pile that wasn't too dirty or wrinkled. Maybe I was picking from the men's pile but didn't know it. No one ever said anything about how clothes are supposed to look or fit. I figured a shirt was a shirt, and a pair of pants was a pair of pants.

I decide that I will take my money, call a taxi, and go to the nearest place called a mall. I've heard that malls have a thousand stores. When I get there, I will buy twelve shirts and twelve pants from the women's section. I figure twelve is a good number because there are twelve months, one for each set of clothes. Then I will throw away all the clothes I got from the orphanage. I can't walk around having people think that I don't know the differences between men and women, at least about clothes anyway.

At the Berkshire Mall, there are all these clothes stores to pick from. I find a place called the Gap, with a million pants folded on the shelves.

I have never been clothes-shopping before, and there has to be a thousand things to buy in this store. I tell the saleslady that I want to go to the women's section, and there I see these pants called corduroys. She asks me what size I am, and I ask her what she means. She says that she thinks I'm a size 10 and gives me a pair to try on.

She says I have to try on the pants in the dressing room. I can feel myself getting red, because I feel embarrassed changing into these new clothes even though she can't see me. I always try to pretend the body doesn't exist.

I try one pair of pants on, which seems to fit. I tell the saleslady that I want to buy one pair of each color. She tells me there are fourteen different colors, and I say I'll take one of each. In addition, I try a shirt on and tell her that I'll take one of each of them to match the fourteen pairs of pants. The saleslady asks me if I am sure. I tell her yes, I have cash in my pocket.

The bill is almost $300, a lot of money out of my fund, but the clothes will last for four years. That leaves me with about $900 for the next four years. It must be expensive to live in the people world.

I don't really have much of a choice, because I don't want to wear men's clothes. I already have enough problems inside me about my female image from the past ten years. For now, I am trying to pretend these things do not exist.

Why is trying to be a female in a people world so complicated? How come there are a thousand and one ways that I am different from my fellow classmates? If I had my mother for those ten years instead of the "shuffle madness," would I have been less unsure about who or what I am?

As I look around me at all the changes in my life since leaving the orphanage, I realize that I have come a long way. I never told my mother about a life lesson I learned when I was a ward of the state, and I still practice it today.

One of the hardest things for me to accept as a child was the fact that I couldn't have a home and a mother like all the other girls I went to school with. I used to be in agony inside my head over the losses that I didn't choose or want. I didn't even have a clue how to get what I once knew with my mother before she went to live with God. It got to be so bad in the orphanage—wanting what I could not have, the ordinary, especially after being with Mrs. Wesson—that I began making myself sick.

Some nights I would bend over, doubled from so much stomach pain that I couldn't even walk. I learned to start talking to myself by saying "It's okay, it's okay" over and over, even though nothing about the world I lived in was okay. After a while, I began thinking that maybe part of my problem, besides everyone abandoning me and hating me for existing, was that I wanted too much out of life.

I decided to try to be thankful for the crumbs of life thrown my way and not to try to get a slice or a whole loaf of bread that symbolically represented life for me.

Maybe kids like me should learn to make the best of what is given to them, like the time Sister Margo in eighth grade was kind to me, even though as a nun, I knew she was not really allowed to care for me in the way I wanted. Or the time that the nice new librarian at the high school brought colored Easter eggs to the orphanage, or the time that Sister Jill allowed the kids to hug her, and she even hugged them back. Maybe if I learn to focus on the crumbs of life, I won't notice how much of the loaf I am missing.

Now, even in college, when I get stressed, I still have those episodes of not being able to breathe, with severe stomach pains, but I just remind myself over and over, "It's okay, it's going to be okay." I try to remember what I now have and how I've made it this far in life. Look, I'm eighteen and in college, when most kids who are wards of the state or foster kids don't even make it out of high school. I tried really hard not to let life make me crazy, though

I must admit that sometimes it is hard work keeping myself from giving in to the darkness that still hovers behind me, just waiting for a moment of weakness. For now, I realize that if I focus on the little things like the crumbs of life, I will survive.

Are my survival techniques a good way of making sure that the darkness doesn't win? How will I know that I can have more than just the crumbs that life throws my way? Is settling for less a way for me to survive but not a way to learn to live? Will the physical pain I feel when I am overwhelmed by life's thoughts ever go away?

As I reflect on my shopping trip and being here at Alvernia College for the past few months, I realize now that the world I was missing is filled with so much life. People are more complicated than I thought. Sometimes it is like I am playing a game of catch-up, but without the rules.

College is a very fast-paced life, and no one checks on me about anything. It is almost as if there are no boundaries for me. In the entire world, there is no one for me to answer to for anything. There continues to be no expectations and no assumptions of success or failure. I could do or be anything I want, and it wouldn't matter to another living soul.

I try to watch the people here at the college so I can learn how to be a human. I want to learn to trust and be comfortable with who or what I am. I am still so lost at times regarding a lot of stuff. Sometimes I feel so overwhelmed by the differences and the lack of knowledge.

One of the college professors stops me one day and asks why I walk around with my head down and why I never look at people when I talk to them. She says that people are going to think I'm strange. She tells me that the teachers know where I come from, and if I want to fit in, I have to look and act normal.

I decide that I will change the way that people see me. I will practice in my room with my head held up and looking forward. I will also try to put on this happy-go-lucky personality, so people won't suspect that I have any problems.

Lately, I have been really trying hard to keep my head up, physically, and to look at people when I talk to them. It is so hard to do this, because when I look at people, I feel like there is a big spotlight shining on me, and they all know I am a freak and an unwanted nobody.

It is so important to me that I somehow blend in with these people who, through their acceptance of me, will make me feel better about myself. I don't know if I can. Will I ever bridge the gulf that stretches between my ability to be a half human and my desire to be a whole person?

I look at these people whom I am beginning to regard as friends. I sense that they welcome me into their midst even with my limitations of not looking at them, not wanting to be touched, not wanting to talk about the past, or even having a lisp when I speak. I wonder how I will ever be able to feel completely comfortable in their company.

My college friends are so different from what I imagined, and they are so excited about life and what they want to do.

There is Matthew, who talks enthusiastically about his great passions in life, his family, studying, singing, and acting. There is Celeste, who, in her quiet way, has taught me that her unspoken love for her husband, who is no longer here, still lives on in her life. The depth of her sorrow and her willingness to move on without denying the person she loved beyond all measure makes me feel okay inside about still loving my mother in ways I can't tell anyone about, lest they think I am crazy.

My other friends are just as diverse and constantly teach me human things that I missed. There are these sisters, Ruby and Jane, who go home every weekend and sometimes invite some of us from the dorm over for dinner or a cookout. They both have neat red hair and are very smart; plus they never seem to get flustered.

Becky will always give me a ride to anywhere I need to go, although I am careful not to take advantage of her or anyone else. My friend Vicki drives this really neat golden-orange Mercury Cougar sports car. She introduced me to the music that is hard on my ears, but I am trying to be open-minded.

Brian is another friend who tells me that for the first time he really has found people who want the same thing out of life that he wants. His parents often have some of us over to their house.

Julie is an English major who has four sisters; she is the baby. She often proofreads my papers, since my mind moves faster than my pen, and I usually skip half of the words on the paper.

There are just so many different kinds of people here, yet they all seem to like and accept me, even if I'm not quite up to where they are as human beings. Maybe I can learn to be better than I am if I continue to learn from people that don't mind me hanging around. Maybe if I can develop at least some of the goodness that they embody, I will be that much closer to becoming a real human being.

Will I ever be able to integrate all the disconnected pieces of my splintered self? Are friends the first step toward being alive, being a person, and being okay?

I'm working really hard on trying to fit in. Thanksgiving is approaching, and I still find myself mesmerized by and scared of people and of the holiday and of what I am supposed to do.

Sometimes I beat myself up inside, because I can't seem to overcome a lifetime of the absence of the ordinary that has set me apart from people. Many of my friends have jobs, date, go to parties, and are in constant contact with their families.

One thing surprises me. I have always believed that when kids turn eighteen, they automatically become adults who are endowed with some special grown-up knowledge, and they no longer need their parents or families. But here at Alvernia, I am discovering that this perception of when a person becomes an adult is way off.

Another way to look at this is that maybe parents and families do continue to be important after eighteen, because their kids, although legally adults, are still learning and growing with their parents' help.

For instance, most of my classmates are in constant contact with their parents, especially their mothers, sometimes on a daily basis. If these people, whom I would certainly describe as more human and complete than me, still need and want their parents to be a part of their lives, where does that leave me? I still feel so far behind everyone. At times it feels like I'm working a full-time job just trying to put the message out that I have everything under control.

I listen to the nightly ritual of conversations on the pay phone. I admire how easily my classmates call their parents without ever wondering if they are good enough or if they are bothering them. It must be really neat to not know the thousand and one ways that I hesitate to approach people, talk to people, or ask questions of people.

Most of the time, it is the little things that the conversations on the phone revolve around, even the homesickness that is prevalent at times. Sometimes I get homesick, but it is for a world and a life experience that ended so long ago, before I was ready to become a full person.

Where are the people that a person like me can call when I am feeling out of the circle of life? If no one will ever let me be in their presence, how will I learn to feel comfortable with who I am, what I am, and who I will become?

Sometimes I think I must appear very foolish to the kids here at college.

Today there is the smell of smoke in the dorm. Being a Good Samaritan, I hurriedly try to warn people to evacuate the dorm.

One of my friends pulls me into a room and asks me what I'm doing. I say, "Don't you smell that fire? It smells like burning leaves."

My friend says that there are some kids smoking joints. I ask her what she means, and she looks at me in a rather funny way. She says, "It is marijuana rolled up like a cigarette. A person could get high and feel no pain." I then say, "You mean there is no fire and that drugs smell like that?"

I feel kind of foolish, running around trying to evacuate the dorm, but I had never heard of drugs that I could smoke. In high school, some kids would talk about these pills that would cause pain to go away, but nothing about these funny-smelling cigarettes. I ask my friend if what they are doing is legal. She says no, but they aren't hurting anyone, and she wouldn't want them to go to jail.

When we both go to where they are smoking, I tell them that they should not smoke because the smell is everywhere in the dorm. They put the joints out and open the window to air the room out. As they are doing this, I notice that they're moving more slowly than usual and wonder if this is because of the drug. When I ask my friend if they are okay, she says, "Yes, just a bit stoned." She says that when people are stoned, they feel great and have no sense of self-control. She tells me it can be dangerous if they are driving, but since they are in the dorm, there is no harm, except when they get caught.

I decide that I will keep away from people who are smoking these funny-smelling cigarettes. I want and need to be in control of my life. I worry that everything I have worked so hard at would be taken away from me if I were caught with this stuff.

Besides, maybe I can look out for my friends and take care of them if I stay clean. With all the problems I have, the last thing I need is an added problem with drugs.

I still wonder how smoking a bunch of leaves could make someone feel no pain. Why are tobacco leaves in cigarettes legal to smoke but not the leaves of a marijuana plant? But then I also wonder what it would be like to lose all control.

Sometimes I feel as if I am always a half step behind the kids at Alvernia College. It isn't that I am not keeping up academically; it is just that I feel this invisible force shield around me that separates me from people when I encounter them.

Although I have been invited to some of the off-campus parties, I don't go, because I'm not sure how I am supposed to act; plus there is drinking. Some of my dorm friends tell me that I haven't lived until I have been drunk.

They tell me drinking would set me free. I don't know about this kind of logic. All I know is that when they come back to the dorm, they walk funny, slur their words, talk and cry about past stuff, and vomit all morning due to a thing called a hangover.

For me it has always been a toss-up as to which is the worst thing for the body, getting a needle or throwing up in the toilet? I really try to avoid both, if possible.

Why anyone would want to lose total control over thoughts and feelings and become emotionally naked in front of other people is beyond me. Yet I wonder if my not indulging in alcohol is another sign that I'm not quite up to my classmates' social development.

My friends date each other from school, or some have romantic friends back home where they come from. I don't know anything about dating, and to avoid it, I make sure I am very busy.

When people date, they end up getting married someday, and that would violate the survival list that I must live by in order not to die. With my past, it is not possible for someone like me to become attached or loved. Besides, there is really nothing about me that would draw the attention of anyone.

I don't want to think about the complications of how to love, especially when I am probably incapable of loving, forming attachments, touching, or bonding in ways that men, women, parents, children, and families do.

Do people know that they need each other, or is it something that is taught by example? Is being a half step behind the constant trade-off for doing as well as I have done thus far?

I never knew that money was so important!

I thought I was so rich with the $1,200 from the orphanage, but it is dwindling fast. I don't think I can live on this for the next four years, even though I try to be careful. After shopping for the female clothes and paying a little extra for a private room, I am down to $600.

I do work on campus, through this thing called work-study program. I clean the music hall under the direction of the music professor. She is nice, as most of my teachers are, but the money goes toward my tuition.

Maybe what I need to do is to sit down and think this money thing out. Obviously I have miscalculated the way money is spent. It doesn't last forever. I am not afraid to work, so I think I need to get a job to work my way through college, at least to pay for the expenses outside of tuition, room, and board.

There is a store called Dominic's IGA, within walking distance of Alvernia, where I could get a job. One of my friends, Stephanie, a math major, said that I could get a job there, working in the late afternoon until closing.

I am nervous about the interview, but all the manager is concerned about is my ability to show up on time and to be nice to the customers. I promise him that I am responsible, and I offer to work for free as a tryout. He says that he will hire me to run the cash register and tells me to remember that the customer is always right.

The manager says that if there is ever a robbery, I should just give all the money, because my life is more important. Can you believe it, Mother? Someone said that my life is more important than money.

I promise to work any hours that he will give me, as long as they don't interfere with my classes. I need to scramble in order to make sure that I don't financially crash.

Sometimes I am so afraid, especially at night, that I will crash emotionally, but maybe if I can control my educational and financial world, then the discombobulated emotional inside world will go away.

How did my mother ever learn the value of money? Why is money necessary to keep living life? Is money really the root of all evil, or is it a way of freedom for those who have little or nothing?

Thanksgiving is very fast approaching, and with it is a big problem. The college dorm is being shut down, and I don't know where I will stay.

I ask the college administration if I could stay in the dorm. I would even be willing to pay. However, I am told that the college closes down for all the holidays.

I try to explain my situation, that I have nowhere to go. I am told that this is a college, and I am on my own. One administrator says that surely someone would take me in during the holidays. Everyone has someone in the world, I'm told. Only I know how hurtful this situation is for me and how I have never belonged to anyone.

Since I never used the phone at the orphanage, I ask one of my dorm friends to teach me how to make a long-distance phone call. This is my first phone call, but I didn't tell her that.

I think the only thing I can do is to call Dad, even though his family hates me. Since Trevor is living there and is now a senior in high school, maybe it won't be so bad if I visit him. When I call the house, Dad answers the phone. I ask him how Trevor is doing, and he tells me that he told Trevor to leave because he was interfering with him and his mother over Alice.

He gave me Trevor's phone number. When I ask about Thanksgiving, he tells me to wait a minute. I can't hear what is being said, but he comes back on the phone and says that Gladys, his second wife, wants to talk to me.

Gladys gets on the phone and says, "You must be incredibly stupid. After all these years, don't you get it? You and your brothers have never been a part of this family. You are the only one left of the four of you that still wants to be in touch with your dad. Get this through your thick head: he is not your dad. He did adopt you, but that ended when your mother died. All four of you have never been, and never will be, a part of this family. We got rid of Trevor, and here you start calling. Don't you ever call here again or ask for anything! Only Alice is our concern. We will be changing addresses and phone numbers so you four can never be in touch with us again. Do I make myself clearly understood? Leave this poor man and us alone! You are eighteen years old. Stay away and out of our lives!"

I never reply. I don't get a chance to say anything. She hangs up the phone at the end of her one-way conversation. I look at the phone in my hand, and I don't know if I should feel let down or angry. I just really feel ashamed and humiliated.

Why do I allow these people to continue making me feel like a failure?

Maybe after all these years of not wanting to believe it, I have to finally accept the truth that the daddy of my childhood and of my heart never really existed. I have to finally accept his rejection.

I know I'm nothing and not worthy of anything in this world, but even though I know this about myself, it still hurts to hear Daddy's new wife, Gladys, talk to me like I'm a piece of dirt. I think I will just put that conversation away inside me. Now at eighteen, I finally have to face the fact that I don't have a daddy.

I have to deal with losing Daddy as I watch all my classmates going home for the holiday. They have no idea how I feel hated, despised, and all alone.

With all the pain that feel, I still have to face the practical problem of what I am going to do about the holidays for the next four years.

I decide to find a hotel to stay in for the holidays. I pick one place filled with people who act like they are drunk. One lady, who is dressed in a flashy short outfit, says this is not the kind of hotel for a kid like me.

One of my classmates, Sam, heard through the grapevine that I was looking for a hotel to stay at so I could study. He told me that he cleans offices in a building called the Berkshire Towers, and they rent out rooms by the week or month.

He said he could use some help cleaning. I could work with him if I wanted to make extra money. I decide to take him up on his kind offer. Now I'll be able to rent a room, plus earn extra money.

I call Sam to see if he needs help. Sam asks why I am not going home. I tell him that I have to study hard for tests. He says that if I need any money, he always needs help cleaning. His girlfriend has another job now, so she is overloaded with work. Things have a way of working out. I've lost Daddy for good now, but when that door closed, another opened. Why don't I ever know what I am supposed to know about life?

Working at the grocery store and cleaning with Sam has been keeping me busy. It costs me almost $200 for Thanksgiving to rent a room, go out for all my meals, and pay for transportation.

I know that I probably could make life easier for myself if only I wasn't so afraid to let my friends know that I have nowhere to go.

One of the fastest things that I have learned is that money can be spent very quickly. In the past couple of months, the $1,200 that had been given to me by the person in charge at the orphanage has almost disappeared.

I know that I spent money on the female clothes; then someone made a comment about my shoes, so I had to buy a new pair of shoes called loafers.

When I arrived at college, I didn't know that I needed towels, bedsheets, pillows, hangers, and a thousand other things that people need when they don't have anything. I had never owned much of anything. At the orphanage, all I had was a metal locker with no drawers, it only had hooks to hang my clothes on, and a metal shelf for my toothbrush, toothpaste, soap, and comb. There had already been sheets and stuff in the storage room.

Every time I turn around, it is as if there is always a new way of living, or something else that most kids learn within the confines of a family. That first night at Alvernia College, I slept on a bare mattress. The next day, I asked Becky to drop me off at a local K-Mart, where I bought the bedding items.

It's just that when I get done paying money for the things that will make me normal, I have very little left. Now I realize that I need to work hard and to have extra money set aside, in case there are other things that I need but don't know about yet.

One of my major concerns is having enough money for the holiday rental fees at the Berkshire Towers. If Thanksgiving cost $200, what will Christmas, spring break, or the summer months cost?

I have to work more so I can have enough money set aside for those times of displacement. Sometimes I get tired from this shuffling, but I have little choice.

How could there possibly be so many ways of not knowing about the ordinary? Why is money so important to living a normal life?

Sleep is so hard to come by at night. I thought for sure a while back that once I left the orphanage, all my problems and all my night dreams would be over. All I want is to sleep restfully and not be caught up in saving my mother from the fire or falling off the cliff or trying to find a way out of the adoption zoo.

I really want my night dreams to disappear, but they continue to haunt my sleeping time and leave me exhausted when I wake up in the morning.

I think that if I stay up all night and study, or if I listen to soothing music or pray the rosary or talk to my mother and God, these will chase away the demons of rejections and abandonment that have become the constant themes in my night dreams.

I sometimes wonder whether the night dreams could be my trade-off for having most other things in my life work out, at least on the outside.

Sometimes I am afraid that I will never wake up. I hate what is played out in my mind when I sleep, because I don't want to be reminded of my not being normal or good enough.

How come I have moved on in my waking moments beyond the "shuffle madness" but not in my sleeping moments? Why can't my life at college erase the reality of the past ten years?

I call Trevor today from the pay phone in my dorm. I ask him how he is doing, and he says that he is having a difficult time making it financially.

Trevor tells me that Dad and Grandma Resuba got mad at him because he told them that Alice was sneaking out with boys older than her and that she was too young at thirteen to be dating.

Trevor says he doesn't care about being thrown out because the Resubas told him that none of us were good enough to be part of their family.

He has a small apartment and is signed up for the navy, where he will go when he graduates in a couple of months. I ask him what he needs. He says he could use help with his rent. Right now he has a part-time job and is going to high school full-time.

I tell him that I will come up to give him money, but I can't stay. He says that is fine with him because there would be no place for me to stay.

I tell him that I would try to get Social Security for us, since no one has ever applied for it. I also tell him that I remember that our mother used to work at a shirt factory in Seymour, Indiana. I am going to get on a Greyhound bus and go to that factory to find out what her Social Security number is so we can get some benefits.

Trevor says that he has an address of some relative who lives in Seymour that I could stay overnight with. He gives it to me and says that he hopes I am able to find out our mother's Social Security number.

Trevor tells me that our mother's family in Indiana knew about the orphanage and Dad giving us up because the Resuba family didn't want us. He reminded me that no one ever offered to take us into their homes in Indiana.

Trevor says that we are totally on our own. He tells me that someday, when he marries and has kids, he will never ever let the stuff that happened to us happen to them.

I tell Trevor that I will be coming up to give him some money at the Greyhound bus stop next weekend. I will give him $80, which will cover his room rent for two months. Then I will try to get Social Security for us.

Sometimes I miss what might have been, and what should have been—a life, a family, and a place to call home.

Trevor meets me at the Greyhound bus station. It has been almost a year since I last saw him.

I remember when Trevor was only seven years old, crying as he was made to walk in only his underwear a half a block in the middle of February because he wet the bed. It is this brother whom I wanted to beat Grandma Resuba up over, even though I was only eight years old. It was the first time I knew what real anger was.

Trevor is now seventeen years old and taller than me. Although only a year separates us, we will soon be going in a million different directions.

I love Trevor, he can be sweet and funny. It makes me sad to know that we have been shuffled in ways that make it impossible for us to be as close as we might have been, if our mother had lived or we had remained a family.

I give Trevor as much money as I can and tell him that for the next couple of months I will send him money to help cover his rent. He tells me that Tyler is in St. Michael's, a reform school for stealing from a store. He also says that he has heard that Billy left for the coast guard. Billy had told Trevor to get away from Scranton as soon as he graduated, so he could live a life without the burdens of the past.

Trevor says that he would be okay, and he doesn't care that Daddy's family despises us, because he is his mother's son, and that is all that counts. "Someday they will get theirs," Trevor says, but he doesn't want them to hold him back.

We hug each other tightly, knowing it may be years before we ever see each other again. As I sit in a window seat on the Greyhound bus waving good-bye to Trevor, I ache for the loss of a closeness that never was and never will be because of the countless separations.

Do brothers and sisters in a family really care about each other naturally, or do they learn to be a family from their parents? How do people know how to be close?

As I travel on the Greyhound bus to Seymour, Indiana, I can't help but feel afraid of being in a town that had at one time embraced us in life and then embraced my mother in death.

I have my mission, and that is to find my mother's Social Security number. The relative that Trevor mentioned says I can stay overnight. They are cousins of my mother's, or something like that.

Although these are my mother's relatives, we are on our own, and I must stay focused on my mission.

I find the shirt factory, and they actually have my mother's Social Security number on file that they give to me.

I figure that since I am in town, I will go to the library and look up the newspaper articles on my mother's death and make a copy. From there, I will go to the funeral home and try to find out how she really died.

Mostly, I just want to get a sense that my mother really lived and was part of a life on this earth.

At the library, I get a copy of the article about my mother's death, which happened as a result of the gas explosion that set off the fire. There is even a picture on the front page of the burned trailer. She never had a chance to make it out alive, and if we had been there, we too would have also been killed.

From the library, I went to the funeral home, where the director says he remembers the funeral because of all the young children running around playing cowboys and Indians. He says we were too young to realize that our mother had died.

I ask him how my mother had died, and he says that he would give me a copy of her death certificate. On the certificate it says she died of smoke inhalation. She was found wrapped in a blanket; she had been trying to escape the fire.

I asked why the coffin had been closed. He told me that there were no burn marks on my mother, but when he put embalming fluid in her, her body turned a grayish black, because she was deprived of oxygen.

I ask him if my mother was aware of what was happening. He tells me that she knew for a few minutes and tried to save herself by properly getting on the floor and wrapping herself in a blanket to stay below the fire and the smoke. He says that because the furnace exploded, she never had a chance, no matter what she would have done.

I ask him if I could have saved my mother if I had been there. He tells me probably not, because the furnace was actually closer to our bedrooms. He says that what saved us was that we weren't there; otherwise, we would have all died. He says that no one lives through that kind of explosion. I thank him for his time, and he wishes me the best of luck in my future.

Did my mother feel any pain on that night so long ago?

The family that is related to my mother is nice, but I am in so much pain over the stark differences of how their children live and how my brothers and I were treated. They say that they knew nothing about the years since she died.

Whenever they asked my mother's two sisters and mother about us, they were always told that we were doing okay, living with our dad in Scranton, Pennsylvania.

Long ago, ever since I was fourteen, my mother's family had ceased to be a part of my heart, because I could never, and never would, understand how they could not embrace her orphaned children. I can never get past their being asked to take us and their saying no.

I find myself wanting this cousin and his wife to embrace me and to make all the pain go away, probably because, somehow, I am still what I don't want to be—the eight-year-old girl child who was left behind.

When I look at my mother's cousins here in Seymour, all I can see is the ordinary, yet all I have ever known and experienced has been the absence of the ordinary. I don't know if I can ever reconcile these two conflicting worlds.

As I get on the Greyhound bus to return to Pennsylvania, I wonder why I love hearing about my friends' families, yet there is so much pain being in the presence of my mother's family. I realize even more how I need to keep focused on making something out of my life.

Is it possible to ever understand the *why* of what people do? How do families continue being families without making room for the more fragile members? I wonder if my mother would have said no if one of her sisters had died? Would she have said no to her children?

I am now battling with the Social Security Administration over the benefits that have been denied my brothers and me.

After returning to Pennsylvania, I immediately apply for Trevor, Tyler, Alice, and me. I spend some time on the bus agonizing over including Alice, because her dad could have applied more than ten years ago, but he didn't. It was he who should have given me my mother's Social Security number, but he didn't.

Finally, I just decide that in all fairness, Alice is my mother's daughter too, and it would be only right to turn her name in for her share of our mother's benefits, even though it lessens the amount that my brothers and I will receive.

Alice, who will inherit everything from her grandparents, is still entitled to a share from the same person that they despise. Grandma Resuba would always say that Alice was the daughter she never had. Well maybe, at least with Social Security, she will never be Grandma Resuba's daughter.

The Social Security Administration doesn't want to reimburse us all the way back to the time of my mother's death. They say that they can only go back one year prior to my application because that is their standard policy.

They tell me that Dad should have applied for it, and there is nothing they can do about it. I try to explain how unfair this decision is, because as orphaned children, we did not have access to our mother's number, and we didn't have anyone to help us. The answer comes back as a denial of the past benefits lost.

I decide to write to the senator from Pennsylvania and to the president of the United States about this denial of past benefits. I tell them that the Social Security Administration knew that my mother died and that they said it was not their job to advertise the availability of benefits.

I wrote that due to the circumstances following my mother's death, it would have been impossible for my brothers and me to have known what to do. We were never told what her Social Security number was.

Both the senator and an official letter from the White House come back with the same reply. They say that while they sympathize with the unique situation that my brothers and I are facing, it was the responsibility of the adults, from our dad to the social workers, to apply for benefits on our behalf.

The letters indicate that it is not the responsibility of the Social Security Administration to actively initiate the distribution of benefits for those deserving. This must be done by responsible adults.

However, due to the special circumstances, benefits would be retroactive for twelve months prior to my application process, but not for the whole eleven years.

I have to be satisfied with what the people in Washington have decided. Besides, I did the best I could, getting some money for my brothers and myself, and even for Alice.

Franklin Roosevelt set this plan up for the widows and the orphans. At least the widows are adult who can look out for themselves, but who can speak for the orphaned children? Why didn't anyone throughout the ten years of the "shuffle madness" protect our rights? Did my mother work hard all those years in the factories, believing that we would always be taken care of?

Tonight, while I am trying to earn money at the local grocery store, three men come in three minutes before closing. I notice them because I am almost ready to close out my drawer and turn the cash over to my boss.

They suddenly come from the back of the store with their guns drawn. They have ski masks over their heads and are screaming for everyone to get down on the floor.

My friend is on the floor with the few remaining customers. My boss has a gun pointed to his head, and there is a gun resting on the back of my neck. The gun barrel feels like a frozen stick touching my flesh.

I can't believe this is happening. It doesn't seem real to me even though I know that it is really happening. The gunman orders me to empty the three cash registers. I empty the first two registers, but not the third.

He starts screaming at me to open it, but I know it is broken and that we have never used it. I try to tell him, but he screams, "Do you want me to use this, girlie!" He then pulls the trigger back. As he is pulling the trigger, my boss screams not to shoot me, that I'm telling the truth. "The register has been broken for over a year, and we only use the first two registers for work."

The whole time, in my head, I start praying that they won't take me as a hostage. I decide that if they do, I would run even if they shoot me. I know that if they shoot me I might survive, but if they take me as a hostage, they will torture me and then definitely kill me so that there are no witnesses.

While they stuff the money into their brown bag, I don't move, because I'm afraid that the gun resting on my neck will go off. Finally, they turn and run out of the story, disappearing into the night.

I don't move for about five minutes. My boss keeps calling my name, until I snap back to the here and now. My friend and I spend the next four hours at the police station. I tell my boss that I can't continue working in a place where I might die before I accomplish my goals.

Do people die from fright? Why did it take me so long to come back to the here and now after being robbed?

I am still reeling from that robbery four months ago. Try as I might, I cannot shake off the feeling of being afraid.

One of the major changes that occurred with the body immediately following the robbery was that there was no period for over three months. In a panic, I thought that maybe I was pregnant; then it started again. Maybe tremendous stress has a profound impact on the body. I have a vague idea that men and women have babies together, and if the blood doesn't come, then that is a sign that a female is pregnant. I don't talk to anyone because how can I ever begin to explain the chaos that exists within me about body issues? I just can't handle everything, so I make choices about what is okay for others to know.

I just know that from now on, I need to manage my stress level so that it doesn't interrupt my everyday life. I don't want anything to interfere with where my life is going.

School is on track, but there are many times when I don't understand things in my personal life. I have only so much energy, and in the three worlds I live in—school, personal, and hidden past—it is impossible for me to integrate them all.

Sometimes in life I have to make choices over what I can handle by myself and what is beyond my ability to handle alone. Usually I think I have everything under control. As a matter of fact, I work really hard at having control, until something like the robbery comes along to shatter my complacency. In those cases, everything that I deem as unimportant or unnecessary comes rushing back to cause me to go into a tailspin of overwhelming chaos. Then I try to reassure myself that the incident is one more reason to keep what has always been kept to myself.

For a couple of moments though, during these past few months, I've began wondering about being pregnant. I tried to tell myself that men and women have babies together. The longer the period didn't come, the more scared I was getting, and there were fewer possible explanations that were available to me. All I vaguely knew was that if there is no period, then the only explanation would be pregnancy. Maybe I should not have made the body one of my trade-offs in life; then I wouldn't be so panicky and could ask someone for help.

How could stress from the outside world continue to affect what goes on inside me? Why can't I control the body like I can control my mind?

When I was young, I used to hunger for a role model. I thought that when I became an "adult" at eighteen years old, my need, or should I really say, my hunger, for a role model would diminish. Instead, I find myself surrounded by people who continue to nourish my fascination with people.

Some of the role models are teachers, or should I say, professors, who, at least to me, are the best at making whatever subject they teach come alive. There are some nun professors and lay professors who make my classes exciting. There is one nun whose family was in a concentration camp, and she draws the most perfect circle on the board. There is also this history professor who is very nurturing, and I have to be careful not to let her know that I crave to still be nurtured.

I don't think I have ever had a teacher here at Alvernia College whom I haven't liked. As adults, they seem pretty nice and appear to be genuinely interested in the subject they teach and in the students. One of the math professors is very laid-back in her manner of teaching mathematical concepts.

Some of the other people that impress me are my fellow students, who are of all ages, races, and backgrounds. I think that it is rather fascinating that we all have the same goals.

While in the dorm, I listen to the different family stories, hoping that I can get a sense of that mysterious world of belonging unconditionally.

What I do now is try to absorb as much from the positive stories I hear and to build in my mind what I think a family should be for me. At least this is a lot different than living with what family had been for me.

The role models, whether professors or students, are showing me an alternative to a reality that I never lived.

I think that it is okay to want a different way of living. So for now, I am like a sponge, soaking up the stories of lives that others have lived.

Do stories teach lessons about living? Is listening to the life story of someone else a way of learning how to live differently? If I absorb those stories of life, will that add more depth to my understanding of who people are and how to get along with them?

This summer I have a job at a company that makes cardboard containers. Last summer I applied for it but did not get it. When I called about the job, I was told that May is too late to apply for a summer job. They already gave the jobs to the children of employees.

The pay for subbing for a factory worker who is on vacation is the same as what the worker is making. At sixteen dollars an hour, that kind of money is nothing to sneeze at. I really need that job.

What I did this year was try to figure out a plan to get myself hired. I applied in November and called the personnel department every Tuesday. One day in March, they told me that I have a summer job. They said that they usually hire employees' relatives first, but since I had been so persistent, they would squeeze me in somewhere. They also told me that I could stop calling every Tuesday because I was in. I am so happy because I need the money for room and board during the holidays.

At the factory, it is hard physical work, even dirty at times. I learn quickly that being a factory worker is not easy. The repetitious work challenges my mind as well as my body.

The older workers are always telling me to stay in school and not to limit my options in life. They tell me that if the factory shuts down tomorrow, they would have no job to go to because of their age and their lack of education.

I watch these workers and realize for the first time what limitations can do to a person. Yet in some ways, I now have a new appreciation for men and women who, in their ordinary lives, spend years at a repetitious job, just so that their children can know a different way of life.

Maybe life's real heroes are the people behind the scenes, those that make every day work. This factory is like many across America. The workers are the unsung heroes who continue to work to make the best of what has been given to them.

When my mother worked at the shirt factory, did she have different dreams for us? Are the people who work in the factories the real heroes who, day in and out, try to provide the best they can for their families?

In college, doing research is really important. My favorite place to hang out at school is the library. Somehow I feel comforted among all these books that contain adventures of lives that I have not yet lived.

An added bonus to hanging out at the library is this new librarian named Lois. She is extremely helpful and also has a bubbly personality. She is always finding something new that I haven't read about.

She works in the evenings. Usually I spend my evenings in the library, often walking out when Lois closes it.

For some reason, we start talking about my background. She asks me where I come from, because she notices how outgoing I am and how I act like I don't have a care in the world. I tell her that I purposely don't want people to know that there is a serious side to me, because I wouldn't want people to think I have any problems.

Lois says she also has noticed that while I will discuss anything from existential philosophy to the political ramifications of a congressional decision, I never ever mention anything about my past. She says she has asked one of the professors about me, and even some of my fellow students. They tell her I never mention my life before Alvernia College.

Lois tells me that she is curious and wonders if I'm doing okay. I tell her that I don't like to talk about where I came from, because people will either think I want attention or they might not like me, because I'm not like them.

I tell her that my mother died when I was eight years old and that the dad that adopted my brothers and me didn't want us. I don't mention the two years in the coal cellar, because I already feel backward sometimes, and I don't want Lois to think I'm not normal because I lived in a coal cellar.

I like Lois a lot. She always engages me in intellectual conversations and believes I'm all right. I could never tell her the whole truth, because I want her to continue liking me.

Lois asks me what happened after my mother died. I tell her about how my Dad had kept his one flesh-and-blood daughter but put the adopted children away in different orphanages on Christmas Eve in 1966.

Lois is really fascinated by my story, so far. She asks about my mother's family, and I tell her that I remember that she had a mother and two sisters but that they wouldn't take us.

Lois wants to know why I keep such secrets to myself. I tell her that in the entire campus here at Alvernia College, and even at North Pocono High School, where I used to go to school, I didn't meet anyone like me who was in a foster care or in an orphanage.

She is curious about the foster homes. I just say that being a foster kid is no picnic, because once you get into the "shuffle madness," you could never get out, unless you had someone who loved or cared about your being displaced from their family.

After ten years in that chaos, people think I should be no different from their children who, thankfully, will never know that kind of discombobulation. I tell Lois that in many ways I am different, even though I would give anything not to be.

The kids here at Alvernia College accept me. I know that they are also curious about me. I am just afraid that if I share where I came from I would run the chance of having them withdraw their friendship. I won't jeopardize everything that I have worked for since arriving here.

Lois tells me that I should write a book someday, because she finds my story very inspiring, uplifting, and fascinating, even though she tells me she suspects that there is a lot more to my story. She says that other people could learn so much from what has happened in my life.

Lois is a wonderful woman who is astute enough to know that I shared only the tip of the iceberg of my life with her. Maybe I will write a book someday. At least people like Lois think I'm okay.

Sometimes I think that God has a way of sending night-lights in the darkness into my life, so that I will know that I shouldn't feel so lonely.

Maybe we all need to have cheerleaders like Lois. I've told her more tonight than I had intended to. Even my friends don't know about the orphanage.

Maybe my friendship with Lois is a stepping-stone out of my prison of a past, which is filled with so much shame and self-doubt.

How can an ordinary person like Lois listen to my partial story and still like me? Why are people fascinated with lives of others who have lived a different kind of life? Why do I like the feeling of someone like Lois championing me and even believing that my story might be worth telling someday?

I think it is really important to learn to drive. I remember how the person in charge at the orphanage wouldn't let me learn. Now it is time to make good on my personal promise to learn how. Some of my friends chuckle at how I approach life; I buy the car and then learn to drive. I just do the best I can with what I know.

A classmate of mine, Maxwell, has offered to give me driving lessons. He is seriously dating this girl named Marla. They are a cute couple.

For the past year, I have been saving money, and I bought this old station wagon, which I nicknamed Bernadette, after my favorite saint. Now that I have my own car, it is time for me to learn how to drive it.

Maxwell takes me to this big parking lot and shows me how to back up, turn, park, and drive safely. He is very safety conscious and very patient. I have a hard time learning parallel parking and remembering to look at my side view mirror.

I do finally pass my driving test, which will help me to be ready for my next adventure after I graduate from college—going to Washington DC for my masters degree at the Catholic University of America.

I am so grateful that I have friends like Maxwell who are willing to share their time and energy to teach me things that allow me to move closer to a normal life. Maybe the driving lessons are, in a way, symbolic of learning to continue going places with the help of others.

I know that as I continue my struggle to emerge from the fog of uncertainty about people, I am continually encouraged by the acts of kindness that allow me to move ahead. Although I may always be a half step behind my friends and not quite up to snuff in the people world I now live in, at least I'm on my way.

So far, aside from my night dreams, I am still somehow doing well in school, making friends, and trying to balance all the ways that are part of who I am. Driving a car offers freedom. I hope that it will take me to places that will continue to surprise and delight me.

Are there all kinds of driving lessons in life? If Maxwell offered his kindness, do I also owe something to another? What kind of driving lessons in life would my mother have taught me?

I have been really physically tired lately. Somehow, in order to have the $1,200 I need for the summer to rent a room at the Berkshire Towers, I need about three jobs.

I work at the factory, wash dishes in one restaurant, and make pizza at the local Pizza Hut. During the school year, I work only two jobs instead of three.

Sometimes my days begin early, and before I know it, I'm crawling into bed at one o'clock in the morning. Many days go by as if they were a blur of speeding headlights.

I'm not sure if I work so much for the money to pay the bills or if I am trying to outrace the hurling darkness of my past, which keeps nipping at my heels.

I definitely need the money, because of all the rents I have to pay for the holidays. I'm also saving for graduate school. Yet I know that whenever I stop, or have a free moment, I am overwhelmed by the spacing out that just sneaks up on me. It takes so much of my waking energy to just stay focused.

It is almost like flashbacks. I'm afraid that if I'm not careful enough I could stay in the past without ever leaving. When I work a lot, I know that my mind will be engaged in another direction, and I don't have to face the thoughts of the past, which continue to haunt me.

I am too afraid of people to let them know my real reason for working so much, getting educated, and just playing the role of a happy-go-lucky person.

Are there different ways of hiding in plain sight? What will happen if I lose my energy?

During the summers at college, I stay at the Berkshire Towers. It is an interesting place filled with rather interesting people. At first I was scared to stay here, but now I think of it as a big dorm. There are so many floors that there is an elevator in this building. The carpet in the building has a certain smell to it, like slightly soured milk. The room is dark, with limited furniture and a bathroom with a stand-up shower that is tight to fit into.

At nighttime I can hear all these strange noises as people come and go. If I listen close enough, I can even get the scheduled pattern of the other tenants that live here. I try not to associate with some of the people here, because they seem strange. The old people aren't too bad. Sometimes I will run to the store for them or carry their packages from the elevator to their room. There are some young men who look shifty to me. I never talk to them or get on the elevator by myself with them.

Outside my window I can see the city of Reading, with its flashing neon lights reflecting back into my room at night. There is a certain comfort as I watch the hustle and bustle of the city even in the wee hours of the morning. The neon lights serve as a night-light for my room, because I am still afraid of the dark, and I like their brightness.

In the mornings, I often have breakfast at the diner next to the hotel. Like clockwork, I arrive at 7:00 a.m. and order the same thing, ham-and-cheese omelet with a side of toast. Even though I have to spend the holidays and summers in a hotel, I am becoming comfortable with being in a building that allows me to be anonymous. Maybe in the end, this is for the best, because I know how to live alone and to be invisible to the world. Being in a family or in a relationship with others would challenge me to live in a way that I have never been prepared to live. I wish deep down that being in a family or in a relationship with others would be something that would be possible, but that is not, and has never been, my reality. What the future holds is still a mystery to me, but at least, in this hotel I am safe.

Is the hotel the closest I can get to living in the people world? Yet why do I yearn to know another way of living?

I have finally decided to make good on the promise that I made when I was fourteen years old. I have always vowed to change my name.

Recently I sent for my birth certificate in Washington DC. Since visiting Trevor and knowing our biological father's name, I was able to get a copy of my birth record.

I also learned that Billy had a twin who died at birth.

It is now the summer of 1976. I will be twenty years old and soon to be a junior in college. I found this really nice lawyer in the phone book. When I tell him the purpose of changing my name, especially some of my past history, he says he will do the work and not charge me the full price.

He says that given the circumstances of my childhood, it should be no problem. I will have to go before a judge and explain my past, then a judgment will most likely be rendered in my favor. The lawyer mentions that he has to advertise in the local paper in Scranton and in Reading to prove to the court that there is no fraud involved in the name change.

I'm not worried if someone says I owe them any money. However, the child part of me is afraid that Daddy's family will see it and write to the judge and tell him that I'll always be a bastard even if I change my name.

The judge is really nice on the day I go to court to get my name changed. I got to sit in the witness chair, like in *Perry Mason*. It is high up from the floor. He asks me why I want to change my name, and I tell him about how my mother died and how Daddy's family, the Resubas, hated my brothers and me. I tell him that if I do well someday, I don't want Daddy's family to take any credit.

The judge asks me if I have a name picked out, and I tell him that I like the name Kennedy, because they, the Kennedys, adopted children and kept them. He chuckles and suggests that I take the name from my birth certificate. I tell him that it's fine with me. Then he officially declares my name changed with the bang of his gavel. He wishes me good luck in my life.

Will this change of name help me to change how I feel about myself? Am I now responsible for bringing honor to this new name?

I keep wondering where I should go after graduating from Alvernia College. Now a junior, I have been thinking about going to the Catholic University in Washington DC for my masters degree. Getting another degree is part of my life plan. I want to study history, because it helps me to have an academic history, since I don't have a personal one.

Now I am more than two-thirds done with college. I have decided that I will go to graduate school so that I can be even more educated. Hopefully this will finally make me almost as smart as other people, maybe even almost as good as them.

I struggle a lot with wanting to have a purpose in my life. The people whom I have noticed doing the most good on a large scale are the nuns that I have encountered. Sometimes I toy with the idea that maybe I should become a nun. This would certainly allow me to live by my survival list. It would also help me to give of myself for the good of others, which is a part of my belief in love and in God.

While I keep turning the possibility of becoming a nun over in my heart and soul, I decide to wait a few years and continue to go to school. Even if I am to become a nun, I need to work on not having any problems, which would make me unacceptable to that way of life.

I have walked a long way together with God in a darkness that was made possible only through the absence of the ordinary. I never ever once felt totally alone, because I always knew that somehow, in spite of who or what made me unacceptable and unlovable in the eyes of people, my mother and he were in my corner, and that was just enough to keep me from going over the edge.

I wonder if faith is just as necessary for surviving as eating and drinking? Would my mother approve of my possible future plans? Can the spiritual desire to serve and do good make all the unfulfilled needs of the orphan child inside me go away?

Often I view life in a military sense, maybe because I was an air force brat before my mother died. Even when I was told at the age of eight that she died and went away on a secret mission with Jesus, I was convinced that somehow she would find a way back to me.

Whenever Daddy went away on secret missions, he always came back, so I just thought that my mother was always on her way home, back to me. Maybe in a way, she was on her way home, but not in the way that I could imagine, understand, or accept.

Even now at the age of twenty, and twenty-one very shortly, I still see life in a military sense. When I was a kid, the nuns always taught me about how I was a member of the army of God. Back then I would imagine that I was in the frontline, ready to give my life. Besides, I figured that I had nothing to lose and everything to gain if I served God, and maybe my serving God would be an act of redemption for my living instead of my mother.

So far, during all these years, I haven't really done much with my life. I haven't made a difference to anyone or anything.

I just want to believe inside me that I am okay beyond all the book learning. I want to leave the world better than I found it. I think about the regular military, but that doesn't have the same kind of intensive goodness as a way of life that a religious life such as that of being a nun has. As a nun, I can change my name and become totally focused on the needs of others, without a thought for my own needs.

Meanwhile, I'm going to graduate school so that I can become smarter and make up for what I have not learned from having a normal life. I need to bring the best of me to wherever I go, and my being more educated will help a lot.

Do you think that if I serve in God's army I will finally be like other people? How am I ever going to know which way is the best to live my life?

Today is my twenty-first birthday, and next month I will be a senior in college. The law says that I am legally an adult, which makes me entitled to the same rights as every adult that I encounter.

If only becoming twenty-one could make me feel emotionally like an adult, then maybe I would feel more together. For me, the only difference is that I can now learn to drink, which I won't because of all the alcoholic orphans that I have met.

The real question from here on out is, "Now what?" This new school year will challenge me in ways that I'm not sure I can live up to. So far academically, I am doing very well. In addition to working around fifty hours a week between cleaning and Pizza Hut, I have a circle of friends who are some of the most fascinating people I have ever met.

I have been able to keep my past distant from my friends, even at times from myself. But my inner world has changed or moved forward very little. Sometimes I find myself whisked back through the flashbacks to the "shuffle madness" of the past. Then I have to spend time convincing myself to come back to this present reality. Often I wonder what I can do to either reinvent myself or do away with parts of me that I either don't want to deal with or cannot deal with.

I hope that with graduation approaching this year, plus graduate school, I will find some kind of direction for my life. Maybe I am just living life too intensely, but don't I owe some kind of payback for surviving both the fire and the "shuffle madness"?

There has to be a way to give my life to others as a way of leaving the world better than I found it. I'm thinking about becoming a nun, a missionary, or a lawyer. I guess I'm looking for a way to confirm that my existence on earth does count for something.

How many now-what's will I have to explore? Is there ever going to be a time when I will feel comfortable with my restlessness? Can I ever really give enough payback for surviving both the fire and the "shuffle madness"? When will I know that I have finally arrived in my relationship with people and life?

This year is going quickly. I took a test called the GRE, the Graduate Record Exam. Like the SAT in high school, all it did was give me a headache. I applied to the Catholic University of America to get my masters degree.

Today I got my acceptance in the mail. I am so happy that the outside world continues to think that I am smart. Maybe two years in Washington DC will help me to find some direction in my life.

Even with the acceptance, I have a hard time shaking off this continuing loneliness that overwhelms me at times. How is it possible to be twenty-one still going on eight? I wish I could will my past not to exist or to creep up on me when I least expect it.

Graduation will be coming soon, and I have to prepare for leaving a place that embraced me without even knowing me. There are separations that surprisingly hurt. More than I care to admit, I like being with these people whom I call friends. Maybe I am still searching for a way to be a whole human being, even though for someone like me, that may be a stretch. At least I know this much, that I have become the best I could make myself into.

I don't know if I will ever shake this loneliness that persists at the core of me, but I will keep trying to be okay. I have done so much in my twenty-one years and feel that there is so much left for me to accomplish.

How could my childhood continue to haunt me in this life that I am trying to make for myself? Will there ever be a time when I will feel comfortable about who or what I will become?

Soon I will be graduating from Alvernia College. Can you believe it, that this daughter of a dead mother has been able to accomplish such a goal? From the moment I stepped off that Greyhound bus four years ago to the present moment, my being here has been a totally pleasant experience.

I really think that Alvernia has provided me with the building blocks for a new life. While I was attending school here, there has never been a time when I have not appreciated the opportunities that have been afforded me.

While it is true that I have been academically challenged, what have made a real difference were the welcoming embraces of the people here who have taught me much more than I ever felt I was worthy of.

Instead of the temporary friends in high school, here I have made real friends. These are the people who invite me along to their get-togethers at the local bar, even though they know I don't drink.

These are people who have reaffirmed my welcome in their presence for the past four years. Each time, I am continually surprised, humbled, and delighted. This means that everything that was told me, all those years, about my not being normal, is not true, at least according to my friends here at Alvernia.

Truly this is the best little college in America, a place where I have felt comfortable and, at times, have been comforted. Where else could a kid buy a car first, then learn to drive, or still be accepted after trying to save the dorm from a fire caused by people smoking marijuana? Blessings often come my way when I least expect them or when I'm not looking for them.

These are the people who have taught me that the people world is as fascinating and exciting as I always thought it was. Even though I have not stepped out of my darkness or learned who or what I am or will become, I am not as isolated as I once was.

The professors; the students; my librarian buddy, Lois; and my Pizza Hut coworkers have all made these past four years an exciting adventure of growth.

Does the college experience always offer more than academic rewards? Are life adventures always as nourishing as my times at Alvernia College have been?

Today is the day that I think will define me as a normal human being. To be honest, there are some parts inside me that are still confused, lonely, and still going on eight years old. I just choose not to acknowledge their existence and to focus on what has brought me to this day.

The only sad part is that my mother is not here to witness my triumph. I have finally accomplished what I've set out to do, and that is to become the best half human that I could be.

The college gives us seven tickets for family and friends to attend the graduation ceremony. I give mine away, because there is no family. The only friends I have are here at Alvernia, and they will all be at the graduation.

I try not to notice how there will be no one to see what I have been able to do with my life, especially people from the past who doubted my success. Here I stand, four years later, at another graduation, a "bastard orphan" soon to be acknowledged as a college graduate.

There is no sweeter revenge on the people who discarded my brothers and me as trash so long ago than to stand here to be recognized publicly as an intelligent human being who is going places.

I haven't learned how to live yet, and I haven't embraced all the different parts of me yet. But I did survive, didn't I? Sometimes I still believe that God and the stars are still shining a light on a path for me.

I do feel a sense of sadness in the midst of my joy, because no one will ever know where I came from and what I have done. There are no permanent travelers in life that often come in the form of family. I still miss not having the mother I always thought I deserved, but maybe education will be as good a substitute as possible.

Why do times of great happiness hold a twinge of sorrow? How come graduations always have accomplishments finished with new beginnings ready to happen? I wonder if my mother and God know that I did this as much for them as I did for me?

Congratulations to the three of us.

I can't shake this feeling of knowing that I must do something soon with my life, before everything I have worked for slips away. So after graduation, I proceed to pursue my graduate studies, and now here I am, and so far, graduate school has been going well. I'm working two jobs so I can pay for it as I go along. I am studying history and religion so that I can possibly teach or go to law school.

For the next two years, I work at the law library during the day. It is a really cool place to work. The people are nice, and I have learned about the different law journals and how to do legal research. The only thing that prevents me from getting into the law profession is that women lawyers look like women. They have a sense of style and self-certainty, which I lack. There is no way I could ever be a woman of that stature, even if I tried.

Time flies, and soon I will be graduating, and it is difficult to believe that almost two years have passed since I arrived here. I have decided that I will join a convent so that I can make real that promise I made when I was fourteen, and that is to serve God and people with my life.

I spend a lot of time in prayer, just trying to discern what all my reasons are for wanting to be a nun. I have always wanted to live my life for a noble purpose and to have purely good reasons for doing what I do. I know that I love God and that he has always loved me. I also know that there is a part of me that feels like there has never really been any other choice in life for me.

There is also a part of me that likes the idea of not needing a past, changing my name, and declaring that the only family that matters consists of the other nuns in the convent. I try to keep these reasons back in the farthest part of my mind, because they don't really matter. All that matters for now is that I find a way to live after I leave the educational institution that has nurtured me since kindergarten.

It is scary leaving the only way of life that I have ever known and felt safe and affirmed in. It never occurred to me that there would ever be an ending to my formal educational experience.

What would my mother have thought about all the reasons for becoming a nun? What happens to a person like me who isn't ever sure about the right thing to do? Is service to others a great substitute for the missing pieces in my life?

Just when I think that I have resolved everything within myself, life has a way of reaching out to tap me on the shoulder saying, "Hey, kiddo, not so fast." Today when I got home, there was a note on my dorm room door saying that I should call this social worker because they have found my mother alive and well. I couldn't believe what I was reading at first, but the eight-year-old kid's heart and mustard seed faith kicked in, and I was ecstatic with the thought that my mother had never died and people lied to me all these years.

I ran to the pay phone, and as soon as the social worker answered the phone, I started gushing with relieved happiness. I kept thanking the social worker for finding my mother because I knew that she didn't really die in that explosion all those years ago. The social worker asked me what I was talking about. I told her that there was a note on my door reading, "Jerri, your mother has been found alive and well, please call this social worker." I told her how I had been told when I was eight that my mother died, and I just knew it couldn't be true, and now someone could tell me where she was.

In a gentle voice the social worker asked for my full name, and I told her what it was. She started apologizing profusely to me over and over, saying that there had been a terrible mistake. The name of the person the note was meant for was Jerri Smith, and she worked in the maintenance department. Her mother has Alzheimer's and had gotten lost over the weekend. The message was never intended for me. She again apologized for the mix-up and for getting my hopes up over an impossible situation.

I said thanks and told her not to mind my unrealistic belief that my mother had been found After I hung up, I thought to myself, There must be something wrong with me if I still, at twenty-three, desperately long for my mother's return. I felt very foolish over this incident.

Will my orphaned heart inside this adult female body ever come to terms with my mother's absence?

Finally, graduation day. It is difficult to believe that I now have a masters degree.

I just wish that I could feel different inside me, more whole, less fractured. This graduation is different from the one at Alvernia College, because I have used my tickets to invite some friends from Alvernia to witness this occasion. I like knowing that I have friends who are willing to travel to witness my accomplishment.

I continue to wish that my mother knew her daughter is doing everything she can to make some good out of her life. I've always wanted her to know that I have never stopped loving her, even when I felt betrayed and angry that she could go and leave me alone by dying. Everything I try to do in life is in part to honor her and God—the two people still in my heart. The twinge of sadness is always present. It is at these public functions when I feel loneliest.

No matter, graduating with a masters degree is an accomplishment that no one ever thought possible for me.

I know deep down inside that this new degree doesn't resolve the messiness that I need to keep to myself. I don't think that I can ever come to terms with or sort out some parts of me that were systematically destroyed by my mother's death.

Sitting here at the graduation ceremony, waiting for my name to be called, I still feel like I am an eight-year-old, wanting, more than anything, for my mother to know how well I've done. I think that by combining my educational accomplishment with my giving of my spirit through service to others a hundred percent, I will have provided my life with some meaning. Now with my two degrees, I should feel a sense of having reached some of my goals.

Is there a limit to the amount of education that can make up for the losses in my life? Will serving God help me get a passing grade as a human being?

This summer, as I prepare to enter the convent, I can't shake off the doubts about whose will I am following—my will or God's will. I am not sure sometimes if I am going in the right direction.

There is always that nagging doubt that some people are right when they say that I just want to join the convent to run away from life or look for a safe place to hide in.

I know that I can always make it on my own financially. Maybe I am afraid of people and never really learned how to live like a normal person in a family. I still have the right to live in the people world that, I must secretly admit, still seems alien to me.

In the depth of my heart, I know my decision is based on how I can best serve God and people in relation to all the trunks that that I have been carrying in my life.

In the absence of this self-confidence, all I can do is to try living in ways that provide structure, rightness, and a sense of belonging, even if it is on the institutional level.

One of the gifts that I must have received from my mother is this sense that God has always been part of my life. However, faith is not always an easy gift, and it comes with many strings attached.

There were times when I have been angry, sometimes in a manner that would come over me so quickly and with such intensity that I would get scared. Even when I would get angry that my mother died and left me before I was completely grown as a girl so I could be a woman, I would talk myself out of being angry, because I figured my mother probably didn't want to die either.

Even with Daddy's family, especially Grandma Resuba, what they were doing, not only to me, but to my brothers as well would almost consume me with rage. I just try not to feel the anger.

All I want is a way to live right so I won't be angry about stuff I can't change. I know deep down inside that I'm still just trying to become a human being.

How is it possible to be twenty-four years old and still trying to learn to live as a person? Why am I always searching for some kind of roots? Will I ever come to terms with who or what I am?

Soon I will be leaving to join the convent. Hopefully, I will not need to struggle with a past that continually haunts me in ways that I least expect.

I have this list of stuff that I have to buy for the convent. It is all so confusing about the sizes of the skirts and blouses and the nightclothes that I don't have. Usually I would sleep in my clothes, get up in the morning, take a shower, and put clean clothes on.

All my life, at least since my mother's death, I have been stripped of a gender identity, which I have been struggling to regain. For the past sixteen years, I have been working hard to reconnect with the female side of me, which either died or withered from the lack of nourishment that my mother or an adoptive mother could have provided.

Emotionally, I think that I am a hard rock, but deep down inside I really know the truth. The truth, which has not set me free, is that I am still a child of multiple ages, still wishing someone would come along to help me.

I try so hard to appear normal, to work for my keep, and to do good for other people. I do worry that the messiness of the broken child inside me will someday overflow my carefully scripted life, and other people will learn that I'm a fraud as a human being. I don't mean to be a fraud or to pretend to be a whole person, it's just that I couldn't fix everything in my life by myself.

Even if I deny my shortcomings in my waking moments, there are always the unrelenting night dreams that remind me of what a freak I really am. I need to do some kind of atonement to make up for a life that I must keep to myself. I must develop my spirit and my mind so that I can do good for others.

Can I be okay if I don't deal with the disconnections that still exist deep down inside me? Will being a nun for good and noble reasons be enough to chase away the ghosts that continue to haunt and tease me?

Tomorrow I begin what I hope is the right way for me to do good for others. Entering the convent should allow me to serve God and people in such a way that it would make me into a whole human being.

I'm not sure what all my reasons are for taking this path in my life. Maybe it is because I don't need a past. I will even be able to change my name. I'll also be able to live by my survival list. Since I'm not able to marry or have children, maybe by being a nun I could serve just as noble a cause.

In the orphanage the nuns, for the most part, were really kind. In some way, maybe there is a part of me that is still searching for the thing called family, which has always been elusive. I know that my entering the convent has something to do with a way of expressing publicly my desires to live a more full life.

Whether it is for hero-worship or because I feel like my choices in life are limited, for now this is a way of giving back for what has been given to me.

It is funny how the search for who or what I am continues no matter how much forward motion I've made. I always thought that when I grew up, all my problems or self-questioning would be over, or at least resolved.

I also thought that if I became more educated than most people, then this would make up for the gaping holes in my development. Yet here I sit with two college degrees, and I'm still searching for a way to be a whole human being, instead of a multitude of fractures that have never healed.

Now I will try religion. I will live a public expression of doing good continually so that I can continue to numb those parts of me that ache with the pain of never quite knowing how to be healed. I hope my spirit is good enough to serve others as a nun and to bring some good into the lives of those I meet.

I don't believe that there is any other way to live a life of wholeness than the one I am now choosing. Well, God, here comes another adventure in the land of the living.

Is serving others through religion the highest calling in life? Will this new life help me to spend what remaining years I have left to live in a way that will bring me closer to heaven? God, how does anyone really know what your will is?

"Service To Others"

Giving, helping, lending, taking time,
Understanding, accepting, encouraging, embracing
People in need of hope and life and welcoming,
Are ways of living and returning the gift of life.

All manner of knowing the human heart,
Is still a journey that is incomplete.
Until that time when disturbances of the soul,
Settle with a peace that is still in process.

Wondering about different ways to give,
What is left after the plundering of her heart.
To whoever journeys on the road with her,
To places that may start somewhere else but end up at the same place.

If only the crystal ball of arriving was more clear,
Then all means of understanding ways to be whole.
Would show itself in the clarity of her journey,
As she tries to keep on the service road to becoming human.

Clouds threaten to obscure the light in her darkness,
Pushing forward through the cobwebs that entangle her heart.
As she moves on a road that allows her to seek ways of being.
Part of the whole and not the splintered ragged edge that tries to
Define her.

God without a doubt always present giving free will,
To challenge her to search out ways to give from within.
To those children who now wonder where they should travel,
As they learn how to heal the life burdens put on them without
Invited permission.

Convent Years: Ages 24 - 34

The Convent Years

(Ages Twenty-Four to Thirty-Four)

Dear Mother,

Today I am beginning what I believe to be a neat way of living. Contrary to what people may think, I know that by being a nun, I will still live by my survival list and do good for the world. Since I am convinced that I will die by the time I am thirty-one years old, it is best that I use whatever time is left serving humanity.

I know that God has always loved me, but maybe it would be better to give back to him a "thank-you" by giving my life for the good of others. My entire life I have been searching for a place where I could belong, where everything in my past will become nonessential. I think that I have finally found a way to live without being noticed.

The only thing I don't like is this vow of obedience. As a nun, I have to take three vows: poverty, chastity, and obedience. At least with poverty, I have always been poor, and with chastity, I never planned to sleep with anyone.

That vow of obedience is really tough. My first difficult moment is when, because I have a masters degree, I am sent out to teach eighth grade near Scranton. When I ask not to be sent there for personal reasons, I am told that it is the will of God that I go. I am also told that the past is over, and nothing that happened before entering the convent matters.

In some ways, there are times when I realize that I have such great expectations of this life. I just hope that I too am able to live up to them.

It seems funny at times how people can reinvent themselves if they are not happy with where they are. I'm not happy with my past and the fact that no matter how hard I tried, I could not find a place called home. Sometimes I wonder how anyone knows that they have arrived at that place that becomes home.

I dread going out on my first assignment, not only because it is a new place, but also because it is so close to the place I swore I would never return to in this lifetime. I will just make myself do the best I can and hope that the person in charge of the convent is right about the past being no longer relevant.

Mother, did you always know that what you were doing was the right choice? God, can doing your will make what I know to be true go away? How does a person know for sure what really is the will of God?

Love,
Jerri

*   *   *

One of the things I like most about being a nun, aside from being able to help people, is that no past is needed. Every year I am sent to a different school to teach.

I have arrived at my current assignment for the year. One thing that is immediately apparent is the age gap between the other nuns and me. There is at least a forty- to fifty-year difference in our ages, but they are very nice.

What a busy life it is, working in the parish. I constantly have to be available for whatever becomes needed. There are eleven nuns here, and I am the only one that drives. It seems that when you are a nun, aside from the prayer schedule and school business, there are constant hospital visits, funerals, and wakes to attend.

The only thing that bothers me is going to the view the dead. I have never been to a viewing, and the last funeral I went to was my mother's. Sometimes I look at the dead, and I can't take my eyes off them, especially their hands. I just try to understand the magnitude of death or nonexistence. In the end, I marvel at the magical life-giving source that makes us human. We are so delicate and fluid in our living and breathing. I still believe that to be human is the most interesting thing in the world.

The only problem that I find on a personal level about parish life is that my assignment is three miles outside the city of Scranton. Try as I might, I still cannot help feeling like that bastard child I tried to forget ever existed when I go out in public. Part of me is always expecting to run into Dad's family and is afraid that they will tell someone that I am nothing and no one. I don't know why, after two degrees and a new life, I still fear them. I have been having intensive night dreams about them lately, even though I try to shut out all these thoughts during my waking hours.

I thought that being a nun would erase everything in the past and make whatever ways I failed to become part of a family obsolete. However, when I go out in public, I find myself with my head down so I won't ever run into any of them. Part of me cringes at the thought of being called a bastard, even though I worked hard not to be.

How come working in God's name doesn't erase the human elements of fear, shame, and self-loathing?

Today is the ceremony where I get to choose a new name, which represents a new life. This will be the fourth time I change my name in my twenty-five years.

Finally, this will be a time when I can be a totally new person, when nothing that has ever happened will be part of my present reality.

I choose the name Bernadette Marie for a few reasons. There was this saint named Bernadette who had a hard life. She had a vision of Jesus's mother appearing to her, and in the beginning, no one, not even the church, believed her.

Thank God, I have no visions. When I was a child, I used to pray that everyone would stay in heaven and not appear to me. I figured I could barely explain how my life was inside me. I knew I could never begin to explain a vision from heaven.

There are so many ways that I can identify with what St. Bernadette was going through, because people didn't want to hear what I had experienced or knew. I picked Marie for Jesus's mother, Mary, and besides, it has a nice flow to it when you pronounce it—Sister Bernadette Marie.

I went from Jerri Diane Sueck to Jerri Diane Zigga to Jerri Diane Sueck to Sister Bernadette Marie. Not a bad track record. Sometimes I do wonder if names are important, boys' and girls' names, religious and secular names, titles that signify stations in life such as Mr., Miss, Mrs., Ms., Sister, Father, and Pastor, along with others. Also, what happens when name or title changes don't quite fit the person?

I also wonder if everyone who changes their name or seeks a title for identification does so for the kind of reasons that I do? From here on out, I must rise to the challenge of being the best of who I am, even if I still am not sure what I should be doing, and whether I am serving God as a nun for all the right reasons.

Did my mother grow when she took on the title of mother or wife? Do names reflect who we are? Am I ever going to learn who or what I am, if I just keep changing my name?

My life is like a blur of frenzied activity, all revolving around doing good deeds. From the time I get up in the morning until the evening, I am constantly on call to drive, teach, listen, visit the sick, and do other purposeful things.

In some ways, I love the nonstop pace of life as a nun, including the prayer time. There is little space for the darkness of the past to come creeping up on me.

There are days that become a blur filled with the frenzy of doing good deeds, so much so that when I go to my room at night, I am tired. The only drawback is that I have to go to sleep. I continue trying to be the best nun, offering everything up to God. I am still plagued by my night dreams of the "shuffle madness" and the two years in the coal cellar.

There are times when I will wake up in the middle of the night exhausted, because I am being chased, questioned, and cornered by events and people who were present in my faraway past. Every morning, even now that I am a nun, continues to be a challenge of wanting to get up and face the day.

One of the most important good deeds that I have done as a nun was to comfort a young boy in the sixth-grade class. His father had died around Christmas, and he was very attached to him. Three months later, when I asked him to do something, he said no, which was not like him at all. I took him to the library and sat him at the table; I leaned over to him, face to face, and said, "You miss him, don't you?" And the kid started crying.

He said no one knows how hard it is for him because he loved his father, and every day it is getting harder to go on without him. He told me I could never understand how he prays and begs God to send his father back. For the first time since leaving the orphanage, I tell him a less detailed account of how my mother had died and my aching hunger and loneliness for her return.

His eyes grew wide, and he said, "Wow, you don't think I'm crazy then for thinking and feeling this way." I told him no, but he should talk to his mother and remember to allow other people to nurture him as his father did. I also told him that he would always feel the sting of his father's absence at various times in his life, even when he becomes a man but that this is okay and normal.

I just said that part of honoring the dead is to keep them alive in our hearts, and our missing them is one way of knowing how irreplaceable they are in our lives. I told the kid his mother might remarry someday. I said that God never meant for any child to remain fatherless or motherless. He should accept the nurturing of another father figure because that is what his Dad would have wanted.

I spoke to the kid's mother on the phone, and she thanked me for talking to him. She said she was worried because he was becoming more withdrawn. I reminded her that just because his father died didn't mean he didn't need to be fathered. She said she had a son who is in his twenties, and she would speak to him about taking his much younger brother under his wing.

How does any kid ever come to terms with the loss of someone who has not finished helping them to grow? Did I do the right thing by letting adults know that this child needed to be touched, nurtured, questioned, and loved even more now than before his great loss?

Today at the high school where I teach, I learn a very important lesson about life. In one of my religion classes, I have two students who have been orphaned by death.

One girl's mother died of a drug overdose when the girl was five, and her father died of an overdose when she was six. Because her parents were not working, there was no Social Security, life insurance, or family that would, or could, take her. She lives in a group home with five other girls and has been a ward of the state for over ten years. She is a really nice girl and a fair student.

The other student's mother died in a car accident, and her father died in the line of duty as a policeman. Unlike the other orphan in my class, her aunt and uncle have assumed guardianship of the children and managed to keep them together.

An important factor in this lucky orphan's situation is that her mother made a will. Both of her parents worked, so there is Social Security for the children. They also have life insurance money for when the children turn eighteen. As a daughter of a fallen police officer, she will receive financial help with college.

I think that the lucky orphan deserves all of this aid and as much emotional support as she can get. I just wish that the unlucky orphan had the same opportunity.

Maybe all parents, when children are born, should be made to construct a will before they leave the hospital. I think life insurance should be mandatory for all parents, with their children being the beneficiary. Finally, I believe that surrogate parenting is a right for every orphaned child, whether within the family or with people who open their homes and hearts.

I think planning and money can go a long way in bridging the gap between the lucky and the unlucky orphans. With enough financial support, the lucky orphan's aunt and uncle are able to provide for all of the children without separating them.

The impact of death is not always equal for all children who are left behind to move on with their lives. Maybe even in death, there are the haves and the have-nots, although it is usually only the orphaned children who know this reality.

Is life always unfair for some kids? Do the lucky orphans know about the twist of fate that could have made them unlucky orphans?

I can't believe that I am still alive. Today I turn thirty-one years old, and I don't die like I thought I am supposed to. I never thought that I would outlive my mother, since she died when she was thirty-one years old. I have tried to serve God and people, yet on this morning of my thirty-first birthday, I still feel so young, so lost, and so confused about a thousand things.

All my life, I figured that my time on earth was limited, so I needed to do as much good as I could before I died. Now what am I going to do?

Sometimes I feel like I am in constant motion, but going nowhere. How is it possible to be always moving but never getting ahead of the darkness that continually nips at your heels?

I have spent years determined to live a good and honorable life, filled with service to others so that I could prepare to die and go to heaven. Instead, here I am, still in the here and now, not regretting anything, just wondering where I will go from here.

What plans do I make as I begin to outlive my mother? The real question is, how do I struggle beyond the limitations within that only I know about? I am still discombobulated. I have tried so hard to pretend that whatever has happened in the past has no impact, but I still don't feel together. The night dreams bombard me, and even some days as a nun are hard.

Maybe I should bury myself in my work and take on even more responsibilities so that every minute of every day is filled. I don't know what it will be like to be older than my mother physically or emotionally. I still feel left behind in the cloud of the "shuffle madness" dust.

What if I made the wrong choice about how to live my life? How do I find a way to live beyond my mother's death age? Will I always be in a circular motion in life, never moving forward?

I met this really neat woman today. She is a radio talk show host in Philadelphia who uses a stage name.

We started a conversation at this meeting place for losing weight. Somehow we struck it off as people who enjoy sharing our views on life. I have started to put on weight, especially since I have turned thirty-one years old and didn't die. I don't care about how I look, but the weight seems to bother other people.

I guess from her job as an interviewer, she elicits some of my past information, which she finds fascinating. For some reason, people find my past interesting. Since we've been meeting at least once a week for the past few months, she and I have become friendly, and I look forward to our chats.

My friend is fascinated with convent life and my past—what little I share with her. She asks me what I am doing for Christmas, because she and her husband, Eli, would be glad to have me over for dinner.

I am deeply touched that she would think of inviting me for the holiday meal. Usually, in the convent, most of the nuns go home to their families, and I spend the time catching up on stuff. Often there is one elderly nun who also stays at the convent. I don't mind the time alone. From my past, I just accept that this is the way things should be.

At one time, I used to think that if I joined the convent, we would all be sisters, like in a family, but it didn't work out that way. No matter how much we do serving others, most of the nuns still go home to their families for the holiday. I guess in all walks of life, people still go home to family. Even for adults, family continues to be an essential part of one's life experience.

I accept my friend's invitation, because she is a person whom I like being around and who makes me feel comfortable. Maybe this is another step in finding a circle of friends, because while doing good deeds and praying does serve God, I sometimes think that my mother want me to be touched by the human experience of friendship. Besides, I have no plans for the holiday, and it might be good for me to get out for a day. It is time to have Christmas with a family. Maybe this is a beginning of celebrating holidays differently.

How do people like my friend know how to extend kindness? Are holidays something that I can still learn to celebrate? Why am I still so afraid of people?

The school that I m assigned to this year is a marvelous place of excitement and life. After seven years of teaching eighth grade, I finally feel that I have found my niche in the educational field.

There is a vibrant atmosphere at this high school that sits in the middle of a struggling neighborhood in Philadelphia, Pennsylvania. Even its name, Little Flower High School, lends itself to the mystique of being important in the midst of the ordinary. There was this woman named Therese de Lisieux, who was called the Little Flower of Jesus because she didn't want to draw attention to herself as she tried to serve God.

I guess the purpose of the school is to help ordinary kids from families who try to show their daughters a moral path to life. The thing that strikes me about being here is the spirit that resonates throughout the hallways and wherever the girls are gathered. Even when there are assemblies in the auditorium, there is an excitement about being here that is electrifying.

I find that there are few stragglers, you know kids who are left to themselves to become loners. Although there is tight discipline, especially regarding cutting classes, the school is dynamic and alive. Sometimes I just absorb the energy from the supportive staff I teach with and from the girls who are always willing to do projects.

One of my favorite projects is Operation Santa Claus, which the school does for Christmas. Each religion class is assigned one family, and they become responsible for providing them with a holiday filled with food and presents.

I feel like I am personally responsible for my five families and try to provide them with a holiday that was deprived of my brothers and me. I make absolutely sure that every child, little or big, is remembered. I especially don't want the teenagers to feel left out. I love doing this Christmas service project, because I still remember the pain of being forgotten on Christmas during my youth.

When we grow up, do we become the Santa Claus for the others in real life? How do I continue doing good for others even as the whisper tears flow to the surface with their drowning currents?

Today I finally met the first human being who I think glimpses the real truth about me and doesn't think I am crazy.

This nun, Sister Leah, is from another community of sisters. She is a counselor by training, and when I start to talk to her, she actually asks some relevant questions.

What surprises me is that she tells me that I have some serious issues to come to terms with. She says trying to forget or pretend that the past never happened is doing more damage than good.

Leah tells me that God never meant for people to live in isolation. She says that certainly any child who has been through the "shuffle madness" is a child cheated out of ordinary life experiences. She says that it would be normal for me to be the way I am and that I would need years of therapy to try to piece back together what some people had deliberately set out to destroy.

Leah says that by refusing to come to terms with such an extraordinary past I am cheating myself out the chance of living as a whole person. No matter how I live my life, whether as a nun, a single person, or a married person, no one can fully embrace these ways of living with the trunks that weigh me down.

One thing I like about Leah is that she is aghast at the way that the "shuffle madness" years, from my mother's death to my high school graduation, have played out. She tells me how lucky I am that I am not crazy, because most other kids would have collapsed under those kinds of unacceptable life losses.

Finally someone has told me what I have always known to be true, that the shattering that took place so long ago cannot be swept under a carpet or forgotten. If I want to be together inside and not always afraid of myself and other people, I need to make some changes.

Mostly, I like knowing that Leah knows that the losses from the time of my mother's death were beyond the ordinary and enough to drive me out of my mind. She confirms what I have long believed, that the "shuffle madness" is not something that I can just walk away from if I want wholeness. She says she will continue talking to me until I can get into counseling where I live. Maybe Leah is another night-light in the darkness.

Will talking about where I have been help me to live with where I am going? Are people still, in the end, an important part of healing? How come there are not more people like Leah who see the complexity of trying to be whole as a difficult but necessary journey?

After doing a lot of soul-searching, I decide that I need more help than either God or I can provide. Maybe in the end it is about people who tried to destroy parts of me and people who have to restore those parts of me that I need in order to be whole. I can no longer go on wrestling with myself night in and night out with my night dreams and not go crazy.

I think that I need to confront a past that I have so little control over. There are so many issues that I know about within me that have never been dealt with, and probably even more issues that I am not even aware of.

I decide that perhaps I need to get some counseling, and although Leah lives in another city, she has agreed to meet me once a month, until I feel strong enough to see someone else. When I approach the person in charge from the province, she is taken aback by my request.

She says that God should be enough and that people who go for counseling end up leaving the convent. When I tell her that I just want to sort out past things revolving around my mother's death, she tells me that the past isn't relevant to my life as a nun because all my energy should be focused on serving God through service to others.

I try to assure her that this is not about God but about some issues that are troubling me. Somehow I feel like I'm asking for the moon. She reluctantly agrees to allow me to see Leah but expects that I should make rapid progress. Her parting shot to me is to remember that whatever problems I have, I brought them with me to the convent. The nuns are not responsible for anything.

I think to myself that no one has to worry about me blaming them. A long time ago, I learned to blame myself for everything, from what has happened to me to the great feeling of shame which continues to haunt me. I don't even know if counseling is the right direction, but I have to keep trying to make sense of who I am and who I am not. Besides, I'm getting tired of running away from myself.

Maybe its time that I tried to come to terms with so much, or at least try to learn how to live with what truths are hidden inside me. I can't go on being afraid of people and myself. This is no way to live, even for someone who considers herself half human.

Is this full-circle time? Why, after so many years, do I end up having to seek healing from people? What happens if I discover things about myself that I don't like?

The person in charge suggests that I take psychological tests over a period of three days in order to see where I stand mentally. I don't say anything, but I think to myself that the order doesn't understand that I have some unresolved issues that I would like to come to terms with.

Of course, I go along with their plan. There are a thousand and one questions asked, along with a memory test for my IQ and all kinds of grids to fill in. There are times while taking this test that I begin questioning myself. There were questions that I didn't know the answer to or didn't want to give the answer.

The person in charge tells me that the final results indicate that I am suffering from post-traumatic stress syndrome, like the soldier who returns from a war. My IQ turns out to be very good, and my memory test result is excellent.

I knew all along that the issue was not only my mother's death but the way I had to cope with everything and everyone in a vacuum without any direction. Sometimes, even as a kid, and now as an adult, I get irked by the assumption that if you try to get what other people have, then you must not be happy.

It is hard to convince someone that I need to deal with these issues. Often I am told that I am strong or tough, and Jesus is enough. However, even Jesus always surrounded himself with advisors and friends. Even his mother was always available to help him do his work. I figure that if Jesus needed a support group, then I am in good company.

Do you think that I am in good company when I try to find the support system that helped Jesus? Why do people assume that asking for help indicates a set of unsolvable problems and acceptable labeling?

Today I force myself to approach the person in charge, and I again request to leave the convent so I can get some counseling.

For the past couple of months, I have seen Leah and realized that I have so many issues that are unresolved, and even issues that are hidden so deep inside. I am still stinging from my initial request of asking to see Leah and being told yes, but that I have brought my problems to the convent. There is no way that I would want anyone to think that I am hiding or using the convent to blame for anything.

I was told that the community wanted healthy people who don't have a lot of issues when they enter. So I think that in order to get some of the splintered parts back together, I will ask for a leave of absence due to health reasons.

When I have my face-to-face meeting with the Mother Superior, she says that it would be best if I stayed in the community and worked toward healing. I tell her that I am being pressured by the person in charge to give her access to all my records, especially what goes on in my counseling sessions. She tells me not to worry about it, because this was confidential between my counselor and me. She will make arrangements for me to have access to a car.

Things are okay for the first month, but then I get an angry phone call from the person in charge of the province, accusing me of going over her head. I try to explain about how she makes me feel intimidated by her demands. I don't want her having access to the counseling sessions, I just wanted to do this quietly.

Inside my head, I am afraid that I am too much of a mess for anyone to understand or accept. She tells me that she has told the superior person in charge that I don't belong under her jurisdiction.

She also says that she will be in touch with the counselor, because as a member of the community, she is entitled to all my information. After she hangs up, I call the superior person in charge, who tells me that she can't help me. She reminds me that she has to be concerned about all the sisters in general, not about any one individual. I don't say anything, I just hang up.

Why are people so changeable? How could someone like the superior person in charge have all that power and still be intimidated by someone who is only second-in-command?

Today in the mail there is a letter from the person in charge, informing me that she has terminated my contract with Little Flower High School. She writes that she hopes that I will be open to serving the community.

I call the person in charge and ask her as to the purpose of this termination letter. She says that it is she who has authority over me. In our conversation, she tells me that I will be sent to the Scranton area to teach eighth grade. She says that if I am a good sister, I will accept this assignment as God's will. When I tell her about my continuing difficulty with being assigned to Scranton, she says the past is a long time ago, and this is my only choice.

When I ask if there is anything I can say to change her mind, she tells me no. I hang up the phone and decide to do a lot of thinking about what to do next.

The person in charge has the right to assign me to whatever job she wants, and if there is a problem with this, then it is my problem. I realize the only thing I can change if I don't like some situation in my life is me. I should have taken a leave of absence like I planned to this past summer, then I wouldn't be in such a quandary about what to do now.

I didn't mean to cause such problems for the person in charge or for the order or everyone, I just wish I can disappear. Maybe it is time to shake the dust from my feet and move on to a place where I can put everything back together. I'm not angry or upset, just a bit hurt, and I feel that I am being misunderstood. I'm truly sorry that my best isn't good enough for the order, but I just can't bear the thought of returning to Scranton with all its memories of unbelievable cruelties.

Why do the boomerangs of the past still bombard me even as a nun?

I'm not sure about anything in my outside world anymore. I wonder if doing good deeds on a full-time basis or serving God in such a public manner is something that I should continue to do?

There are times when I feel as if everything I have so carefully worked toward is coming back to beat me up. I think that what I need to do is to settle myself down and spend some quiet time doing a reality check of where my life has been, where it is, and where I need it to go so that I don't crash.

Tonight, as I lie here trying to find where my spirit needs to go in order to grow, I realize that it is the complete denial of my past that has brought me to the brink of making a life-altering decision. There is no way I can continue to be a nun if I cannot understand or accept my own humanity in its fullest.

I also realize that leaving the convent won't solve my problems, but then neither did entering it. The nuns deserve better than I can offer. I need to spend time confronting my own demons, even the ones given to me by others.

I need to get into counseling, because as much as I love my mother and God, what people have done to me and what I think of myself as a result, need people's intervention and help. In some ways, maybe counseling is possible because my mother and God will be there, supporting me. I must search for a way to not feel so condemned all the time.

Tomorrow I will petition for a leave of absence due to health reasons. I have spoken to the Vicar for Religious, and this was her suggestion. There are no regrets, no second doubts. If I am not whole, then I cannot give a hundred percent of who I am to the order, and they deserve my best efforts. If I just do not know how to be whole, then how could I ever expect to give fully to the works that would please God?

It is not that I wanted to have this life of mine, but I forgot to take care of the cards handed out to me at birth—being motherless and being shattered. I thought not picking up the pieces would be okay and less painful, but I can't be a real person without coming to terms with the whole of me.

Can I go back and heal my damaged heart? Why, after religion, do I still need people to bring me to life?

Tomorrow I leave the convent, a way of life that I was not really prepared to join.

It isn't that I have any regrets for what I have done for the past ten years, because I don't. It's just that maybe a person should be totally together if they are going to publicly serve God and not be discombobulated inside like I am. I'm sure that the convent deserves to have what I have been told they wanted, and that is somebody who is a whole and healthy person.

One lesson that I have learned is that at thirty-three years of age, instead of beating myself up for not being good enough, I will shake the dust from my feet and move on.

There are no good guys or bad guys in my inability to continue in a way of life that I thought would bring peace to my heart. The truth is that I was messed up a long time ago, and neither education nor religion can undo the damage that continues to haunt me today.

At least I do walk with my faith and my relationship with God intact. These ten years have been a learning experience, and even though I wasn't whole enough or good enough, at least I tried to be the best nun, giving service to others as best as I could.

I'm not sure where I go from here, but there will be no turning back, no regrets, no second-guessing of my decision. How I will live from here on out is not yet known to me, but this may be an opportunity for new growth and for experiencing life in another dimension.

I know that no matter what I do I must somehow lasso the past and harness its destructive energy and channel it into something positive in my life. Maybe I'll even write a book someday, like my friend Lois has always told me I should.

Now it looks like I have a whole new adventure before me. I hope that I can stop being one of the walking wounded and become a walking healer who makes other people feel better for having known me.

How often does a person come back from the darkness to start a new life? Are the lessons from years past stumbling or building blocks to the future? God, will I still be able to learn to be whole, or at least learn how to live with my fractures?

"Living My Life"

Laughter, acceptance now the norm
Where once was dark, now is light
Pain and loneliness no longer constant
Companions for the journey are present.

Up and down, life is no longer chaotic
Road maps offer a certain clarity
That allow new life to begin to be lived
Second-guessing fades away into the past.

Travel, children, home, family, pets, friends
Offer an excitement of living never before experienced.
Now is her turn to seek what has been denied
Tasting the deliciousness of life is the new plan.

Where or why no longer needs answers
Motion forward in permanent direction.
Sand replaced by solid ground for roots
Growth continues as life bathes her in its' light.

Hope replaces despair, emotions now acceptable
Toughness replaced by strength of character now emerged.
No longer hidden behind absences of the ordinary
Now is a new path that offers an embrace of what should have been.

New life, new beginnings, new tomorrows
Wipe away the whisper tears hiding in her heart.
A new day, a new start, a new dream of hope
That offer a change rooted in certainty of self.

My Emergence Into Life
Ages 34 - Present

My Emergence into Life

(Ages Thirty-Four to Present)

Dear Mother,

Today I am thirty-three years old, and I have left the convent. I have a small apartment that has two bedrooms, which I share with a roommate. I met my roommate while teaching at Little Flower High School. She is engaged to a nice guy.

The first thing I do today is get a kitten that I name Molly. I have always wanted a pet, something I could cuddle and feel responsible for. An additional reason for getting the kitten is that I am trying to teach myself to be attached.

Since I'm not sure if I am able to become attached to human beings because of the missing pieces inside me, I thought I would practice by having a pet. Maybe if I can become attached to Molly and feel a bond with a her, then it might be possible to move on to a dog, and then people.

I know I sound so childlike with how I try to heal myself, but I don't know what else to do. Having no money, I have taken on three jobs—one is caring for the elderly on the weekends, the other is working at night at a locked psyche unit in a state hospital, and the third is substituting at a local high school during the day.

One of the reasons I want to work so much is to tire myself out, if this is possible. My main purpose is to stay awake as much as I am able to. I'm not sure what direction I want to take in my life, but I need to find a way out of these self-imposed and other isolations in this life that I now live.

I will be looking for a counselor who might be able to provide me with some help to put back together what so long ago was blown apart. The reality is that if I ever intend to make an attempt at living in the real world of people and not in institutions of education and religion, I need to accept everything about my life and learn to make the best of whatever truths I discover.

Truth is a fickle thing at times, because when I go searching for answers to questions, I may not be prepared for what I need to accept as real. It's just that my denial of who or what I am and where I came from is no longer working for me.

I have to believe that deep down inside is a human being worth salvaging. If I am to live in the real world of human beings, with their complex mixture of mind, gender, spirit, emotion, and dreams, I can't keep running from myself. I have to struggle to bring all the splintered parts of me together.

Why is it so hard to know who or what I am? Will learning about my complexities help to glue back what was broken so long ago? Why does my spirit still seek that magnetic pull of wholeness?

Love,
Jerri

*   *   *

I am finding life in the adult world to be very stressful. Maybe I just missed out on some important lessons growing up. Between money and trying to learn how to manage my time, I am feeling overwhelmed.

I think that there must be something wrong with me. I should be thinking about seeing a therapist. I feel like this eight-year-old inside who doesn't know how to say no with money and time. Maybe I am stuck in an emotional past that I've never outgrown.

Even though I work a lot, I don't have any money. When people ask me for money, I feel obligated to give whatever I have, even if it means dipping into my bill money.

I am trying to learn not to believe people. Three times I sold an old car along with the title. The people always promised to make payments, because they didn't have all the money. All three times I didn't get the payments as promised. I also sold my air conditioners, which were brand new, and I didn't get any payment. I have to learn not to let people take advantage of me.

It isn't that I want their approval or have the means to do this. There is something inside me that feels that they wouldn't ask if they really didn't need the money, and I should think of others before myself, even if it hurts me.

One of the reasons that I think I have figured out how to do well in school and in my job is that school has always been a consistent event in my life, without traumatic interruptions. The move from education to a professional job market was a natural flow for me.

Work and school never really depended on where I came from or who I was inside. All I ever needed was the proper paperwork certifying that I have completed whatever was necessary to fulfill the requirements needed.

Being human, or at least accepting the multitude of pieces that make a person someone, is more than just a name or a face; it is much more intricate. The real question is, how do I go back and undo the survival list, which is still a central part of how I live and how I fail to live?

I still feel like I am in a fog sometimes, trying to learn the language of the living. I have learned the language of working, but to live and to work are not always the same.

How is it possible for the past to still anchor me down, even when I desire to reach out and grow? Why do I still feel like there are just a million pieces of me that I can't match together? Will there ever be a time when the question of who or what I am will be answered?

My life is becoming a little more settled on the outside. I have finally been hired as a full-time teacher in Philadelphia, and I have been able to pick a good school.

I've cut back to working weekends at the hospital and am now taking care of only one elderly person. I've kept one old lady under my care, because she is so mean and nasty that no one else is willing to work with her. Maybe it's Catholic guilt, but I feel responsible for her because no one wants to deal with her.

When she is not being mean and nasty, she is nice. She is in her eighties and just feels lonely and abandoned. Her son visits her, but she wants someone to be with her all the time. I hope that if I ever live as long as she does, I will at least be gracious to those who are caring for me.

One thing that I have learned is that she likes going for rides and looking at houses. She loves to tell me about how her life used to be and how she doesn't belong in this world anymore. I get her out of the house by taking her wallet and throwing it in my car. She always follows me out of the house for her wallet, and then she gets into the car.

She always asks me if I am going to quit. I just say that I'll stay until someone else comes along, although I don't see anyone in the horizon yet.

I look at this lady and wonder what is in store for me in my future. She must have been young once, madly in love, cherishing her parents and her son. She loves to tell me about the time she took three different buses on a fifteen-hour trip to visit her son for two hours on parents' day at the camp he was attending. I thought what a wonderful act of motherly love. I don't think she is really mean and nasty deep down, it's just that she is tired of being left alone. Most of her friends are dead.

Now at eighty-nine, she struggles to see a purpose in her living. Constantly, I remind her of her family. She has a beautiful granddaughter. It is hard sometimes to lift her spirits because of her comparison of life now with life from the yesteryears.

One lesson I have learned from my old friend is that it is important to age gracefully and welcome the changes that come, even if they are a reminder of the slowing down of life. There was a nun friend whose mother I used to help care for, and she was the picture of aging gracefully. I hope I end up like her mother and not like the woman who acts mean and nasty out of loneliness.

Where are the words that can comfort someone who has experienced a life of living and now sits for hours alone, wishing for a past that no longer exists? How do I bring meaning to the life of someone who just wants to die? How come after working hard all through one's life, there is so little energy left to enjoy the fruits of one's labor?

Sometimes I count my blessings and realize that I have been lucky in some ways. At times it is pure luck, other times I make luck work for me.

I teach in a large high school in Philadelphia, where the students and teachers continually teach me about different life experiences. I teach history to juniors and seniors and sometimes help out with some activities.

There is a certain spirited camaraderie at the Franklin Learning Center. I would guess this bond exists at most schools. The unique collection of characters is really what makes a building into a place of learning and living. We are all here for a shared purpose, and most of us enjoy each other's company.

I have never met any two people who are the same. Maybe that is why I have always found people to be so fascinating. Sometimes I'm not sure who is more interesting, the staff or the students.

My vice principal is like a battery that doesn't quit. She has more energy than I will ever possess, and she has excellent taste in clothes. The principal is a very formal person, but he is approachable and has this dry sense of humor, a bit too dry.

One of the teachers is always assigning other teachers nicknames such as Queen of Ma Bell and Queen of the IBM Lab, just to name a few. There are teachers who are strict and others who are lenient, teachers who are approachable and others that keep their distance.

Even among the students there is an abundance of personalities. One kid comes every morning to see me, because he wants to make sure he is going to college and is doing everything right to get in. Another kid comes to talk to me about how she just wants to be in Hollywood someday and worries that it is too big of a dream. Of course, I reassure both students that all things are possible, if they want it bad enough and are willing to pay their dues to make their dreams come true.

They always ask me why I believe in their dreams, when even at home, they don't get this nurturing enthusiasm. I just tell them that I have come from nowhere and from nothing, and if I can make something out of my life, then surely they can also.

There is nothing that cannot be accomplished if they are willing to work toward the dream. Half the fun of dreaming is enjoying the ride toward its fulfillment.

Is passing on encouraging words a way of sharing the echo of who we are? Can sharing the energy of others bring more life into the world I live in?

There are times when I encounter a student who needs something more from me than just the academics.

One of my boys in class has begun talking to me on almost a daily basis since he has been in ninth grade. His mother was killed in a plane crash during the winter of his freshman year in high school.

It was just by chance that I struck up a conversation with him about his mother and her devastating death. One day, before school, he came to ask if he could talk to me and said that he thought I might be able to help him.

Fred said that he had heard me talk about the hand of cards in life that we are all dealt and how we have to play the hand. He wanted to know if I knew how hard it was not to have a mother and yet to be surrounded in such a mothering society.

I told him about my own mother's dying and how my entire universe became altered by that one defined and irretrievable moment. He looked relieved and said, with tears glistening in his eyes, "Finally someone who knows what I am talking about."

I asked Fred what he missed the most about his mother. He said that he used to sit at the dining room table doing homework, and his mother would walk through, tousling his hair, patting him on the back, getting him in a bear hug, and telling him that he was a great kid.

I told Fred that those are what I call the mother touches and that they are normal, healthy, and essential to every kid. He almost started crying again when I told him that just because his mother died, it doesn't mean that he also died.

"Her death in no way negates the continuing need of the mother touches," I said. "Just because you were fourteen when she died, you didn't stop being a son, a kid, or a human being still searching for a way to be a person or a man."

Fred told me how his sister cried the night before her prom, and how on every occasion he feels like there is something missing from his life. I told him that the greatest way to remember his mother is to talk to her spirit and to allow her to come along for the ride as he goes through life becoming the man that he is meant to be.

Missing her, even aching for her return, is normal, and few people will ever understand the depth of his sorrow; but it is okay to want her and to want to be nurtured.

I encouraged him to seek out people who can help him compensate for his loss. The mother touches are still essential to his growth. I told him to allow his aunt, grandmother, or whoever to continue what should be continued and to embrace their nurturing spirits.

Fred said that sometimes, late at night, he tries to imagine how different his life would be if only he can turn back time. He wondered if he had done something wrong for her to die. I told him that in life things just happen. I said that I don't believe that there is a grand plan to orphan certain children. It's just one of those things in life that are beyond our comprehension, but not beyond our continuing sorrow.

The key to everything though is not just that his mother died, but that he lives in a way that honors everything she has taught him, dreamed for him, and sacrificed for him.

I said that she would want him to look for nurturing from others, and to accept other mother touches in abundance, because it would take a lot to make up for what she would have given him, if fate had not stepped in.

I also told Fred that he will always feel loneliness and a sense of loss, especially at graduation, his wedding, and the birth of his children.

I just said that these moments, instead of being depressing, are an opportunity to be touched with the feelings that continue to honor her presence and her absence in his life.

Fred and I have talked many times throughout his four years in high school. He thanked me for listening because after his mother died, he wanted to die too. Now he knew that he must make something of his life.

I told him that I was thinking about writing a book someday about my experience of being without a mother, and he said that was good because maybe other motherless children won't feel so lost like he did.

Fred said he loves his father, but he is not his mother. He said that most kids don't know how lucky they are and how in a split second, their whole universe could be altered forever, with no opportunity to go back to how it was.

I love Fred because of his honesty and his willingness to try to understand the world that he must live in. He is willing to honor his mother by becoming a man in the image that would have pleased her had she lived.

Maybe I am taking what happened to me and helping other kids not to believe that they are alone, crazy, or left behind.

Do I pass on my mother's spirit when I nurture a child struggling to find his or her way without the greatest cheerleader that every child deserves? Will Fred ever know that the depth of his feelings for his mother is a wonderful tribute to the presence that she has been for him? Will he ever know that by his becoming the man that he is destined to be this will be the greatest way to honor his mother?

At the psychiatric hospital, where I have been working part-time for a few years, there is this really neat guy I work with.

After I left the convent, I really needed to work for hours in order to pay the bills. Mark was in charge of scheduling, and he always made sure I had plenty of time to work.

He is married to this beautiful woman, and they have two little girls.

We have been working together for a few years, and he has always complained about this pain in his knee from an old football injury.

He often tells me that he has a good life. In our conversations he would tell me how amazed he is that given my background of orphanage and foster homes, I'm not a psychiatric patient.

I just say that in many ways, I am lucky because I just refuse to be beaten by life. I make whatever I have work for me and try to compensate for what I did not receive and still do not have.

Mark went to the doctor to get his knee checked out, because he almost dropped his baby daughter when his knee buckled underneath him. He told me he had been diagnosed with MS—multiple sclerosis. He said he will have to learn to live with this disease.

I asked him the other day how he was doing. He said that he remembered what I said a while back about being orphaned and alone and that I just do the best I can, and about how I look for those things or people that can make up for what I have lost. Mark said that this is the way he figures it too. He said that he is the luckiest guy in the world with his MS, because, looking on the bright side, it is affecting only his legs.

With his arms he can hold his daughters and hug his wife, and he is able to work on the computer at the hospital. The way Mark thinks is that even when his legs go completely, there is his wheelchair, and who knows what treatments are on the horizon for MS.

Mostly though, Mark said that his losses don't begin to compare to what I have lost. He is especially fortunate to have a large family that is always there for him.

His brothers and sisters always make sure that he is included in all family plans and adventures. In addition to that, he has his work, family, and the administration staff at the hospital, who have been very supportive of him.

When I think about Mark, I have to believe that he too has made choices about how he lives with the sucker punches that life deals out sometimes. One thing about Mark is that he has always been as gracious a person as he was the day before he found out he has MS as the day after.

I continue to be fascinated by the depth that the human spirit can go to in order to find a way to live with what is outside of the ordinary.

It is people like Mark who continue to reaffirm my journey toward healing as a realistic one. As he continues to live a gracious life, I hope that his spirit will always outlast whatever physical limitations are sent his way.

How do some people like Mark accept the cards dealt them without bitterness? Do his work family and childhood family give him strength? Why, in the end, is someone like Mark, or even someone like me, able and determined to try to make our way toward the light, when others are content to stay back in their darkness?

Today, when I get home, there is a phone message from my mother's youngest sister.

For the past few years, Billy has been periodically in touch by phone. He has given my unlisted phone number to Mother's family in Indiana.

Although I have not seen Billy since I was ten years old, I still talk to him every now and then. He lives in Alaska with his wife. He says he hasn't been out to Indiana in years but had decided to let bygones be bygones.

My friends are my real family.

I know that Billy gave her my phone number, because he said that they wanted to get in touch with me. I tried to explain to him that they are dead to me because of their abandonment of us as children.

Billy really holds not our mother's family but Dad's family responsible because of their abuse and neglect.

I debate within myself for about a week before calling Indiana. In the end, I decide that I must know one thing about my mother, and that is whether she ever loved me. Even now, in this adult body, there are these children of my heart who yearn for the truth about who she is.

When I do call, my mother's youngest sister answers the phone, as though the past thirty-two years never happened. I cut her off at the pass with her, "Oh, how have you been?" with "Did my mother love me?" There is silence on the other end. Then she says that my mother loved her children deeply.

She says that she would like for me to come out for a visit. I say I would have to think about it because they are dead to me. She says that Grandmother is nearing eighty years old and would often cry because I am the only one of my mother's children who never comes back to visit, or to be in touch.

I ask her why I should go visit an old woman who was forty-seven years old when she said no to taking us, or my mother's two sisters who were in their twenties when things changed.

My mother's youngest sister says that I need to understand that her mother had her hands full with her husband, and she and her sister had their own families. She says that at that time her life was in turmoil with a divorce and remarriage. I tell her that if she thought her life was in turmoil, she should try living like my brothers and me. Our lives gave new meaning to turmoil.

She asks me if I am bitter or angry. I tell her no, because I never got past trying to understand the unexplainable. How could they sleep at night, knowing that we were put out? This aunt of mine says I should be more like my brothers and realize that for the sake of my mother, and my grandmother, I should come to give her peace before she dies. She also adds that I could see my mother's grave. I tell her I will have to think about it because of the promise I made to myself a long time ago.

My mother's sister says that my mother would have forgiven them for not taking us in, and I should also be able to forgive them. I tell her that sometimes forgiveness is more complicated than just the spoken words.

My mother's sister says that our mother did love us deeply, and the shock of her death devastated her family. Maybe it's me, but I can't imagine having a daughter or a sister dying and leaving four orphaned children without making sure they are checked on and taken care of. She tells me that life for adults is different than for children, and sometimes the timing is off.

I tell her that I would think about coming out for a visit since, I work a lot and have to sort some things out in my mind and my heart. When I hang up, all I can think about is where she was when I was eight, ten, twelve, fourteen, and so on.

I find it interesting that none of my brothers have returned to Indiana to live there. Sometimes I wonder about my mother's relationship with her family. I can't understand why they would not seek us out or take us in our time of desperate need.

I think that I might consider going back, maybe as an effort to retrace my mother's steps. Perhaps if I can learn more about who she was, then I can make more sense of these jumbled family ties that do not exactly bind.

All I know is that it will be a while before I make this trip out to the people who did not do right by us and by our mother. One positive point of returning to a place and people who knew my mother is that I will finally learn where she is buried.

Often I have wanted to go and stand at her grave to try somehow to come to terms with her death. Since I plan to start writing a book soon about the journey that the three of us—Mother, God, and I—have undertaken since her death, I will come out to read to her at her gravesite.

It is only fair that I share my writing with the one person who, although is not physically present, has never let me give up on myself. Maybe I will try to learn who she was so that her story can also become a part of my story.

Why can't I just pick up the conversation with her family in Indiana as though the past thirty-two years never happened? How could my mother's mother, sisters, and the other members of her family not search for us in our time of need? How do I balance my adult conversations with the brokenhearted emotions of the child I once was?

I decide that I will go to Indiana to give peace to my mother's mother and to her family, although I am not sure they have a clue about their moral lapse when it came to her children. Mostly, I now look at this journey as an opportunity to retrace my mother's steps in order to learn what I can about who she was and my place in her world.

Since I am considering writing a book, I want to stand by her grave for the first time since her burial so long ago and seek her blessing for this possible adventure. In the end, I am going to her family for her sake and to try to right a great injustice.

I say for her sake, because she broke bread with her mother the night before she died, and maybe she would want me to let that old woman off the hook. While she is in her seventies, I will always remember that she was in her forties and my mother's sisters in their twenties when my mother was killed.

When I arrive, I am greeted like I am this long-lost relative who was on a sightseeing tour of the world and have returned in triumph, sharing the stories of my adventures. I have long conversations with them, explaining that their lack of action contributed to the splintering of the family that my mother had started.

The greatest blessing that I receive is learning how horrified my mother's nieces, whom she has never met, are because of the consequences of their mother's and grandmother's inaction. My mother would have liked her two nieces who tell them straight up that they would never have come back to Indiana if they had been me.

At least the next generation in my mother's family doesn't believe in sweeping everything under the carpet and making peace at any price. I do like these cousins who have children of their own and who are willing to put themselves in my shoes for a while and not accept the rationalizations that are offered as excuses.

I try to learn about my mother from the stories that her sisters tell. They say that they are much younger than her and weren't around her that much. They say that her first cousins from Kentucky, who grew up with her, would know more.

I take Grandmother to visit her sister in Kentucky so I can retrace my mother's footsteps. I want to learn about the challenges in life that she faced. I also want to try to understand what her family had been for her.

How could different people within the same family think and feel so differently about so many things? Will learning about my mother help me to come to terms with the great losses that life has handed to me? By retracing her footsteps, will I finally do justice to her name and her life?

I have been thinking about forgiveness and its role in my life. Ever since my mother's family in Indiana tracked me down, I have wondered if they are owed forgiveness, or if I really have any bitterness in my heart.

There has never been a time that I hated them. How could I hate people I don't know? It's just that this whole thing has never been based on hatred.

This sense of total abandonment, sadness, and disbelief is what I have always been busy trying to figure out. It is my mother's family, Daddy's family, and Mrs. Wesson that I have never figured out.

While I believe that I have spirituality, the complications of forgiveness make me wonder whether it is right to allow people to believe that there are no hard feelings concerning that which was done so long ago.

The problem is not that I hate people, it is just that I don't understand how some people, even my mother's family, sleep at night. One of her brother-in-laws told Billy that we all got educated. All I want to know is, don't people in Indiana get educated?

Beyond the forgiveness is the murkier question of trust. If they want forgiveness and ask for it, I can give it, but I won't feel anything different. All I will be doing is parroting words that will make others comfortable, but nothing will change anything for me, because they've made their choices in life, and I have made mine.

I don't harbor resentment or jealousy, I just never got to those feelings. I am still back at the child-level emotions. I'm trying to understand what they could never explain to my satisfaction or to my mother's.

In some ways, I feel like they disrespected her more than me. She had bonded with them, she knew their stories, she shared their family culture and history. I'm sure she would have assumed that her four older children would have been absorbed into her extended family if there had ever been a catastrophe that only death could initiate.

Forgiveness is available, but the issues of trust and re-bonding will always be matters which will challenge my soul and my heart. They broke her trust, which was her birthright, and failed to protect her greatest gift, her children.

Why did people who embraced her in life change when death came to claim her? Do the people who neglect, abuse, or turn their backs on children in their hour of need have the right to ask for forgiveness?

In the process of learning who my mother was, it has helped me to understand, but not accept, the reasons why her mother and sisters entered into a world of silence about our existence.

Her family are good people who failed to rise to a difficult choice when faced with a moral challenge to become the family for her orphaned children. Her family had a way of keeping things under the carpet, even if these things were the shattered lives of the children she once nourished.

My mother was born when her mother was fifteen or sixteen, and she was given to her grandmother to raise. Apparently, she had bonded with her grandmother in a way most children would have bonded with their mother. While living with her grandmother, her best friends and playmates were her first cousins.

When she was five, her mother married her stepfather, and then she went to live with them. Apparently, her years with her grandmother had split her heart, and she felt more comfortable at her grandmother's home.

Neither her mother or her sisters told her first cousins about our need of a home. All I can figure out is that the resentment between my mother's grandmother and mother over her kept her mom from telling the rest of the family about us.

From my grandmother's explanation, she felt that my mother was spoiled and always wanted to live with my great-grandmother. Even today, my mother's mother, who is in her seventies, still speaks with such venom over what she perceives as the interference of my great-grandmother in her life, in matters regarding my mother. This lifetime hidden hostility may have contributed to her not taking us, or her not telling Mother's first cousins about the request to take us.

I also learned that my mother was a person who was impeccably dressed at all times. Her sisters and cousins said that she was never without her makeup or jewelry.

They said that she always chose us over anyone who tried to hurt us. Our biological father was abusive to us, and our mother took us away from him.

She loved to travel and always wanted to be on her way to somewhere else. It's funny, but her mother loves to travel also, and so did her grandmother.

I just think that my mother's mother was so young when she had her, and her mother was so strict with her that in Grandmother's eyes, my mother's grandmother was easier on her, even doting on her. There was probably some jealously over my mother that had simmered for years and, I believe, had never resolved itself within my mother's mother.

I guess when you learn what the family secrets are, it is easier to understand how their ramifications can still be felt years later, even if some of the people are no longer alive. I do forgive my mother's sisters and her mother, although I'll probably never understand or accept their actions.

Why do family secrets have a way of keeping people from coming to terms with themselves and their families? How come secrets still boomerang years or decades later, especially on people who weren't even around for the event that set them into motion?

While writing this book, I realized what a gift it was to have the company of my three brothers in the early days of after our mother's dying. In hindsight, she would have been so proud of them.

At first, Trevor, Tyler, and Billy all tried to figure out what we had done so wrong that made our mother's family and Daddy's family turn their back on us. In the early days of our displacement from the inner circle of family, we supported and encouraged each other.

Billy, as the oldest, worked constantly to protect us as much as any ten-year-old could. He was always trying to figure out ways to run away and find someone to save us. Often he would go with Trevor or Tyler down to the outhouse, because they were too young and terrified to be out in the dark alone.

He would try to keep our spirits up by saying that even if our mother was in heaven, she would make God use his special power to save us. Billy was always telling us to huddle close, like in football, so we could keep the biting wind from freezing our faces. He taught us how to blow into our hands to warm our faces for a few seconds, then to stuff our hands in our pockets.

Often, when he thought I wasn't looking, I could see him almost crying when either Trevor or Tyler would ask him why Grandma and her family hate us so much, or when I would say that I was making a list of the mean things they were doing so that I could tell our mother when she came back from living with Jesus.

Later, when we got separated, I never saw Billy again. But what a wonderful big brother. Trevor and Tyler and I eventually were also separated by the "shuffle madness" that comes when you are a ward of the state.

Today Trevor is happily married with four children and living in Iowa. Tyler is still trying to come to terms with the past and working on getting his life together. He lives in Iowa. Billy is married and living in Alaska.

The greatest irony about all of this is that years later, without telling each other, Trevor and Tyler also changed their last name. Maybe each of us is trying in our own way to change what we can so that we are not imprisoned by our past. All three of my brothers have kept their promise about not returning to Pennsylvania.

Even though we, in our separation, never became family again, I am thankful that during those two dark years of abandonment, abuse, and neglect, I had these companions for the journey. Trevor, Tyler, and Billy, thank you.

Alice, I understand, married someone twenty years older than her when she was nineteen. She has four sons. She also, after thirty years, got in touch with me. Financially, she struggles and does ask for help. I told her that she needs to go back to school. She had more opportunities than Trevor, Tyler, Billy, and me, yet she is struggling to get herself together.

How could four children descend into a harrowing darkness and madness and come out alive in more ways than just physically? Why was the company of my brothers able to help me to survive? Did Billy at the age of ten show more manhood than Daddy who was supposed to be our protector?

I must find a therapist who can help me deal with all the versions of me in different ages that are within me. I know I have matured in my professional and educational life. However, in other less observable ways, I am immature and not the same age as that of the person I am in my professional or educational world.

Deep down, I realize that I function at different emotional ages, and I still need to grow up in many ways. I have seen several counselors, and although they have been somewhat helpful, I need to really sort out what kind of healing I need.

I know the deficits that exist within me and what I want to work on, especially because I live by the survival list I made when I was fourteen.

Some hard truths about myself are my distrust of people, my fear of attachment, my need to explore the issues that almost destroyed me as a child, my gender, and the realization that I am not half human.

I still feel intimidated by people. I live in a house instead of a home. I have never taken a vacation. I feel like I don't deserve anything pleasurable, because I have to make restitution for living.

As long as I live like this and not make any changes, I will never be whole. I need to embrace what I feared the most as a child, and is these are the female self and the woman I am meant to be. Somehow I must merge the children in different ages into one person who is able to hold her head up high and believe that her existence has a purpose.

From here on out, I will no longer allow myself to think that I am half human because that gives victory to all those who tried to destroy me. I will seek a counselor who can help me touch the whisper tears that are held back by a dam of stoicism.

Now I know that there has to be another way for me to live. There needs to be a clearing out of the messiness inside that keeps me imprisoned in places of my heart and soul that no longer need to exist for self-preservation. I must seek ways of living a full life as a whole human being.

How do I find someone to show me the way to move from merely surviving to living a life full of friendship, joy, contentment, and fun?

A long time ago, I decided that I would be an observer in life and not a player.

Back then I didn't think I had the skills to be like other people, or that I had even the raw material to develop those skills. But now I think that I was going in the wrong direction with this choice. Maybe the truth is that I have just as much opportunity to enjoy life experiences as others do, only, I have not surrounded myself with people who can nurture me.

I will no longer allow the limitations that have been imposed upon me to continue holding me back. I have been born for something greater than the losses that have been dealt me. Never again will I settle for observing life at a distance.

I'm not exactly sure how I will change from being an observer in life into being a player, but it should be exciting to watch how I change. I have my cat and my dogs, and I am very attached to them. I swear that my cat looks at me with questioning eyes sometimes. She probably wonders why I do things the way I do.

Recently I bought a little row house in Philadelphia. The area around it is filled with at least fifty thousand people. This little house will have to do until I build my dream house, a log cabin that is on the list of past wishes.

Part of the reason that I know I am still not where other people are is that I don't know how to turn this house into a home. There are times when I feel overwhelmed by having to care for it. Probably, the reason is that I never grew up in a house or a home. One part of it that I especially try to avoid is the basement. I know I don't like the basement.

Although I tell myself I am physically an adult, emotionally, at times, I'm back to a much younger age. I work hard at trying to get everything together. I have learned that I have to let friends share the journey of this adventure called life. Then I won't feel so overwhelmed by what other adults consider ordinary, everyday living.

I wonder if it will be possible to turn "the house" into "my home"? What will it take to help me accept life in ways so many other adults take for granted?

Philadelphia is where I make my home these days, although sometimes I feel like I am on my way to somewhere, only, I'm not sure where it is that I am going.

Every Friday, the *Philadelphia Inquirer* has a presentation written about a child or sibling group who are available for adoption. Often I study their pictures and their story and wonder about the hopes and dreams that bring these children to the point of publicly putting themselves out in full view to ask for adoption.

As I read about the others, I realize that my obsession with being adopted was not so out of the ordinary. Each week I notice that, although the years have changed, each of our stories, my past and their present, is filled with the losses and sorrows that are beyond measure.

As I look at the pictures of the older children, I applaud their courage at saying, "Look, I know I'm not young, cute, or adorable, but I am good, honest, and just as hungry to be in a permanent relationship as the younger children." Their refusal to continue living with the absence of the ordinary and to seek a way to be rooted, to belong, and to be part of a family is proof that their human spirit is alive and well.

Maybe someday, when I feel more steady about who I am, I will be able to open up my home and heart to one child, or a sibling group, that is on that assembly line of the "shuffle madness." Who knows, my mother may have grandchildren of the heart, who will reflect all the survival and living choices that I have had to make because of her absence.

I will continue to read "Friday's Child" and pray that this service will touch the hearts of others so that there can be less loneliness in the world. Getting the message out to America about children who are seeking permanency is an underappreciated service.

In the end, the success of even one story ending in adoption is a tremendous boost to everyone else who waits for their turn. My turn never did come, but I have fought for a way to compensate for the lack of permanency with friends, counseling, education, my mother, and God.

How come there aren't more people getting the message out about the "shuffle madness" kids? Do public stories of heartache really touch the people who are capable of offering a life of the ordinary to a child who has known only its absences?

Today I do something that I never thought I would do. I go back to Scranton, the city of my childhood displacement. My friend Cleo and her husband, Louis, drive up with me so I can take pictures for the book I am writing about my life.

Even though I am now in my early forties, I still cannot shake this overwhelming desire to put my head down in shame. I decide that I must force myself to hold my head up and to look at this place just as I do everything else.

There has got to be more goodness here than evil. Now I realize there were people who did try to help us. The neighbors who tried to help us when they reported Daddy's family for their abuse and neglect of us far outweigh the people who chose not to accept us. My teacher in the third grade who gave me candy to pass out on my birthday. The last cop who told them that he would take all the children, including Alice, if he was called out to the house again. They all represent people who tried to do right by us.

Maybe it is time to forgive Scranton. There were people who tried to interfere in the viscous cycle that we children were stuck in. When I was at the orphanage and the high school taking pictures, I realized that I have come a long way from the darkness I once knew.

Only at Grandma Resuba's house do I realize that there are still places in my soul that are fractured. I can't even get out of the car to take any pictures. Cleo takes them with her camera. The coal bank is still there, along with the house, painted the same color, and the white coal cellar door.

Even now, although I have come a long way in my life and emotional development, at this moment, staring at the house of my nightmares, all those memories of alienation and shame come rushing back before I could stop them. I guess even in my healing process, I still need to continue making progress.

For now though, I am grateful that by revisiting Scranton I have learned to remember that most people were not, and are not, filled with hatred. Some even took a proactive stance in dealing with Daddy's family. Maybe we are alive today because of the neighbors' constant calls of complaints. So now I will think of the city of Scranton in a different and more hope-filled light.

Can going back to places of my childhood allow me to be less frightened by the memories? Why do return visits to places of extreme neglect still evoke feelings of childhood terror, even though I am now an adult?

When I was young, I used to think that if the mother in the family died, then everything fell apart. As I continue to learn about people, I realize that what happened to my brothers and me was an aberration.

Most family members will absorb the orphaned child. They will even embrace him or her with additional love and affection, to try to make up for the greatest loss any child can experience. Most times, when tragedy hits a family, they smother the child in a protective cocoon.

I have a friend, Margaret, whose natural mother died when she was five years old. A year or two after her death, my friend's father remarried a woman who raised her as if she had been born to her.

Recently we were talking about the eightieth birthday party that Margaret was planning for her mother. She said that she owes everything to that woman.

When she was young, her mother stepped in and treated her as if there was no other child in the world. She considers her mother to be her best friend.

She has always called her Mom, and even though she is technically her stepmother, she really has been the only mother she has ever known. Even after her father died and her mother remarried, Margaret remained her number one priority.

She said that now that her mother is older, when she looks back on her life, she realizes how lucky she has been. This woman entered her life when she was a child and chose to provide the continuing of the ordinary that every child so desperately seeks.

She hugged her, nurtured her, disciplined her, and stayed the course throughout her whole life.

Margaret says that she doesn't remember her birth mother, but she was never without a mothering presence in her life. She had two great women who provided safety nets for her growing-up years, and although they never knew each other, they had so much in common.

One woman started the ordinary events in her life. Another woman made a deliberate decision to step in and continue the ordinary so that one child could know wholeness and nurturing, which are the birthright of every child.

Margaret says that no matter what she does for her mother, she can never really give back as much as was given to her. She feels blessed that her mother raised her as her own.

I salute all women who mother children, their own as well as those of other women's, especially when the child has been set adrift by the death of the natural mother. That is why I say mothers of the heart are just as important as mothers of the flesh.

Why are some women able to nurture children not born to them? And why wasn't I fortunate enough to be raised by one of them?

The biggest question for me has always been, how do people love others who are not genetically related? Maybe there are different kinds of DNA. Besides the genetic connection, I believe that there is emotional DNA, historical DNA, knowledge DNA, and story DNA, all of which make some people bond beyond the physical DNA.

I just refuse to believe that only genetics can be the reason for caring and becoming intimately involved in one another's lives. Surely, what makes a family is the conscious decision to gather together to remember the past, to experience the present, and to work on a future.

My brothers and I were not born to our adoptive father, but at one time he showed his care and concern and his love for our mother, and he introduced us to his family as his children. Most of all, it was his emotional DNA that was our connection to him as long as our mother lived, but it withered after her death.

What he never remembered was that he had invited us to bond with his heart, and we accepted him as the father of our hearts. In the brokenness of this sacred trust and bond, he used the excuse of genetic DNA; he ignored that when children accept you into their hearts, they aren't thinking about physical DNA.

My brothers and I were remembering the story DNA of him pushing us on the swings, taking us for rides, and showing us the airplanes at the airports. We were remembering the historical DNA of him being part of our lives with our mother. I knew the shared emotional DNA of him sitting by my bed during all those hospital stays because of my cleft palate operations.

Yet after our mother died, all Daddy and his family could focus on was their genetic DNA. I couldn't understand the rejection of the other kinds of DNA in exchange for a life that limited experience of family.

Does the adoption DNA have the same lineage as the genetic DNA? Can the fusion of all the different kinds of DNA—emotional, knowledge, story, and historical—make a family, even though the genetic DNA does not exist?

I have decided to share our story. Maybe by telling an insider's view of the "shuffle madness," I may help another child. I also hope to encourage adults who are responsible for children's lives to be more aware of the positive or negative power that they hold in their hands.

Sometimes when a story is told, it is so tempting to want to leave things out, especially parts that might make one look foolish. I made a choice that I would sit down and write the story as it unfolded, with no censorship.

Maybe there is a book inside of everyone waiting to be written and shared. This is my moment in time to do what I have always been drawn to do. When I was a kid in the orphanage, I was always writing in notebooks about what was happening. I would write bits of poetry in between.

When I would read what I wrote, I worried because it was always about the loss of my mother and a way of life that I craved for but would never know. People were always telling me that the past was over, but they just never got around to showing me how to live in the present.

I approached my friend Cleo, who is a counselor in the high school where I teach, and asked her to read a few pages. She came back telling me, "I think you have something here, kiddo." She thought the other kids might be helped, if they knew that their experience could be validated by my sharing what my mother's presence and absence in my life had meant.

I also want to use this gift of writing to right an old wrong. Daddy's family's portrayal of my mother as a person was that she was nothing but a loser with four bastards who would never amount to anything.

My mother's presence in this life was important, and her children have made something out of the ashes that were left after the total destruction of the family that she started.

It is important for foster kids to know that the feelings of abandonment, alienation, and desperate desire for the ordinary are normal. It is healthier to struggle to come to terms with the unexplainable than to hover in a darkness of fear and isolation.

This book is my way of telling about my struggle to live in a way that keeps me from being swallowed up by the pain of the past.

Can any book really adequately explore the human condition of loss, loneliness, despair, and hope? Would my mother have been all right with my sharing of our story about the ramifications of people's decisions?

I think I am discovering the difference between a house and a home. As I wrote earlier, after several years I finally purchased my first house. I say my first, because someday I am going to build a magnificent log cabin.

For a long time, I had such a hard time figuring out what to do with the house for the first few months, because if I used just a little bit of hot water, then there was no more. When I mentioned this oddity to a friend of mine, she said something must be wrong. She got a friend of hers to come over and look at the furnace. What they found was that a valve that said Vacation/Regular had been turned to Vacation. They also showed me the phone line that wasn't connected properly and a few other odds and ends that go into making a house run more smoothly.

One of the things I really want to work on is making my house a home that has a welcoming spirit. Maybe because I have never really lived in a house, let alone a home, I find it difficult to make the conversion. Maybe as I become more comfortable with who I am and my place in the world, then learning how to be at home with my house will become more natural.

When I first moved in, I was overwhelmed by the responsibility of something so big. For the first two years, I slept on the couch in the living room for fear that something like a fire would happen. Gradually, I began playing country music and soft music, which helped to soothe me and make me become more comfortable in my surroundings.

I added some candles to the house and pictures on the wall, and even some flowers in my two-by-four front yard. I then had a photographer recopy some of the few pictures I have of mother so that they could compliment my home. There is a big one of my mother that will go above the mantlepiece when I build my dream home.

Maybe someday I will know how to make the feeling of home second nature, but for now I keep learning about ways to move the spirit of home into the house where I live. Even my four-legged friends are eager to greet me at the end of a long day. They add something to the house that brings life to it.

One thing I have learned, as I begin to enjoy my home, is that the spirit of the owner is most important of all. I wonder if my mother agrees with me on this?

Often, I am asked if I feel angry or bitter. To be honest, what I feel most at my basic core of existence is a sense of being cheated out of so many things.

From the day of my mother's leaving and dying, my brothers and I were not only deprived of her presence in our lives, we were also deliberately and consciously set outside of any family experience. We never did get back to a place of the ordinary that we once knew with her.

Sometimes I have to admit that I got angry with her for dying and at God for having all that power and not using it. Often, the anger subsided when I realized that I was getting angry with the only two people who knew and cared that I existed.

I have tried to be really careful not to become angry, because I have met some bitter people who started out being mad at the world. They aren't nice to be around, and I didn't want people to be repulsed by me any more than they already were.

I began to realize that maybe there is righteous anger. This means that some people have gone out of their way to destroy parts of me because they thought they were better than me. The truth is that the people who did wrong by us four older children deserve anger. However, I have to be careful not to let them put their tentacles of hatred in my soul. Righteous anger for me means that what they did was wrong, but I will let them answer for their deeds to a higher power, so that they don't drag me into their world filled with acid-laced bitterness and destructive anger.

Does anger serve a purpose? How do other human beings deal with people who deliberately set out to destroy them?

Sometimes I learn some hard lessons about who I am and how much work there is left to be done to become who I want to be. I had worked at a health care facility where some workers were not treating the people they were in charge of properly. After really struggling for months over this situation, I resigned with a letter of explanation.

What I took from this experience was the realization that I would never again tolerate the mistreatment of an individual. The fact that I struggled for months before I spoke up troubles me and makes me question my values and deplore my willingness to tolerate what I knew to be wrong. The biggest lesson I learned from this experience is that I have developed what I call a K-Mart attitude in life. Basically, no matter what happens on a job, no amount of mistreatment or harassment will ever be tolerated by me again.

This newly developed way of thinking will help me to keep grounded in always doing what is right. Never again will I allow myself to let other people intimidate me. I will not let what I know to be wrong to exist in my presence. I discovered that the "uh-oh" voice that lives in my conscience is what I need to always make sure to listen to.

There is a certain feeling of freedom within myself now that I know I will never allow people to abuse others. I like knowing that I have drawn a line in the sand that I will not step over, or let other people step over, especially when it comes to the well-being of others.

I work in many positions where the welfare of other people is directly in my hands, and I always must be vigilant in doing what is right in keeping whoever I am responsible for safe and secure. These jobs have taught me that there are times when I have to step up and speak up on what I know to be right. The truth is that I will always be haunted by not doing the right thing immediately when I should have spoken up. I don't beat myself over that situation anymore, because sometimes life is about learning lessons of growth when I least expect them.

I have come a long way since my convent years, and I am still growing through my life experiences. There are times when I realize that the best lessons are learned after some terrible mistakes. It is in the learning that I know I can win another opportunity to grow and change for the better.

I wonder if my mother ever had to swallow her hurt in order to learn not to let people intimidate her? What was her attitude about the welfare of other people? How did she manage to give me these strong feelings about doing the right thing and protecting those who need protection the most?

Somehow, the jobs that I have been attracted to have always been in the area of providing service. For the past several years, I have been working at the psychiatric hospital on the weekends, teaching full-time, and working at this social work job part-time in the evenings.

Each job challenges me in ways that I hope will help me to grow. I have to admit that for me, working at the psychiatric hospital is at times a very humbling experience. Most of us are just a fine line away from admission ourselves. My heart really breaks when we get a person who is currently in foster care or had been for most of their childhood. I don't say much, but I realize how easily I could be where they are if I didn't hold all my pieces together inside me. I ache for these patients who have been fractured by a life of disconnections. Sometimes I wonder if I am stronger than they are or just more stubborn about not letting the darkness beat me. Mostly, what I witness when I see these particular patients, whether they are twelve or sixty, are lost children still trying to find their way to that place called family.

I have a social work job where I am responsible for helping families to stay together. I try really hard to convince parents to make positive changes in their lives so that their children will not become wards of the state. Most of the time, I am successful in helping a family turn around, but there have been times when the family and the environment have become poisonous to the child, with no chance of change. It is these cases that make me lie in bed agonizing for hours, wondering whether something else could have been done, even though I knew I did my best. One thing about learning to be an adult is that sometimes your best is not good enough if other people won't take advantage of the opportunities to do better for their children.

The job that really makes me feel good is teaching. For me, it isn't really about the subject, or even the discipline, it's about making a difference, sometimes years after you have taught that student. For instance, Jordan, a former student of mine whom I had been begging to go to college for two years, called me out of the blue one day. He told me he got a scholarship and was going to become a history teacher because of me. I was touched. My students became my cheerleaders when they found out I was writing a book. Of course, they all wanted to be mentioned. They're not a shy bunch. They cried when I did a reading for the senior English class, some even offered to "take care" of Daddy's family. I think they were joking. It is a lot of fun sometimes being a teacher.

What lessons of living do other people get from the jobs that they work at?

One of the smartest things I have done is to seek a way to live so that I won't always be so emotionally crippled. As much as my mother and God have been my companions on this journey, there are other ways for me to continue to grow with people.

I am now working with a counselor who lives nearby, and she is helping me to undo the shame that I took upon myself, which really belongs on the shoulders of the people who did not choose to add to my life. She is building on what other counselors have started to do. It took me years to accept other people's help. I'm just glad I'm not where I used to be.

I think that for most of my life I have been as hard on myself as other people have been on me. There is a great unfairness in my self-expectations being based on those people who have never had any vested interest in me.

One of the greatest fallacies that I hear constantly by well-meaning adults is that children are resilient or adaptable. This statement isn't the truth at all, because kids change forever. Who I would have become with my mother's presence has been altered in a million splintering ways by her absence. Instead of being resilient and adaptable, I became a survivor, trying always to find the ordinary that I once knew. I have no regrets on what I have done to survive and not go crazy.

Is the search for who I am a victory against all those people who mistreated me? Was my mother's advice about life what I needed, instead of the counseling I am working on now?

One of the most heartbreaking revelations for me occurred when I was reading some selections from this book I'm writing to the senior English classes in the high school where I teach and having students come up to me, whispering that they are in foster care but asking that I not tell.

I find it sad that there are over 580,000 children in foster care and almost 200,000 available for adoption. Today the average kid will be in foster care for up to eight and a half years, which is a significant number. Age, race, sex, and all the reasons that years ago kept me mired in an unrelenting wave of displacement still continue today.

What I find really disturbing is that close to 70 percent of foster kids will never finish high school, and only 3 percent will ever finish college. If any one racial or ethnic group were to have almost 70 percent of its children not graduating from high school, this would be called a national emergency. Teaching here in Philadelphia, the dropout rate of almost 50 percent, is constantly meriting media attention. Yet nothing is ever mentioned about who these foster children in school are, and there are no special support systems for them.

Forty percent go on to become the chronic homeless that fill our shelters and ironically, most of their children go on to become wards of the state. Up to 60 percent of the boys will go on to experience legal trouble.

Yet this is not because there is something inherently wrong with these children, it is the system that deliberately sets these kids up for failure.

It is so hard for me to accept the reasons that allow this system not to change. I believe that money becomes a factor, with the average foster place being paid an average $1,200 and up per month. There are some places where foster parents can go on vacation with their kids and family while the foster child is left behind at a foster respite center.

When I went to the hospital, there was a treatment team assigned to me so that I didn't stay any longer than was absolutely necessary. When I became a ward of the state, whether I was provided an actual foster place or residential care, there was no team, only some overburdened case worker who, even with the best of intentions, could never find the right home that would offer the permanency that I so desperately sought.

The wounds that have turned to scars line both my heart and my soul and continue to haunt me as I try to come to terms with the losses that should never have been.

I realize that there are some good people who try to become a temporary refuge for a kid who is traveling that journey to a place called home. However, there are far too many people in this foster care system who are here for their own reasons, be it money or personal fulfillment. Most foster kids will experience ten to twenty placements over a long period of time. The best home gives the child a glimpse of kindness and how life should be, but to not invite the child into this circle of permanency can cause great despair.

The saddest tradition that is still carried out by this "shuffle madness" system called foster care is, like what happened to me before them, telling twenty thousand kids on their eighteenth birthday, "So long, good luck, we don't get paid to keep you anymore."

How is it possible to send children, and these are children, out into a world where they are not prepared to live physically or emotionally?

The sad thing is that foster care, in a house or a group home, is America's shameful and dirty little secret. These children who are publicly invisible to their past families and present reality can only hope that the limbo they are thrown into will not totally crush their spirit.

For any child to spend more than one or two years outside of a permanent family circle, as we in America define family, is to invite an emotional hurricane within that child's heart. That child then will probably spend the rest of his or her life trying to find enough pieces in order to put himself or herself back together.

Some flesh-and-blood families are toxic to their children, but we as a country should never allow the exchange of one nightmare for another.

These kids are our kids who just got a bum rap in life, and becoming wards of the state really places all these children within our collective public-responsibility circle.

Not everyone can go out and adopt a kid. However, we can all support changes in laws that do not economically reward a system that encourages the drowning of children in a system that dooms them to failure.

Even now that I'm an adult, there will always be an ache in my heart and a fracture in my soul, because I could never find that place called home or family. Somehow I hope to take what has been my experience and champion others to continue making new permanencies where once only temporary sadness existed. On behalf of all kids like me, I thank all the people who do try to make a difference.

How come there continues to be the shedding of whisper tears in a country filled with such compassionate people? Why don't more people of the heart open their lives to some child who only seeks what is the birthright of every child—a place called home, a place called family?

One of the most difficult jobs that I have is to work to repair the shattered image of myself that I was given as a child.

Within the past few years, I have tried to put together within myself an image that is reflective of who I have always wanted to be. Now I have learned how important it is to allow friends to nurture those parts of me that have remained undeveloped yet hungry to grow. Had my mother been there she would have done the thousand and one things that would have set me on the road to a life that is not filled with so many self-doubts. It is her absence and the continued missing mothering that never took place that forced me to find other ways to build a self-image that is whole and self-accepted.

My friend Jazmin often says that when children miss out on any developmental stage as a child, they carry those missing pieces into adulthood. Her husband died when her two sons were very young, and she has always tried to surround them with strong masculine people. As a teacher, she has had foster kids in her classes who have been in multiple placements who seem to be missing the constant steady nurturing that her two sons receive. She says it takes forever to socialize her own children properly and to consistently teach them about manners, how to take care of themselves, and how to treat other people.

I have surrounded myself with female friends who have helped to nurture that feminine identify that I thought was lost or destroyed so long ago. I have one friend who is really into shopping. My friend Lois is always calling, asking me if I took my vitamins and checking on my health. These friends and others nurture me in ways that I have rarely known but need in order to continue growing.

I even practice looking in the mirror now and then, trying to connect with the face staring back at me. I don't know if I will ever become what I might have been if my mother had not died when I was so young, but the good thing is that the bullies of my childhood and my night dreams no longer have a dominant place in my psyche.

Why don't people caring for them realize that children are so fragile in their self-worth and self-image? Is it necessary for me to go through all the stages I have missed in order to become whole?

Allowing people to add to my life has helped me to feel secure about who I am. Removing those who try to subtract from my life has helped in the healing process. No longer do I feel so alone or so scared at times. Friends do have a way of building my self-esteem.

Often, when I reflect on how I should learn to celebrate my life, I realize that the only mirror I have had was other people. For a long time, in the endless darkness of childhood and adolescence, I mostly heard echoes of "second best," "maybe someday," and "not now" from them. I realize more and more how destructive were these people who subtracted from my life. I will no longer allow these voices from the past to keep their intractable claws on my psyche.

Now, today, if I feel someone is unhealthy for me or tries to make me feel uncomfortable about who I am, I just don't give them my energy. I figure I have paid my dues in the survivorship game of life, and now it is time to allow a different attitude and approach to surround me.

I am beginning to enjoy the fact that some people think that I am okay the way I am. They don't begrudge my efforts to change and grow. In fact, people like Lois and Cleo and others cheer me on when I try to make the life given to me work for me.

Writing and sharing my story has, in some ways, become a blessing in disguise. Most of my friends were aghast to learn about my childhood experience and really believed that it was a story worth sharing with a wide audience. They felt that it might help other children who struggle with the "shuffle madness" of being "wards of the state." They didn't think less of me or as a freak, like others thought I was.

Will allowing people to add to my life move me farther away from the darkness that I once knew? How can I keep the "subtracters" from becoming part of my life? Am I an "adder" or a "subtracter" in my friends' lives? What about in the lives of all that I come in contact with?

I have always believed that there are angels in this world. They don't have wings, but in their human form, they become what I call night-lights in the darkness. There are people who have somehow made my journey less lonely and helped me to gain the strength to keep on keeping on. Part of my list includes these special people and their special kindness.

The first night-light in the darkness after my mother died was the old woman on the bus who shared her sandwich with me as we traveled to Scranton, Pennsylvania. I was really hungry, and she even shared with me a small pillow she had brought with her. There was little else in that darkness that followed for the next two years. It was only the kindness of this one teacher who looked out for us that made me feel like I wasn't a total alien in this world that seemed to turn on me when my mother died. Of course,

Trevor, Tyler, and, especially, Billy were night-lights for as long as we were together. Sister Margo came along in eighth grade in her blue habit. She always made me feel welcomed, although if she knew what a freak I was inside, she might have thought differently. She always really made me feel good when she didn't laugh at my desire to have an adoptive mother and didn't tell me that at thirteen I was too old.

In the summer of 1970, in Wichita, Kansas, there was the neighbor who would tell me that she felt bad for me. There was the old couple at the club who cleaned the room for the happy hour and gave me a soda. They helped me feel less alone. Even the social worker who came out to the house to send me back to the orphanage from Wichita, Kansas, became a champion in my eyes when she told me in the car that Mrs. Wesson was wrong for hating me and trying to destroy me.

In high school, there was the assistant librarian who brought colored Easter eggs to the orphanage; my teacher in my freshman year, failing me in English the first quarter; and some of the nuns in the orphanage, from Sister Jill to Sister Linda—they have all become night-lights in the darkness. They lit a path in my darkest moments, and this was enough sometimes to energize me just to get to the next day.

Even today, I still encounter what I call the night-lights in the darkness. They are people who continue to have an impact on my life. These people, guardian angels, have often provided a buffer between my stumbles in life.

Are the night-lights in the darkness God's way of helping me to continue in my life? Why did these guardian angels in human flesh choose to add to my life at a time when so many others withdrew their lights from me?

Often I used to think that everything I needed to learn about life I would learn from people. In the past few years, I have become increasingly involved in some animal-rescue work with this loose-knit group of people who try to repair the damage done to our four-legged friends. This experience has taught me life lessons not only about animals but also about people.

The first time it happened, I was driving down a busy interstate highway in the middle of a snowstorm, and I saw this beagle sitting by the side of the highway. What could I do? Of course, I pulled over and coaxed her to come to me. She was crying, smelled terrible, and looked emaciated. Since I was on my way to work, I took her with me. She whimpered throughout the entire ride, cowering against the passenger-side door.

Whenever you stop to help someone or some animal, I believe that there are universal laws that make you responsible for helping as much as possible. When I arrived at the psychiatric hospital, everyone fell in love with the beagle. Margaret and I finally convinced her daughter to adopt the dog whom she promptly named Rudy. We helped to pay to have her fixed up, which included three baths, shots, spaying, and the removal of eight teeth. The vet believed she was around nine years old and was used as a breeder then dumped because of her age.

Donna took Rudy everywhere. Rudy had her own passport so she could go to Canada twice a year with Donna for vacation. Rudy lived for seven more healthy years, slept on Donna's bed, and was loved by her cats. I think Rudy felt she died and went to heaven. She loved Donna with the kind of passion only a rescued animal could love someone who saves them and gives them a better life. When Donna told me about Rudy's death, she was crying, and I gently told her that she needs to remember that she gave Rudy seven years of heaven on earth, which was denied her by some jerk who abandoned her. Rudy spent every day, from the time of her rescue until her death, following Donna with the devotion that few people ever give in a lifetime to another person.

Callie was one of the first cats I rescued. I heard all this noise outside my apartment building one evening. When I looked outside, I saw a group of young boys trying to shove this cat down a sewer drain. I yelled at them to "leave my cat alone," and they dropped her and ran away. When I picked her up, she began purring and clinging to me. The next day, I left her at the vet's office and proceeded to search for an adoptive home. Since she was multicolored, I named her Callie. Eventually, she went to live with my friend Eleanor. I never saw those boys again. Somehow I can't help but wonder if cruelty isn't learned, and whether somebody had hurt those boys so badly that now they act out against innocent animals.

My other four-legged friend that I saved and kept was a black cat named John—not Johnny, not Jack, but John. I heard about this cat being shot with a BB gun and decided to take him in. He was, by far, the ugliest-looking thing that I have ever seen, but his eyes could look through your soul. I had as many of the pellets as possible removed, and due to the surgery, he looked like someone had crisscrossed him in a sword fight. Much of his fur was missing, and the vet said he had only two teeth left. She said that there were pellets left in him and that eventually he might die of lead poisoning. In the meantime, she said he was feeling good and gaining weight, and he loved to sit right beside me.

So John, as I now called him, came home to spend a life with my menagerie. The four-legged friend he loved the most in my home was Nina, my sixty-five-pound pit bull. I had taken in Nina when she was five years old. She was being sent to the SPCA (Society for the Prevention of Cruelty to Animals) because her owner was tired of breeding her. At the SPCA in Philadelphia, all pit bulls are killed automatically, no matter what, because of their bad reputation, which is due to some jerks training them to be mean. Sometimes I wonder why animals suffer life and death consequences just because someone trained them to be mean or tortured them into meanness.

John actually liked Nina's food; of course, this was much to her dismay. I would laugh watching Nina bark and whine, looking to me for help while seven-pound John had his face in her food bowl. Aside from that, they slept together and would hang out at the same corner of the couch—Nina on the cushion and John on the armrest with his front paws dangling over, resting on Nina's head while they both slept.

When I would come home, John would hold this entire one-sided conversation with me. I guess he figured that only his opinion counted. About three years later, I could see that his health was failing, so I took him to the vet, and she said that the lead poisoning was starting to kick in. She wanted to keep him at her office for observation. He ended up being the unofficial mascot, and everyone fell in love with him.

I would bring Nina down once a month for her visitation time with John, and he would come right over to her, sit at her feet, and begin this conversation for which I have no translation. Nina would cock her head and look at him, probably still thinking that John always had to have the last word. When we would leave, John would put his right paw on her foot as if to say good-bye. After about six months of living at the vet's office, John passed away in his sleep. I have no regrets about having him as a part of my life, because I have become richer for knowing him, even if he was from the four-legged family.

John and Rudy taught me about people's deliberate cruelty, which can extend beyond just children. They both also taught me about the incredible kindness that lurks in the hearts of human beings. Life lessons of childhood and adulthood, of children and animals, of people and their intentions—good or bad—continue to play out before me as I try to blend into this "ballet" called life.

Do my four-legged friends like Callie, Rudy, John, and Nina reflect a way of change and gratitude that comes with experiencing kindness and healing?

I have decided that there are things in life that I want to do now because I have moved from surviving to living. Some things, such as buying a house and a car, I have accomplished. Yet, increasingly, I find that there is much more to living a life filled with excitement and growth opportunities.

So, as usual, I have made what I call my dream list of ways I want to change and things I want to do. Making lists continues to be a wonderful way for me to do some goal setting and dream making. I think the following are good things to dream about:

1)   I want to allow people to be a part of my life up front and personal, not just observing from a safe distance.
2)   I would like to make a difference in the lives of children who start out in life with strikes against them by being wards of the state.
3)   I want to visit every zoo and no-kill animal shelter in America.
4)   I want to become an established writer about the human condition.
5)   I want to build a log cabin that would become a home where there is a spirit of welcome for my two-legged and four-legged friends.
6)   I want to visit every state in the United States.
7)   I want to remain open to the possibility of an adult relationship, which could involve friendship and romance.
8)   I want to visit every major league baseball park in America.
9)   I want to learn about computers and technology so that I don't have to handwrite my next manuscript.
10) I want to have a family of the heart through adoption of a child or children.
11) I want to build a gravestone that truly honors my mother.
12) I want to have a thank-you dinner someday for those who have been night-lights in my darkness.
13) I want a purple metallic motorcycle and a purple metallic helmet.
14) I want to continue on the road to emotional recovery, never returning to the nightmare from which I barely escaped.
15) I want to surround myself with my family of friends.
16) I want to become the woman that so long ago started developing and to begin to walk with my head held high.

These are just a few ways that I am trying to turn what was once a life filled with people-imposed limitations and self-limitations into a life now filled with endless exciting adventures of living in the here and now. I will never again allow the darkness that once nipped so close at my heels to ever share any of my personal space.

Will I ever completely be able to fulfill my reality dream list to my complete satisfaction?

One of the terrible habits I used to have was taking time off from people. When I had left college and graduate school and entered the convent, I let go of the friendships that brought me great joy and pleasure. I have discovered that maintaining friends is hard work and part of what adds to my being human.

A few years after leaving the convent, I decided that I had to make changes in my life. One of the first things I did after I decided to write this book was to work on reconnecting the disconnections in my personal life. I got myself into counseling, worked on getting out of debt, and, more importantly, started to get back into contact with the friends I made in college.

Of course, the first one I called was my old friend Lois, just to thank her for inspiring me to tell my story. From that phone call, I established contact with other friends who are now married, with children of their own. Some are librarians and social workers, others are teachers or are in business.

Lois was so excited to hear from me and said that from now on, there will be no more taking time off from people. She has arranged for a monthly gathering of a support group for renewing our friendship and for reading line by line, paragraph by paragraph, the story she told me I was meant to write.

Most of the time, when we get together, there is a spirit of renewal and celebration about what I have managed to do with my life. Lois—along with Celeste, Jason, Ruby, Leanne, and Marlee—was initially taken aback by my story, because I kept so much about where I came from and who I was to myself. However, they began to share that reading what I wrote helped to explain so much of what they observed during my college years. Celeste, especially, tells the story of how she first met me and our interaction, about my not wanting anyone to touch me.

These friends, along with others who do animal rescue or work with me at my various jobs, have taught me that having a good time together, or sharing a common interest, is okay. Lois said she would never allow me to walk away again. I told her she won't have to worry about that because I have learned that I want to be involved in my friends' lives. I also learned that it is normal and healthy to have good times in the company of others. Trying to reconnect with others who are healthy for me is one of the best ways to take care of myself.

What kind of disconnections of the heart and of friends happened when I had to choose survival over living? Are the friendships in our lives the safety nets that emerge in adulthood? Is friendship something we always must work at in order to keep it alive?

From the life-altering event of my mother's dying and the subsequent ways that I had been abandoned, I have now found ways to make peace within myself. Maybe life has a way of balancing what people dish out, even if it has been filled with chaos and, seemingly, does not have any direction.

I think that luck, gifts of mind and heart, and, mostly, hard work have enabled me to turn what surely could have been a life of disappointments and failure into a wonderful celebration of survival and now life. I have always tried to pick and choose my battles because I learned a long time ago that I would destroy myself if I tried to win at everything that came my way.

One of the hardest lessons I learned early was that no matter what I do, what I say, or who I become, there will be people who will not like me or believe in me. Usually this is a lesson that most people learn as adults.

When I was eight years old, I realized that no matter what I did, Daddy's family would never love or accept my brothers or me. It didn't matter if I got straight As or was the quietest girl in the world, I learned that you can't change people if they have already decided not to change.

One of the reasons that I tend to roll with the punches is that life has taught me to be patient and to remember that as tomorrow comes around, it is another day of opportunity. Teaching really has taught me to take this "go with the flow" to the level of a high art form.

When I was a child, I waited for my mother to return, for Daddy's family to like me again as they appeared to do when my mother lived, for my mother's family in Indiana to come, and for the long-sought-after prize of adoption to become a reality. Now, as an adult, I wait for people to change and grow. I have found that sometimes, if I wait long enough, people do change. Yet I also learn another hard lesson, and that is that some people don't even recognize their need to change.

I have changed in many ways. No longer do I harbor any resentment of the people in my past, because that gives them power and control over me even when they are not part of my life now.

One of my earliest foster caretakers, Mrs. Smith, calls periodically because she worries about one of my brothers. She had told me that she had been jealous of me because I would accept her husband but not her, because adoption wasn't going to be possible. She also acknowledged that, working full-time, she had allowed herself to bite off more than she could chew and became overwhelmed with five children. After I left that foster home, she had her hands full with one of my brothers, and he left a few months later. I told her that I didn't hold any hard feelings and that I should have never been forced upon her as part of a package deal. She did right by the one brother she kept, and that is what is important. So we have come full circle to the point where she calls periodically, and both of us can even laugh about her son and me competing against each other as kids when I lived there.

With my mother's family in Indiana, I have chosen to make a new history, because I will never understand or accept their reasons for not taking us. When I do visit, I will focus on the here and now, enjoy my visit, and talk to my mother at her grave. Coming full circle has challenged me to work at finding ways to be with people even if I have to remind myself to not look back.

Does coming full circle mean a new way of forgiving and moving forward? How do I maintain my protective barrier from people yet learn to accept them as they are?

Whenever I try to take stock of my life, I can really see how important my reading books have been for me. It isn't that books have solved my problems. It's just that being a passionate reader has allowed me to travel to worlds I would have never known.

I probably have to give my mother credit for instilling in my heart a love for learning and for dreaming. When I spent those two years in the coal cellar, Trevor, Tyler, Billy, and I were always reading these books we got out of the school library. Sometimes I could almost leave the life and world I lived in and escape to places where there were no questions, no pain, and no doubt about where I belonged.

Especially at the orphanage and foster homes, reading became a refuge within the "shuffle madness." Books always offered me a sense of hope and of wanting more than I knew.

Now that I am no longer a child, reading remains a passion for me. Sometimes books allow me to feel right in my way of thinking, and about living life to the fullest. There is this book I read called *The Ditchdigger's Daughters,* it is about a black couple who were determined that their daughters would be highly educated and become professionals. What struck a common cord with me was their intensity in pursuing the dream and the reality that if you are black, or orphaned, the need to fulfill the dreams is the same.

I have a good friend, Jazmin, who shares my passion for reading. At times, through our discussions of what books have to offer and what the writers meant, I learn more than from just what I read. Even Jazmin, as a single mother of two boys due to the unexpected death of her husband, has had to struggle to make her dreams a reality in her life.

I wonder how I could have ever sustained my will to be more than what was expected of me if I had never been able to indulge my hunger for learning. Just as when I was a child I couldn't wait to go on some exciting adventure through a book, I still, even today, feel the same excitement, the same passion for being adventurous. Maybe there are gifts of my childhood that follow me into my adulthood that are good and healthy. I hope that the child parts of my heart will always be open to healing, whether through people or through books.

Do all people feel as passionate about the simple things in life, such as reading, as I do? Are people like Jazmin a living embodiment of a book that has yet to be written?

I don't know if I ever told you how lucky I feel. There is a realization that I have always had companions for the journey. Some people, especially for a long time after my mother's leaving, were only temporary, and others will continue to be a part of the healing circle that surrounds me.

There has never been a time when I felt totally alone, if for no other reason than that I always had a sense that my mother and God were somehow part of my life, even if I couldn't see or talk to them. Now as I continue to emerge from a darkness that once held me in a death grip, I realize that there are people who will support and nurture parts of me that have been waiting to be told that "it is okay, no one will ever hurt you again."

I don't know where life will lead me, but I do like the direction in which I'm going. Am I still furious at a system that is set up to fail so many children who become wards of the state? Yes, but I no longer feel the shame that paralyzed my voice and kept me from speaking out about the great hunger and sadness that exists for over a half million American children.

The people, those companions who tell me that I am okay, welcome, and at home in their presence, allow me to have the courage to shrug off the cloak of silence, embarrassment, and shame about something I have avoided all my life.

It is Lois, my cheerleader from the Alvernia College library; Cleo, my proofreader; Jazmin, my writer and reader friend; and so many others who empower me to do what I must do, and that is to tell others about my journey so that other children might know something different. There is a certain steadiness about surrounding myself with safety nets made up of people who believe that the message and the messenger have something to say that will add to the places in our hearts and souls.

Will I ever know the peace that I have sought for so long? Are companions the "people food" that encourages humans to be more than they could ever dream to be?

For a long time, even when I was little, I tried to find a definition of family that fit the reality I was living in. But it was never the kind of family that would take a kid like me into their hearts or offer me the kind of permanency that I so desperately desired. Now that I am an adult; I have had years to reflect on what my definition of family was or should be. First and foremost, I needed to define my version of family so that I could develop a sense of being at home with others who shared their welcoming spirit with me.

Family will always be those friends who have encircled me in their embrace, often even protecting me from myself. One of the great drawbacks of living outside of the ordinary is the lack of boundaries when it comes to the many areas in my life. Whether it is the inability to handle money, the way I shop, or even the way I let other people intimidate me, I had to make changes and to allow my friends to teach me what healthy boundaries are all about.

When I visit with these friends, it is so different from what it used to be in my life. I have invitations for the big holidays such as Thanksgiving, Christmas, New Year, and Easter. Family should assume that someone is included and that this is how friends make me feel.

Maybe the great gift that I have discovered is that there is such depth in people who are willing to invite me into this experience of family. My greatest heartache as a child was seeing good people with their children and knowing that I was not being treated nicely, and I wished it were not the case. One person who taught me that the need inside me to be mothered and nurtured was normal is Leah, a counselor and now a friend from my convent years. She understood those areas of my heart that I have always tried to hide even from myself. I learned from her that who I was, who I am, and who I will be is always dependent on accepting the whole of me. She looked inside me and chose to help me to sort out my confusing existence. This unconditional acceptance is the closest to a family experience that I have had.

This family of friends that now have become a link in my spirit offers me a chance to learn what should have been learned so long ago. Sometimes I pinch myself at my good fortune, that people like and care deeply about me. Perhaps the truth is that I, like every other person, have always been entitled to knowing security, nurturing, and embracing. I hope that someday my definition of family will help someone else expand their outlook and invite others to be a part of their lives.

Did my mother ever struggle over the meaning of family? Why do people have to limit what family means?

I have spent a lot of time wondering how I could honor my mother in death that would do justice to her. There have never been the Mother's Day cards or the Christmas presents, things that could adequately and concretely express the appreciation and love that I feel for her.

I decided that there were only three things that I could give to her in order for my heart and soul to be able to say to her, "Debt paid in full." The first two are easy in comparison to the last one.

Since I have never been able to honor my mother in life, I have decided that I would first write a living testimony about my mother, God, our travels, and myself as I searched for a way to survive without my mother.

Then I intend to sit by her grave and read it first to her before anyone else. I figure that the least and most I can do is to offer her a first look and a first listening to what I want to say about the celebration of who she was in the life of one of her children.

The second way that I wish to express in a concrete manner that her existence is worthy of recognition is to buy her a unique tombstone. On it, I would like to engrave a letter that would express the tremendous ache and sadness and loss that her dying and living has had on me. I have never believed that it was God's will that I be motherless or that her presence on earth was an aberration or a mistake. As her child, in her life and in her death, I feel a responsibility to acknowledge the gratitude I have always toward her.

Finally, I know the best way I can celebrate who my mother was and who she is in my life is to live in such a way that honors everything that she would have wanted for me. I have been in the process, these past few years, of trying to step out of the shadows that hide all the parts of me that somehow became a continuous ball of confusion.

I am working on celebrating the gift of who I am and the spirit that has never allowed the darkness of despair to become a permanent part of me. The only way I, as my mother's child, could ever do justice to her presence on this earth is to live an honorable and happy life.

I am learning to celebrate who I am as a female, as a woman, and as a whole human being. I have always believed that like every other mother, my mother probably wanted her children to know a happy and secure life. I have grown tired of believing that I was a disappointment to her and now believe that I have been a gift in her life and in her death.

Does she know in heaven that her life has been celebrated on earth? I wonder if she knows that I celebrate all mothers when I honor who she was and who she is in the depths of my heart and spirit?

*   *   *

Dear Mother,

How do I thank you in the written form, when words could never begin to express the gratitude I feel for our shared journey? There were many times, even years, when I thought I would go crazy from all the trauma of a childhood filled with the absence of the ordinary.

I really believe that my making a special place for you and for God inside my mind and heart allowed my soul a chance to heal and to grow. When you died, I tried desperately to find you in the poignant ways that only an eight-year-old orphan could.

I tried to ask Daddy's family about you, and as you know, that wasn't a good idea. I asked God to send you back, I even bargained with him with two-for-one proposition. Apparently, he liked you better.

Then one day, as I was talking to you, I realized that your spirit had to be somewhere listening to my whispered pleas. Even when you didn't answer, I knew that I felt better talking to you. I kept talking to you so I wouldn't lose the connection I once had with you. I knew that you were fading fast from my memory, so I tried to keep you alive in my heart. Then I learned that along the way, I wasn't so lonely even though I lived in a continuous state of confusion.

When I was a child, I would always tell Daddy's mother that someday I would tell you everything, and maybe through this book, I finally have. This written story is for you, for all the mothers who mother, and for all the children who have known the abandonment that allow them to live lives filled with the absence of the ordinary.

One of my favorite movies is Beaches with Bette Midler. In the end, she takes the little girl's hand and becomes a mother of the heart to her best friend's orphaned daughter. I must have seen it about twenty-one times. Somehow it helps me to know that the ending is what allows that little girl to continue the ordinary. The song "Wind Beneath My Wings," which is sung so hauntingly by Bette Midler, best describes how I feel about you and God. I too can truly say, You have been the wind beneath my wings.

Thank you!

Love,
Jerri

Jerri Age 8

Jerri age 10 – in the orphanage

Front of Orphanage

Waiting Windows

Jerri's High School

Gussie "Sandra" Zigga
1933-1964

JERRI D. ZIGGA
''Jerri''
History and Philosophy

High School Graduation Photo

rri - College Graduation

SUMMARY

The Bureau of Children's Service first became involved with the   . children on December I4, I966 when a request for service was received indicating that the children were possibly being neglected. The complaint also stated that these children were being discriminated against by the parents of their stepfather while the natural child of Mr.   was receiving the proper care.

On December 20, I966 Mr.   : visited our office requesting help in placing the children. The   . children were entrusted into the custody of their mother after her divorce from the children's natural father. Mr. and Mrs.   . were married in July, I960 in the state of New Mexico. At that time Mr.   was serving with the United States Air Force. On November II, I964, Mrs. Zigga was killed in a fire and explosion in their house trailer while she was residing in Indiana. Mr.   at that time was stationed in Montana. Shortly after his wifes death Mr.   resigned from the Air Force and returned with his five children to live with his parents in Scranton. Mr.   's parents are not accepting of the four children by his first wifes marriage during the past two years things have deteriorated to such a degree that Mr.   no longer feels that the children should remain in the home.

CATHOLIC SOCIAL SERVICES

MOST REV. J. CARROLL McCORMICK, D.D.
PRESIDENT
REV. KENNETH T. HORAN, M.S.W.
DIRECTOR

Social Summary

SCRANTON MIDVALLEY OFFICE
300 WYOMING AVENUE
SCRANTON, PENNA. 18503

RE: Gerri Diane Zigga
D.O.B: 7/16/56

Mr.   met his wife, Gussie, while he was stationed in
Mississippi with the U.S. Air Force. She had been divorced and
had four children. They were married in July 1960, in Roswell,
New Mexico and Mr.   adopted the four children. In 1962 a
daughter,   was born to the couple. Mr.   was sub-
sequently transferred to Montana while his wife and children remained in Indiana, living near her parents in a trailer. On
November 11, 1964, the children were staying overnight with their
grandparents, a fire developed in the trailer and Mrs.   was
killed.

Mr.   returned to Scranton, seeking help from his parents.
They did not feel that he had any responsibility towards his adoptive children, only towards his natural child.   Mr.   ,
went to work, leaving the children in his mother's care, resulting
in neglect and abuse, until neighbors reported the situation to
Lackawanna County Bureau of Children's Services, Scranton, Pennsylvania.
Mr.   voluntarily placed the four adoptive children but his
parents threatened him with court action if he placed   so
she remained with her grandparents.

The three youngest children were initially placed in Our Lady
of   ,   , Pennsylvania and   the eldest
was placed in   ,   , Pennsylvania.
Because long term placement was believed to be an appropriate solution

to the difficulty. Gerri and the twins were placed in the home of
Mr. and Mrs. _____   under the supervision of Lackawanna
County Bureau of Children's Services.   adjusted to the
home but Gerri and ___ did not and the county agency called on
Catholic Social Services to provide a foster home for Gerri.

I visited with Gerri several times before the preplacement
visit with ___ was arranged. I found her to be outgoing,
bright, and quite congenial except when the conversation turned to
Mr. and Mrs. _____ This subject she would not discuss.

After the pre-placement visit, the _____ and Gerri were
equally accepting of each other and placement began on December 9,
1969.

Gerri adjusted very well at first and she made noticeable
progress at school. However, in February 1970, when Mr.
accepted a transfer to Kansas, Gerri became apprehensive about her
future and even experienced some respiratory difficulty due to the
anxiety. Mrs.   assured her that she was a member of the
family, and as such would accompany them, if Bureau of Children's
Services approved and if Gerri herself wished to go. Gerri seemed
torn between her desire to go and her desire to remain loyal to her
father. This was worked out with Mr. ___ who had maintained
minimal contact with Gerri throughout her placement, the last time
being two years before. Although he expressed love and concern for
Gerri he had not formulated any plans for her return nor did he
have any idea when such a plan could be made. He decided that Gerri
should be allowed to make her own decision regarding the move.

Mrs. _____ was also very upset at this time due to the
separation from her husband and the responsibility of selling the
house and preparing to move. She became critical of Gerri and Gerri
reacted with hostility during the stress situation.

In several private interviews with Gerri she was finally able
to express repressed feelings of love for her mother and the terrible
years of loneliness and unhappiness since her death. She expressed
her fear of risking herself in a close relationship and her distrust
of people in general. She also disclosed that she had deliberately
contrived to be removed from the _____ home because Mrs.
made disparaging remarks about Gerri's mother and father. Following
this, there seemed to be a marked improvement in her behavior and
especially after the house was sold in June and definite plans were
made for the move to Kansas.

We consulted with our agency psychologist who is familiar with
Gerri and the   and he recommended strongly that they be
allowed to remain together.

Mrs. _____ worked closely with our agency and relied on the
caseworker's supportive contacts. She has a tendency to over-react

to Gerri's behavior which is sometimes merely a manifestation of
adolescence.

Sincerely yours,

(Mrs.)
Caseworker

JM/sp

cc

Re: Zigga, Gerri

4-6-67

Gerri at ten appears much older looking than the average child in that age bracket. Her face is not as animated as a child of ten. Her front teeth are missing due to an accident. She a speech handicap. As she walks, her left leg seems to drag. It was due to some accident. Gerri is an average student but applies herself. She causes no difficulty in her department She accepts responsibility and does her assigned tasks well. Because Mr,   was in the Air Force, the children traveled extensively.

Otis Quick-Scroing Mental Ability Test - Beta Form B administered, May 10, 1967
    Chron. Age   Mental Age   I/Q.   Grade 5
     10-9·   11-10   110

7-10-67

Gerri was promoted to the 6th grade. Her grades were average. She spent one week at the Little Flower Camp for girls. Gerri enjoys her visits with Mr.

8-20-67

She was baptized on August 18th and received her First Holy Communion on August 20th.

9-6-67

Gerri was enrolled in our 6th grade with ▆▆▆▆▆▆▆ as her teacher.

11-5-67(a report from the group mother and teacher)

In general a very responsible individual. She shows some tendency to sensitiveness. She i well adjusted to the Home. Her weakness is that she is a "busy body". She enjoys reading dancing. In fact, she is interested in all sports. In school she is serious about her work. Her progress is good in the 6th grade.

Certificate of Baptism

✝

Church of

Saint Eulalia

Elmhurst, Pa.

❧ This is to Certify ❧

That ___ Gerri Diane Zigga

Child of ___

and ___ Gussie Green

born in ___ Washington ___ D. C.
(CITY)   (STATE)

on the ___ 16th ___ day of ___ July ___ 19 56

was **Baptized**

on the ___ 18th ___ day of ___ August ___ 19 67

According to the Rite of the Roman Catholic Church

by the Rev. ___ Mr. Richard B. Comiskey

the Sponsors being { ___

as appears from the Baptismal Register of this Church.

Dated ___ August 19, 1967

___
Pastor

No. 314 F. J. REMEY CO. Inc. MINEOLA, N.Y.

Notations

FIRST COMMUNION
- Date August 20, 1967
- Church St. Zulalia's
- Place Elmhurst, Pa.

CONFIRMATION
- Date October 25, 1967
- Church St. Eulalia's
- Place Elmhurst, Pa.

MARRIAGE(S)
- To ___
- Date ___
- Church ___
- Place ___

SUBDIACONATE
- Date ___
- Church ___
- Place ___

RELIGIOUS PROFESSION
- Date ___
- Order ___
- Place ___

Re: Gerri Zigga

October 13, 1970

Mr. _____ came here to discuss the needs of his children. He is being pushed hard by Mrs. _____ caseworker, to take Gerri into his new house. He barely has a shell there, for he is building it himself, no plumbing, no heat - and no partitions yet. We can't believe that Mrs. _____ would want to do that to him again - and make Gerri miserable in such an environment. Gerri is a bunch of nerves from the two bad foster homes she experienced, and she has just begun her high school work. She needs all the time, peace and quiet to adjust herself to the studies. Mr. _____ needs time to finish the house and to furnish it properly before he brings anyone there to live. It will take him another year or so. Besides, Mr. _____ has had enough trouble over these children with his mother. If Mr. _____ will visit Gerri here, and know that is happy, he can work on his house peacefully, but he does not need another lash-up with his mother, with the children and in a messy shell of a house. It is strange to think that someone could imagine such a ridiculous plan.
Mrs. _____ the foster mother - - - , must not interfere in our plan at _____ .

September II, 1970

Mrs _____ called about a week ago that she would return a girl to Fatima on Sept. 9. At that time we did not know who the girl was.
On Sept. 9th Mrs. _____ arrived at Fatima with Gerri _____ . She met her at the airport. The girl flew in from Wichita, Kansas.
Gerri is 14 and a "B" student. Her foster parent, Mrs. _____ , suggested that Gerri repeat the 8th grade. We do not think that would be right, since the girl has been promoted into 9th grade.
Today, we talked to Mrs. _____ , Guidance Counselor at the school, and we hope Gerri will be happy in her social group.
Later, Mrs. _____ -?, caseworker, visited _____ . We talked about Gerri's future, and decided not to upset her again. If group-living will prove beneficial to Gerri, she will remain at _____ through high school. Unless Gerri herself will indicate she would like to try another foster home, she will not be disturbed. She had gone to I5 different schools already, and has had her share of foster homes.

September 30,1970

Mrs. _____ : visited with Gerri. She told Gerri she has a foster home for her. Gerri was upset when she returned to her department. She said she will not go to another foster home, but she did not say that to Mrs. _____ ., because Mrs. _____ told her she will not expect an immediate answer from her. She gave her a week to decide.

October 8, I570

Mrs. _____ called and asked if we would like her to bring _____ .., Gerri's brother, here to _____ to show Gerri some pictures they brought from Indiana - mother's grave and maternal grandparents and family. She said those people live in dire poverty, but they have love and warmth for each other. The entire trip cost $400.00, but Mrs. _____ feels it was worth it for _____ ..

February 22, 1971

Geraldine Zigga

7-16-56

Our Lady of ██████

Aug. 70   Feb. 1971

LCID

5   1

2-15-71

123 lbs.

Visits her Orthodontist
regularly

Occasional headache and common cold. Says she is nervous and gets upset easily
Should return annually to Cleft Palate Clinic.

Fair. She is much calmer now, and her prognosis is good
for the future.

Fair   9th

Geraldine passed her mid-term test. As she is becoming calmer,
we hope sh e will do even better in the second semester. She does try.

She enjoys any activity planned for the children by the University
Club. She prefers the rougher games — but she likes sewing, too.

Very good. She enjoys living with her peers. Like her brother,
she would never adjust to a foster home.

It would be profitable for this girl to complete her high sch
at Fatima , and then go on her own.

Geraldine is an intelligent person, but she has a mind of her own, and
could become emotionally disturbed, if sh e had to bear too much pressure. She wants to
be quite independent, and she is able to assume much responsibility. She likes her stepfather, but she would not like to be dependent on him nor on anyone.

Nov. 21, 1971

Gerri Zigga

7-16-56

Our Lady of ~~Fatima~~

Feb. 1971   Nov. 1971

LCID

5   1½   127

2-15-71

Oct. 1971. Seen frequently by Dr.   and Dr.

Has occasional headache and common cold. Was at Cleft Palate Clinic Aug. 4, 1971.

Mentally, she is doing well. Emotionally and socially, she has come a long way, but she still has much to learn — she is very opinionated.

Good   10th

Gerri is very ambitious and she uses her time well. She is doing well in school.

She likes to draw and read, but she enjoys work, too. Gerri likes to assume responsibility, and she is dependable.

Well adjusted, helpful, and dependable.

Gerri seems to be at home living here with her brother. They work well together, shop together, and enjoy each others company. We would recommend continued living together for Gerri and her brother.

Re: Gerri Zigga

April 13, 1972
        Mrs.   , Counselor, from North Pocono High School talked about Gerri Zigga.
She said the girl has a very poor attitude towards life. She is burning up with hostility.
She had to be sent for to come to the office for guidance concerning her roster for
next year. She made a very poor impression when she came and carried on. She said she
wants Police Work or Law Enforcement. Mrs.   said she could obtain some catalogs
for her and she can talk it over with ███████ at ██████. She threw herself in defiance
at that and said she need not show anything to anyone. It is her own decision. Mrs.
        cut her short here saying that all girls and boys in their school share their
plans for the future with their parents, but since she is not with her parents, she
should know enough to share it with those who take care of her - who are concerned
about the braces on her teeth, who clothe her so well and who take care of all her
other needs.

        An appointment was made for her with the secretary for a Personality Rating Test.
She comes out very poor. During the appointment she was heard muttering "hypocites,
hypocrites." When asked what she was saying she became defiant. She was told she
would be out in the cold, but she has no appreciation for anything nor anyone. She
is just full of hostility towards those who are kind to her.
        I told Mrs.   I would talk to Gerri and try to convince her to reduce her
hostility for her own sake.

April 15, 1972
        Gerri seemed to be reached by what I had to say to her today. She recognized her
problem and promised to change her attitude to those who wish her well.

May II, I972
    Mr.   -   caseworker, talked about plans for   and Gerri. It seems that Mrs
, Gerri's caseworker, from Catholic Charities, has been working with Mr.   ,
and she has plans to send Gerri and   to live with him in September. He is also
to tak   .. the boy from St. Michael's. We do not think it is a good plan to saddle
this man with the three Zigga children, for they are all very wilfull and difficult to
guide and supervise. However, it will be up to Mr.   ' to find that out. I understand,
the   . boy at   's has one more year to finish high school. He will be permitted
to remain there, and then he plans a military career.
    and Gerri will go with Mr.   . to visit their brother   on Sunday at St.
Michael's at I:00 (May I4).

May I3, I972
    Mr.   called and said he has arranged to take the children to visit at St.   ae
tomorrow. We told him it is O.K. with us.

July I4, I972
    Mr.   , caseworker, has arranged for the   children to return to their father
before school begins - during the Labor Day week-end. Since they will be released to their
father then, there will be no vacation planned for them. The father has been told that by
the caseworker, Mr.

August 22, I972

    Yesterday, Mr.   ., caseworker, called and said he would like to come in and see the
children for they are making arrangements to release them to their father.
    Mr.   came in today and spoke to both - Gerri and   Before speaking with them,
I told Mr.   that we did not know what Gerri will want, but we definitely feel that
    would have to be moved from Fatima now for he no longer fits into our program. He
would probably fit better with his brother at St. Michael's. His life style is too old
for us to cope with.
    After speaking with Gerri and   Mr.   reported to me that Gerri has mixed
feelings about her father and   . She enjoys living at Fatima, and she would like
to continue her high school education at North Pocono. Mr.   told Gerri that the
decision will be hers. She can talk it over with her father on Sunday.
    When Mr.   left, Mrs.   ~ Public Health Nurse, came in to inquire
about Gerri. She wondered if she would leave Fatima, for Mrs.   , Gerri's caseworker
told her Gerri would be going to live with her father. We told Mrs.   that Mrs.
    has planned this, and she is pushing it all the way, but we do not agree with
her, for there is no genuine interest in these children by Mr.   and his mother.
He was actually stuck with these children when he married their mother, but there seems
to be no actual attachment and no love. The children are all strong headed and he and
his mother are aware of that. If Gerri wants to remain at Fatima, and study at North
Pocono, Mrs.   should not work so hard in trying to change her mind. The boys, too,
will not be easy for anyone else to handle.   should go to   's where his
brother is, and stay there until he can go on his own.

June,1972   Our Lady of ▓▓▓▓

Gerri Zigga   Nov. 1971   June,1972

7-16-56   LCID

          5   2   130 lbs.

          2-15-71   5-26-72

App. good.   Visits Dr. _   . every month for orthodontic work.

                    She is a bright girl, honest and dependable, but
                    there is still some hostility.

Good   She is promoted to —   11th   IQ   110

          She does quite well in school.

          She likes sports, outdoor activit ies, reading and excursions
          into the unknown. She works, and takes responsibility for her
          chores seriously.

          Good, but she has strong opinions and does not allow easily
          for compromise.

                    Gerri and her brother are very happy living together. What-
                    ever plans are made for them, they should continue to be
                    together. They need one another, since there aren't any
                    other close ties in their life pattern.

Re: Gerri & ▮▮▮ Zigga

Sept 1, 1972 —

Mr. ▮▮▮▮▮▮▮, stepfather of the ▮▮▮ children came to
▮▮▮▮▮. He said he was pressured to take the children to his house,
but he remembered he was not able to cope with them when they were
small, and his mother had a rough time with them too. As it is,
he said he has a hard time with ▮▮▮ his only child of that marriage.
She poses some difficult behavioral problems with which he cannot
cope. We advised Mr. ▮▮▮▮ to see the Director, which he did,
and he was convinced there that ▮▮▮ had to leave that same afternoon, Sept. 1, 1972, since it was almost time for school and he
could no longer remain at ▮▮▮▮.

Gerri was told that she was free to make a decision — to go
with her father or to remain at ▮▮▮▮▮, and finish High School.
Gerri decided to stay at ▮▮▮▮▮. She has been communicating and
cooperating much better for some time now. She identifies herself
with the staff, and tries to be helpful. We feel Gerri has made
the right decision.

Sept. 13, 1972 —

Mrs. ▮▮▮▮▮▮, School Counselor, inquired about Gerri today.
We told her about Gerri's decision and about the change we have
noticed about her. She was pleased to hear that Gerri's attitude
has improved since last year. We feel Gerri likes to be independent
and she enjoys being free at ▮▮▮▮. She goes to school where she
is accepted; she earns money and saves

still has much work to be done in the Cleft Palate Clinic and by her
Dentist.

Jan. 1973

Jerri Zigga

7-16-56

5   2½

7-24-72

Appetite good

Our Lady of ████

June 1972   Jan. 1973

LCID

131 lbs.

Next appointment
1-26-73. Dr. ████ and
Dr.

          Mentally, she does very well. Socially, Jerri still
harbors some hostility. She has gained insight to her problem but has not overcome it.

     Good   Junior H.S.   I.Q.110

          She does apply herself to her studies and does quite well.
She is already looking beyond her senior year and into college possibilities.

          She likes sports and understands boys better than girls. She
knows right from wrong, so there is no problem.

          Good. But Jerri is quite independent and insists on her own
life style. We trust she will find her way in life.

          To continue at ████ until she completes high school.
She will try her wings from there – if all goes well until then. This girl
is sincere and she does want to earn her own living. She does not want
to be obliged to anyone in her family. She is generous and would rather
give than receive.

Re: Gerri Zigga

February 5, 1973 - Mrs.   R.N. Department of Health, came to
to talk about   's leg problem. We also discussed Gerri Zigga.
I told her Gerri would like to go to college if she could get a scholarship.
Mrs.   feels Gerri would be eligible for scholarship through the Bureau of
Vocational Rehabilitation. She will speak to Mr.   about it, and he will
come to talk to us. We hope Gerri can keep her marks up that she may qualify
for College Entrance Exams. She told me today, that she is thinking of Alvernia
College.   She says if she cannot
get into college, she will g o into service, and if she gets into college, she
will go into s ervice after college. She is interested in history, law and
politics.   Maybe she should go into service
first to learn law and order. She needs to learn to both. Sister
finds her defiant and uncooperative in the dining room. She insists on sweeping
crumbs off the table on the floor. The others are learning to do the same.

June 1973

Jerri B. Zigga

7-16-56

Jan. '73   June '73

Bureau of Children Services

5   2½

132

7-24-72

Sees Dr.
every month.

Apparently good.

Good. It seems Jerri has finally shed the rest
of her hostility. She is a much more pleasant girl. It took a long time but it
was worth it.

Average

to   12 - I.Q.110

Jerri has just brought in her promotion card. We are all
glad for her. She is making plans to go to college, and
we are helping her to reach her goal. She needs to brush up a little in English
grammer and spelling. She is aware of her weakness and is doing something about it

Jerri enjoys going to town once in a while. She likes
outdoor activities, reading and taking responsibility for the smaller ones in her
department.

Very good. She knows what she wants, what her responsibilit
are, and she feels free at ~~Bureau~~. She is a generous girl, who cooperates well with
the staff.

To continue within our program until she graduates
from High School. We hope she does well during her final year. We
believe she will - with the help of God. This poor girl deserves all
the good there is in store for her.

LACKAWANNA COUNTY INSTITUTION DISTRICT

506 Spruce Street, Scranton, Pa. 18503

REPORT ON CHILD IN CARE

Date June 1973 .... Institution [redacted] ....

Report On Jerri D. Zigga .... Period from Jan '73 ... to June '73 .....

Birth Date 7-16-56 .... Referred by Bureau of Children Services ....

Physical Development: Height 5 ft. 2½ in. Weight 132 lbs.

Last Physical Examination 7-24-72 .... Last Dental Treatment Sees Dr. monthl

Ilnesses Apparently good. ....

==

Mental and Emotional Development Good. It seems Jerri has finally shed the rest of he hostility. She is a much more pleasant girl. It took a long time but it was worth it.

School Progress Average ....To. Grade 12 .. I.Q. 110 ....

Achievement and Remarks Jerri has just brought in her promotion card. We are all glad for her. She is making plans to go to college, and we are helping her to reach her goal. She is aware of her weakness and is doing something about it. She needs to brush up a little in English and spelling.
Activities and Interests ....
.... She likes outdoor activities, reading and taking responsibility for the smaller ones in her department.

Institutional Adjustment Very good. She knows what she wants, what her responsibiliti are, and she feels free at [redacted]. She is a generous girl, who cooperates well with the staff.

==

Recommended Plans for Child ....

Adoption ....

Release ....

==

Remarks and Additional Information To continue within our program until she graduates from high school. We hope she does well during her final year. We believe she will- with the help of God. This poor girl deserves all the good there is in store for her.

IN RE: PETITION OF JERRI : IN THE COURT OF COMMON PLEAS OF
DIANE ZIGGA FOR CHANGE OF : BERKS COUNTY, PENNSYLVANIA
NAME : CIVIL ACTION - LAW
:
: NO. 365 AUGUST TERM, 1976, A.D.

O R D E R

AND NOW, TO WIT, this /4th   day of August,
1976, after hearing the within Petition and in consideration of
the motion of Francis F. Seidel, III, Esq., Attorney for the
Petitioner, and upon presentation of proof of publication of
notice as required by law, together with the proof that there are
no Judgments or Decrees of record or any other matter of like
effect against the Petitioner, and appearing that there is no
legal objection to the granting of the Petition, it is found as
a fact that the requirements of the Act of April 18, 1923,
P. L. 75, as amended, 54 P.S. Section 1, et. seq., have been
satisfied and

IT IS HEREBY ORDERED AND DECREED THAT the name of
Petitioner be and is hereby changed to Jerri Diane Sueck.

BY THE COURT:

_____
                              J.

Francis F. Seidel III		IN RE: PETITION OF JERRI DIANE ZIGGA	July 14, 1976, Petition for Change of Name of
		FOR CHANGE OF NAME	Jerri Diane Zigga, filed. EoDis: Order, filed. AND
		TO	NOW, TO WIT: July 14, 1976, upon consideration of the
365		JERRI DIANE SUECK	aforegoing Petition and upon motion of Francis F.
			Seidel, III, Esquire, Attorney for the Petitioner
		:	above named, it is ordered and decreed that the with-
		:	in Petition be heard on the 23rd day of August, A.D.,
		:	1976, at 9:30 a.m., in Courtroom No. 1, and that
		:	notice of the filing of the within Petition and of th
		:	aforesaid date of hearing be published once in the
		:	Berks County Law Journal and the Reading Eagle-Times
Seidel	aus Ct 15.50	BY THE COURT:/s/W. Richard Eshelman, President Judge	at least one month prior to the date of said hearing.
Seidel Sat. due Ct 3.00		taken, Searches and Proofs of Publication, filed. EoDis:	August 23, 1976, Hearing held, testimony Order to be filed by Attorney for Petitioner
Law Journal Pd 14.01		Hess, J. EoDis: Order, filed. AND NOW, TO WIT, this 14th day of September, 1976, after hearing
Rdg Eagle Pd 10.00		the within Petition and in consideration of the motion of Francis F. Seidel, III, Esquire, Attorney fo
Seidel (Order) Pd 6.00		with proof that there are no judgments or decrees of record or any other matter of like effect against the Petitioner, and upon presentation of proof of publication of notice as required by law, together
		the Petitioner, and appearing that there is no legal objection to the granting of the Petition, it is
		found as a fact that the requirements of the Act of April 18, 1923, P. L. 75, as amended, 54 P. S.
		Section 1, et. seq., have been satisfied and IT IS HEREBY ORDERED AND DECREED THAT the name of Petitio
		er be and is hereby changed to Jerri Diane Sueck. BY THE COURT:/s/Warren K. Hess, Senior Retired
		Judge	

Alvernia College

Reading, Pennsylvania

To all who may read these Letters
Greetings in the Lord

The Board of Trustees of Alvernia College
on the recommendation of the Faculty has conferred upon

Jerri Diane Suerk

the degree of

Bachelor of Arts

with all the rights and privileges pertaining to that degree

Given at Reading, Pennsylvania this twenty-first day of May,
nineteen hundred and seventy-eight.

_____
Dean

_____
President

THE CATHOLIC UNIVERSITY OF AMERICA

UPON THE RECOMMENDATION OF THE FACULTY OF

THE SCHOOL OF RELIGIOUS STUDIES

WITH THE APPROVAL OF THE ACADEMIC SENATE
HAS CONFERRED UPON

JERRI DIANE SUECK

THE DEGREE OF

MASTER OF ARTS

WITH ALL THE HONORS, RIGHTS AND PRIVILEGES PERTAINING THERETO.
GIVEN UNDER THE SEAL OF THE UNIVERSITY, BY VIRTUE OF THE
AUTHORITY VESTED IN THE BOARD OF TRUSTEES BY THE CONGRESS
OF THE UNITED STATES, AT WASHINGTON IN THE DISTRICT OF COLUMBIA
THIS TWENTY-NINTH DAY OF FEBRUARY, NINETEEN HUNDRED AND EIGHTY.

_____ PRESIDENT

_____ CHAIRMAN OF BOARD OF TRUSTEES

_____ REGISTRAR

Edwards Brothers, Inc.
Thorofare, NJ USA
September 21, 2011